Stalag Luft III

STALAG LUFT III

THE SECRET STORY

ARTHUR A. DURAND

LOUISIANA STATE UNIVERSITY PRESS
BATON ROUGE and LONDON

10 9 8 7 6 5 4 3 2 1

Designer: Sylvia Loftin
Typeface: Primer
Typesetter: The Composing Room of Michigan
Printer: Thomson-Shore, Inc.
Binder: John H. Dekker & Sons, Inc.

Library of Congress Cataloging-in-Publication Data

Durand, Arthur A., 1944–
    Stalag Luft III : the secret story / Arthur A. Durand.
        p.   cm.
    Bibliography: p.
    Includes index.
    ISBN 0-8071-1352-2 (alk. paper)
    1. Stalag Luft 3 (Żagań, Poland : Concentration camp)   2. World
War, 1939–1945—Prisoners and prisons, German.   I. Title.
D805.P7D87 1988   87-33871
940.54′72′430943—dc19   CIP

The paper in this book meets the guidelines for performance and
durability of the Committee on Production Guidelines for Book
Longevity of the Council on Library Resources. ∞

To those who suffered captivity
so others could remain free

Contents

Illustrations

The American flag raised at Moosburg
Stalag Luft III reunion, 1965

FIGURES

Acknowledgments

I am indebted to many persons for their assistance in the preparation of this study. Major General Delmar T. Spivey, USAF (Retired), and Lieutenant General Albert P. Clark, USAF (Retired), who originally suggested the topic, generously granted me full access to their personal papers and freely gave of their time in personal conversations and in critiquing the manuscript in its various stages of completion. The interest, patience, and understanding exhibited by these two individuals have been of inestimable value. I also would like to thank a host of other former prisoners of war: Alexander MacArthur for his constant support, encouragement, and unflagging friendship; Major General Arthur W. Vanaman, USAF (Retired), Colonel Charles G. Goodrich, USAF (Retired), John Wells, Ronald L. Delaney, Willard L. Heckman, David Pollack, Robert Weinman, Elwin F. Schrupp, Ralph H. Saltsman, Norman L. Widen, George Sweanor, Roland L. Sargent, Norville J. Gorse, Clifford Hopewell, Arthur Dreyer, Loren E. Jackson, Reginald Pettus, Jerry Sage, Donald L. Stillman, Eugene M. Wiley, Donald G. Charland, and all the many others who assisted my research, generously consented to lengthy interviews, or took the time to write to me. In addition to the former prisoners, I would like to extend a special note of appreciation to Henry Soderberg from Sweden, who granted me extensive interviews and free access to the notes and diary entries he made while serving as a YMCA representative in Germany during World War II. His graciousness and objectivity stirred in me a new awareness of the invaluable role neutrals can and do play in the midst of international strife. I also would like to thank the many persons who aided my archival research, among whom are: Edward Reece and others at the Modern Military Branch of the National Archives; the personnel at the Diplomatic Branch of the National Archives; Bill Lewis and Bruce Ashkenas at the Washington National Record Center, Suitland, Md.; Hannah Zeidlich at the U.S. Army Center for Military History, Washington, D.C.; Wayne Robinson, Allen Striepe, and Elinore Peets at the Albert F. Simpson Historical Research Center, Maxwell Air Force Base, Ala.; Charles Warman and Royal Frey at the Air Force Museum, Wright-Patterson Air Force Base, Ohio; Jimmie H. Hoover, Roberta A. Scull, Jane P. Kleiner, and Olar Bell at the Troy H. Middleton Library, Louisiana State University; and Duane Reed and Donald J. Barrett at the U.S. Air Force Academy Library. I am especially indebted to Duane Reed, in the Special Collections Room, who gave me unstinting support above and beyond that normally associated with archival research. His assistance and cooperation in establishing and maintaining the Stalag Luft III collection have been pivotal to the task of ensuring continuing access to invaluable historical documents pertaining to the camp. An equal measure of appreciation must be expressed to General Clark and the Stalag Luft III Ex-Prisoners of War Association for sponsoring the archival program and providing a financial grant. I owe a special debt of gratitude to the late T. Harry Williams, who was for me a dynamic and visible model of what the true historian can and should be. A special thanks also is due Burl L. Noggle, David F. Lindenfeld, and Cecil L. Eubanks, who also gave invaluable assistance in the early stages of research and writing. A particularly heartfelt thanks goes to John L. Loos, who has been a special source of comfort and inspiration to me throughout the years I have known him. I wish to express my sincere gratitude also to Colonel Alan L. Gropman for giving me a vote of confidence that has led to rewards far beyond anything I ever could have imagined. I shall always be grateful for what he taught me concerning the need to hold to one's convictions. An equal note of thanks goes to Brigadier General Alfred F. Hurley, USAF (Retired), for providing me the opportunity to pursue the studies and research that served as the foundation for this historical account. Several individuals read the manuscript in its various stages and provided invaluable insights and suggestions. For their painstaking efforts, I would like to thank John Toland, Dennis E. Showalter, Richard Campbell, Thomas Fitzpatrick, Steven Weinberg, James Keeffe, B. A. James, Lyman B. Burbank, Lieutenant General Walter G. Johnson, USAF (Retired), and Major General Robert M. Stillman, USAF (Retired). The errors that remain, of course, must fall to my charge alone. I also wish to thank Les Phillabaum, Director; Beverly Jarrett, Associate Director and Executive Editor; and Catherine F. Barton, Managing Editor, all of Louisiana

State University Press, for their interest, encouragement, and assistance. Their unending patience with my missed deadlines was truly magnanimous. I am particularly indebted to Barbara O'Neil Phillips, also of Louisiana State University Press, for her meticulous work and close cooperation in the final editing of the manuscript. We shared a mutually enlightening association, a blessing that made a traditionally onerous task most enjoyable and rewarding. To her I extend a very special thanks. I wish also to thank the following individuals: George W. Wenthe for excerpts from his daily log and diary; Ronald L. Delaney for excerpts from the *Gefangenen Gazette*; Emmett Dedmon for his poem "Willie Green and His Flying Machine"; Joseph Boyle for his poem "The Fate We Share as Prisoners"; the late Elisabeth von Warburg von Lindeiner for granting me free access to her father's personal papers and memoirs; and Berthold Geiss and Barbara Riley Cunningham for their excellent translation of difficult and lengthy German texts. Most of all, I would like to express a very inadequate but wholehearted thanks to my family: my wife, Phyllis, who spent countless hours reading, making suggestions, and typing the manuscript in its many stages and who remained at the same time a constant source of inspiration and a loving wife and companion, and our three sons, Brennan, Darin, and Ryan, who cheerfully forgave their father for remaining in his study far too long. My mother and father also deserve a special thank-you for their constant love, encouragement, and support, as well as the priceless love for learning and the enduring values they passed on to me and countless others through the years.

Stalag Luft III

Introduction

When Colonel Delmar T. Spivey entered Stalag Luft III in late July, 1943, he was a full colonel and twice the age of most of his fellow inmates. The senior staff immediately realized that his seniority and West Point training would catapult him into prominence as a leader. To reduce the chances of his inadvertently giving away important secrets to the Germans, the staff quickly briefed him on the entire spectrum of camp activities, including the vital covert intelligence and escape work that had been painfully developed during the three years since the first Allied fliers were captured by the Germans.

Spivey stood transfixed as he looked into the gaping hole of the entrance shaft to tunnel "Harry." It descended thirty feet straight down, shored every inch of the way with bed boards taken by quota from the prisoners. He was told also about its overall design—projected three-hundred-foot length, electric lights, self-contained storage and work rooms, and specially designed railroad trolleys to carry the dirt back out of the tunnel as it was being dug. He was even more surprised to learn that the tunnel he was staring at was but one of three such undertakings, and that the entire effort was tightly orchestrated by an interesting character code-named Big X. During succeeding days he learned all about the prisoners' forgery operation, covert communications with London and Washington, impressive education and theatrical programs, and robust play on the athletic fields.

Two weeks later Spivey assumed command as Senior American Officer (SAO) of Center Compound. Still dazzled by what he had seen, he reflected on the need to record for posterity the amazing activities he saw at every turn. If nothing else, he reasoned, the account might make it easier for the next generation of prisoners and save them the trouble of having to "invent the wheel all over again." As logical and intriguing as the idea sounded, Spivey knew there were great risks. The Germans obviously would love to get their hands on so revealing a document. He nonetheless decided to proceed with the effort, knowing that everything hinged on the careful observance of numerous precautions and safeguards.

As a first step he appointed three lieutenants to serve as compound historians: Thomas E. Mulligan, Lyman B. Burbank, and Robert R. Brunn. Their task was to record and enter in a log everything of significance that happened each day. To preclude the log's falling into German hands in any usable form, certain information was coded by means of a simple but effective technique. After the three men agreed on the items to be recorded and were satisfied with the way it all looked on paper, they initiated a clever routine. One man took the first word of the text and every third word thereafter and wrote them on a sheet of paper without any capitalization or punctuation. The second man started with the second word and did likewise, and the third man wrote down every third word. The three strings of nonsensical prose, of and by themselves, meant nothing and revealed nothing. The three sheets of paper were then hidden in separate locations, some in hollowed-out table legs, others in prepared wall cavities, and still others found their way into nooks and crannies of every imaginable description. There they remained until the camp was hastily evacuated in late January, 1945. They were gathered up and transported westward with great effort and considerable risk as the Germans marched the prisoners away from the rapidly advancing Russian armies. These documents served as the basis and initial impetus for the true story related here. In addition to these documents, I drew upon numerous other firsthand accounts gathered from personal interviews, diaries, logs, and letters, both private and official, as well as recently declassified government documents. Every effort has been made to let the evidence speak for itself.

1

Through the Eye of the Needle

It was Friday the thirteenth when Wing Commander Harry Melville Arbuthnot Day led his squadron's first mission over Germany in October, 1939. Not a man given to superstition, Wings Day, as his friends called him, felt it was his responsibility to carry on the tradition set when his predecessor had led the squadron's first raid against Germany in World War I.

The previous day Wings had been placed on standby orders and knew the mission was imminent. For Wings's peace of mind, it would have been better if the task had been immediate. Standby orders gave him time to think, and serious doubts welled up in his mind about Command's wisdom in assigning his squadron to "strategic" reconnaissance. On the surface it seemed simple enough: the intelligence briefer had waved a hand vaguely across a huge map of Germany and said, "So far as we know, there's nothing very much there." The area referred to consisted of the Ruhr Valley and up toward the North Sea, the route home. But Day recognized the plan for what it was—suicidal. The task was beyond the capability of his squadron's Blenheim reconnaissance aircraft, which did not have the speed, the armament, or the climbing power of the enemy fighters. Carrying only one Bren gun fixed in the wing and another in the turret amidship, the Blenheim was no match for Messerschmitt fighters armed with four wing guns and one cannon. Furthermore, the Blenheim's 200-mph top speed made it an easy prey for the 350-mph Messerschmitt. Conceptually, droning steadily along in a Blenheim over the heart of industrial Germany—at war, in daylight—was *asking* to be shot out of the sky.

The premission weather briefing predicted solid cloud cover across all of Germany, but Wings soon found himself in clear skies. He was not surprised when his gunner reported over the intercom that sporadic flak bursts were coming their way. Wings held his course but glanced around when the intercom clicked a second time and emitted a cryptic "Flak." Suddenly he realized that the flak was guiding fighters to his aircraft. It was an old trick, and as a former fighter pilot he should have been onto it. He was furious with himself. Three Me-109s in line astern turned in on him. Wings banked and turned as tightly as possible toward them, but it was too late. He heard the sharp explosions of cannon shells slamming into the Blenheim. The outcome never was in doubt: Wings and his crew were about to pass through the eye of the needle, that indescribably small window between life and death that virtually all downed fliers had to squeeze through on their brutal journey from cockpit to prison camp.

Wings jammed the throttles forward to emergency power, swung the Blenheim into a dive, nose hard down and engines screaming. The first acrid wisps of smoke began filling the cockpit as the self-sealing tanks caught fire. In seconds, smoke masked his instruments, his hands, and even the sergeant sitting beside him. Wings had seen the sergeant clip on his chest parachute and yelled to him to get out. He then groped through the smoke and found the right seat empty. Flames began to lick at him, searing his shoulders and face. With frantic deliberation, he pried back the escape hatch above him and forced himself up. The dreadful thought of being impaled on the tail fin flashed through his mind. But with one final kick he was away, his sprawled body tumbling over and over. In the next terror-filled seconds he reached for the rip cord, his lifeline. At the same time he glimpsed the Blenheim, one wing buckled, rolling and disintegrating. He also saw a savage Me-109 and relaxed his grip on the rip cord to reduce the chance of again becoming a helpless, easy target. At about fifteen hundred feet he pulled the rip cord and experienced the welcome shock of being suspended beneath the billowing white canopy. Parts from the Blenheim fluttered past him like huge pieces of ash. Directly below was a small woods in the middle of fields; not far from there was a scraggly village. Near the woods a man driving a tractor was looking up, and Wings knew there was little chance of making a run for it. Across the fields men, women, and children were running, waving, and he could hear clearly their excited cries. With a tearing snap of branches he plunged into the woods. He hit the ground hard and struggled to his feet, automatically trying to unclip his parachute harness. A horde scrambled into the woods. The first man to reach him was a Forest Guardsman, Walter Becker. He paused as Wings murmured, "Englander." Then Becker, grinning, reached out and shook him warmly by the hand.[1]

The war had lasted only five weeks when Wings was shot down. But already the Germans had taken 700,000 prisoners in Poland.[2] And by war's end they would take literally millions. In comparison, the number of Allied fliers held by the Germans would remain relatively small for years to come, partly because the air campaign over German-occupied territory got well under way only after mid-1943, but also because fundamentally different circumstances surround the capture of airmen. Army and naval personnel usually fall into enemy hands en masse while fighting side by side with their comrades. In isolated situations they may be taken singly, but such cases are the exception. Aerial combat is highly individualistic by nature, and, for the defeated, so is the aftermath. Warplanes cover great distances and are shot down randomly, the hapless crew members further dispersed by the fast forward motion of the plunging aircraft and by the prevailing winds. During World War II, prior to the advent of small survival radios, downed crewmen seldom reestablished contact with one another unless brought together by their captors or reunited by members of the underground or resistance movements. Airmen came out of the sky one by one and usually faced their captors the same way, adding a significant dimension to an already traumatic experience.

But that was only one part of being shot down and captured. Other aspects are recalled vividly to this day. Often the airmen were the victims of cruel and brutal forces; on occasion the recipients of unusual kindness; at yet other times privileged witnesses to the humor and tragedy of human folly. The thoughts, motives, and actions of the prisoners confined in Stalag Luft III can be understood only by sharing, at least vicariously, the hopes, fears, anxieties, and horrors, both real and imagined, experienced by the men in their last days of combat and early face-to-face encounters with the enemy on the ground. War seemingly possesses no powers of discrimination, often reversing the roles of victor and victim for no apparent reason. The fliers who ended up in Stalag Luft III understood these truths as

1. Sydney Smith, *Mission Escape* (New York, 1969), 1, 7–9.
2. Peter Young (ed.), *The World Almanac Book of World War II* (New York, 1981), 40.

well as anyone else, perhaps better than most. They witnessed the vagaries and the disaster of war firsthand. Their individual stories are their corporate testimony.

Albert P. Clark, Jr., answered to the nickname Bub. But he also answered to either Junior, which many thought more appropriate in view of his youthful appearance, or Red, for his flaming hair. Tall and thin, Bub responded good-naturedly even when someone called him Flamingo—at times his lanky legs did seem to bend a little backwards at the knees. The nicknames in part described and in part belied the character of the man. Behind his kid's grin and youthful looks was an officer who rightfully wore the insignia of a lieutenant colonel at the early age of twenty-seven. Outwardly shy and unassuming, Bub was a quiet, self-assured leader who could be effective without drawing attention to himself—the kind of man one would like to see in the intelligence business. In the early summer of 1942, however, that sort of work was probably the farthest thing from Bub's mind. His full attention at the time was devoted to surviving as a fighter pilot under the tutelage of the veterans of the Battle of Britain.

Fighter pilots must be prepared to fight alone. Bub knew that and had the constitution for it. But common sense and experience told fighter pilots and bomber crews alike that the enemy would be quick to gang up on any plane found beyond the protective firepower of its parent formation. In spite of their best efforts, however, fliers sometimes did find themselves alone and, not unexpectedly, outnumbered. It happened to many. Lieutenant Colonel Clark was one of them.

On Sunday, July 26, 1942, members of the 31st Fighter Group, to which Clark was assigned, were ordered to conduct a sweep over the Continent, the objective being to surprise and destroy the enemy in his own territory. The target area, Abbeville, France, was one of the primary bases of the Richtofen Gesehwader and its one thousand German fighters then deployed along the coast.

Just off the French coast, the Spitfires climbed rapidly to eighteen thousand feet. Wing Commander Johnny Walker broke radio silence, asking for the location of enemy fighters. RAF radar reported "50 plus" Focke-Wulfs above the invading force. The element of surprise clearly lost, the entire formation entered a 180-degree left turn over Abbeville. Suddenly the Canadian commander of Yellow Flight, with Clark as Yellow Two, spotted an attractive target—German aircraft taxiing on the runway. He peeled off, and Bub followed quickly. The switch in direction occurred so abruptly that Yellow Three and Four never really caught up. The two aircraft in the lead dove to the deck and skimmed low over the airfield, firing just as a number of FW-190s were taking off. One German aircraft apparently went down, but Yellow One obviously did not stay around to confirm the kill. Knowing he had flown into a hornet's nest, he slammed the throttle to emergency power. Again Clark had to play catch-up, but by now the gap between them had become too great. He was on his own.

Instinctively Clark headed straight for the sea at full throttle, fifty feet off the ground. In spite of the advantage he seemed to have over the enemy fighters, several FW-190s soon closed in and scored one hit in his left wing, cutting the ram-air supply to his airspeed indicator. The needle stuck on 320 mph. Bub called for assistance, but no one responded. Yellow One, Three, and Four were nowhere in sight. In desperation, Clark made a tight 180-degree turn, engaged in two head-on firing exchanges, then made another run for the sea. Crossing the coast, he was jolted by flak and found four more aircraft gaining on him. Bullets fired by his pursuers created tiny waterspouts all around the low-flying Spitfire. With Clark almost clipping the waves, the enemy could not gain an altitude advantage and still go after him. Knowing the FW-190 was faster than the Spitfire at sea level, Clark did a sudden loop and came down on the tails of a pair of FWs breaking right. He emptied his guns at them. The other pair, apparently shaken by his surprise move, broke left, and all four flew off. Somewhat relieved after all the jinking, Clark also headed for home—land was in sight, presumably the English side of the Channel. He saw no more German aircraft, but suddenly had another crisis. The engine began to fail with high engine performance readings, apparently from being operated for so long at full emergency power.

The running battle had carried Bub some distance out to sea. And the Spitfire was a notoriously rapid sinker. He recalled all too vividly that exactly one week earlier the distinguished Irish ace, Padde Fanucane, had been seen alive and well in the cockpit as his Spitfire settled on the water. But it sank in the fleeting moment before the pilot could escape. Bub quickly gave a Mayday call and attempted to jettison the cockpit canopy. The rusted jettison handle broke in his hand. The canopy would not open. Turning directly toward land, he put his feet on the dash in preparation for whatever came next. Dead ahead lay the low bluffs that shield the coast just south of Cape Gris-Nez near Ambleteuse, Pas de Calais, France. The Spitfire maintained barely enough airspeed to clear the bluff before crashing into a field. Shaken and exhausted, Clark struggled once again with the canopy, got it open, and leapt out. Greeted immediately by German soldiers manning the coastal gun batteries, he sadly realized that there was no place to go. Having faced the enemy alone in the air, he now faced them alone on the ground. Like so many of his colleagues, he had found the gateway to prison.[3]

War is full of surprises, but few are welcome. Clark could vouch for that—and his experience certainly was not unusual. Until their own planes were hit, most airmen engaging the enemy felt they were mere observers at a bizarre satanic affair. All around rained death and destruction, which for some inexplicable reason were passing them by. As if in a dream they watched other unfortunate airmen plunge to fiery deaths, amid debris and ruin, mangled and bloody. With tightened stomachs and sweating hands they watched in awe . . . and waited . . . methodically and frantically engaged in the mechanics of combat but nonetheless suspended in time. At times they almost wished the seemingly inevitable would come, so the uncertainty would end and their long awaited fate would at last be revealed. They prepared as best they could for the madness, steeling themselves physically and emotionally, knowing all along that their preparations were anything but adequate. Surprises occurred, usually in rapid succession, and were almost always bad ones—a fact of life for airmen. Only on the rarest of occasions did fliers find otherwise. First Lieutenant Norman L. Widen, known as Cy, was one of the few who did.

There were two things almost everyone knew about Cy: he was always hungry, and he was afraid of water. Flying a single seat P-38 as an escort for John Morely Bennett's B-17 bomber flight when the formation crossed the North Atlantic, and later during orientation operations around the coast of England, Cy busied his mind with ways to survive in the event he was hit. He could not swim, and water bothered him. Like the Spitfire, he was a natural-born sinker.

3. Interview with Albert P. Clark, July 4, 1984; General Clark Scrapbook, in Albert P. Clark Collection, 1942–1975, Special Collections Room, U.S. Air Force Academy Library, Colo.

Cy had little confidence in the sea survival gear provided at that time by the United States Army Air Forces, which consisted primarily of a navy-type inflatable dinghy and the standard inflatable Mae West life jacket. He was impressed, however, with the equipment provided to British crewmen. So when the American gear left him floundering during routine training in a swimming pool, he knew what he had to do. A quick midnight requisition gave him a British Mae West that contained special flotation devices in addition to a better mechanism for oral inflation if the CO_2 cartridge did not work. He also obtained a British dinghy and outfitted it with survival aids he thought would be helpful: a fluorescein dye to repel sharks and visually assist rescue planes, a whistle for summoning surface vessels, a mirror to shine toward aircraft that might be searching for him, a skull cap with a yellow top visible from above, a can of bully beef and some iron pills for strength, a little telescoping flag to signal surface vessels, a flashlight with an extra bulb, a .45 automatic pistol, a razor, a toothbrush, and photographs that could be pasted on false identity cards. Then in the extra dinghy he sat on he carried a machete, a first-aid kit, a compass, maps, fishhooks, and a water bag. He even made sure he had a British parachute. In the water it took two hands to unfasten the American chute; the British had redesigned theirs so that one hand could release it in two quick movements. Perhaps some of his fellow fliers thought him a little too cautious. Actually he was only being prudent. Thousands of crewmen lived to curse the day they failed to make such preparations.

On December 18, 1942, Cy climbed into his P-38 in North Africa to fly cover for a bombing mission against a nearby docking facility on the Tunisian coast. Cy's plane was clearly marked, the ground crew having painted Great Gut in large letters on one boom and Chow Hound on the other in affectionate recognition of his constant longing for food. Noting a malfunction as he ran up the engines, Cy opted for another plane. Unfortunately, it was not much better. Apprehensive from the start, he nonetheless took his place in the formation.

At about 31,000 feet the fighters were jumped by Me-109s. In the dogfight that ensued, Cy maneuvered into position and hammered bullets into an enemy fighter with telling effect. The Me-109 struggled for a time, but then went down. Cy did not see the outcome. While still zeroed in on his quarry, he felt the sudden impact of enemy fire striking his own left engine and looked up just in time to see it burst into flames. At the same moment he saw the pursuing Me-109 and immediately started sharp inside turns to shake it off. But the thickening smoke and flames creeping into the cockpit warned him he had to get out—and soon.

Getting out of a burning, twisting P-38 was a fighter pilot's nightmare. The booms were connected in the rear by a horizontal stabilizer mounted directly in the path of an ejecting body caught in the windstream of the plummeting aircraft. Since there was no powered ejection seat, the best a pilot could do was turn the aircraft upside down and slide out with just enough downward motion to slip under the stabilizer or with enough force to go over it. Unfortunately, Cy's plane was already in a screaming dive and out of control. He could no longer turn it over, but hoped he could slide under the cleaver that would be slicing toward him the instant he left the cockpit. Seconds counted now. As he released the canopy and stood up, a 400-mph wind slammed and tore at him as he struggled to kick free.

What followed surprised him. Miraculously clearing the stabilizer, he tumbled into a new world. The noise inside the airplane had been deafening, as though one were rolling down a steep hill in an iron barrel, on fire, with a lot of people throwing rocks. A split second later everything became peaceful and quiet, churchlike. The silence was reassuring and revealing. From below he could hear an airplane running up its engines on an airfield near Tunis. He also heard a bell ringing somewhere, and a dog barking. It all seemed unreal.

But reality soon reasserted itself. Earlier Cy had discovered he could feel the rudder controls better if he dispensed with the encumbering footwear. So that day, as usual, he had left his shoes off and was wearing only his loose-fitting winter flying boots. Just after he pulled the rip cord, the shock from the opening parachute forced his boots off. Feeling the tug on his feet, Cy instinctively glanced downward. It was then that he saw the water. The thought of his careful preparations comforted him greatly. But another source of anxiety appeared immediately as Cy looked back up to see his assailant's Me-109 closing in. Fearing the worst, he was astonished to see the aircraft enter a circular pattern around him. The German pilot grinned and saluted as he passed by.

Cy quickly turned his attention back to the dreaded water landing. He had rehearsed it well in his mind and knew exactly what to do. In a crouch with feet held together in case there was floating debris, Cy splashed down. For the third time in the space of a few minutes he was surprised. He had landed in one foot of water and two feet of mud.

With the Mediterranean at his back and Germans coming toward him with weapons drawn, he attempted to sink his maps and other escape aids. But the items refused to sink in the shallow water and remained in clear view. Cy raised his hands and proceeded slowly toward his captors.[4]

In the early months of the war, the Germans had to pull the airmen in one by one. But as the years passed, the numbers began to mount. As might be expected, a few "strays" got mixed in their ranks from time to time, confirming that many paths led to captivity. Less than two months after Cy Widen was shot down, a drama unfolded that would send an army officer into the midst of the air force prisoners. In early 1943, Eugene L. Daniel, Jr., an army chaplain assigned to the 34th Infantry Division, found himself sitting on a barren mountain, square in the path of General Arnim's advancing 5th Panzer Army. His unit had been moved to Mount Lessouda about sixty-five miles from the coast of Tunisia to watch for signs of German movement westward out of Faïd Pass, where the enemy was entrenched. Another battalion had been placed on Mount Ksaira, a number of miles to the southeast, to watch for the enemy in the mountains to the east. In addition, both battalions were to serve as "islands of resistance" in case of an enemy breakthrough.

On February 14, Valentine's Day, the 10th Panzer Division came through Faïd Pass about dawn. They engaged and defeated a force from the American 1st Armored Division and within two hours arrived at and surrounded Mount Lessouda. It was Sunday, and Chaplain Daniel had made plans to go to each platoon area to conduct worship services. Instead he had to scurry to the top of the mountain and dig a foxhole for protection from the German assault. When the Americans repulsed a hastily prepared German infantry attack, the enemy backed away and began to shell the mountain. The artillery fire continued throughout the day, all night, and all the next day. The Americans were dug in well, so casualties were light. In fact, the small defending force managed to locate and capture a number of Germans wounded during the earlier attack. Since he could not conduct services, Chaplain Daniel sent to the units that could be reached messages containing Scripture lessons and some thoughts he felt were appropriate.

4. Interview with Norman L. Widen, April 11, 1979.

Late Monday afternoon a lone American fighter plane flew low over the isolated platoon and dropped a small container attached to a long yellow streamer. The message inside said "TANK DESTROYERS AND INFANTRY WILL OCCUPY POSITION T AT 6363 AT 2200 HOURS TONIGHT TO COVER YOUR WITHDRAWAL. YOU ARE TO WITHDRAW TO POSITION TO ROAD WEST OF BLID CHEGAS WHERE GUIDES WILL MEET YOU. BRING EVERYTHING YOU CAN." The position to which they were to withdraw was some seven miles to the west, and the area in between was occupied by the Germans. The commanding officer decided to take everyone, including the wounded German soldiers captured on Sunday.

Following normal procedure, Chaplain Daniel joined the medics and wounded men. Most of the wounded could walk, but the egress route took them down into gullies ten to twenty feet deep that had been washed out straight down the side of the mountain. Two seriously wounded Germans had to be carried on stretchers, and before long the fast-moving main column was far ahead. When the first streaks of morning light appeared, the small party stopped to discuss their situation.

Chaplain Daniel proposed that the medical sergeant stay with the prisoners who could not possibly walk and then turn them over to the Germans. The sergeant respectfully declined, noting that he had joined the army to serve American sick and wounded and did not want to stay with the enemy wounded. Daniel understood the objection only too well. At the same time, he felt that it would not be right to simply leave the German POWs to die in the scorching sun. Reluctantly, he decided to stay with them himself, assuring the others that the Germans probably would recognize him as a noncombatant and return him to the American lines under a flag of truce.

After everyone had left, Daniel began making plans to get the two wounded men into the hands of the German medics. They were lying in a deep ravine and could not be seen by the German troops on the desert plain and on a paved highway about a mile away. He crawled carefully up to the rim and peered out. German vehicles were moving up and down the highway, and foot soldiers could be seen advancing westward toward the American lines in the distance. Daniel went back into the gully and tried to explain the situation, but their puzzled expressions convinced him they did not understand English. Frustrated, he decided to brew a cup of tea before contacting the Germans for help. When the tea was ready the Germans begged for a swallow, and the three of them quickly consumed the single cup of tea.

The idea suddenly came to Daniel to carry one of the wounded German soldiers with him for protection. He chose the man who seemed to be injured the least and tried to explain the plan to him. The German's repeated reply was "Nicht verstehen." Finally, in desperation, Chaplain Daniel reached for the entrenching shovel strapped to his belt and threatened the prisoner, saying "You must go." The German looked up at Daniel from his stretcher and grumbled in English, "If I must, I must." Obediently he arose and climbed out of the ravine.

Waving a white flag, arms around shoulder and waist for support, the chaplain and his prisoner walked slowly toward the German lines. After they had gone a half mile or so a German motorcycle patrol spotted them and came speeding in their direction. The motorcycle was equipped with a sidecar and had a small machine gun mounted on the handlebars. When the driver stopped about one hundred yards away, the rider dismounted, drew his automatic pistol, and proceeded toward the pair. The wounded German called out, apparently assuring his rescuer that the chaplain was unarmed. The soldier put his pistol back in its holster and approached cautiously. While waiting for the soldier's arrival, the prisoner said in broken English, "I want to say something." Daniel said, "All right." The German repeated this statement, and each time Daniel urged him to say what he wanted to say. Finally the wounded man clearly and deliberately responded, "Americans are very gentlemanly."

It was late afternoon before the Germans allowed Daniel to lead them back to the other wounded German. In the interim they questioned him at length about forces remaining on Mount Lessouda. Chaplain Daniel sensed that the Germans were delaying an important operation until they could be sure no further threat existed there. Accordingly, he was careful not to let it be known the defenders had vacated the area. The Germans, in turn, sensed that he was being coy and lectured him on the nature of warfare, saying that he did not seem to understand the seriousness of the situation. They assured him they would kill every American on the mountain, if necessary, in order to clear it. For the first time in his life, Chaplain Daniel began to realize that there was such a thing as an "enemy." Previously he had believed that no one wished him ill. Now he began to perceive that the Germans considered him their enemy and that they would kill him if he did not do what they wanted. If any doubts remained, they were put to rest when Daniel reminded the Germans that he was a noncombatant and that the time had come to send him west to his own lines. The Germans sent him east to their regimental headquarters. Chaplain Daniel had turned over two prisoners and now had become one himself.[5]

The war in North Africa continued until May, 1943. The Allies then moved up through Sicily and into Italy, where a stalemate developed that lasted until the final days of combat in Europe. Flight activity in the Mediterranean remained intensive, supporting the Italian operation and the strategic bombing attacks against the Ploieşti oil fields in Romania and other lucrative targets throughout the Balkans and southern Germany. But as 1943 progressed, the emphasis began to shift back toward northwestern Europe in preparation for the inevitable invasion of the Continent from England. In addition, air operations took on a new and ominous character that spring as the long awaited combined British and American bomber offensive got fully under way. In ever larger numbers and with increasing intensity, the Americans continued their high-altitude precision-bombing attacks by day and the British struck with saturation-bombing raids throughout the night. And month by month the Allies extended the range of their operations until virtually every square mile of Axis territory was exposed to the relentless pounding. The growing effort, in turn, took its toll on the airmen. The agonizing decisions that crewmen had to make on every death-defying mission now became just that much more wrenching. Already prone to judging themselves harshly when things went wrong, they found that the longer, ever more difficult missions provided proportionally greater opportunities for making wrong decisions. For Flying Officer George Sweanor of the Royal Canadian Air Force, March 27, 1943, was a day of wrong decisions.

By early 1943, George was a veteran who had flown his share of tough missions. He had been to all the hard targets except the one that held a special fascination for everyone—Berlin. It was the heart of Nazi Germany, and to many the thought of hitting it seemed worth the risk of flying deep into enemy territory.

5. Interview with Eugene L. Daniel, Jr., April 14, 1983; Eugene L. Daniel, Jr., *In the Presence of Mine Enemies: Memoirs of German Prisoner of War Life, February 16, 1943 to April 29, 1945* (Attleboro, Mass., 1985), 1–7.

George got his chance just when he wanted it least. A fatiguing flight schedule the previous week and a serious bout with the flu and stomach cramps made him wish for a night to recuperate before undertaking another mission. But Flying Officer Pat Porter, the captain of the crew and a man George felt exceptionally close to as a result of shared experiences, was nearing the end of his tour. Probably he would have only this one last chance to hit Berlin. Loyalty overruled judgment, and George went too.

Pat's crew preferred to fly in their Halifax aircraft nicknamed Kitty. Each plane had its own personality—Kitty was frivolous—but they felt comfortable because they knew her every whim. Unfortunately, Kitty was in for extensive repairs, and they drew an airplane designated "E" Edward, which they assessed immediately as having a rather seedy character. The flight engineer, with an eye for detail, noticed that the ax normally mounted near the escape hatch was missing and ordered the ground crew to find one. In the interim the radio operator complained that the set was temperamental.

The raiders crossed through moderate coastal flak without too much trouble and started inland. About an hour later they ran into a very heavy flak barrage south of Bremen. At twenty thousand feet, nearby blasts rocked the aircraft, and a sheet of flame shot at them as a Lancaster exploded on their port side. It seemed ages before they broke through to a quieter sky.

On the ground a mile and a half ahead, near Rotenburg, a young high school student, who did night duty as a flak gunner, had been recalled from a birthday party to man his gun. The four-gun battery's radar operator worked feverishly to separate the contacts that congested his screen. Finally he concluded he had a single target and fired.

The rounds scored and "E" Edward's starboard outer engine went silent. Noting their position just southeast of Bremen, George suggested they do a solo raid on the city and go home rather than try to finish the long haul to Berlin on only three engines. Another crewman added his thought that they should run southeast to northwest over Bremen, bomb it, then cut between Wilhelmshaven and Emden, a distance of only seventy miles to the sea and four hundred miles home (compared to eight hundred miles via Berlin). But Pat disagreed. They'd gone through hordes of flak and fighters thus far and would waste it all if they didn't press on to the target. He was persuasive, and the remainder of the crew accepted his logic.

The damaged aircraft lost altitude continuously until the crew had to struggle just to keep it at ten thousand feet, barely above the clouds. "E" Edward was still twenty minutes away from the target when the Battle of Berlin opened. A Halifax, illuminated by a dozen searchlights, was weaving frantically, but ended up a mass of earthbound flames. The raid was in its final stages by the time "E" Edward arrived, and already the heat of the fires had burned off some of the cloud cover. George could see two areas on the ground engulfed in flame. The closest one, he concluded, definitely was a city, most likely the western part of Berlin, but the remaining clouds, smoke, and glare from the sheet of flame made it impossible for him to know for sure. To keep from losing any more altitude, he released his bombs with the usual prayer that they would fall only on military targets, though he had small hope it would be answered.

With the weight of the bombs gone, the crippled aircraft slowly gained altitude. But by now it was well behind and below the mutual protection offered by the other ships in the formation, which had flown homeward. The flak batteries spotted the straggler, but somehow missed. The navigator gave a course for home that would cut corners and increase their chances of catching up with the others. During a few quiet moments the crew drained fuel from one tank to another and George slid out of the front turret to lie prone in the nose in order to glance back into the blind spot underneath, the most likely place for a fighter approach. The radio had gone dead, and the operator kicked it. Just then, four streams of fire shot over the full length of George's prone body. He felt a sharp sting in his left leg as cordite fumes filled the aircraft. He had seen no fighter, but the pattern of fire led him to conclude that one had raked them from behind. The radio operator thought his set was exploding after the kick he had given it and set to work putting out the fire in his compartment. But George noticed that the navigator was bleeding as he worked over his desk.

Pat swung the aircraft toward Sweden and called the roll. The main stream of fire had missed all of them, but several crewmen had been wounded by small pieces of metal. The hydraulics were gone, the bomb-bay doors had dropped open, and the undercarriage had fallen. There were numerous little hydraulic oil-fires in the midsection, and Pat could tell that all the engines had gone dead. The altimeter began to unwind with frightening speed. He fought the plunge and turned back inland, knowing they were somewhere near the coast and wanting to avoid ditching in the cold sea. At the same time he gave the bail-out order.

George slid down to the front escape hatch to find that shrapnel and ice had fused it to the aircraft. He tugged with all his might, but could not budge it. No one else could either. Another crewman tried the rear escape hatch and it also was jammed—the handle had been shot away and there was nothing to release the lock. George placed Pat's parachute beside him, opened the hatch above his head, suggested Pat get out that way while the others got out the rear, wished him luck, and raced to the back of the burning plane. There he found the rear gunner already at work with the ax that had been replaced just before takeoff. Everyone knew they were racing toward death. Finally the door gave. Falteringly but with deliberate speed, each crewman slid or leapt into the black night. George was last. Assuming Pat had already jumped from the front, he sat for a moment on the edge of the back door, realizing he was leaving his only means of getting home. Then, knowing the plane must be nearing the ground, he too rushed out into the night.

The slipstream caught him as a sheet of flame passed over—he had not realized how bad the fire was. The drill called for a ten-second wait before pulling the rip cord, but he knew he did not have that luxury and pulled it immediately. Right after the parachute opened, there was a second muscle-tearing jerk as the canopy caught the upper branches of a tree. "E" Edward crashed and exploded in a field. George could feel the heat—had he delayed his jump by only a second or two, he knew he would still be aboard the aircraft. A tall tree, the only one in the vicinity, broke his fall and saved his life.

A gun emplacement, about two fields away, was still firing shells, even though the aircraft was burning furiously amid the crackling explosions of the machine-gun ammunition. George could hear numerous German voices not too far away and realized that his parachute draped over the branches pointed clearly to his position. He released his harness to drop to the ground. The tree was taller than he had imagined, and he went crashing down. He got up, dazed, and tried to get his bearings. The leg wound was becoming painful and was bleeding badly. Only seconds had passed since they were hit, but it seemed that many eternities had come and gone. All he knew for the moment was that he was on solid ground and alive and that it was raining. His escape seemed miraculous. Pausing in the rain, he breathed a prayer of thanks.

He knew he had to get away and hoped that nobody would think to look for him beyond the plunge path. There were sharp pains in his leg, but he could not tell how serious the injury was. George tied a scarf tightly around his leg to stop the bleeding and immediately made for a small orchard. Five Germans were standing at its edge and George almost bumped into them, but luckily one of them spoke when he was only a few paces away. He froze, then inched backwards to try another route. He soon found that the field was surrounded by houses and people, and from the blacked-out motor traffic he figured he was in the suburbs of a city. Escape would not be easy.

Before long he stumbled into a long irrigation ditch. The water was up to his thighs. Crouching, he waded its length to pass, undetected, the circle of people converging on him. By the time he left the ditch, he was soaking wet, and the continuous rain guaranteed he would stay that way. It was a cold March night, so he walked as quickly as his throbbing leg would allow. An hour later he was a mile away.

Then George followed a railroad track to a closed station, searched for schedules, and fled again when two motorcycles with sidecars drew up, their headlights illuminating the building. He found a heavily traveled road and was shortly in another suburb. Heading southwest by compass, he hoped to get clear of the Greater Hamburg area, where he assumed he was. But as dawn approached, his leg began to give him considerable pain, the stomach cramps had returned with a vengeance, and the rain was sapping his already low spirits. He stopped briefly in a cemetery, adjusted the scarf on his leg, and then pressed on. A few minutes later he was beside a long, dark building, and the stomach cramps were fiercely insistent. He squatted there. But then a door opened suddenly, and he was trapped in the light. He had no choice but to sink to the ground and freeze. Seven Wehrmacht officers strode out of the building, laughing and joking. Their heavy boots hit the pavement only a yard or so from his head, but they did not see him. Perhaps their eyes had not yet adjusted to the dark after the brightly lit barracks. But their noses surely should have told them he was there. He got up and staggered away.

As dawn approached he found himself still in the suburbs. He walked boldly along city streets, taking advantage of the light and the lack of pedestrians. Then in his path was a bridge guarded by Germans, so he turned toward a large park, hoping to spend the day there reconnoitering. A family suddenly emerged from a side street and headed right for him. "Guten Morgen," they murmured as they passed, but they paid no further heed. It was Sunday morning, so George presumed that they were on their way to church and were still half asleep. Surely a blood-stained, soaking-wet, malodorous Canadian uniform merited more curiosity than they had shown.

George managed to stay clear of children and lovers throughout the day, but not without difficulty. As he searched for a suitable place to cross the river he could see the couples sitting or standing, but had trouble spotting those lying on the ground until he almost stepped on them. Having finally located a probable crossing spot, he settled down to wait for nightfall and dry out his boots. Later, while putting his boots back on, he saw two members of the Hitler Youth coming his way. He was so intent on watching them that he was startled when a sweet voice behind him asked, "Was ist los, Herr Leutnant?" (What's the matter, Lieutenant?) He swung around and saw a slender, attractive young woman with beautiful blond hair looking at him. He knew no German, so he muttered unintelligibly as he tied his boot laces and rose to saunter off. She shouted for help. A group of people appeared from nowhere and headed toward George. The Hitler Youths, knives drawn, came running. George increased his pace, the Germans fanned out to surround him, and he ran toward some young spruce trees that he had scouted earlier in the day. He raced into the east end of the woods, went halfway through, then circled left, then back, hoping to outfox his pursuers. But the blonde and two men had anticipated his tactics. George twisted away from them, but his leg collapsed momentarily, and they were on him. Seconds later ten more people arrived, the older ones restraining the Hitler Youths, who wanted to jab him a few times with their daggers. Knowing any further attempt at escape was futile, George slowly struggled to his feet, shrugged his shoulders, and spread out his hands to indicate surrender.[6]

By comparison, some missions undoubtedly were easier than others. Everyone welcomed these "milk runs," which counted toward tour completion just as the deep penetrations did. And they were good missions for beginners, giving a taste of things to come without overwhelming them the first time out. In reality, however, there was no such thing as a milk run: every mission was fraught with danger, and the first flight into enemy territory frequently became the last. It certainly was for Colonel Delmar T. Spivey.

A commanding officer at a large flexible-gunnery school in Florida, Spivey joined a secret investigative team that was going to Europe to discover why their graduates were reportedly not proving out well in

6. Interview with George Sweanor, February, 1979; George W. Sweanor, *It's All Pensionable Time: 25 Years in the Royal Canadian Air Force* (Woodland Park, Colo., 1979), 96–106.

battle. Some, it was said, couldn't hit the broad side of a barn, much less a moving aircraft. Spivey was determined to find out why.

He got airborne on August 12, 1943, as the guest of a highly experienced crew. Pilot Eugene Wiley had completed fourteen missions, co-pilot Emmitte Wells nine, bombardier Overman four, navigator Bob Broach thirteen, and most of the enlisted men fourteen. It was Spivey's first, but the trip was to be a milk run over the Ruhr, and Spivey was pleased to be flying with real veterans.

The first sign that all would not be easy appeared as the B-17 began to roll down the runway. The supercharger on number-one engine ran away. The plane lurched sideways and headed across the field at about a sixty-degree angle to the runway. The plane had not gained flying speed, so Wiley was forced to keep going and clear a brick building on the edge of the field. The takeoff woke everyone up in rapid order.

Once on the way toward the target in the Ruhr, Spivey could not help noticing how peaceful the countryside below looked. He also noticed that the Spitfire escorts had barely turned back to England before the German fighters appeared. They, too, looked peaceful at first. Spivey's hands were clammy as he gripped the nose gun and began to search for a target. In addition to watching the Germans, he kept an eye on his fellow gunners and former students. The Germans peeled off and headed directly for the formation. Spivey cursed aloud when the gunners opened up while the fighters were a good two thousand yards away. But the closing speed was so great that he joined in himself only a few seconds later. The FW-190s began to fire and almost immediately turned on their backs and pulled straight down away from the formation. Brief though the exchange was, Spivey had the answer he had come looking for. He stared in disbelief as the gunners sprayed their bullets across the sky. Firing at a moving object from another moving object is tricky business. Further, trajectories differ, depending on whether one is shooting out of the left or right side of the aircraft fore or aft. The scientists and engineers who built the equipment for flexible gunnery designed the gunsights to compensate for such problems. The school taught the young gunners to use the sights, but in the heat of battle the sights too often were forgotten. The urge to "hose down the enemy" obviously was strong.

Spivey knew he had made an important discovery, and the school could dramatically improve the gunners' success rate. He saw other matters the school should address. At one point a plane with an obviously dead or unconcious pilot flew right through the bomber formation without firing a shot. The trigger-happy gunners deluged him and, in the process, shot up one another.

As the plane reached the target the fighters faded back and the ground gunners took over. Spivey was impressed as he watched the huge boxlike smoke puffs appear and disappear in the sky, one too low, one high and to the left, and another one, seemingly created by a thousand guns, bursting high and to the right but much closer. He also saw the bombs fall away, released with a mighty oath by Overman. As he watched them keeping up with the forward motion of the plane, a burst of flak jolted the entire aircraft. The armor plate on which he was kneeling smashed up against his knees. The impact knocked off his steel helmet and sent the ammunition boxes flying. His nose gun came to rest at a crazy angle. Broach saw a very large hole in the right wing and before long the cowling ripped off in the slipstream. Wiley announced over the intercom that he could not feather (stop) the propellor, and that the resulting drag would make them unable to stay in formation. Pulling out to the left, he stuck the nose straight down, evading and twisting as he went, trying to get into the thin stratum of clouds at five thousand feet before fighters could do them any more damage. All the crew could do was hang on and fight off the ammunition boxes. The tail gunner, who was badly wounded, asked permission to bail out to get help. The chances of getting back looked dim anyway, so Wiley told him to jump. The sky was full of fighters, but only two pursued them. They reached the clouds with just one 20-mm hit in the waist that did not injure anyone.

By now the whole ship was vibrating badly, but Wiley and Wells still had it under control. They took a heading of 300 degrees in order to get back north of the Ruhr and out of range of the flak. After ten minutes they prepared to turn left and fly out over the Dutch coast. At this point number-three engine caught on fire. Then number four went. The fire in number three began to spread, and within a minute or two the wing, red-hot, began to glow. With two engines now out, the plane started to lose altitude rapidly. Wiley saw no choice but to give the bail-out order. Within ten seconds Overman had the escape hatch open, but did not jump. The intercom system gave out, leaving Spivey without any further means of electronic communication. Fortunately, Lieutenant Broach, always quiet and efficient, heard Wiley issue new directions and countermand his earlier order to jump. By now the plane had descended to well below a thousand feet, and Wiley commanded everyone to prepare for a crash landing.

As Wiley and Wells initiated landing procedures much as they would for a normal strip approach, the others scrambled for the radio compartment. In the rush, Spivey's chute harness caught in the bomb racks—for an instant it seemed he would not get free. Being in the bomb bay when the plane crashed would no doubt have been fatal. But he cleared himself, rushed across the bomb-bay doors without using the catwalk, and reached the radio room when the aircraft was no more than fifty feet above the treetops. He frantically tried to open the door, shouting to those inside to let him in. It opened and he squeezed in. Spivey flopped down in a sitting position and took the full impact when the head of the man in front of him snapped back. His dental bridge broke and several teeth began to swim in blood and saliva. The plane crashed through telephone wires and hit the ground, slowly churning to a halt in a wheat field. Everyone then moved in desperation to get out before the plane exploded.

The ten remaining crew members scattered like a frightened covey of quail. But it was too late. The plane had come down near the German-Holland border, in a rich farming district. Germans and Dutch alike converged on the site from nearby fields. Spivey turned toward a hedge, but a Dutch farmer overtook him. In one hand he held a hunting rifle, in the other a pitchfork. The flight for freedom came to an abrupt and early end—the old farmer's pitchfork rested uncomfortably hard against Spivey's back.[7]

Whether a tough mission or a milk run, there always existed the danger of going down at sea. The unfortunate drowning of Padde Fanucane in his sinking Spitfire had served as a strong reminder to Clark that the sea was an enemy to be feared as much as the Germans. Cy Widen did well to prepare for survival at sea, even though he did not use his equipment in the end. The North Sea and the English Channel in particular held special dangers for downed air-

7. Interviews with Delmar T. Spivey, 1973–1981; Delmar T. Spivey, *POW Odyssey: Recollections of Center Compound, Stalag Luft III and the Secret German Peace Mission in World War II*, ed. George Gibb and Hilma Gibb (Attleboro, Mass., 1984), 1–8; Bob Broach, "The Last Mission," 1943 (MS in possession of the author); Eugene M. Wiley to the author, July 1, 1980.

men. In the winter, survival time in the water was only about three minutes; even if one had a raft, the chances of staying alive were not good. Ditching in the sea in the summer was not so likely to be fatal, of course, but even then the sea proved to be temperamental and dangerous. Second Lieutenant Norville ("Johnny") Gorse and his crew were among the unfortunates who had to face the dreaded North Sea waters.

In bad weather and heavy cloud cover, their mission got under way at 0530 hours on July 28, 1943. Gorse sat in the left seat and served as pilot for takeoff and formation rendezvous. More than three hundred bombers participated in the raid against the Oschersleben FW-190 airplane plant, but the number should have been much larger. The formation Gorse joined was scheduled to put one hundred planes over the target. Only twenty-eight made it, the rest being lost to aborts or listed as missing in action.

Once in formation, Gorse turned the controls over to First Lieutenant Bill Nance. Flying over the North Sea and turning east to align their course with the Frisian Islands, the formation spread out in the clouds and re-formed when the skies cleared. The group leader was hit by Junkers JU-88 40-mm cannon fire that blew away most of his tail section. The group re-formed on the deputy leader's plane, but its right wing ended up with a long hole from cannon fire, and a fuel line broke in one of its engines. The group re-formed again. Gorse took over the controls just before the number-two plane in their flight was hit and fell back out of formation. He edged his plane into its place. There were discussions about an additional move, but Gorse argued that they already had flown in four different positions and were surely attracting fighter attention. Nonetheless, another change was agreed upon. Gorse was in the process of making the alteration when the top turret gunner shouted that they were being hit in the left wing with 20-mm cannon fire. Three enemy fighters had attacked from six o'clock high, out of the sun, and were shooting down on them. Gorse started evasive action and slid under the lead ship for protection, but not quickly enough to avoid cannon fire through the radio room and out the right wing. Technical Sergeant Maxwell had time to blow up the lead fighter, but the other two got away. Three more fighters pounced on the damaged bomber. Maxwell and the tail gunner, Staff Sergeant Ed Youngers, each hit one. But the fighters also had hit their mark. The forty minutes of combat were over.

Nance called the navigator for a heading home while Gorse pointed the nose down to dive and blow out the fire that had started. Maxwell yelled that the left wing flap had burned away, the main spar was exposed, and the left wing was on fire. Suddenly, huge quantities of fuel poured out of the left wing tanks; the crew felt a large bump when the fuel ignited, and then all four engines stopped. Nance started toward the rear exit, collided with Maxwell coming out of the turret, and shouted, "Let's get out of here." Gorse saw that the fuel coming out of the wing was burning about three feet behind it, not in the wing, and suggested that ditching the plane and having the dinghy would be better than attempting to survive the North Sea without the boat. Joe Hudson, the navigator, came out of the nose and said they were sixty miles from the coast and sixty miles west of Heligoland, confirming the need to ditch rather than bail out.

Gorse continued a redlined-airspeed-indicator dive, and the flames slowed with the fuel loss from the ruptured tanks. Meanwhile, Youngers came out of the tail after the explosion and reported that four of the gunners had bailed out. Then he returned to his position and shot down two of the three fighters pursuing them. Apparently sensing victory and seeing no more opposition from the bomber, the fighters had closed to within 150 feet of the tail. Youngers' gun coming alive caught them by surprise.

By the time the plane reached sea level, most of the fuel was gone and the wing fire appeared to be out. Leveling off to ditch, Gorse propped his side window with his elbow so it would not jam. That would be his escape path. The warm outside air rushed in, condensed on the cold windshield, and turned to frost. Gorse scraped at it. He set the plane down on the water while checking height and water conditions through both the open window and the partially frosted windshield. The water was calm with a slight swell, and he ditched the plane smoothly.

Most of the flames were out when the two dinghies were released. But one fell into some burning fuel and sank. Nance, Maxwell, and the rest of the crew escaped through the radio hatch while Gorse squeezed out through the pilot's window. The six boarded the remaining dinghy and checked their gear—paddles, a Very flare pistol, a hand-powered radio, two parachutes, a survival kit with fresh water and chocolate bars, and miscellaneous minor items. The plane sank, then exploded under water. Three oxygen bottles and some empty ammunition cases surfaced. They salvaged two of the bottles, opened a parachute, made a sea anchor from part of it, and tied the bottles to a trailing shroud line to measure drift.

The navigator pointed out that the North Sea current was counterclockwise and that they would drift toward Jutland, so they steered toward the North Channel. They wondered whether an RAF patrol would find them the next morning. Hudson mentioned that his watch had stopped at 1105 hours. They began their trip by cranking the hand radio and paddling in two-hour shifts.

Late that afternoon, a shark struck one of the trailing oxygen bottles and hit it several times. The crew clearly saw its dorsal fin and mouth: it was ten to twelve feet long. The shark swam in a wide circle and then came to within a few feet of the boat, but did not touch it. Everyone sat still until he swam away, then continued paddling and cranking the radio.

Early on the morning of the second day they watched a German fighter climb out over the Frisian Islands. A storm descended upon them shortly afterward and continued until the following morning, bringing with it fifteen-foot seas that threatened to capsize them. But the crew kept the boat pointed into the waves and managed to stay afloat.

Later in the day, British fighters bombed Jutland. On their way home they flew down close to the boat but did not see it. The Very pistol had been lost in the storm and arm waving was not enough to attract them. Toward evening the dinghy passed a buoy marking the North Channel.

That night, a stream of British bombers flew over on their way to Hamburg. One was shot down in flames, broke into two parts, and fell not far from the boat. The storm and rain continued intermittently. The crewmen were partly protected by the parachute silk, but not from the drenching spray of the breakers. Bailing became one of their regular chores—and then an endless job when a bootheel poked a hole in the bottom of the boat.

The rain stopped on the morning of July 30. They had drifted east of their former position and were awakened by explosions along the German-held coast. Three JU-52s, each with a huge mine-detector ring under it, were exploding mines with machine-gun fire. One spotted the dinghy and left the formation. The others dropped green and yellow sea markers around the boat. A Dornier DO-24 twin-engine seaplane soon returned and landed nearby. Two guards stood on the pontoons with machine guns and motioned for the crew to board the plane. One guard watched with his gun pointed at them while the other cut up the dinghy and threw it back into the water. The men were now prisoners, disappointed they had been captured but nonetheless thankful to be alive. They knew their ordeal would have ended much sooner and far less favorably had they fallen into the North Sea at any time other than midsummer.[8]

Whether on land or at sea, every downed airman able to walk or swim thought first of eluding capture and getting back into Allied hands. The chances of success were slim, but virtually everyone felt he had to try. Understandably, the closer a crew member was to the Low Countries, France, or Spain, the better his odds. Even then, it was seldom possible to predict who would make it and who would not. Lieutenant Ralph H. Saltsman and one of his fellow crew members, Josepe Emanos, apparently landed in the same field. The Germans happened to stumble upon Saltsman, but Emanos, shot down on July 14, 1943, was back in England by December 1. He was the last one back of the six in his crew who got out of France. According to intelligence reports, he also was the nineteenth crew member to return from that raid.[9]

Few were so fortunate, and most fliers knew that. Perhaps that was why Captain Roland L. Sargent felt such surprise when he suddenly discovered he was on the road back to England. But in war-torn Europe, it was by no means a certainty that the road you were on would get you home. For him, the historic Schweinfurt raid, launched on August 17, 1943, and doomed to be one of the longest and most costly attacks of the war, seemed to drag on forever.

Shot down after the bombing run, he hit the ground hard on the outskirts of Saint Huebrichts-Hern, a small village north of Liège, Belgium. His left ankle badly sprained, he was unable to get to his feet before a man dressed in rough work clothes, evidently a farmer, approached him. Sargent raised himself up on one elbow, and the man raised his hand, as if to indicate he meant no harm. Soon other men gathered and stood in a semicircle, looking at him but saying nothing. Sargent motioned to his ankle, but the onlookers gave no

8. Norville J. Gorse, "There I Was," n.d. (MS in possession of the author).
9. Ralph H. Saltsman, "My Story," September 14, 1944 (MS in possession of the author); Josepe Emanos to Colonel Saltsman, February 9, 1976, copy in possession of the author.

sign that they understood. He then tried a few words in faltering French, asking whether or not this was Germany. They shook their heads, one man said "La Belgique." Feeling encouraged, Sargent tried to get up, whereupon they immediately reached down to help him. Using his meager French, he conveyed to them that he was an American pilot. They responded warmly, smiling, nodding their heads, clasping his hand, and saying, "Bonjour," "Courage," "Bonne chance."

One of the group was a middle-aged woman who knew a little English and seemed to have some authority. When another man approached, the group grew uneasy. The woman spoke in a low voice to Sargent—this man was not to be trusted, and Sargent was to say nothing to him. The man stopped some distance away and just stared, the group all the while shielding Sargent from the unwanted intruder. Nobody spoke to the man at all.

By this time Sargent had become anxious to get out of such a conspicuous spot. Genevieve DeSchatsen and Henri Snellings got on either side and helped him toward a large wooded area nearby. As they entered the woods two figures appeared on the path ahead of them. One was Captain Robert McNeely, Sargent's navigator, and the other was a Belgian who had seen McNeely parachute down and was trying to hide him from the Germans. Together, Sargent and McNeely were kept in the woods until about midnight, when Lieutenant Keith Byington, co-pilot on the crew, was brought in to join them.

The Belgian with Byington could speak English well enough to tell them they had to move to another spot in the woods, which Genevieve DeSchatsen's father owned. Concluding that Sargent could not make the trek because of his bad ankle, the Belgian, a stocky, muscular man, offered to carry him piggyback. In seemingly tireless fashion, the Belgian tromped through the underbrush, under low-hanging branches, along rough trails, stumbling and staggering at times, but never once stopping or falling. He led them to a crude shelter and left them there. He returned periodically with food and water.

Several days later a Belgian farmer brought a straight razor and shaved the three fliers without lather or water. Since each had a four-day growth, it was a painful operation. But they were going to be taken to a village some distance away and so their looks must not arouse suspicion. That argument made sense to the Americans. Much of what followed did not.

By this time the men had given up their flight outfits and put on civilian work clothes. While their shaves still smarted a well-dressed middle-aged man came to see them. He spoke English well and told them they were next to go by truck to another village. At the same time, however, he strongly urged them to get back their military uniforms and give themselves up to the Germans. He argued that they had very little chance of evading capture and in their civilian clothes they could be shot as spies. The Americans were shocked to hear such words coming from a Belgian, especially from one as highly educated and intelligent as this man appeared to be. They would have been even more surprised, had they known at the time, that the man was none other than Genevieve's father.

The trio indicated they wanted to continue their efforts to get back to England. The man seemed disappointed, but argued no further and simply left. Later that morning they were led to a dilapidated old truck. The men said brief farewells to the country people who had risked so much to help them, climbed aboard, and bounced off. Out of hiding for the first time, they felt completely vulnerable and out in the open where they could be seen by anyone—a definitely unsettling sensation. Eventually they arrived in a fair-sized village and stopped in front of a modest dwelling. They were quickly ushered inside. The driver returned to the truck and drove away, never having spoken a single word.

Their new guide and caretaker, apparently a lawyer in his mid-thirties, peered through the lace curtains to see if anyone had noticed their arrival. Then turning, he smiled, greeted the men in stilted English, and said they were welcome as allies and friends under his roof.

One evening a local gendarme and several others who were in the resistance movement visited the home. Everyone sat around the dining room table with a shaded lamp suspended over the middle and conversed in a mixture of poorly spoken French and English. The gendarme knew only one sentence of English, "I am the teacher and you are the pupils," which he proudly demonstrated. All the visitors carried concealed guns, which they freely showed, boasting that they had killed Germans and wanted to kill more. In the next breath they asked if the Americans were afraid of the situation in which they found themselves. With a sense of false bravado Sargent said no.

Soon the host announced that the next stop was Liège. Again the men expressed their heartfelt appreciation and said good-bye. A new guide escorted them to a nearby tram, bought their tickets, and led them on board. The tram was filled to capacity, and a fair number of the passengers were Germans in Luftwaffe uniforms. Sargent found himself squeezed between two of the uniformed men. What would they do, he wondered, if they knew they were rubbing shoulders with an American pilot? Occasionally his eyes would meet those of a German; the glance was momentary, an expressionless exchange. Understandably Sargent was most uncomfortable with the whole situation. Then a group of girls, also in Luftwaffe uniforms, boarded, and Sargent felt more at ease when all the German men directed their attention to the girls.

Deep in the heart of Liège, the guide led the men off the tram. Strung out in a line, not wanting to appear to be together but not daring to lose sight of one another, they followed as the guide wove his way through the twisting streets. Once a German officer walking toward Sargent startled him by saluting smartly. Sargent had the presence of mind not to return the salute. He found that several German enlisted men were walking behind him. The officer apparently had only been returning their salutes. Sargent found himself perspiring more than the temperature of the day warranted.

Finally arriving at a large public square, the group was taken to a café on the first floor of a two-story building. The owner, who lived upstairs, was the Liège link in the underground that the men had so unexpectedly found. Because of the August heat, the windows of the second-story room in which they stayed were usually open onto the square. The Americans themselves could remain invisible to the people below. But the owner sat by the window with the volume turned up, listening to BBC radio broadcasts. Every time the words "Ici Londres" boomed out, they cringed. It seemed probable that everyone around the square would hear it, and they thought surely some German authority would soon be pounding on the door to investigate. But none ever did.

For the next move they were to go by themselves around to the next block from the square and wait for a car. They did as they were told and looked around for their contact. They stood together for an awkward minute or two. Suddenly a voice with an American-sounding accent asked, "How's it going, fellas?" Taken aback, they saw some men they had not noticed before, sitting in two parked cars. The fliers were flabbergasted at this casual greeting and quickly walked over to the first car. The driver told McNeely and Sargent to get in and directed Byington into the other car. They immediately pulled out for Brussels, the next stop.

Once again the Americans were surprised and chagrined by the seemingly reckless way their guides conducted business—clandestine activities should be conducted as inconspicuously as possible. The men sat rigidly in mounting disbelief as the two cars sped through the city and into the countryside. Inexplicably the drivers acted like madmen, at one point forcing a large group of Hitler Youth and their accompanying officers off the road. The Americans turned white with apprehension.

Once in Brussels, they drove to a residence in a thickly settled neighborhood. They were greatly surprised to find about twenty other Allied fliers, some of whom they knew, waiting inside. False papers identifying them as French workers were being prepared, complete with the necessary official stamps, travel permits, and photographs. The man who drove them from Liège apparently was in charge of the Brussels operation and had an air of easy confidence. He talked freely about past successes and sounded so encouraging, the men became convinced that they were as good as back in England. In fact, a group that had left shortly after Sargent arrived at the house had reportedly cleared France and now were safe in Spain. The Americans were elated and impatient to get started.

Then suddenly ten of them were briefed for departure. They would be driven to a large railway station where they would meet their guide, who would have already purchased their tickets, and board the train. They were asked to give up the one thing they still possessed that could identify them as military personnel—their dog tags. It was a difficult request to comply with. While not overtly resisting, the men discussed it among themselves and expressed real concern. But they had been told in England that if they were ever shot down and made contact with the resistance organizations, they should put complete trust in them and do everything precisely as asked because the lives of everyone involved might depend upon it. So they reluctantly turned their identification tags over to their host.

The first part of the plan worked without a hitch. The ten American and British fliers got on board and took seats in two separate compartments partly filled with civilians. During the uneventful ride through the countryside, the men exchanged glances only occasionally with their guide, who remained standing in the corridor. As the train neared the French border, however, several gendarmes announced that everyone would have to get out there for a routine check. The men had been told they would not have to leave the train. Their guide motioned for them to stay put.

When the train stopped, all the civilians got off, leaving their luggage. Soon two gendarmes peered in, looking at the baggage, and asked the fliers whose it was. No one said a word. The gendarme was standing in the doorway, and his companion was looking over his shoulder. Silence. Again he put the question to the speechless men, gesturing impatiently. The silence was heavy. Finally one of the group answered in French, with a noticeable British accent, that the suitcases belonged to those outside. The reply resulted in an immediate demand for identification. Each of the fliers handed his papers to the gendarmes, who glanced at them and handed them back. They then turned to the guide and questioned him at length. In the meantime, the civilians reboarded the train and it pulled away, clacking over the rails. But there was a difference. Sargent could still see their guide standing in the corridor, but now he was flanked by gendarmes and stared gloomily out the window. The civilians seemed unaffected by it all, but in each of the men an uneasiness grew as they sped along to a future that had suddenly become very uncertain.

Eventually, after what seemed hours, the train entered Paris. The men watched the civilians get off and the gendarmes, with the guide between them, move along the corridor. The guide glanced back, his wordless look telling the men to follow him. They stayed far enough behind to avoid attention but were close enough to spot further signals about what they should do. As they entered the large station teeming with people, the guide looked back at them once more and nodded his head toward a young boy standing slightly to one side. The men moved in the boy's direction. Their guide disappeared into the crowd, the gendarmes still at his side. They never saw him again or learned what happened to him.

The boy, who appeared to be in his mid-teens, crossed the terminal toward the exit. The fliers followed, again trailing out unevenly but remaining acutely aware of where the man immediately ahead was going. They crossed the square in front of the station, walked along a sidewalk, and saw the young guide go through a doorway. One by one, the men ahead of Sargent reached that unimpressive sanctuary and disappeared from sight. Then he too stepped through it and found a rather narrow hallway that led to a registration desk of sorts. The boy in whom they had placed their trust was talking to a man behind the counter. The last of the ten-member group came into the hall. Together, they stood in a line stretching from the door to the desk, waiting for their accommodations. The boy and desk clerk continued talking in low voices.

A figure darkened the doorway, and a man in civilian clothes came inside. He was followed by another, then another, and yet another. The fliers were all looking at them, wondering who and what they were. They were not aware at that moment that there were exactly ten men. But they found out abruptly and violently when the men walked down the hall until one of them was in front of each flier. Suddenly, as though on signal, they turned, pulled snub-nosed automatics, jammed them into the fliers' stomachs, and harshly demanded "Hands up!" The fliers were stunned. It all occurred unexpectedly and very fast. Hardly believing what was happening, they raised their hands above their heads while the intruders frisked them roughly. In uncomprehending shock, none of the fliers uttered a word. Sargent thought for a moment he saw one of the men patting their erstwhile young guide on the back as though in appreciation for a job well done, but he could not be sure.

Still in a daze, Sargent thought wildly that the whole scene was a trick being played on them by the underground. But the thought fled rapidly when they were taken outside to a waiting bus alongside which stood a German officer. At that moment Sargent had every reason to believe that for him the long Schweinfurt raid was finally over and that he, too, would now be numbered among the thousands who became prisoners of the Luftwaffe. That day would surely come for Roland Sargent—but not yet.

Grueling days were to pass before Sargent found comparative refuge in Luftwaffe hands. The words of Genevieve's father must have echoed in his mind many times as he suffered at the hands of the Gestapo, who did indeed treat him as a spy. There seemed little help for him in the coming weeks. It might have been some small consolation, had he known, that the route for most downed fliers was uncertain from the point of capture until they arrived in a permanent Luftwaffe camp. Each man who passed through the eye of the needle prior to capture was subjected to yet another highly unpredictable and emotionally trying experience as he encountered the enemy face to face on the streets en route to the interrogation cell.[10]

10.   Interview with Roland L. Sargent, June 24, 1980.

2

Down Uncharted Roads

The reception given Allied fliers in the European theater varied, depending on the stage of the war and the attitudes of the people who captured or otherwise had access to them. Airmen dreaded the thought of landing near the target they had just attacked. But whether or not they managed to get clear of the target area, their first encounter on the ground made a considerable difference. If soldiers arrived, capture was imminent, but the flier's safety usually was assured. If civilians got there, the chances of making contact with the underground improved, but so did the risk of being beaten with clubs and pitchforks or being lynched by irate citizens not accustomed to the self-control exercised by the military.

Germany was not unique in this regard. Even in England the crowds occasionally became unruly. In March, 1941, the German submarine U-99 was forced to the surface by depth charges in the Atlantic. The crew was taken captive and transported to Liverpool. Word of their arrival preceded them, and as they were marched toward an interrogation center a sizable crowd gathered. Liverpool residents had suffered from the blockade, had lost citizens in ships sunk by U-boats, and had seen the dead and wounded brought from other ships struck by submarines. The crew literally walked the gauntlet when the crowd released its pent-up fury, attacking with brooms, pokers, shovels, and garden forks. The police tried to stop the people, but in the end the party had to make a run for the nearby jail. As a policeman said, apologizing to a crewman whose nose had been broken in the fracas, "Sorry, old boy, they're usually very nice people."[1]

In England this apparently was a relatively isolated incident, no deaths resulted, and the British government neither condoned nor

---

1. A. J. Barker, *Prisoners of War* (New York, 1975), 58.

encouraged the action. The same could not be said of Germany, especially in the latter days of the war. As Allied bombing attacks intensified, the fate of each airman became increasingly uncertain. One could hardly have predicted the extent of that uncertainty based on the warm handshake Wings Day received from his captor in October, 1939.

After Forest Guardsman Walter Becker released Wings's hand, two Luftwaffe youths with rifles hesitantly requested that he put his hands above his head. He did so, his face blackened by smoke, eyes swollen, eyebrows burned away. Hatless, he walked down the hill with them to the village of Langweiler.

At the grocery store, the shopkeeper produced some face cream and smeared it gently across Wings's scorched forehead. A Luftwaffe doctor arrived, an elderly, kindly man, and introduced himself as Hauptmann (Captain) Hermann Gauch. Wings had continuously asked about his two crewmen, and now he got his answer. The captain led him outside. There in the back of a truck, amid a heap of scorched parachute silk, lay both their bodies. The chattering onlookers in the street fell silent. No one moved as Wings snapped to attention and saluted the crewmen. As Wings turned away, Gauch gave him his arm and uttered, "I am sorry." He assured Wings that they would be given a proper military funeral.

Later that afternoon the Germans took Wings to a pleasant villa in the village of Fischbach-Weierback. A stocky Wehrmacht major and his wife greeted them in the hall. The major, also a doctor and cousin of Gauch's, explained that Wings was to wash, have his burned face dressed again, and properly compose himself before being handed over for more official medical treatment and interrogation by German Intelligence. After a wash and a fresh bandage, Wings looked and felt better. These people, he thought to himself, were treating him like one of their own men.

Later Wings asked for the location of the bathroom and was told it was down the hall. No one followed, and Wings momentarily thought of escape, a move he would have been prepared to make had people been unpleasant. But he was being treated like a guest of honor. For the next two days he remained in this strange twilight of captivity, in contact with people not accustomed to being jailers, who were faintly apologetic about and embarrassed by the precautions they were called upon to observe. Even after being taken to the hospital, Wings found the situation congenial and unreal. Reality came only at night, when he was alone in his hospital bed and there was a sentry in the open door. And in time there came the inevitable entry into the barbed-wire enclosure of an actual prison camp. But even there, Wings had every reason to believe he would be treated as an honorable and professional soldier.[2]

Bub Clark also found himself somewhat surprised by the sequence of events after his capture in July of 1942. After being checked in by a POW processing officer who took his name, rank, and serial number, Clark was taken to an officer's quarters to await the Luftwaffe. He was given a Sunday-night supper and then driven by a senior Luftwaffe officer and two guards to the Luftwaffe Officers' Club in Saint-Omer, one of the main bases of Fighter Command West. There he was interviewed by fighter pilots who had been involved in the afternoon fight and by an intelligence officer. Their primary interest, he concluded, was to discover who shot him down, as each one wanted credit. From Saint-Omer Clark was taken to the army military jail in Boulogne for the night. Early the next morning he was put on a train, the Dunord, and escorted to Brussels by one NCO and two privates. From there he took an evening train to Germany and, after two nights' traveling, arrived at Frankfurt. In a few hours he would be in Dulag Luft, the main Luftwaffe interrogation center, tired and harried, but certainly not abused.[3]

Perhaps the gentlemanly reception given these two officers had something to do with their being fighter rather than bomber pilots. In fact, unless a fighter pilot was shot down while executing a strafing attack, he usually benefited from that strange sense of camaraderie that prevails among airmen, whatever their nationality. That principle certainly seemed to hold true for Cy Widen when he waded ashore to his waiting captors in North Africa in December, 1942.

As Cy approached the Germans he extended his gun to them, butt first. He had walked only a few feet when a photographer drew near and a jeep suddenly appeared with a pilot dressed in desert flying gear. The pilot was introduced to him as Sergeant Hafner, the man who shot him down. Hafner offered Cy a cigarette. Not a smoker but still dazed, Cy took the cigarette and lit it. Then, noticing that Cy was an officer, Sergeant Hafner saluted him. A friendly discussion ensued, a mixture of pleasantries and questions about where Cy was

2. Smith, *Mission Escape*, 10–13.
3. General Clark Scrapbook.

born. Cy considered himself a "name, rank, and serial number" man and refused to give away information he thought might be used against him later. He named the city of Philadelphia, a place he had never even visited. During the conversation the photographer took pictures at a furious rate. When Cy commented on the helmet a German was wearing, they asked him if he wanted to try it on. He said he would; he put it on and smiled. The photographer quickly captured the scene.

Cy was impressed by the man who had shot him down. Seeing something hanging around the sergeant's neck, he hesitantly asked if it was a Ritter Croix (Knight's Cross). Hafner said it was. Upon closer inspection, Cy noticed the Eichenlaub (oak leaf) cluster as well. The sergeant was a highly decorated veteran. When he pointed out he was aware that Hafner must already have a distinguished military record, Hafner replied, "Yes, you're the eighty-second airplane I've shot down." Although not liking the outcome, Cy was somewhat relieved to learn that he had been outgunned by a true ace.

After Cy commented on some of Hafner's other decorations, Hafner made a complimentary remark about Cy's set of wings. Cy immediately removed them from his uniform and said, "Here, you can have them if you like. I don't think I'll need them where I'm going." Then in a gesture of magnanimity, Hafner reached for his wings, saying, "Here, you can have mine too." At that point, however, an officer stepped forward and said, "No, you can't give this man anything— he's your prisoner." Undaunted, Cy asserted, "You tried to extend a friendly hand to me and I to you—if we both survive this war and our nations are back at peace again, come to the States sometime and visit me." Then everyone present, including Cy, walked over to examine the ruins of his airplane.

Upon leaving the scene, Cy was escorted to a house on rue de Plus in Tunis and incarcerated on the second floor. The windows were barred, and the guards appeared to be Hitler Youths or very young airmen, who were distinctly inclined to act like toughs. Cy wished his guards were more experienced soldiers, people who had been around long enough to recognize man's inhumanity to man and who, he believed, were likely to be more lenient. Somewhere along the way he ran into just such a person, a man who had worked as a butcher in Milwaukee and knew the area where Cy's two brothers lived on Fond du Lac Avenue. Cy appreciated the extra pieces of bread the man gave him from time to time and never forgot him.

In addition to his concern about the guards, Cy knew that food, or rather the lack of it, was going to be a problem. Supper that first night consisted of one slice of German black bread and a little piece of sausage. In keeping with one of the names on his airplane, his gut began to growl and never stopped. Shortly thereafter, on the train to Rome, the transition from K-rations to German black bread and sauerkraut began to have its predictable effect. The ride north in the crowded cars was miserable for both him and the guards.

Before continuing their journey, several thoughtful and trusting guards let Cy visit some of the sights in the Vatican. Once back on the train he traveled up the Po Valley and through the Brenner Pass. His impressions of captivity thus far were largely formed by the memorable exchange with the impressive young sergeant who shot him down.[4]

The unusual circumstances that led to Chaplain Daniel's "capture" also greatly affected his first days in captivity. Arriving at the German regimental headquarters, he was taken to see Oberst (Colonel) Schmidt, the commanding officer, who sat behind the center of a long table. There were three staff officers on his left and three on his right. Daniel was both scared and fascinated: this obviously constituted a formal interrogation session. Colonel Schmidt offered him a drink and a cigarette. Daniel declined both.

Colonel Schmidt began by asking several questions about Daniel's regiment and the American forces in the area. Getting little satisfaction, he commented to the others that a chaplain probably would not possess information of value in such matters anyway. Then the colonel asked, "Why did you Americans come to North Africa when you already have a great rich country?"

"We came to help get at the enemy. The United States has no territorial designs on this area," Daniel replied.

"I am not going to be a hypocrite," Schmidt retorted. "We are out to win Africa for ourselves. We want the riches of Africa."

"Why don't you buy the raw materials you need from Africa on the open market, like the other nations of the world?" Daniel asked.

"You really are naive," Schmidt snapped. "Don't you know that Britain and America control the seas and the raw materials of the world? Germany cannot buy what she needs." Amplifying his point,

---

4. Interview with Widen, April 11, 1979.

he then asked, "Don't you Americans have chocolate, bananas, and coffee every day of your life?"

Daniel admitted that they did.

"Don't you think the Germans would like to have these things too?" Schmidt asked. "Well, this time," he said with great feeling, "we intend to have them."

At that moment the telephone rang. Schmidt was obviously pleased with the caller's message. He slammed down the receiver, pounded his fist on the table with glee, and announced, "Our troops knocked out 75 U.S. tanks today and are advancing rapidly to the west."

"How far are you going on this drive?" Daniel asked.

Confidently and proudly Schmidt replied, "To Casablanca!"

Somewhat emboldened, Daniel asked, "Why do you think Germany can win this war when they were not able to win World War I, especially since America and the West have grown even stronger since 1918?"

"The West has grown stronger industrially," Schmidt admitted. But then he quickly added, "There is one factor that is different this time, and that is our 'Fuhrer.' Adolf Hitler is a specially gifted man, a military genius who will out-smart the Allies and develop secret weapons that will put the Allies to flight."

Daniel realized that Schmidt's adoration of Hitler bordered on religious worship. The interview ended with this lecture, and Daniel was asked to wait while some papers were drawn up. He wondered how the documents would affect him, feeling that little good could come from such a pompous, self-righteous Hitlerphile. When the stenographer finished, Schmidt gave the papers to Daniel. Later the interpreter read the contents aloud, and Daniel learned to his surprise that the note thanked him for aiding the wounded German men whose lives he had helped save. It also spoke of the good treatment the German prisoners had received while being held as POWs by the Americans. It was signed by Schmidt.

The next morning the Germans drove Daniel eastward some fifteen miles to a barbed wire enclosure that already contained several hundred Americans captured in recent days. At the gate a German officer said in good English, "Chaplain, we have heard about you from Colonel Schmidt. You are the 'no smoking, no drinking' American chaplain. We heard what you did for the wounded German prisoners who were in your hands. That is the most Christ-like act that I have ever heard of. Colonel Schmidt said that you were to have whatever you wanted. What do you want?"

At first Daniel did not know how to interpret the offer—it seemed too open-ended. The officer explained that the chaplain could have whatever he wanted and go wherever he wanted within the compound. Daniel appreciated the seemingly genuine spirit of good will that prompted the offer, but also saw the obvious irony. The compound was nothing more than a large barren enclosure without so much as a single tree or protection of any kind from the hot desert sun. Nonetheless, he was grateful for the opportunity to walk freely among the prisoners and tend to their needs. Furthermore, once he realized that the camp held many badly wounded who did not have enough to eat or drink, he collected French money from the Americans and bought tangerines, dates, and "pancakes" from the Arabs who had gathered with their wares outside the compound.

After several days, the Germans took all the prisoners to Sfax on the coast. There, the Germans made Daniel no special offers. He now was just another POW.[5]

By the time George Sweanor was shot down and captured in March, 1943, he had heard tales of prisoners being sadistically treated by German civilians. When the crowd gathered around him on the edge of the woods, he immediately asked to be taken to the police station. The Germans replied that they had every intention of doing just that.

Other than the two Hitler Youths, the group appeared to be friendly and formed an escort. George and the blonde who had spotted him carried on a conversation of sorts. He was embarrassed by the brown stains that he had been unable to clean from his uniform.

Partway to the police station a woman cyclist stopped to question him. She spoke English and took over as interpreter. Everyone wanted to know why Canada was making war on Germany when Germany had nothing but good will for Canada. They also wanted to know how many raids he had made on Germany and whether he had ever bombed Hamburg or Harburg. Their reference to Harburg told George where he was.

After many questions the woman commented: "You are lucky; for you the war is over. Now you will go to a nice camp and play tennis and enjoy yourself." Both Hamburg and Harburg had suffered greatly

---

5.   Interview with Daniel, April 14, 1983; Daniel, *In the Presence*, 8–14.

from the bombings, and George was impressed to find the people so friendly.

At the police station George's escort turned him over to the chief. George thought the big man looked comical in his Prussian-style helmet. He searched George in a perfunctory manner, failing to find any of the escape aids stowed in his clothing. Later he took his new prisoner out along the street, clasping George's belt in his big right hand to forestall any ideas of escape. The chief proudly pointed out where a Halifax had crashed and, in the next block, a Wellington's resting place. As the chief continued the talking tour George found himself thinking, "The old boy's not so bad."

Arriving at a Luftwaffe post, George was handed over to a young lieutenant who signed a receipt for him. Having a few jobs to do, the German asked George to accompany him. The first task was to bring in the German flag. They stood at attention while the lieutenant saluted. Having never seen a real Nazi flag before, George gazed at it and admitted that it looked smart rippling in the breeze.

Returning to the office, the lieutenant made George turn out his pockets and take off all his clothes. Again he managed to conceal his escape aids—all, that is, except the marine light wired around his waist. The lieutenant winced when he saw the wires connecting the two cylinders. There was nothing classified about the aid, so George started to explain that the device, which lights up and floats, was used for rescue at sea at night. Offering to demonstrate, he started to twist the knob. The German officer leapt toward him and slapped it out of his hands. The two soldiers standing by covered him with their rifles. Laughing, George insisted it was harmless and added, "I'm not a saboteur." The Germans were not convinced.

With one of the guards carrying the device, the lieutenant took George to another building where a major and a captain were questioning two other members of George's crew. He was relieved to see they were all right, but the Germans would not let them talk to one another. Instead, the two were taken out. Then the major turned to George.

The lieutenant spoke first, describing the explosives he had found. The guard produced the marine light. The major, recognizing it for what it was, took the cylinders and wire, and turned the knob. The light came on, nothing more. The lieutenant blushed, muttered an apology, and left.

Since the conversation centered around the idea that it was flak and not a fighter that brought him down, George decided that the major was a flak officer. Suddenly, in a loud voice, the major changed the subject: "Why are you sullying the good name of Canada by flying over peace-loving Germany and murdering women and children?" An argument ensued, with the major concluding, "We should hang you as a murderer, but instead we send you to a rest camp; Germany is too generous!"

Realizing that arguing would get him nowhere, George listened patiently until the major wore himself out. He then asked about the rest of the crew. "You were the last, but now we have captured all," the German boasted, "except for one charred body in the pilot's seat." George's spirits plunged. His good friend Pat obviously had fought the plunging aircraft long enough for everyone to get out. He had deliberately sacrificed his life to save the others. What other explanation could there be? Pat was too smart to think he could ever crash-land a burning, badly damaged aircraft at night and in low clouds mixed with rain. George shed tears for his friend as two guards led him to another building where they locked themselves in with him for the night.

By this time George had not slept for thirty-six hours, but it was the shock of Pat's death that engulfed him in weariness. He stretched out on a wood bench. The guards, however, were too curious to let him sleep. In broken English they asked him many questions about Canada. They were very polite and friendly, so George answered them as best he could. Up to that point he had met more than thirty Germans, and most of them, in fact, had been polite and friendly. If these were the ardent, sadistic Nazis, he concluded, they were doing a good job of fooling him. Even the major, who was, he thought, a big windbag, appeared basically harmless.

Before long, one of the guards asked if he would like a drink. George answered yes, and the German returned shortly with a canister containing a cold brown liquid. Eagerly George gulped it—then summoned tremendous facial control to hide his reaction. It was terribly bitter. This was his first taste of German ersatz coffee. Thirsty as he was, he would gladly have thrown the rest away had it not been for the smiling, helpful faces of the guards. "Gut, ja?" they said as they drank theirs. "Ja, gut," George lied as he suffered finishing his. To George's horror, one guard, eager to please, took his empty canister and rushed out to refill it. Determined to be philosophical, George convinced himself that if the Germans could drink it, so could he. Besides, he might not get anything better for years.

George got no sleep again that night. Shortly after midnight he was taken to the train station to begin the trip to Dulag Luft, some 250 miles south of Hamburg. On the way he encountered his fellow crew members once more, but was separated from them at the station. The only officer, he was taken to a first-class carriage; the others were led to a third-class car. Choosing a compartment that was full of civilians, the escorting officer told two of the passengers to leave. The idea of civilians meekly taking orders from the military was new to George. He apologized to the couple, who now would have to stand. He doubted that they understood his words, but he felt better for having done so.

As the train gathered speed he could fight sleep no longer. Closing his eyes for a nap, he awoke only when the train stopped at a large station two hours later. There the escort gave him his ration for the day, white bread, a piece of garlic sausage, and a small bottle of soda water. Thinking this was awfully meager fare, George was surprised to learn, sometime later, that this was preferential treatment because no common German was permitted white bread. The tiny loaf he was given was in deference to his officer status. It was the last white bread he was to see for as long as he was in captivity.[6]

In many respects, Sweanor's passage to Dulag Luft marked the end of an era. Spivey's trip only a few months later presaged the journeys others would experience. The war had raged for some time now, and more than a few nerves were beginning to fray.

With pitchfork and rifle, the old man who captured Colonel Spivey marched him down the road toward home, which was about a mile from the crash. They entered his kitchen, and there was much loud talking and gesticulating between him and his wife, none of which Spivey understood. But he was pleased when they seated him and the woman brought him weak coffee, rich milk, and good bread. A halfhearted attempt to give him eggs was abandoned when he declined the offer.

By this time a distinctly friendly attitude seemed to prevail in the kitchen. Suddenly Spivey recalled that the briefing officer had told them that the Dutch and the French were friendly and might put

6. Sweanor, *Pensionable Time*, 106–10.

them on the underground road to Spain. He got up, having rinsed his mouth with the coffee, and removed his helmet, and placed it on top of the cookstove. Then he spotted an old coat hanging on the wall. With much talk and waving of hands, he made it clear he wanted to put on the coat and get on with whatever was to come next. To his horror, the old woman let out a shriek as he moved toward the coat. In the same instant the farmer reappeared through the door, gun in hand and wearing a natty Landwehr uniform. He barked out a command in German. Spivey quickly realized that he was indeed their prisoner and made one desperate break for the door. Just as quickly the old man and his son barred the way.

They took Spivey to the local constabulary of a nearby village. Soon he was joined by the rest of the crew, all except the gunner who had bailed out earlier than the rest to get medical aid. An attempt was made to load them on a Model T Ford bus to drive them to another village. But after a mile or so, the bus quit running, and everyone marched the rest of the day. As they walked, Spivey admired the way the Germans had managed to plant every square foot of soil along the way and kept their fields extremely neat.

After a cold night of interrupted sleep, the Germans woke them about four o'clock in the morning, conducted a second search, and put them on another bus. This time the destination was a Luftwaffe station near the town of Rheine. There they were given a drink of water, some sausage, and black bread and were put in solitary confinement in the post guardhouse. It was Spivey's first chance to think. Reflecting on the events of the past thirty-six hours, he thanked God that they all were safe from serious injury and death. Then he thought of his wife and son and found his throat closing tightly. He buried his face in his old winter flying cap and fell asleep.

When Spivey complained of not feeling well, the Germans sent him to see the surgeon. His mouth and head hurt from the blow received in the crash, and his bowels had not functioned for three days. He asked for a laxative, but the Germans did not understand him—nor did he understand them. Efforts to communicate in French also failed, so he used sign language to tell them what was wrong. The Germans thought his bathroom antics hilarious and finally exclaimed, "Ja, ja, ja!" In no time they produced a glass of milky liquid, and Spivey drank it. Then he realized they had misunderstood and had given him bismuth and charcoal to check the diarrhea they thought he had. He was truly in trouble now. He went through the whole pantomime again, this time even getting so red in the face that blood vessels stood out on his neck and forehead. The Germans at last caught on and nearly burst with laughter. Spivey, however, looked at the box of pills they gave him. He clearly could see the word *cathartic*. As he was dismissed from the hospital he overheard someone remark, "The colonel is not sick; he is crazy!"

The fourth day they were given two days' rations and put on the train to Frankfurt. Spivey was surprised that the commuters paid them no attention at all, especially since they were closely guarded and readily recognizable in their aviators' togs. All ten of them were put into two compartments of a third-class train. As they proceeded he gazed at the damage inflicted upon hundreds of factories along the railway and wondered how long the Germans could take such a beating before they quit. At the same time he was amazed to see how quickly they had cleaned up the debris and how well the people were dressed.

About midnight they came to East Cologne. There the fliers were taken off the train and led along dark, bomb-torn streets filled with soldiers. They crossed a huge bridge over the Rhine and suddenly realized they were standing beside the famous cathedral. The group paused for a moment to look. Suddenly four drunken German officers appeared and began to rant in German in a manner that made the Americans both angry and fearful. They picked on Spivey, presumably because he unmistakably was the oldest and a colonel. When they got no response, one of them resorted to English. Breath laced with alcohol, he stuck his face close to Spivey's and told him what they were going to do to Luftgangsters who bombed their women and children and magnificent churches. Spivey could see that the cathedral had been hit several times and that not much remained of this once-beautiful city. Lieutenant Wells started to answer back, but Spivey thought it best to remain quiet. The guards seemed to want to walk a fine line, cheerfully telling all inquirers who the Americans were and interceding only when they were about to be manhandled. In due time, the guards moved the group along—to everyone's relief.

Spivey had never dreamed that such total destruction was possible. Every building they saw from the Rhine to the far western side of the city was ruined. And once they got lost in the rubble. One guard rousted some men who were sleeping in a basement and asked the way. By this time the Americans were so bewildered and frightened, it would not have surprised any of them if the Germans had shot them on the spot. The provocation, Spivey thought, must have been great enough for the inhabitants to commit such an act. Finally they got back on the main path. Even there, where walls on either side stood more than four or five stories high, the first light of dawn was clearly discernible through the upper windows. It was a horrible sight. Yet in all his fear, confusion, and apathy, Spivey could not help feeling a fierce pride in the Allies' awakening military might. Audible expressions from the men confirmed his own feelings, and more than once he quieted them as they mumbled, "This ought to teach the bastards!"

The group reboarded a train in the busy station on the west side of the city, and Spivey was glad to leave the nightmarish world of Cologne. In contrast to the eerie atmosphere of that hellish, war-torn city at night, the daylight ride to Frankfurt was like traveling through a fairyland. The scenery was beautiful, and the war had not yet touched the area. Even under such difficult circumstances, Spivey appreciated the magnificence of the countryside.[7]

It would be some time before Captain Roland Sargent shared any of those comforting feelings. From the moment the Gestapo rammed their revolvers into him and his fellow travelers in the Paris hotel, he knew he had every reason in the world to anticipate the worst. They were put on a bus that went south to the outskirts of the city. The ride ended at a massive iron portal set in a high stone wall. Inside, there was a brick courtyard in front of some dingy, stone buildings. The big gates closed behind the bus as it entered the yard. The men were taken into a two-story structure and placed in a room, with their captors still in attendance, to await questioning. One at a time they were ushered into the presence of a man in civilian clothes who sat behind a desk.

Standing alone before the man, Sargent did not know what to expect. Speaking fluent English, the man told Sargent he could sit down and proceeded to ask just who he was and what he was doing in France. Sargent said that he was an American flying officer, that he had been shot down, and that he had been trying to evade capture and get out of Europe. The interrogator asked for military identification. Sargent, of course, had none—not a blessed thing to prove he was indeed a member of any nation's armed forces. He understood only too well the predicament he was in. This was the infamous

7. Spivey, *POW Odyssey*, 8–16.

Fresnes prison, also a Gestapo headquarters, which housed primarily political prisoners, saboteurs, spies, and members of the Resistance and French underground. Prisoners from the Spanish Civil War were still there, serving as forced labor for the Germans. In fact, anyone caught in civilian clothes had a good chance of ending up in Fresnes prison, and ending his life there as well. When captured, Sargent had been wearing such clothes, and he had no military identification. But he insisted over and over again that he was an American pilot on a military mission over occupied territory. The interrogator was just as insistent that he produce some form of military identification.

Finally, shaking his head sadly, the interrogator said Sargent obviously was a spy and, of course, would be shot. He demanded all Sargent's false papers, his wristwatch, belt, and shoelaces. He looked at the gold ring on Sargent's left hand and asked if it was a wedding ring. Sargent said yes. The man did not ask for it. He put the watch in an envelope, set it aside, and then told Sargent he was sorry but there was nothing he could do for him.

A soldier waiting outside led Sargent to a large, high-ceilinged room containing partitioned-off, roofless cubicles, each a little larger than a telephone booth. The soldier opened the door, pushed Sargent inside, locked the door, and left. Alone, Sargent groped for some shred of hope. His mind was in a turmoil, his stomach tied in knots. Periodically he heard heavy footsteps and then the opening of a door, gutteral commands, and the sounds of someone being marched away—to what fate he could only guess.

Eventually a soldier with a rifle over his shoulder beckoned Sargent out and led him through a dimly lit tunnel. As they walked, an old man and a young boy approached, pushing a two-wheel wagon, with a German soldier impatiently bullying them. Apparently the two were moving too slow—the guard gave the old man a vicious kick. He took the punishment without retort and continued to struggle with the cart. Sargent could hear the soldier's abusive voice for some time as they continued along the way. Finally they stopped in front of several doors that lined the corridor. The guard unlocked one, pushed Sargent inside, and closed and locked it. As daylight faded the room became completely dark, and again he was left to contemplate his fate. He thought of his wife, their hopes and dreams. They had been married only a few months before he left for overseas. And he felt he had to face what lay ahead in a manner that would reflect honorably on his mother and father.

The next day Sargent was taken to a cell on the third floor. Much to his relief, Byington and another American, Technical Sergeant Ralph Stease, were already in the cell. Simply seeing someone he knew boosted his morale, though it did not change the uncertain future one bit.

In the weeks that followed, the three were almost constantly hungry. Each day before dawn they were awakened by the sound of metal wheels grating on the concrete floor outside their cell, signaling the arrival of breakfast. A cart carrying a large kettle of dark, lukewarm liquid labeled coffee and slices of German black bread smeared with jam was pushed along the hallway by some Spanish Civil War prisoners accompanied by an armed guard. The entourage stopped in front of each cell while the guard opened a little cutout in the door. A small shelf on the inside was used for the metal cups into which the liquid was ladled. If no cups were on the shelf, the delivery crew was not in the habit of reminding the prisoners. A slice of bread for each occupant was slapped down on the shelf, and the door slammed shut. Most of the time the liquid tasted like burned wheat seeds. Late in the afternoon the second and final portion was brought around—warm thin soup with some suggestion of vegetables, occasionally a piece of some kind of meat, and another slice of black bread and jam. That had to suffice until early the following morning. Not surprisingly, most of their conversation was devoted to food.

Fleas plagued the prisoners day and night, from the moment they arrived. Those elusive, maddening little creatures invaded their mattresses, blankets, clothes, hair, and bodies. The men developed scabs from scratching bites, and they spent much of their time searching for fleas in the seams of their clothes, which they removed and turned inside out. But it was a losing battle and simply became one more thing that had to be endured.

One day several weeks into their imprisonment, a fourth prisoner was put in the cell, a fellow by the name of David Whytehead. He said he was an American, a first lieutenant who had been shot down while flying with a British unit as an observer on a night bombing raid. Byington, Stease, and Sargent questioned him carefully, distrusting him from the outset. His answers proved unsatisfactory and they treated him coldly for a while. Finally, after a rather awkward period, he became noticeably nervous and confessed that he was an American para-commando captured on a sabotage mission. Although he had been in civilian clothes, his story apparently sounded credible enough to deceive the Germans, at least for the time being. Whytehead felt he needed to perpetuate the fabrication as long as possible, and therefore told the same story to Sargent and the others. Whytehead was fluent in French, however, and talk in the prison indicated that his colleagues on the mission were being tortured and probably could not conceal the truth much longer. Fearing the worst, he decided to confide in the others so that they could get word home should they ever get out.[8]

Over the years the unfortunates in this large institution had developed a means of communicating with their fellow prisoners in the other buildings. They talked or yelled through the barred window to all those within earshot whatever messages they wished to convey. Thus Whytehead was informed that three young Frenchmen in an adjoining cell were to be executed for committing acts of sabotage. Then he learned that they had asked the Germans to allow Whytehead and his cell mates to eat the food they would leave behind. The next morning the Americans heard the guards coming to get the Frenchmen. They listened in silence to the clomping boots, the squeak of the door as it was opened, a few brisk commands, and fading footsteps. Almost immediately the door to their cell was thrown open. Two guards impatiently motioned them out, propelled them into the Frenchmen's cell, and indicated they were to take what they wanted. The Americans grabbed what they could—some bread and some sort of meat—all the time feeling queasy about what they were doing at the very same moment the Frenchmen were facing death. Back in their cell they found they could not eat the food right away. In time, out of necessity, they knew they would, but not just then.

One day the cell door was opened, and a man in the doorway said, "Roland Sargent, you are to come with me." Sargent was ushered into a small room downstairs and presented to an officer in a blue Luftwaffe uniform. The officer beckoned him to a chair and then sat down at a table. In good English the German explained he was attempting to locate certain Allied Air Force personnel whom the International Red Cross had reported as missing in action after air raids over Europe. He said the records of Fresnes prison showed that Sargent claimed to be an Allied officer shot down during a daylight mission and picked up by the Gestapo in civilian clothes without military

8. The information Whytehead gave them was later transmitted back to the States, but Sargent never heard anything more or discovered what happened to him.

identification of any kind. In order for that identity to be established, the officer went on, it was absolutely necessary for Sargent to give certain information—his name, rank, serial number, crew position, squadron and group, target, place shot down, time of day, where he hit the ground, who helped him, and the route he followed to get to Paris.

Sargent knew he was in a tough spot. No one except the Gestapo and a few other Germans knew he was in that prison, or even alive, for that matter. He had, to all intents and purposes, simply vanished from the earth. The Gestapo, he felt, could easily classify him as a spy and shoot or otherwise dispose of him, and no one would ever know the difference. Unless he could somehow gain the support of this Luftwaffe officer, he would be totally at the mercy of the Gestapo.

Sargent searched carefully for words he could use to establish his identity without giving any valuable information to the enemy or endangering the lives of the people who had risked so much to help him. And, of course, what the Germans knew or did not know was a mystery to him. So he gave the date of the mission, approximate time of day, general area where the plane went down, and the names of the crewmen. The rest of the questions he did not answer. The interrogator looked disappointed and said the answers were unsatisfactory. Sargent must say more about who was involved in the underground. When Sargent refused, he was impatiently dismissed.

Byington and Stease were taken out separately and similarly interrogated. Whytehead was not. Back in the cell, they discussed the happenings and hoped and prayed that the Luftwaffe officer would come to believe their story in time and rescue them from the hands of the Gestapo.

Some days later they were abruptly informed they would be leaving the prison the following day and should be prepared for an early departure. They said their farewells to Whytehead and tried to offer him words of encouragement, but inwardly were not optimistic about his chances. The next morning, guards escorted them from the cell, leaving Whytehead still there. They were marched into the yard at the rear of the prison. Others were being brought out at the same time, including most of the group that had been with Sargent in Paris. Unfortunately, McNeely, Sargent's navigator, was not among them. Sargent wondered why, but was told nothing. Taken by bus to the rail yard, the men were loaded into a boxcar. Eventually the train began to move toward Frankfurt and the main interrogation center located nearby. At last, Roland Sargent's long Schweinfurt mission was over.[9]

Until the end of 1943, there were only isolated cases of prisoners being severely abused or killed by irate citizens. Thereafter, however, disconcerting evidence of mob action condoned, and even encouraged, by the German government began to sift through the foreign and domestic press and official channels. Henceforth, the uncharted road that stretched before every crew member gained yet one more unknown, the ever-increasing possibility of abuse or death at the hands of a hysterical mob.

On May 17, 1944, an American pilot was brought before an assembly of Nazi party officials at Altludersdorf and subjected to intentional abuse, public curiosity, and violence. Finally a German official asked, "Is there a manure pitchfork available to kill this individual?"[10] Several days later, Paul Josef Goebbels, Hitler's propaganda minister, published a front-page editorial in the May 27 edition of *Völkischer Beobachter,* charging that Anglo-American air attacks over Germany were no longer warfare but murder pure and simple. "Only with the aid of arms," he asserted, "is it possible to secure the lives of enemy pilots who were shot down during such attacks, for they would otherwise be killed by the sorely tried population. . . . It seems to us hardly possible and tolerable to use German police and soldiers against the German people when it treats murderers of children as they deserve."[11] And on May 30, 1944, Martin Bormann, Hitler's closest confidant, issued a circular admitting that British and American fliers had in fact been lynched by the Germans: "Several instances have occurred where members of the crews of such aircraft, who have

9. Interview with Sargent, June 24, 1980.
10. State Department to American legation, Bern, August 10, 1944, in File 711.62114 A/7–2544, "United States Prisoners of War Detained by Germany," Record Group 59, Diplomatic Branch, National Archives. No information is available on the flier's fate.
11. *Trial of the Major Criminals before the International Military Tribunal: Nuremberg, 14 November 1945–1 October 1946* (Nuremberg, Germany, 1948), IV, 50, hereinater cited as *IMT*; New York *Times,* May 27, 1944. In November, 1943, the Germans reportedly found an excellent propaganda item that, if true, reveals unnecessary antagonism on the part of a flier. The incident was widely publicized throughout Germany as "typical of the cynical American youth which is destroying Europe's cultural monuments." A young airman had stenciled the name of his plane, Murder, Inc., on his jacket, the sight of which led to deep resentment by the German people and government. J. Stafford Redding to Cordell Hull, December 29, 1943, in File 711.62114 A/195, RG 59.

bailed out or who have made forced landings, were lynched on the spot immediately after capture by the populace, which was incensed to the highest degree."[12]

The prohibition against military and police involvement in the rescue of downed airmen from hostile crowds received its strongest endorsement on February 25, 1945, when Albert Hoffmann, a national defense commissioner in Westphalia, addressed all county councilors, mayors, police officials, county leaders, and county chiefs of the Volkstrum. Tersely he stated, "Fighter-bomber pilots who are shot down are in principle not to be protected against the fury of the people. I expect from all police officers that they will refuse to lend their protection to these gangster types. Authorities acting in contradiction to the popular sentiment will have to account to me. All police and gendarmerie officials are to be informed immediately of this, my attitude."[13]

German officials were fully aware that such statements were an open invitation to murder and that they represented gross violations of Article 2 of the 1929 Geneva Convention, which clearly states that POWs are under the control of the hostile power but not of the individuals or corps that captured them. The same article says that at all times the prisoners must be humanely treated and protected, particularly against acts of violence, insults, and public curiosity. After several airmen had been killed, Nazi leaders attempted to rationalize their position: "The German authorities are not directly responsible, since death . . . occurred, before a German official became concerned with the case." Furthermore, these same Nazi officials were confident they could doctor the evidence for the newspapers and depict the affair in "an appropriate manner," stating that, among other things, the dead airmen had indeed been "terror fliers."[14]

In this propaganda effort, carefully outlined acts were identified as characteristic of terror fliers: attacks on the civilian population, firing

---

12. *IMT*, IV, 51. For specific information received by the State Department about individual beatings, torture, and killings of airmen immediately after capture by civilians, military personnel, and police, see official correspondence in RG 59, Files 711.62114 A/7–2444, 711.62114 A/589, and 711.62114 A/6–1644. The last also contains summaries of press reports from Sweden deploring the Germans' actions.

13. Hoffmann quoted in *IMT*, IV, 51.

14. Ambassador Ritter to the Supreme Command of the Armed Forces, June 20, 1944, in U.S. Office of United States Chief of Counsel for Prosecution of Nazi Criminality, *Nazi Conspiracy and Aggression* (Washington, D.C., 1946–48), Supp. B, Sec. III, pp. 526, 56.

on airmen still descending with their parachutes, attacks on passenger trains engaged in public transportation, and attacks on military hospitals and hospital trains clearly marked with the Red Cross. In practice, however, little effort was made to determine if a particular aircraft had indeed been involved in such actions. Ambassador Ritter noted, "In the cases of lynching, the precise establishment of the circumstances deserving punishment [was not considered] very essential." They were, in fact, not the least bit essential, as indicated by Bormann's observation that "no police measures or criminal proceedings were invoked against the German civilians who participated in these incidents."[15]

Figures are unavailable concerning the number of crewmen who were killed by lynch mobs. However, Allied fliers were very much aware of the danger to which they might be exposed should they fall into the hands of civilians, especially near the end of the war. And this awareness increased their apprehension as they faced their captors for the first time and later traveled through the towns and countryside en route to Dulag Luft.

Lieutenant James Keeffe was one of twelve captured fliers who experienced the ire of the crowds in August, 1944. From a Luftwaffe field headquarters building in Brussels, they were sent by train to Frankfurt. They arrived about eleven o'clock at night, and even in the dark Jim immediately saw that the station was badly damaged. The fliers were a motley group: they wore a variety of mixed dirty uniforms, flying suits, and civilian clothing, some covered with bloodstains; several wore bandages; a few suffered from burns. After spending the night on the tile floor in a workmen's washroom in the basement of the station, they were herded back up onto an empty platform very early the next morning. Hungry and unshaven, they looked even more disheveled. The commuter train they were to board for Oberursel came in loaded with factory girls dressed in gray overalls. When the girls saw the captured fliers on the platform, they gathered around with the fiercest look of hatred in their eyes Jim had ever seen. Emotionally wrought up by the sight of the captives, the girls pleaded with the guards for four or five prisoners, eventually reducing the number until they were shrieking, "Just give us one,

15. Chief, Supreme Command of the Armed Forces, to the Foreign Office, June 15, 1944, *ibid.*, 530; Ritter to Chief, Supreme Command, June 20, 1944, *ibid.*, 526; *IMT*, IV, 51.

just give us one!" Jim watched warily as the girls swung lunch buckets and spit at them. Finally the guards, who initially just told the girls to go away and leave the airmen alone, now used their burp guns broadside to push them back. Then the guards managed to get all twelve fliers safely on board the train.

The respite was short-lived, however. After the twenty-minute ride from Frankfurt to Oberursel, the group disembarked and was paraded through the town to a small park where they were to wait for a tram that would take them the short distance to Dulag Luft. Most of the prisoners sat on the ground while a few stood not far from the lounging guards. Jim noticed that the people walking by were quiet and stoic, though a few would stop and stare for a minute or two before going on their way. But one middle-aged man, dressed in a civilian suit and using a cane, came into the park and began to circle the prisoners. As he walked he started to work himself up emotionally, just as the girls at the station in Frankfurt had. He began to shout, and the guards and the prisoners ignored him. Finally he stopped, directly in front of Jim. The man shouted and screamed in German about their being terror fliers, Luftgangsters, and murderers of women and children. Then he backed off and spat right into Jim's face.

That had never happened to Jim before. He immediately went into a boxing stance and cocked his right fist. The man raised his cane and began shrieking again. Out of the corner of his eye, Jim saw one of the guards drop his cigarette onto the grass, grab his burp gun, and charge toward them. Expecting the worst, Jim was surprised when the guard rushed past him, shoved the muzzle into the man's chest, and started shouting, all the while backing the civilian out of the park. Jim was fairly fluent in German and understood the guard to say, "You damned civilian, get the hell away from these airmen and leave them alone! At least they're fighting for their country and that's more than I can say for you."[16]

Lieutenant Keeffe was never beaten, stabbed, or lynched, but he did find out directly what angry civilians could do. Usually, however, the prisoners received rather routine treatment. Once captured and in the hands of the military, each one could expect to hear repeatedly the heavily accented stock phrase, "Fur you, da var ist ofer" And in the

16. Interview with James Keeffe, March 12, 1979.

days ahead the prisoner became accustomed to hearing himself referred to as a "Kriegie," the shortened version of the German word for prisoners of war, *Kriegsgefangenen*. Eventually the prisoner arrived at the main interrogation center, Dulag Luft. As one observer noted at the time, the prisoners were brought there "on foot, by train (first-class, second-class, third-class, prison car or boxcar), by truck, by car, by air, by submarine, by tank, and even, in some cases, by dog cart."[17]

17.   Lyman B. Burbank, "A History of the American Air Force Prisoners of War in Center Compound, Stalag Luft III, Germany" (M.A. thesis, University of Chicago, 1946), iv.

3

Dulag Luft

Tail gunner Alexander MacArthur knew that the Germans would make good use of the letter tucked into the knee pocket of his flight suit if they found it. He had gotten the letter from his brother, who was stationed in the Pacific, and had taken it with him—an unpardonable sin for fliers. But he had never thought of it during the frantic hours of the mission or later on the ground in northern Italy as he twice fled from being shot and finally fell into German hands. Now as his captors' jeep rumbled toward the nearby Gestapo office, he remembered the letter. Hoping the others would not notice, he carefully unzipped the pocket, eased the letter out, and slipped it outside the jeep. No sooner did it hit the ground than the driver slammed on the brakes and rammed the jeep into reverse. MacArthur's sleight of hand failed, and the Germans had a prize they knew the interrogators would appreciate: precious insights into the private life of their next victim.

Alex relaxed somewhat at the thought that the letter contained nothing of intelligence value. In fact, after his terrible day, it seemed ironic that his brother thought Alex should finish "that sideshow over there," join him, and "pack snowballs" for the Pacific team. To Alex the comment was just brotherly jiving. The Germans were not so easily convinced. Name, rank, and serial number be damned, they wanted to know the real meaning of what they were sure was a code. In time the interrogator tired of asking about packing snowballs and moved on to other subjects. But Alex knew they would come back to it—and they did, again and again.

From the outset Alex felt that he was misunderstood. Having failed to explain something as simple as packing snowballs, he knew it would be futile to try to say anything about the rubber device found in his pocket. The explanation for it also was quite simple, had he chosen to give it. The temperature in a gunner's turret at high altitude often reached sixty degrees below zero, and the little microphone in each man's helmet repeatedly frosted over from breath condensation. To clear it, one had to remove the helmet and a glove, suffer exposure in the bitter cold, and risk dizziness from lack of oxygen. A condom over the microphone allowed an airman to simply reach in and snap it once, clearing the frost quickly and cleanly. Sometimes, however, the condom would break, and experienced airmen like Alex usually carried an extra. Understandably not perceiving its military use, the thorough Gestapo agent found the rubber item, placed it on the counter in plain view, paused a moment in utter disgust, and then blurted out, "Ach, you Americans, you think you have come to the land of paradise!" Alex knew better than to try to defend his virtue. Blushing, he let the matter ride, enjoying some inner satisfaction at the thought that his captors were the victims of their own propaganda. They saw him as yet another Luftgangster who had landed on their soil, ready for any kind of action.

Accepting MacArthur's claim that he was a downed airman, the Gestapo soon transported him to the Luftwaffe interrogation center at Verona, Italy. There, he again tried, in vain, to explain that packing snowballs had no military significance. The persistence of the interrogators both annoyed and intrigued Alex. They obviously were wrong on this particular issue. But he also recognized that they definitely knew their business. They were thorough, systematic, and extremely well informed. Convinced they would learn nothing important from him, he nonetheless was glad when he was sent on his way to Stalag Luft III. His stint in Verona left lasting impressions on him. And it was only an outpost, or branch office, of Dulag Luft.[1]

The name was actually an abbreviation of Durchgangslager der Luftwaffe (transit camp of the air force). Originally designed as an experimental farm, Dulag Luft was located near Oberursel at the foot of the Taunus Mountains.[2] To get there, most prisoners traveled first to Frankfurt and then another ten miles in a northwesterly direction by train to Oberursel, a small town of about twenty thousand people.

1. Interview with Alexander MacArthur, September 7, 1979.
2. "Dulag Luft," n.d. (MS copy in Delmar T. Spivey Collection, 1943–1975, Special Collections Room, U.S. Air Force Academy Library, Colo.), 1. This manuscript was sent by First Lieutenant Stanley L. Webster, Jr., of the 513th Intelligence Corps Group, Camp King, Germany (the name given to Dulag Luft after its occupation by American forces), to Lieutenant Colonel James H. Keeffe, Jr., at the latter's request. It was written by an army officer stationed there in 1959–60, whose name is not presently known.

Once there, the prisoners marched to a small park where they boarded a tram that made the trip out to the camp almost hourly. If the tram had just left the station, the prisoners started on the two-and-one-half-mile walk to the camp. On the way they passed a Shell filling station that had many Coca-Cola signs. The weary men often tried to drink from the water spigot at the station, but an old woman habitually posted herself nearby and would chase them away.[3]

Upon arrival at the gates of Dulag Luft, the prisoners were channeled in several directions, depending upon the physical layout of the camp at various junctures during the war. In September, 1939, the German army took over the experimental farm and used a single building to house a few French prisoners. Control of the camp was transferred to the Luftwaffe in December, 1939. As the number of downed airmen grew in 1940, four wood barracks were constructed across the road from the interrogation center to house the overflow of prisoners who had been questioned and were awaiting shipment to a permanent camp. Soon it became apparent that a high percentage of the captives would need medical attention, and a portion of Hohemark Hospital, located about one mile west of the camp, was requisitioned—about sixty-five beds were reserved for wounded prisoners. Several private rooms in the hospital were set aside so high-ranking Allied prisoners could be interrogated in circumstances that the Germans reportedly considered appropriate to their respective ranks. The hospital, which had been a sanitarium, was well equipped and surrounded by a beautiful park.

These facilities soon proved inadequate, and the transit portion of the camp was moved to several other locations in succeeding years, including one outside the nearby town of Wetzlar. The acquisition of additional buildings and the relocations of the transit camps created some confusion about the proper name of the camp. Originally, the term *Dulag Luft* designated the interrogation center proper and the transit camp across the road. The prisoners, however, continued to use the term without distinguishing among the interrogation center, the hospital, and the transit camps. It was natural for them to do so. In

---

3. "Auswertestelle West," A.D.I. (K) Report 328/1945, frame 0468, microfilm roll A5405, and "Great Escapes", Doc. F164, both in Newspaper and Microfilm Room, Troy H. Middleton Library, Louisiana State University, Baton Rouge; Broach, "The Last Mission." One prisoner recalls the gas station as being an Esso station (Spivey, *POW Odyssey*, 17).

addition to being conveniently short and easily recognizable, *Dulag Luft* represented an experience as well as a place.[4]

Shortly after the war began, stories and reports filtered back to Allied Intelligence about what was going on near Oberursel. In time the news reached the fliers, and the combination of factual information about the interrogation center and its rumored effectiveness created an almost superstitious dread about what would happen to them there.[5]

Actually, the accounts themselves were quite confusing. Accord-

4. On September 10, 1943, the transit portion of the camp was moved from Oberursel to the edge of a park known as the Palmengarten in the very center of a residential section of Frankfurt. This change placed it only 1,635 yards northwest of the main railroad station, which was an Allied target area, thereby endangering the prisoners' lives. This transfer was in violation of Article 9 of the Geneva Convention, which prohibited the housing of prisoners in combat zones. Evidence that Germany considered the city of Frankfurt susceptible to enemy attack is found in the systematic evacuation of citizens from this and other urban centers at this time. The anticipated consequences were not long in coming: in March, 1944, a bombing attack on Frankfurt destroyed the transit camp and reportedly killed one or two prisoners. More will be said later about placing prisoners of war in the center of cities as a means of warding off enemy air attacks. Although this became a serious threat in late 1944 and 1945, the prisoners may have been placed in Frankfurt for this or some other reason. The transit camp was then sited approximately two miles northwest of Wetzlar, a small town on the Lahn River about thirty miles north of Frankfurt. As happened when the Frankfurt prison camp first opened, the prisoners had to stay in tents for a time until the new facility could be constructed. A.D.I. (K) Report 328, frames 0461–63; "Dulag Luft," 6; American Embassy in Berlin to Department of State, November 8, 1941, in file 740.0014 EW/2247, "Prisoners of War—European War, 1939," RG 59; International Red Cross report, March 4, 1943, File 740.00114 EW/3977, RG 59; Bern to Secretary of State, May 23, 1944, in File 711.62114 A/565, RG 59; Camp Report No. 6, "Dulag Luft," June 12, l944, File 711.62114 A.I.R./6-l244, "Reports of Inspection of Camps for American Prisoners in Germany," RG 59; "American Prisoners of War in Germany," prepared by Military Intelligence Service, War Department, November 1, 1945 (Copy in Archives Division, American Red Cross Headquarters, Washington, D.C.), 5. After the Germans launched their attack against Russia, a similar interrogation center was opened in the East and became known as Auswertestelle Ost (Evaluation Center—East). Accordingly, the interrogation center near Oberursel was renamed Auswertestelle West (Evaluation Center—West), and the name Dulag Luft thereafter should have been used only to designate the transit camps at their various locations, first across the road from the interrogation center, then at Frankfurt, and finally at Wetzlar. William W. Ingenhutt, "Something was Missing" (Thesis, Air Command and Staff School of Air University, Maxwell Air Force Base, Ala., 1948), 61; A.D.I. (K) Report 328, frame 0462. Around April 15, 1945, the interrogation center was moved to Nuremberg-Buchenbuhl, but the organization had by this time deteriorated to the point that it no longer deserved to be called an evaluation center. A.D.I. (K) Report 328, frame 0461.

5. A.D.I. (K) Report 328, frame 0461.

ing to some, conditions were exceptionally good at Dulag Luft— never more than four men in a room, and often only two; hot showers in the barracks; a separate barracks that was a communal dining hall; a communal sitting room that had upholstered chairs; Red Cross supplies so plentiful that gala four- or five-course dinners had to be given at least twice a month during the early years so food parcels would not accumulate; wines and spirits, which the Germans liberated during their invasion of France, given to the prisoners as long as stocks lasted; until 1942, birthday parties were common, and one could have white wine, claret, or whiskey; skiing during the first two winters in the nearby mountains with German officers; occasional summer sojourns into the woods to collect berries and firewood; and weekly parole walks and visits to church.[6]

Exaggerated as the stories undoubtedly were, they nonetheless had some basis in fact. Lieutenant Bob Broach, the navigator on Colonel Spivey's plane, was subjected to a brief, superficial interrogation before being released into the transit camp. He found his crew mates there, and they reported together to their assigned barracks. It was Saturday night, and most of the prisoners had gathered in the mess hall "for a little brew and close harmony." After the experience of the past days, the news sounded too good to be true. There was a race to the mess hall, and within five minutes Bob had guzzled several glasses of beer. Emmitte ("Willie") Wells, the co-pilot, led sundry verses of "Sing Us Another One, Do." The beer, he recalls, was very mild, but Bob thought it a fine introduction to prison life. The revelry continued until eleven o'clock, lock-up time. By then, Wells had established his reputation for possessing a large repertoire of miscellaneous ditties.[7]

In reality, such accounts left much unsaid, and the prisoners quickly perceived that concessions of this nature were but a part of the total environment designed to snare the unwary, bewildered captives and cause them to revise their preconceived notions of the "cruel Huns," thereby sapping their aggressive spirit. To some extent these conditions existed in the transit camp near Oberursel and to a lesser degree at Frankfurt and Wetzlar, but not in the interrogation

6. Inspection Report of the International Red Cross, March 4, 1943, File 711.62114 A/3977, RG 59; "Dulag Luft," 29, 31.

7. Wiley to the author, July 1, 1980.

center. Furthermore, the luxuries, enjoyed primarily during the early years of the war, were of long-term benefit only to the few prisoners who served as part of the permanent staff at Dulag Luft.[8] Most of the prisoners retained far more vivid memories of the unpleasant atmosphere in the interrogation center.

After the guards who escorted the prisoners to the camp secured a receipt for their delivery, the captives were sent to the Reception Office. There, the staff's first task was to attempt to get the prisoners to reveal their identity, usually by ordering the officer prisoners to step forward and the "other ranks" to line up behind them "to insure that they would not be separated and to allow them to go to the same camp."[9] If this ruse worked, and apparently it often did, the Germans had successfully completed an important first step in the interrogation process. Knowledge of who belonged with whom on the various crews was a valuable tool in the interrogator's hands.

One by one, the prisoners then filed into the Transport Office, where some personal information was noted and each man was thoroughly searched. All clothing down to their underwear was removed and methodically examined for weapons, escape aids, and personal property such as papers, pictures, and money. Nevertheless, George Sweanor again managed to safeguard his hidden treasures. No sleight-of-hand artist, he exercised care in the order in which he undressed, handing over his clothes a piece at a time and moving the contraband as he did so. He worried most about the hunting knife he had hidden in the stocking that covered his leg wound. Strangely, the guards who searched the clothing in minute detail and calmly probed rectal areas disdained to pick up the blood-soaked stocking, and the knife went into the cell with him.[10]

If the prisoner's comb, cigarettes, matches, money, etc., had not been taken earlier, the Germans now took such items, placed them in an envelope with his name on it, and gave assurances he would get them all back. Then each man was photographed and fingerprinted. From the Transport Office, the airmen moved to one of three likely

8.   "Dulag Luft," 31. For an extended discussion of the permanent staff and an explanation of German aims and techniques in providing such "generous" care to selected prisoners at Dulag Luft, see Smith, *Mission Escape*, 21–52.

9.   A.D.I. (K) Report 328, frame 0469.

10.   Sweanor, *Pensionable Time*, 110.

locations—the transit camp, the "snake pit," or a solitary confinement cell—depending upon the number of prisoners on hand at any
one time.[11] At the beginning of the war, virtually all prisoners went
directly into the interrogation center. But their numbers increased
from the dozen or so that arrived during the month of December,
1939, to an average of 2,000 each month in 1944.[12] When all available
space in the interrogation center was in use, the camp staff sent
prisoners to other places. Those thought to know little went to the
transit camp after being briefly questioned.[13] Prisoners who appeared
to be a valuable source of information, but could not be immediately
placed in solitary confinement, usually went to the snake pit, a one-
story building used as a way station. Spivey was sent there, and its
nightmarish features were apparent right away, from the dirty rooms
to the nasty guards. The small rooms contained an iron bed, a small
table, a few chairs, and a slop jar. The single window was closed and
locked, and the solid wood shutter, which opened and closed from the
outside, was shut tight. The morning and evening meals usually
consisted of one slice of heavy black bread with a thin coating of
oleomargarine or ersatz jam, and a cup of lukewarm ersatz tea (made
from various mixtures of hay, carrots, and parched grain) or ersatz
coffee (composition unknown). For the noon meal, there was a good-
sized dish full of potato soup with large pieces of potatoes but no meat
or fat. Spivey was not allowed to shave or brush his teeth, and only
after much shouting and pleading did a guard let him out to use a
filthy straddle latrine.[14] Fortunately, the prisoners had to endure the
snake pit for only a few days before being sent to the interrogation
center.

The center housed a confusing array of conditions and various
forms of treatment. After 1941 the most prominent feature of this

11. Dulag Luft was susceptible to wartime needs just as the rest of Germany was,
and the disposition of the prisoners varied from time to time, depending on such factors
as the inmate population and the facilities available. There were frequent exceptions to
the routine of handling prisoners, and it would be impossible to account for them by
outlining all experiences of all prisoners.
12. A.D.I. (K) Report 328, frame 0467. According to that same report, the peak
month was July, 1944, when more than 3,000 Allied airmen and paratroopers passed
through the center. The yearly totals were: 3,000 (1942), 8,000 (1943), and 29,000
(1944). "Dulag Luft," 6.
13. Broach, "The Last Mission," 14.
14. Spivey, POW Odyssey, 17.

portion of the complex was the "cooler."[15] This structure contained some two hundred forty solitary confinement cells into which each prisoner was thrust without ceremony. This was to be his home for an undetermined period of time during which he was cajoled, threatened, fed well, starved, treated to cigarettes and chocolate, or left to suffer nicotine fits and ponder his fate. All this was part of a sophisticated interrogation process that developed over months and years. During the early days of the war, attempts to obtain information in subtle ways were inefficient and feeble. Near the war's end, the operation was so effective and thoroughgoing that it produced for the Germans almost every bit of information they desired from the crews.

Different explanations have been given for the center's success. Some say the prisoners talked because of fear or, conversely, because of German kindness.[16] Others suggest that the captured airmen's security training had been inadequate, and so they were not prepared for the techniques used upon them during interrogation and either consciously or unconsciously gave away important military secrets.[17] Hans Scharff, an interrogator at Dulag Luft, claims that the prisoners talked because the Germans' methods were "almost irresistible."[18]

In 1941 a German flier, Franz von Werra, visited the center. He had been shot down and captured in England and was put through the British equivalent of Dulag Luft, the British Air Interrogation Centre at Cockfosters, before being sent to Canada, where he was to be held as a prisoner of war. He escaped and made his way through the United States and Mexico and returned to Germany from South America. Hermann Göring then ordered him to visit all RAF prisoner of war camps in Germany. Von Werra concluded that the interrogations conducted at Dulag were superficial, reporting to Göring that he "would rather be interrogated by half a dozen German inquisitors

15. This term was used by both the Allies and the Germans to designate the solitary confinement cells found in prison camps throughout Germany. One German noted that it was easier to pronounce than *Offiziersbesprechung*. Hans Joachim Scharff, "Without Torture," *Argosy* (May, 1950), 88.

16. See David Kahn, "World War II History: The Biggest Hole," *Military Affairs*, XXXIX (April, 1975), 75.

17. An excellent discussion of the problems that obviously existed in this regard is found in Ingenhutt's study, which was based on information gathered from informal interrogations of between 1,500 and 2,500 American officers and NCOs who, like him, passed through Dulag Luft before being sent to Stalag Luft III. These informal interrogations were part of an internal camp intelligence effort.

18. Scharff, "Without Torture," 87.

than by one RAF expert." The formal report in which he recommended certain changes in the camp's procedures came back from Göring's desk with the notation "will be carried out." And Dulag Luft did indeed adopt many of the organizational features and methods of interrogation used by the British.[19]

Scharff's claim that the methods were almost irresistible is credible in the sense that the interrogation effort at Dulag Luft did not consist of a single act. The extended engagement was conducted by skillful men employing clever tactics of which the man being questioned often was totally unaware. A British report went so far as to credit the Germans with sometimes completely disguising the adversarial character of the interrogation. When this was achieved, the prisoner, after exhaustive and usually productive questioning, often wondered when the actual interrogation was going to begin.[20]

The interrogation process began innocuously when a man pretending to be a Red Cross representative entered the prisoner's cell and asked him to fill out a lengthy form. After the Allies protested such false practices, the interrogator no longer mentioned the Red Cross, but the illegal form continued to be used, apparently until the end of the war. According to the Geneva Convention, prisoners of war were obliged to give only their name, rank, and serial number. The German forms asked for this information first, but gradually verged into other areas. Most prisoners gave the required data, paused a little on the questions about their home address, the names of next of kin, and civilian employment, and stopped writing altogether when they came to questions about the number and location of their flying units and other military information.[21]

The Germans made maximum use of this preliminary session. In addition to the information obtained on the "Red Cross" form, they had an opportunity to evaluate the prisoner's character. After leaving the cell, the men conducting the session often wrote telling statements that helped in later interrogations, describing the prisoner as

19. Kendal Burt and James Leasor, *The One that Got Away* (London, 1956), 238–39.

20. A.D.I. (K) Report 388, "German Methods and Experiences of Prisoner Interrogation," microfilm roll A5405, in Newspaper and Microfilm Room, Troy H. Middleton Library, Louisiana State University, Baton Rouge.

21. A.D.I. (K) Report 328, frames 9–10. This report asserts that until about the spring of 1944 the majority of "Red Cross" forms were for the most part completed. After D day, however, fewer and fewer of the forms were filled out (*ibid.*, frame 10).

"a heavy smoker" or noting that he was "unsure of himself and susceptible to flattery." Furthermore, when the prisoner announced he
could not supply the requested information, the interrogator usually
displayed a pained look. How else could they prove the prisoner's
claims that he was in fact a flier and not a spy or a saboteur? Surely
the airman was telling the truth, but (in a lowered voice) the Gestapo
was not so easily convinced. Some of the ways in which the Gestapo
secured information did not bear thinking about, especially since the
interrogator too was a military man, a man of honor, and understood
such things in a way the security police did not. The object of this
entire exchange, of course, was to impress upon the prisoner the
importance of giving sufficient information to establish his identity
beyond any doubt. The interrogator argued that at the minimum, the
prisoner had to reveal his flying unit. Then, alone in his cell, he
contemplated the last words about the Gestapo.

The small cell was ten and one-half feet long, five and one-half feet
wide, and had an eight-foot ceiling.[22] The airman sat alone with his
thoughts. There was nothing to divert his attention. The furnishings
consisted usually of a bed, one stool, and two blankets. No reading or
writing materials were available, and the one light was turned on and
off at random from somewhere outside the cell. Outside switches also
controlled the temperature of the heaters, a source of much suffering
for the prisoners. Frequently the temperature in the room became
almost unbearable, rising high enough at times to singe a towel laid
on the radiator and making the bed and all metal hot enough to
scorch bare flesh. The thick cement walls retained the heat like a
sauna, and the one window in the room was painted over.[23] The
Germans insisted that the construction of the walls prevented communication between the prisoners and that the occasional high temperatures resulted from breakdowns in the heating system, explanations considered inadequate both during and after the war.[24] The

22. A.D.I. (K) Report 328, frame 0472. Some sources list the dimensions as ten
feet by four feet (see "Dulag Luft," 23). On a recent visit to Camp King, however, I was
escorted through several rooms and found that the larger dimensions were more
accurate.
23. Bern to Secretary of State, August 17, 1943, in File 711.62114 A/45, RG 59;
A.D.I. (K) Report 328, frames 0472, 0478.
24. Bern to Secretary of State, August 17, 1943, in File 711.62114 A/45, RG 59;
A.D.I. (K) Report 328, frame 0472. At the Nuremberg trials, it was brought out by
Major Cline, a mechanical engineer from Cambridge who inspected the cells, that the

effect on the prisoners was predictable. When the time came for them to be taken from their cells for interrogation, they were relieved and thankful just to be momentarily out of confinement. This feeling of gratitude played an important role during the second session.

The first interrogator had by this time turned over all his data to another, one carefully chosen to deal with the particular prisoner. The man who now conducted the interrogation was a specialist who handled only crewmen from bombers, or fighters, or whatever his area of expertise might be. All the interrogators spoke excellent English and had lived for extended periods of time in Allied countries. Most of them were good judges of character and had a large array of techniques to employ against the captives.

Taking advantage of the prisoner's sense of relief at being let out of solitary confinement, the interrogator usually began in a friendly manner, offering cigarettes or chocolate and engaging in light conversation about war's unfortunate effects, sports, music and art, some aspect of life in the captive's native country, or the mutual problems of military men. Skillfully the interrogator sought to make the prisoner feel safe and relaxed.

These circumstances made it difficult for the prisoner to stick to name, rank, and serial number. Officers found it particularly hard to remain silent, for the majority felt that their breeding and background required them to duel verbally with the interrogator on such obviously innocent matters. Unfortunately, every word they spoke to relieve their sense of being ill at ease gave the interrogator a handle. Not unexpectedly, the enlisted prisoners did not respond in the same way. As one report noted, the sergeants mostly "felt no compunction about being stubborn to the point of downright rudeness: they were less easily flattered than officers, and they had fewer delusions about the real purpose of the interrogator's conversation. The average sergeant felt instinctively that he was not sufficiently important to warrant as much attention out of pure chivalry, and to this extent officers as a class were easier to interrogate" than were the enlisted men.[25]

If the prisoner was able to withhold the desired information throughout extended friendly conversations, threats of violence

---

1.5-kilowatt heaters installed in the cells were far in excess of the requirements, and that a 500-watt heater would have been sufficient to produce a comfortable 65°F. As it was, temperatures rose to as high as 129° ("Dulag Luft," 16).

25.   A.D.I. (K) Report 328, frame 0475. Ingenhutt reached the same conclusions.

abruptly followed. The primary threat, that the captive would be turned over to the Gestapo, was employed most effectively when the prisoner refused to identify his unit. The interrogator repeatedly insisted that this information was needed to prove the subject's claim that he was an aviator. Until such proof was given, he reminded the prisoner, no word would be sent out regarding his capture. This thought naturally caused considerable anxiety, since the men knew their loved ones back home had received word they were missing in action, but not that they were alive and well in a German prison camp. Furthermore, they knew that until the Red Cross received information about their captivity, the Germans could kill or otherwise keep them hidden away for years, all the while claiming they had never been captured. Jews were told they might be subjected to persecution, and whenever the Germans learned a prisoner had relatives in German-held territory, they suggested what might happen if he did not talk. Usually the session served to create a great deal of uncertainty in the prisoners' minds.

Except in rare cases, the threats were not carried out. Nor was physical violence relied upon—the possible exception was an occasional slap on the face. The interrogators prided themselves on being able to get the information they wanted without resorting to such vulgar tactics. And the results seem to bear out their claim. A man captured in civilian clothes did not need to be tortured. He only needed to be reminded of how the Gestapo treated spies. One interrogation report noted: "Under mental pressure because of his civilian-looking flying clothes, the [prisoner] told all."[26] And among groups, such as the eleven-man B-17 crews, it was not unusual for at least one of the men to reveal the identity of his squadron. And if the crew stepped forward as they were asked to do at the Reception Office, the Germans gained an important piece of information they wanted about all eleven men as a result of one indiscretion.

Although violence was seldom used, there were other forms of physical persuasion. The prisoners' diet was woefully inadequate and had the cumulative effect of weakening their resistance during repeated interrogation sessions. And after a time, the high room temperatures and other irritations of solitary confinement often made the

26.   A.D.I. (K) Report 328, frame 0477. The civilian clothes were usually obtained from the underground, and trying to conceal the donor's identity placed additional mental and emotional strain on the prisoner.

men anxious to leave their cells even though it meant submitting to more questions. The solitude created a need for conversation of any kind, and the interrogators were only too happy to oblige.

The Germans also used subtle but effective bribery to capitalize upon the prisoner's awareness of his physical discomfort. The offer of a cigarette, a drink, a parole walk or trip to the camp cinema, a promise to expedite notifying the prisoner's next of kin that he was safe, or a pledge that members of a crew would be allowed to remain together, all served to throw the prisoner off stride. The Germans knew better than to ask for something directly in return. They were satisfied that prisoners accepting such favors would likely feel a little indebted to them or would at least be inclined to view them in a more friendly and trusting way than before. An interrogator would turn this asset to his own use at a later time.

At times, bribery was disguised as chivalry. High-ranking captives often received preferential treatment at Hohemark Hospital and at a hunting lodge outside Frankfurt. Or they were wined and dined at the officers' mess, all the while being subjected to discreet efforts to obtain information. More frequently, however, they were simply displayed at these places, the intention being to portray to newcomers a contented group of senior officers enjoying the "comradeship of the Knights of the Air" of which the Germans so frequently boasted.[27]

Sometimes the interrogator totally disarmed the prisoner by demonstrating how much the Germans knew—so he no longer needed to remain silent. Much to the prisoner's dismay, the interrogator usually possessed an amazing arsenal of facts. It was demoralizing that the Germans could often cite the prisoner's unit number, the location of the unit, the name of its commander or other notable personnel, the types of aircraft it possessed, the missions it had undertaken, possibly some of the missions planned for it, and a seemingly infinite list of other details that left the prisoner astonished and convinced that the Germans did in fact know everything they wanted to know.

Colonel Spivey was indeed surprised by what the interrogator knew about him. Saying that Spivey really did not have to worry about giving away any secrets because the Germans already knew all about him anyway, the interrogator produced a picture of the flying person-

27. A.D.I. (K) Report 328, frame 0478; Eric Friedheim, "Welcome to Dulag Luft," *Air Force*, XXVIII (September, 1945), 43.

nel of an 8th Air Force group and the group commander and his staff. He told Spivey about the group he had flown with and the names of the crew members, that he had a wife and a child whose birthday would come two days later, where he had been throughout his service, and wound up by saying Spivey should have had his big feet on his desk at Maxwell Field, Alabama, instead of trying to find out why so many Allied bombers were being shot down over Germany. The information shocked Spivey. He was in Europe on secret orders and was certain that not a person on the crew knew about his job or mission, much less anything about his wife or his child's birth date. Somewhat awed, he filled out the "Red Cross" form, leaving out the data concerning his group. The interrogator obligingly filled it in for him. As a parting shot he told Spivey he was lucky his previously scheduled mission to the ball-bearing works at Schweinfurt had been scrubbed twice, because the Luftwaffe had been waiting and would be again whenever the attack took place. Spivey had in fact been posted to go on one of the flights. And the next day his spirits plummeted when he heard the anti-aircraft guns and saw American bombers being viciously attacked by German fighters as they engaged in the shuttle raid from England to North Africa that was a diversion for the long-awaited Schweinfurt raid.[28]

In the aftermath of the interrogations, the prisoners naturally wondered where the Germans got their information: from spies in Allied squadrons or from stool pigeons among the prisoners, from microphones in the walls, or from airmen who talked too much? It actually came from a wide range of sources, and the most obvious were among the least important.

An estimated 80 percent of the information the Germans obtained was produced by the Document Section, the most efficient and productive division in the center.[29] The staff scoured Allied newspapers, books, and periodicals, the pockets of captured personnel, and material from airplanes that came down in their territory. No item was too small or insignificant, and every scrap was scrutinized with extreme care.

The results were startling. A one-way railroad ticket between two

28. Spivey, POW Odyssey, 22–24.
29. This estimate was given in a staff report drawn up for the Counter Intelligence Corps, U.S. Strategic Air Forces in Europe, and made public in Friedheim, "Welcome to Dulag Luft," 17. See also A.D.I. (K) Report 328, frame 0485.

English villages gave the Germans an important clue about the impending transfer of airmen attached to a British Wellington bomber group. The Luftwaffe subsequently learned that the RAF was shifting a number of these planes to antisubmarine patrol duty. The Document Section's experts became so resourceful and methodical that they could identify a flier's unit by the manner in which his ration card was marked. At one base, for instance, the clerk always used a heavy black pencil, and since the PX counter was constructed of rough board, all the cards from that group showed its distinctive grain in the pencil marks. Air crews were told not to transport papers and other extraneous documents, but the men persisted for a variety of reasons. The most serious violations involved diaries. One diary revealed the number of crews undergoing training in the United States, as well as how many heavy bombers were available for that purpose. It also divulged highly secret data about the heavy bombardment program. The photographs furnished airmen to facilitate their escape through the underground sometimes served to identify their unit also. Photographs from the 91st Bomb Group, for example, had a particular brown color. Everyone from the 95th Bomb Group wore the same checkered civilian coat when he had his picture taken.[30]

Numerous other sections plied their trade at the center, and they all added pieces to the puzzle. The Yellow File Section collected biographical information on Allied personnel, using newspapers, award lists, magazines, radio broadcasts, and censored mail, and carefully cataloged it for quick reference. The Squadron History Section gathered data on every Allied squadron and its historical development—facts on past and present location, postal addresses, names of its leading personalities, and the special equipment it was known to operate. The Attack Section prepared a map each day displaying the Allied air operations of the preceding twenty-four hours. Based chiefly on German radar tracking and Observer Corps reports, the map showed targets, courses, results of missions, numbers of aircraft involved, and even canceled actions. Information obtained from interrogations in progress was incorporated into the display so that each interrogator had access to the work of the others. Two Situation Rooms also contributed to the interrogator's arsenal of knowledge. One attended to British activities and the other to American actions.

30. Friedheim, "Welcome to Dulag Luft," 17, 43; A.D.I. (K) Report 328, frame 0464.

Maps showed the locations of recent raids, the progress of raids still taking place, and the front lines of the opposing armies. They even gave the fullest possible details of ferry flights and transport movements. A staff of translators in the Press Evaluation Section went through all copies of Allied newspapers and magazines, looking for pertinent information. The Photograph Section developed and printed all film found on a prisoner, as well as any that was recovered from the gun cameras of downed aircraft. The Technical Section maintained a library and a museum of Allied equipment. Files were kept for every known crash site in Germany or in German-occupied territory. Each crash received a number, and the file contained the type of aircraft, location of crash, and such details about the personnel on board and the home unit as emerged in later interrogations. And finally, a group of linguists listened to the airmen's wireless communications around the clock seven days a week—plane to plane, plane to base, and base to plane—recording and transcribing the conversations and the radio frequencies along with their place of origin.[31]

Armed with such information, the interrogators confronted each prisoner. The object was not to learn any great secrets about grand strategy or similar matters. It was commonly understood that the average airman was not privy to such information. Rather, the interrogator sought tactical and operational information that would help the anti-aircraft gunners place their weapons, assist in the evaluation of the latest technical equipment used on the missions, determine important targets, and gather small talk that would assist them in breaking down the resistance of future prisoners.

Hans Scharff later emphasized that to the best of his knowledge, no American pilot talked through fear or through any ignoble hope of bettering his condition as a prisoner. He estimated, however, that all but about twenty out of the more than five hundred men he interviewed did talk, telling him exactly the things he was trying to find out.

Unfortunately, the record shows that there were prisoners who knowingly revealed military secrets. One prisoner provided the Germans with a page and a half of technical details about the P-47's

---

31. A.D.I. (K) Report 328, frames 0463–66; Scharff, "Without Torture," 90. Other sections at Auswertestelle West, such as the Political Section, are described in Scharff, "Without Torture."

combat flying range, its supercharger, its armament, and the tactics its pilots employed. One bomber crewman revealed the form of attack they most feared: one from in front and twelve hundred feet above them meant only the top turret could then come into action. And the German interrogation reports include other cases of airmen freely divulging information on equipment, the types of formations flown against various targets, and the meaning of important code words.[32]

In view of the center's reputation for success, it is indeed ironic that Dulag Luft let slip an opportunity to discover the biggest intelligence plum of the war, the news that the Allies had broken the German cipher code. This fact, known as project Ultra among the few who were aware of it in the West, was considered the ultra secret of the war. It so happened that Brigadier General Arthur W. Vanaman passed through Luftwaffe channels as a prisoner of war. He had been briefed on the existence of Ultra just a short time before he was shot down and captured.[33]

What happened to the prisoners at Dulag Luft constituted yet one more ingredient in the bond of experience shared by the men sent to Stalag Luft III. Most of them did not leave Dulag Luft burdened with a sense of guilt, sincerely believing they had not given any important information to the Germans. They did, however, leave with a heightened respect for German thoroughness, organization, and intelligence-gathering ability.

After a stay of one or two weeks (but sometimes as long as a month or more), the prisoners were sent to a transit camp and then on to a permanent camp, usually in groups or "purges" of fifty to one hundred men. The three-hundred-mile trip from Dulag Luft to Sagan usually proved to be another ordeal. Frequently the men were packed into the forty-and-eight boxcars taken from the French (marked "40 Hommes—8 Chevaux"). The cars had often been used to haul livestock, and it was not unusual to find fresh manure or an inch of black dirt on the floor. Sometimes the Germans ordered several prisoners to clean out the cars. There were a few boards for the prisoners to sit or lie down on, and the arrangement depended on the number of people.

---

32. Edwin A. Bland, Jr., "German Methods for Interrogation of Captured Allied Aircrews" (Thesis, Air Command and Staff School of Air University, Maxwell Air Force Base, Ala., 1948), 13–15.
33. Personal conversation with the author. General Vanaman was the highest-ranking American officer in captivity and later became the senior officer at Stalag Luft III.

Since the cars were almost always filled beyond capacity, the majority had to remain standing or sit on the filthy floor.

The prisoners suffered other discomforts on the trip as well. Although there usually was enough food, drinking water often was withheld for periods of twenty-four hours or longer. There were no toilet facilities, and the men were unable to relieve themselves except perhaps in a nearby woods or a marshaling yard when the train stopped. Little effort was made to provide any privacy for the prisoners, and often there were women in the vicinity.[34]

The cars were poorly ventilated and the inside became oppressive as the train proceeded on its jerky way. Since this transport was assigned a low priority, the prison cars were hitched to the end of one freight train after another and shunted on and off railroad sidings. The trip took two days or longer, and often exposed the prisoners to bombing and strafing attacks by Allied aircraft.

When the train finally arrived at the station in Sagan, the tired and dirty travelers got out and walked the short distance to the camp. While at the transit camp, many had heard detailed accounts of the country-club atmosphere at Stalag Luft III, which reportedly contained swimming pools and golf courses. Few prisoners entertained any delusions about what lay ahead, and they certainly did not believe such stories, but they did look forward to seeing their new home so they could size it up for themselves. They also welcomed being able to establish some kind of routine after the hectic uncertainty of recent days. And they knew that old friends would be there, many of whom they had thought were dead but whose names they had seen on the register at the transit camp. With a swirl of such thoughts running through their minds, the prisoners stepped beyond the edge of the forest separating the railway station from the camp and gazed for the first time upon the maze of barbed wire and gray buildings of Stalag Luft III.

34. Spivey, *POW Odyssey*, 29.

German camps

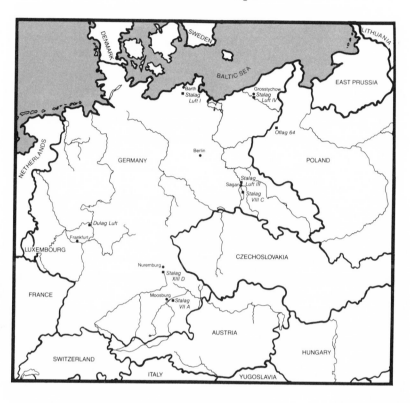

4

Before the Gates Opened

Allied prisoners occupied Stalag Luft III from April, 1942, until February, 1945, a period of almost three years. During this time the camp grew rapidly from a small enclosure containing two compounds, a service area, and a section for the German staff to a sprawling complex of six compounds. The prison population mushroomed from several hundred men to more than ten thousand. British and Commonwealth troops were in the majority in the beginning, but by the time the camp closed, the Americans were. Relations with the German staff went from good to bad and mediocre, influenced by the pace of the war, the prisoners' conduct, outside interference, and personnel changes. And the prisoners themselves altered their way of life from time to time in accordance with the availability of supplies and the tasks they set for themselves.

The phenomenal growth of the camp and the frequent physical changes largely explain the difficulty of rendering an exact account of the conditions and events associated with Stalag Luft III. In strictest terms, everything should be viewed in reference to time and place. Doing so, however, obscures the real essence of the camp's history, which is found in the continuous rather than the broken lines of development. The opening of new compounds and the shifting of populations within the camp interrupted the scheme of things, but only momentarily. For when these events occurred, only a brief time elapsed before the prisoners created or, more correctly, re-created an existence much like that found in the older compounds, complete with a sense of community spirit and a wide range of activities.

This continuity was possible primarily because each compound contained approximately the same facilities and was occupied by a relatively homogeneous group of people who possessed a sense of purpose and self-identity. The men did have in common their national heritages, for example, and their role as comrades-in-arms. But these things in themselves do not account for the community spirit that existed in the compounds of Stalag Luft III. Talent, leadership, and experience all had a part in its development.

The matter of experience is important. From the beginning, Stalag Luft III housed prisoners who were by then all too familiar with life in captivity. By the time the camp's gates opened for the first time in April, 1942, some of the men who passed through them had been behind barbed wire for two and one-half years. During these thirty months, leaders emerged and asserted themselves. Also in that time, both the Germans and the prisoners formed opinions about one another in their respective roles as captors and captives, devised various concepts and techniques to assist each side in achieving its own ends, and established policies that had an impact on later events.

Along with Wings Day, a few other British fliers were captured by the Germans in the fall months of 1939. Among the first were Tommy Thompson and Wank Murray, who were shot down while flying over Berlin with a load of leaflets. Much to their surprise, they were taken to see Göring himself, who in typical fashion received them cordially and complained they had disturbed his sleep and had obliged him to take shelter. He assured them, however, that he appreciated the chivalrous way the Royal Flying Corps had fought in the last war and said he intended to see that Royal Air Force prisoners were treated correctly. Soon they were nevertheless locked in Spangenburg Castle, sleeping on straw mattresses, and living on the lowest scale of German rations. There, they met the other members of this earliest group of downed airmen. Among them was Wings, clearly outranking and, at forty-one, twice the age of most of them. Before long, it became evident he would direct the way the British adapted to prison life. [1]

The course that British prisoners were to follow in the days ahead was typified by Wings's decision on how they should conduct themselves, at least in the beginning, during the daily head count taken by the Germans. When the German officer in charge of Appell approached, Wings snapped his little squad to rigid attention, turned sharply, and

1. Smith, *Mission Escape*, 4, 15. Smith's book, originally published in Great Britain in 1968 under the title *Wings Day*, is an excellent biography. Although Smith never goes so far as to state explicitly what I have just asserted about Commander Day's role, one quickly gains this impression from his book. From what can be gleaned from other sources, there is every reason to believe that Wings deserves the eminent position claimed for him here.

rendered an impressive salute. Wings felt that if he ever needed to insist on the rights granted to prisoners by the Geneva Convention, his position would be stronger if he had at least outwardly fulfilled his own obligations, one of which was the observance of military courtesies. Even more revealing is the statement he made on November 10, 1939, when the British and French prisoners in Spangenburg paused for a brief but meaningful ceremony commemorating the end of the last war. Facing the small gathering before him, he declared: "Nineteen-eighteen may seem a long way off to some of you. At the beginning of that year it looked as though we had lost the war. It may seem to some of you now that you have already lost this one. But we beat the Germans in 1918 and what you have already done will help to beat them again. For you the war is *not* over. Vive la France—and England."[2]

In the second week of December, 1939, Wings and some of the other RAF prisoners were transferred to Oberursel, where Dulag Luft was just being opened. The Germans assigned him to the permanent staff that operated the transit portion of the camp, and he again became Senior British Officer (SBO). It was therefore one of his tasks to establish policies regarding various aspects of prison life. As a trained and experienced military man, he knew the official answers to most of the questions that arose. In the days ahead, however, he encountered situations that rendered the official positions inadequate or inappropriate. And when such matters came to his attention, he attempted to set procedures in accordance with the facts as he knew them, even if that meant violating the rules. Wings did very well—most of these early decisions remained in effect throughout the war.

One of the most difficult questions Wings dealt with involved signing a parole slip in return for the privilege of taking walks outside the compound. He knew that officially parole was not to be given under any circumstances and feared that he would be liable to a court-martial after the war. Before many days passed, however, he concluded that his indefinite restriction to the tiny Dulag justified parole. It was a matter of mental health.

The manner in which the Red Cross food parcels were distributed also affected the prisoners' health and welfare. In the early days of the war the parcels were addressed to each individual by name. Since the

2. Smith, *Mission Escape*, 18.

rations provided by the Germans were inadequate from the beginning, only those officers who had been in captivity long enough for their names to have been entered in the addressing system could expect to receive sufficient food. To offset this inequity, Wings ordered that the food in the Red Cross parcels be pooled. The old prisoners thereby gave up their favored position in order that new arrivals would receive better rations, an important factor in their recovery from being shot down and interrogated. This policy later was in effect at Stalag Luft III as well, even after the compounds were divided by nationality.

And Wings's decision on using coded messages to relay intelligence information home provides evidence that the prisoners meant it when they asserted that for them the war was not over. One day during the spring of 1940 an airman passed through the camp and told Wings about a special code the prisoners could use to send and receive messages to and from London. Wings had never heard of the system before, but immediately asked that he and several other officers on the permanent staff be registered as code operators. In time, valuable information reached London in coded form by means of the prisoners' letters home. When new prisoners reached the transit camp, Wings and his staff queried them about the tactics of the fighters that had brought them down and the methods used by the interrogators who questioned them after their arrival at Dulag Luft. The data were then transmitted to England and helped the Royal Air Force devise effective countermeasures. This amounted to an open-and-shut case of espionage. The Germans would have been fully justified in putting on trial as a spy anyone caught in coding activities.[3]

These policies and measures were indicative of how strongly the British believed that the enemy's efforts must be frustrated, resisted,

3. *Ibid.*, 17–18, 24, 30; William E. S. Flory, *Prisoners of War: A Study in the Development of International Law*, with an Introduction by Norman H. Davis (Washington, D.C., 1942), states: "It is recognized in customary international law that persons otherwise entitled to the status of prisoners of war may forfeit the right to such status by the commission of certain acts such as espionage, violation of parole, and war crimes. The quality of a military spy is dependent upon four conditions: 1) he must either be in search of or have obtained information; 2) he must intend to put the information in the hands of the enemy; 3) his mission must carry him into the zone of operations; and 4) he must be acting clandestinely or on false pretenses" (p. 37). For further information on this question, see Morris Greenspan, *The Modern Law of Land Warfare* (Berkeley and Los Angeles, 1959), 326–32.

or circumvented in every possible way. Fostering escape activities was a logical extension of this conviction. It was considered to be the duty of every British officer to attempt to escape. But not everyone possessed the temperament or talent for such a difficult task. Furthermore, it was a duty for which virtually none of them had been trained.

Interestingly enough, the Germans were almost as much in the dark when it came to preventing escape. Consequently, the opposing sides developed their skills through prolonged trial and error. Wings was joined in this task by a highly talented group of individuals. Lieutenant Commander Jimmy Buckley was a Dartmouth graduate who had a remarkable aptitude for sorting out complicated problems. He was the major organizer of escapes until he disappeared at sea during an escape attempt in 1943. Squadron Leader Roger Bushell, a South African–born lawyer, was a graduate of English and French universities, and a former British ski champion and rugby player. He had an eye for detail and spoke fluent French and German with a Swiss accent. Bushell later masterminded the mass escape from Stalag Luft III in March, 1944. Flight Lieutenant John Gilles also spoke German fluently and was a chartered accountant. Flight Lieutenant Harvey Vivian, a graduate of American, English, and German universities, spoke German like a native. And Major Johnnie Dodge, an American-born nephew by marriage of Winston Churchill's, turned out to be an avid escaper.[4]

By June, 1941, this select group had collected a quantity of German money, used their parole walks to gather information on the paths and roads in the surrounding countryside, obtained train schedules, and completed a tunnel out of the camp. Including Bushell's escape from a goat shed near the exercise field, a total of eighteen men, including Wings, made their way out of camp in early June and caused a furor in the Reich command structure. It was the first successful mass escape by British prisoners.[5] Heinrich Himmler did not miss the opportunity to point out to Hitler that the Luftwaffe obviously was incapable of doing its part in protecting the security of

4. Three books contain further information on these men and are the sources upon which I drew: Smith, *Mission Escape*, 36ff.; Paul Brickhill, *The Great Escape*, with an Introduction by George Harsh (Greenwich, Conn., 1950); and Aidan Crawley, *Escape from Germany: A History of R.A.F. Escapes During the War* (New York, 1956), 27–31.
5. Anything involving five or more prisoners was considered a mass escape.

the Reich. Unfortunately, all eighteen were recaptured. The Germans, not surprisingly, decided to transfer them elsewhere.[6]

Following their recapture, most of the escapers from Dulag Luft ended up in Stalag Luft I, a permanent Luftwaffe camp located at Barth in the province of Pomerania on the shore of the Baltic. Opened in the summer of 1940, it had good and bad qualities. The facilities were adequate, and the two hundred or so officers living there generally got on amicably with one another and enjoyed cordial relations with the German administration. But there also were moments of turmoil and unrest. Flight Lieutenant B. A. ("Jimmy") James arrived there soon after it opened and remembers the first year as a "dreary and soul destroying period." Penned up in a small dusty cage (about one hundred by seventy yards), the prisoners watched and waited from afar as the seemingly unstoppable German armies prepared for the assault against their homeland. And since no Red Cross parcels arrived that first year, food was always scarce. Such conditions, James recalls, "were bound to exacerbate any incipient feelings of bitterness or remorse and fuel any paranoid fantasies about other prisoners that might exist, such as occurred when the Dulag 'crowd' arrived, guilty in the eyes of the prisoners at Barth of 'living it up with the Germans.'"[7] In addition to having reservations about the Dulag crowd, the original inhabitants had begun to suspect that some of their number were collaborating with the Germans, especially when tunnel after tunnel was discovered and destroyed. By the summer of 1941 relations between the Germans and the prisoners also became tense. Parole walks had been discontinued after two prisoners escaped on a walk for which they managed to avoid signing the parole forms. In addition, the men had fused a microphone system the Germans had installed to listen in on the prisoners' conversations, and a series of reprisals followed.

Again Wings Day was the Senior British Officer. He quickly realized that corrective action had to be taken to eliminate the unrest. In light of his own tunneling experience at Dulag Luft, he concluded that the prisoners' security measures were inadequate. The Germans

6. Smith, *Mission Escape*, 48–50, 55.
7. Gustav Simoleit, "Prisoner of War Camps of the Air Force in World War II," Pt. I, May 5, 1969, enclosed in Simoleit to Spivey, May 5, 1969, in Simoleit Folder, Spivey Collection; B. A. James to the author, August 6, 1982. For a complete account of James's experiences, see his biography, *Moonless Night: One Man's Struggle for Freedom, 1940–1945* (London, 1983).

learned a great deal about the location and progress of the tunnels through a microphone system placed in the ground along the perimeter fence. But they also benefited from the factionalism in camp. Would-be escapers wasted time and energy in feuds and jealousies. It was obvious to Wings that all their attempts would be doomed unless they tightened security and coordinated their efforts.

Increased discipline, however, clearly was not the answer, for here the commanding officer could not impose the King's Regulations. Furthermore, the men did not need to be directed as much as they needed the benefits of experienced leadership. No one of his age or level of experience had been in camp before. In this case, his mere presence would help. And he did what he could to settle the unrest among the men. He formed boards of inquiry to investigate the charges of corruption and collaboration the prisoners had lodged against one another and handled the findings in such a way that the gnawing doubts were largely dispelled. Then he did something that, perhaps more than anything else, served to develop camp spirit from that point on: he designated "escaping" as the "operational function" of the camp.[8] Virtually everyone understood this terminology. Every prisoner was a military man and knew that the use of the word *operational* meant that as a unit they were back in the war. Many of them had felt guilty that they had been shot down, thinking that if they had banked their aircraft a little harder, dived a little farther, or climbed a little faster during that last flight, they might still be serving their country as operational members of their squadrons.[9] Now they had a chance once again, both as individuals and as an operational team. Individually they could accomplish little, but together they might create considerable havoc within the Reich. Now a person who never thought of escaping could feel that he was contributing something merely by helping others to escape.

This kind of feeling was precisely what the prisoners needed to pull them together. Wings himself calculated that no more than 25 percent cared to venture escape at all; of those, only 5 percent could be considered dedicated escapers, fanatics who thought, dreamed, and talked of nothing else and availed themselves of every opportunity to get away no matter how appalling the risks. The others were neither

8. Smith, *Mission Escape*, 58–60, 65–76.
9. Interview with Albert P. Clark, April 7, 1973; James L. Cole, "Dulag Luft Recalled and Revisited," *Aerospace Historian*, XIX (June, 1972), 62–65.

afraid nor lazy but were convinced they simply would not get very far. However, if asked to do so, they would work for the benefit of those who did wish to try to escape. Wings felt that at least 50 percent of the prisoners would help. As things turned out, his estimate was correct—perhaps even a little conservative.[10]

Thus the prisoners' escape activities came to have a twofold objective: to help individuals who wanted to escape, and to give the prisoners a feeling of doing something positive toward bringing the war to an end. Everyone knew the escape attempts forced the Germans to abandon any ideas about economizing on the guarding of Luftwaffe prisoners. Most prisoners had long since tired of being told that for them the war was over; escaping was one more way of telling the Germans that such rhetoric was only wishful thinking. Only 5 percent of the population may have been avid escapers, but it was a highly active group. Besides, there were many others who periodically caught the fever.[11]

Wings soon realized there was no lack of interest in escape at Barth. He correctly perceived that he was "shut in a kennel with a good pack of foxhounds. They were over, round and on top, bursting with energy, sniffing at every nook and cranny. Eyes bright and sterns up and waving, all looking to be let out."[12] All they needed was organization. Wings invited Jimmy Buckley and one Barth old-timer into his room, and the three of them interviewed everyone who had anything to do with escapes or had anything to say about escaping. It took nearly a week. Wings appointed Buckley to head the Escape Committee, and he, in turn, selected two other officers to help him. In addition, each barracks elected its own three-man committee.

The prisoners started forty-eight tunnels at Barth before the Germans took them by train to Stalag Luft III in April, 1942. Unfortunately, Barth sat right on the seashore, and they would hit water at four or five feet below the surface. Consequently, the Germans destroyed most of the tunnels by driving heavy wagons around the compounds. At least one tunnel proved worthwhile, however. Flight Lieutenants John ("Death") Shore and Jimmy James dug what was

10. Smith, *Mission Escape*, 65–66. Albert P. Clark (interview, November 8, 1975) indicated that between 60 and 70 percent of the prisoners at Stalag Luft III worked in one capacity or another on the escape activities.

11. Smith, *Mission Escape*, 65.

12. *Ibid.*, 66.

known as a "blitz" or lightening tunnel out of one of the brick incinerators, and though James was caught immediately, Shore made a
"home run" all the way to England.[13]

Other methods of escape also verged on success. Flying Officer Pat
Leeson tried to march out of camp dressed as a German chimney sweep
while the real sweep was still there. That effort failed. Undaunted,
Leeson tried again just six weeks later. This time he dressed as a
German interpreter who was escorting two prisoners to the dentist in
the town of Barth. Unfortunately, there was a flaw in his fake gate
pass, and he was caught a second time.[14] On another occasion, two
prisoners decked themselves out in homemade German uniforms, jackboots made of cardboard covered with black shoe polish, and dummy
wood rifles. They joined a night platoon of guards closing the wood
shutters on the barracks windows. The prisoners got through the
gate, but then something unexpected happened. The guards were not
supposed to talk. When a guard nevertheless asked one of the prisoners a question, the reply was inappropriate. The German got suspicious and soon uncovered the prisoners' disguise. At this point, all
the guards (including the second prisoner) stopped marching and stood
around in a group, roaring with laughter and slapping one another on
the back. The second prisoner joined in the fun and fortunately found
it unnecessary to speak. Just as the march was about to resume,
however, a German officer appeared, and the whole story had to be
recounted. The officer enjoyed the joke with the rest, but ordered a
second check and found that there was still one too many. Chaos
ensued and every German feverishly accused his neighbor of being
an impostor until finally the second prisoner was unmasked.[15]

There were even instances in which officers attempted to escape
during blizzards, hoping the swirling snow would hide them while
they climbed over the fence. One man in January, 1942, and then two
men in March got beyond the wire, but all were recaptured soon
thereafter.

The escape organization also helped people who wanted to
"escape" within the camp by means of the "ghost" system. First used

13. Brickhill, *The Great Escape*, 19; Smith, *Mission Escape*, 73.
14. A fairly complete account of Leeson's chimney-sweep escape is given in
Crawley, *Escape from Germany*, 65–66. See also Smith, *Mission Escape*, 74; B. A.
James to the author, August 6, 1982.
15. Crawley, *Escape from Germany*, 72–73, 55–56.

when Shore got out through the incinerator, this system aimed at keeping the Germans ever uncertain about the total camp strength and the total number missing after a particular escape. When an escape took place, one or more ghosts immediately went into hiding. When the Germans next counted the prisoners, the ghosts would be among the missing, supposedly having gotten away. So there were now extra men in camp, and they could escape at the next opportunity without the alarm being raised. This was important during those first few hours after a break when the escaper needed to get as far away from the camp as possible. If the Germans learned of but had not identified the ghost escaper, another ghost would go into hiding at once, and the Germans would put out the description of the wrong prisoner. The first ghost remained hidden for three weeks before he was discovered in the roof of one of the barracks during a routine search. A second effort stretched out for six weeks, until the ghost dressed himself up as one of the Germans who worked inside the compound and walked out the main gate. Much to his dismay, however, he soon met face to face the man he was impersonating and took his customary turn in the cooler. Only a dedicated escaper would be likely to volunteer for a stint as a ghost, for the role entailed hard work and considerable mental and physical strain. It meant hiding in cupboards, in tunnels under construction, under mattresses, and in other such places.

Another practice that frustrated the Germans' attempts to keep close tabs on the prisoners was the "duty pilot" system. Eventually a permanent institution in many Luftwaffe camps, the system reported the arrivals and departures of every German. The terminology was said to have stemmed from pilots at RAF airfields being assigned extra daily duty. Duty pilots had to monitor all air activities, including weather forecasts, refueling, and other matters pertaining to airplanes and air crews. At Barth the duty pilot sat at a window that offered a good view of the front gate. He had sketches of all the known German camp staff and their names, a logbook showing times of entry and departure, and a staff of runners who would follow the Germans through the camp. Runners not only gave this information to the duty pilot, they also told prisoners engaged in various kinds of forbidden work. The Germans concluded that there was little they could do about the duty pilot and let the practice continue.[16]

16.   Smith, *Mission Escape*, 78.

In some instances the prisoners at Barth had begun to organize themselves as a community even before Wings arrived—for example, in the way they handled their financial affairs. Whenever officers and enlisted men were held in close proximity, the Germans had a ready-made situation for creating dissension between the two groups of prisoners. In accordance with the Geneva Convention, officers alone received regular pay while being held prisoner. So they could purchase useful items on the German market that were unavailable to the others. To help correct this inequity, the officers set up a fund to finance NCOs' purchases of musical instruments, sports equipment, theatrical supplies, and other items. The commandant approved the plan, and the funds were handled by two chartered accountants, Flight Lieutenants Bob Stark and John Gilles. The aid to the NCOs assumed two forms: direct grants to the senior NCO for general camp use, and loans to individuals for buying cigarettes, food, and toilet articles. When Wings arrived, he discouraged the personal loans, and soon they were seldom used. In return, the grants to the senior NCO were increased.[17]

Camp conditions as a whole seem to have been adequate at Barth from the time Wings arrived until the prisoners moved in April, 1942. The prisoners were issued wallpaper, which they put up in their sometimes crowded rooms. A large sports field located outside the compound provided some relief from the routine when German escorts were available. And an ice hockey rink was constructed between two barracks. Games were available for indoor use, and a good library existed, stocked in part with privately owned books. Now and again, there were performances and concerts in a big theater hall located in the NCOs' compound.[18]

Wings took a dim view of one of the plays that was presented at Barth, though the Germans who attended the performance seemed to like it. Wings sat in the front row between the commandant and the German camp adjutant. The title of the play was *Alice and Her Candle*, and "the first four lines of the dialogue dispelled all hope of innocent fun," for "with every line it grew more vulgar and lewd."

17. "Financial Policy and Statement," June, 1943, Index A, Short Summary of the Developments of the Financial Policy Adopted in German Prison Camps, in File 711.62114 A/21, RG 59.
18. Report of visit by Dr. Folke Malmquist, October 7, 1941, in File 740.00114 EW/1902, RG 59; B. A. James to the author, August 6, 1982.

Cringing with embarrassment, Wings looked at the Germans' faces, which all registered concentration without a glimmer of a smile. He feared the commandant would rise in righteous indignation to protest such a "lecherous and libidinous performance." Instead, after it was over, the Commandant complimented Wings on "the fine standard of the Shakespearean English and the acting." Wings remained unimpressed and told the cast the next day that the Germans might have been struck with their skillful "reversion to the robust humour of earlier centuries and . . . use of short descriptive Anglo-Saxon words," but he himself was not. Wings recommended that they not do the play again. [19]

The prisoners obviously learned much at Stalag Luft I about community spirit and escape. So did the Germans. They learned a great deal about how to prevent escape and about how to handle a bunch of crafty prisoners. Some telling insights appear in a brief by Gustav Simoleit, a German officer who served on the camp staff at Barth. It is interesting to compare his impressions with those of the prisoners.

Simoleit, a professor of history, geography, and ethnology in civilian life, served on the staff of an anti-aircraft unit before reporting for duty at Barth in August, 1940. He spoke English and several other languages and speculated that his linguistic ability was a primary factor in his assignment to a prisoner of war camp staff. When he received his orders to report to Barth, he was extremely unhappy and apprehensive about the kind of men he would have to serve with in his new capacity as a jailer. He was greatly relieved to discover that his new position gave him "important duties and responsibilities" and that "the P.O.W. camp in Barth was one of the few places in the world where, during a merciless war, soldiers of both fighting armies could meet and establish personal contacts" and could become acquainted with "many reasonable and well-educated people of other nations."

The living quarters in the officers' compound, Simoleit recalled, were divided into many small rooms, each occupied by only two, three, or four men. This system "enabled the prisoners to equip their rooms according to their own taste and fancy with furniture, pictures, bookshelves, and flowers."

The Americans served as the protecting power for the British at the time, and Simoleit remembered their visits to the camp on inspection trips. When they arrived, the commandant and his staff cordially

---

19. Smith, *Mission Escape*, 77.

received them and invited them inside for breakfast or coffee. Both then and later in the day after the inspection had been completed, the Germans and Americans discussed the prisoners' complaints "in the highest degree of understanding and cooperation."

Unfortunately, Simoleit with some sadness wrote later, "this relatively satisfactory life and the good relations between the prisoners and the German personnel resulted in difficulties and troubles." It seems that the "military and civilian authorities, especially the [political party] functionaries had little understanding concerning the good relations between the prisoners and the camp staff," and accused the latter of being "too lenient" and even suspected them of engaging in "dangerous collaboration" with the enemy.

The first victim of this attitude was the camp's second commandant, Major von Stachelski. The major, Simoleit later recalled, liked to spend the dull evening hours in the barracks, sometimes drinking a little too much. One evening he started feeling sorry for the "poor prisoners" and resolved to help them. Although it was strictly forbidden to give the prisoners any kind of alcohol, he had several boxes filled with beer bottles and took his gift himself to the officers' compound, where he was received with great joy. A few days later the young German camp doctor visited his superior medical officer, who was on the staff of the commanding general of the military area, and told him the beer story as a good joke. The doctor's superior, however, reported it to the general.

The next morning the general suddenly appeared in Stalag Luft I and started an intensive investigation that led to the commandant's dismissal. Simoleit, at the time second-in-command, was appointed commandant. Much surprised by the unexpected honor, Simoleit was not happy in his new position. The commandant had a colonel's power to command and discipline, but Simoleit was only a captain in the reserve. Furthermore, he was assuming his new duties at a difficult time. Rumors had spread over the country, especially in the neighboring military units, that at Barth there were unbelievable fraternization and even drinking bouts with the prisoners. Numerous visitors, majors, colonels, and generals, all wanted to see the strange camp where such things could happen, and their numbers wore Simoleit down. They were surprised to find a mere captain in charge. And Simoleit found it hard to convince them that the infamous drinking bout was an isolated affair and that the staff's work and humane attitude were not treason but were fully expected of the signatories of the Geneva Convention.

Captain Simoleit felt outgunned in his quarrels with senior officers over such matters, so he repeatedly demanded that a higher-ranking officer be appointed. Finally, a Major Burchard was named as the new commandant, and Simoleit resumed his more palatable duties as second-in-command.

The camp had only seven officers assigned to it: the commandant; his adjutant; the Abwehr officer, responsible for security; and four officers in a department known as the Lagerfuhrung, of which Simoleit was in charge. The Lagerfuhrung (roughly, compound control office) served as the constant intermediary between the prisoners and the commandant and the other departments.[20] Understandably, the people assigned to this office came into close personal contact with the prisoners.

Surprisingly, Simoleit himself was none too confident about the loyalty of the men working for him in this capacity. Captain Hans Pieber was an Austrian who had lived for a long time in Central and South America. "His experiences in foreign countries," Simoleit asserted, "made him especially able to have excellent contacts with the prisoners." Lieutenant Buckwich, he recalled, was "the genuine type of a liberal, merry, light-hearted Austrian." Further, "the relations of [these] two Austrians to the prisoners were so very good that they were not far from becoming risky and dangerous to both sides." In a strange sort of way, Simoleit was more correct than he ever could have imagined or, if he did know the truth behind his words, ever let on.[21]

One day shortly after his arrival at Barth, Wings was dumbfounded to learn that a young officer, Paul Burke, was under sentence of death by his own prison mates for suspected collaboration. Burke, it seems, had been spending a great deal of time with Lieutenant Buckwich.[22]

20. Simoleit states that the literal translation would be "camp leadership," but since the real and highest leadership post belonged to the commandant, Lagerfuhrung should perhaps be translated as "camp organization" (Simoleit, "Organization and Administration").

21. Gustav Simoleit, "Prisoner of War Camps," n.p.

22. In *Mission Escape*, from which this account is taken, Smith gives Buckwich's name Buckvig and lists him as an Abwehr instead of a Lagerfuhrung officer. It is possible that he is correct and that Simoleit is wrong in both cases, but this seems

Burke told Wings that he and Buckwich had become close friends and that Buckwich had even taken him into a room that contained the primitive seismograph the Germans were using to detect tunneling. Burke had reported this incident to the camp leaders, but they refused to believe him, feeling that no German officer in Buckwich's position could be so indiscreet. Buckwich then provided Burke with some maps and a magnet for making crude pocket compasses, gave him advice on where they should be hidden, and tipped him off about the times and places for several German security searches. With the exception of the time Burke and Buckwich viewed the seismograph, Burke's three roommates were present whenever he met Buckwich. Nevertheless, the Germans' continuously discovering tunnels created an atmosphere of suspicion in the camp, and Burke was told that the prisoners would hold a court of inquiry on him. Burke argued that Buckwich was not a German, that he was in fact an Austrian who hated Nazis. A week later Burke was advised that the prisoners considered him a collaborator. Burke suffered as an outcast from that moment until Wings arrived.

Wings immediately appointed a board to inquire into the charges, and it concluded that there was no real case against Burke. He had been found guilty "on a mass of hearsay, suspicion, gossip and a certain amount of the unthinking malice born of discomfort, hunger, boredom and a need for leadership commanding respect." Buckley agreed with Wings that only mass rivalry, with the resulting lack of security, had been responsible for the tunnel discoveries. In a formal gathering of all the officers in camp, Wings officially exonerated Burke, who in time apparently was accepted back into the fellowship of the other prisoners. Other developments suggest that it was indeed Buckwich and not Burke who was the collaborator. But he was not alone, for Simoleit's other subordinate, Captain Pieber, also committed "indiscretions" by helping the prisoners in ways that bore fruit later.

One other German officer became well known to the prisoners at Barth, Lagerfeldwebel (Officer Compound Sergeant Major) Her-

---

unlikely—Simoleit was Buckwich's supervisor. One explanation is that Buckwich became an Abwehr officer as a result of the personnel changes that occurred after Major Stachelski was relieved of command. But the Abwehr was a distinct service command and its members were somewhat out of the camp's normal command structure. The facts of the case otherwise seem correct. See Smith, *Mission Escape*, 62–63.

mann Glemnitz. He took care of many details of camp administration, including everything from the distribution of Red Cross parcels to maintaining the list of occupants in the cooler. Sometimes referred to as "Dimwits" by the brasher young prisoners, Glemnitz was anything but dim-witted. A World War I infantryman and pilot, he spent the interwar years working as a blacksmith, a ship machinist, and a field technician for a plow company. That last job took him on frequent and extended trips to South America, the United States, Spain, and North Africa. Those experiences paid rich dividends in the prison camps. Extremely observant, intelligent, efficient, and absolutely loyal to his country, he was respected by the prisoners as a professional soldier. Even though he caused them much anguish, they found that he was one of the few Germans they came into contact with who possessed a genuine sense of humor.[23]

The Germans, like members of prison staffs throughout the world, fell victim to the prisoners' love of nicknames and argot. Thus, the German soldiers assigned to anti-escape duties became known as "ferrets." A German officer or soldier, especially a member of the prison staff, was a "goon." The guard towers were "goon-boxes," and the act of provoking the enemy was "goon baiting." The Germans never quite understood the implications of the word *goon,* and the prisoners gave them little to go on. Once when the Germans asked what it meant, someone answered that it was simply an abbreviation, G.O.O.N., or "German Officer or Non-com." Actually, the word gained wide currency with a comic strip in the *Daily Mirror* that depicted "goons" as low-browed, primitive apemen of great strength and stupidity. The Germans apparently never knew where the word came from, and neither did very many of the later prisoners. That made little difference, for it served the prisoners as a shorthand expression for a host of undefined but generally negative feelings toward their German captors.[24]

Events at Barth continued at an interesting pace (monotonous on the surface, hectic behind the scenes) right up until the camp was evacuated in April, 1942. One morning after Appell, the NCOs were

23. Interview with Hermann Glemnitz, conducted by Albert P. Clark and Elwin F. Schrupp in Berlin, April 9–10, 1984 (MS in Clark Collection); Smith, *Mission Escape,* 62–63, 78–79.

24. John A. Vietor, *Time Out: American Airmen at Stalag Luft I* (New York, 1951), 108; Smith, *Mission Escape,* 62.

ordered to pack up their belongings and parade at four o'clock that afternoon with their luggage. When they reported, they were told to pick up their baggage and march—around and around inside the compound. With each round the prisoners discarded something. This process continued until their path was littered and the Germans calculated that the prisoners were carrying real necessities. They then marched the prisoners back into the barracks and had some Russian prisoners pick up the debris in the compound. It is not known whether the Russians were allowed to keep their newly found treasure.[25] Two days after this incident in the NCOs' compound, the first contingent of officers left for Stalag Luft III. The other officers and NCOs followed soon after.

25.   Smith, *Mission Escape*, 79.

Looking from South Compound toward North Compound
Courtesy of U.S. Air Force Academy Library

North Compound
Courtesy of Harold Kious

Lieutenant General Gottlob Berger
Courtesy of U.S. Air Force Academy Library

Colonel Friedrich-Wilhelm von Lindeiner
Courtesy of U.S. Air Force Academy Library

Major Gustav Simoleit
Courtesy of U.S. Air Force Academy Library

Sergeant Major Hermann Glemnitz
Courtesy of U.S. Air Force Academy Library

Colonel Charles G. Goodrich
Courtesy of U.S. Air Force Academy Library

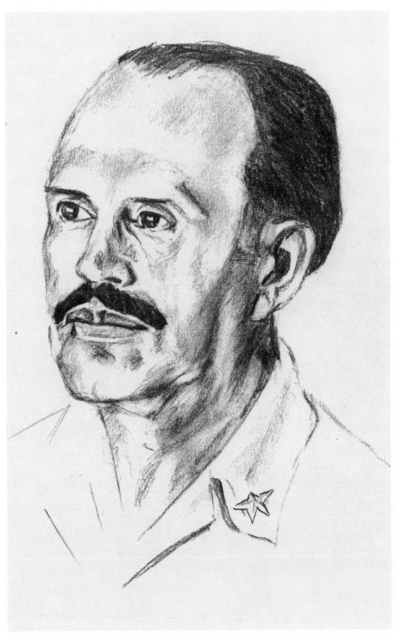

General Arthur W. Vanaman
Courtesy of U.S. Air Force Academy Library

Lieutenant Colonel Albert P. Clark
Courtesy of U.S. Air Force Academy Library

Colonel Delmar T. Spivey
Courtesy of U.S. Air Force Academy Library

Henry Soderberg (*left*) with American POW
Courtesy of U.S. Air Force Academy Library

A wash hut
Courtesy of Richard Kimball

A typical room
Courtesy of U.S. Air Force Academy Library

5

The Kriegie's Domain

Tension was high when Bub Clark walked into East Compound of Stalag Luft III in August, 1942. It was not a good day for a new prisoner to arrive. Everybody's nerves were on edge. There had been a direct confrontation between the prisoners and a large contingent of heavily armed guards earlier that morning. The focus of attention had been Douglas Bader, the famed legless fighter pilot who antagonized the Germans from the moment he was shot down. Having earlier lost his legs in an airplane crash, he had tin ones made. Then he had defied the odds and learned all over again to fly. When his plane was hit and he discovered the tin legs were caught, he simply unstrapped them and bailed out. He both intrigued and angered his captors. Having allowed an English aircraft safe passage to drop him another pair of legs, they were rewarded with Bader's continuous escape efforts and the most antagonistic personality many of them had ever encountered. Once in Stalag Luft III, Bader riled the prisoners so much that the Germans decided they had to move him to Colditz, a prison reserved for the most avid, troublesome escapers. Bader threatened to jump in the fire pool so the Germans would have to swim in after him, an act calculated to embarrass and humiliate them. The Senior British Officer talked him out of it, but Bader received satisfaction anyway. Feeling that his forced removal might cause a riot, the Germans took the precaution of sending armed guards to lead him out. Bader sneered with glee as he left, knowing the other prisoners would not miss the significance of two columns of armed Germans escorting one solitary man who had no legs. So the prisoners had their day, but lost the battle of keeping Bader with them. Consequently, their mood was almost as foul as the Germans'. Bub was led into the camp and shown to his bunk. Still almost warm, it was Bader's.[1]

---

1. Interview with Albert P. Clark, April 15, 1976.

The camp, about ninety miles southeast of Berlin, was approximately one-half mile south of the town of Sagan, which boasted a population of about 25,000 people, in the province of Silesia. It was near the old Polish border and on the Bóbr River, a tributary of the Oder. The area was well forested, but the trees added little beauty to the setting, since they were primarily thin and scraggly pine.[2]

The camp had apparently not been located there by accident. The spot was well away from all combat zones, and even farther away from any friendly or neutral territory. The soil seemed designed to thwart tunnelers. Fine gray topsoil mixed with an accumulation of pine needles contrasted sharply with the earth below it, which was equally sandy but very light in color. This definite problem for would-be tunnelers was an obvious asset for the Germans in their efforts to detect such activities. Furthermore, extensive shoring would now be needed to prevent the tunnels from collapsing on the diggers. To the tunnelers' delight, however, the soil was virgin and had not been permeated with burrows, and water was to be found about three hundred feet below ground level. Equally important, Sagan lay at the juncture of six rail lines. Bringing the prisoners to the camp was therefore easier, but so were their numerous escape attempts.

The prisoners quickly noted the anti-escape devices built into Stalag Luft III. The perimeter fence consisted of two separate and parallel barriers about seven feet apart, each about nine feet high with an overhang at the top pointing inward and consisting of barbed-wire strands approximately six inches apart horizontally and two feet

---

2. The description is a composite of numerous reports and narratives, many of them rendered by the prisoners themselves. Where conflicting data appeared in the sources, either the most commonly found information was used or a deliberate determination made based upon the best information available. The following sources were relied upon unless otherwise noted: Smith, *Mission Escape*, 81; Brickhill, *The Great Escape*, 21; Charles G. Goodrich, "History of the USAAF, Prisoners of War of the South Compound, Stalag Luft III," 1945, Annex II (MS in Albert F. Simpson Historical Research Center, Maxwell Air Force Base, Ala.), hereinafter cited as "History of South Compound"; Spivey, *POW Odyssey*, 31ff.; and "A History of Stalag Luft III," a document whose author is known but cannot be named at this time. The document was written just after World War II. Verification of its authenticity, as well as comments on its strengths and weaknesses, can be found in Paul Clark to Colonel Alfred F. Hurley, October 15, 1974, which is filed with a copy of the document in the Special Collections Room, U.S. Air Force Academy Library. Although this document pertains primarily to escape activities, there is other information of value. Friedrich-Wilhelm von Lindeiner, "Memoirs of Colonel Friedrich-Wilhelm von Lindeiner-Wildau, Kommandant, Stalag Luft III," n.d., trans. Berthold Geiss, ed. Arthur A. Durand (Copy of MS in possession of the author), 92.

apart vertically. Between these fences lay barbed-wire tangles that were two to four feet deep. Inside the camp and approximately thirty feet from the perimeter fence, a warning wire, stretched some two feet off the ground, marked a no-man's-land. The Germans solemnly declared that anyone stepping over the wire in the direction of the perimeter fence would be shot without warning. Outside and along the fence stood guard towers, one at or near each corner and others at intervals of approximately one hundred to one hundred fifty yards. Each one had powerful searchlights, and each guard had a rifle, a semiautomatic weapon, and a machine gun at his disposal. The barracks were built off the ground so inspections for tunneling were easy. Also, they were in the center of the compound, at least forty yards from the fence. Outside, the clearing extended one hundred feet or so to the edge of the woods.

The camp itself was new and well designed for efficient operation. It contained four distinct areas. On the west side, a large area, called the "Kommandantur," was for the Germans. In the northeast corner sat the "Vorlager," which contained facilities for the prisoners, such as the cooler, sick quarters, bathhouse, coal shed, and storage buildings, as well as several barracks for Russian prisoners who were used as camp labor. In the southeast corner was the officers' compound. Because of its location on the east side of the complex it came to be referred to simply as East Compound. And in the lower center of the complex was the NCOs' compound. Again, because of its position, it became known as Center Compound (see Figure 1).

The inclusion of officers in Stalag Luft III meant the camp's name would thereafter be misleading. The designation "Stalag," a contraction of the word *Stamnlager,* can be interpreted to mean a prison for the "common stock" of the army or servicemen below officer ranks. Few NCOs and lower-ranking prisoners enjoyed the relative comfort of Stalag Luft III, the majority being sent to other Luftwaffe camps or work camps. In view of the men who actually occupied Stalag Luft III, the camp should have been called Oflag (officers' camp). At least the Germans were consistent, though: all the Luftwaffe camps were labeled "stalags."

The groups occupying the two compounds were a mixed lot. British airmen were the largest group, but other services and nationalities were present. Commonwealth troops from Canada, Australia, South Africa, and New Zealand arrived in sizable numbers. They were sometimes identified as being from their respective air forces, but in

Figure 1.
Stalag Luft III in April, 1942

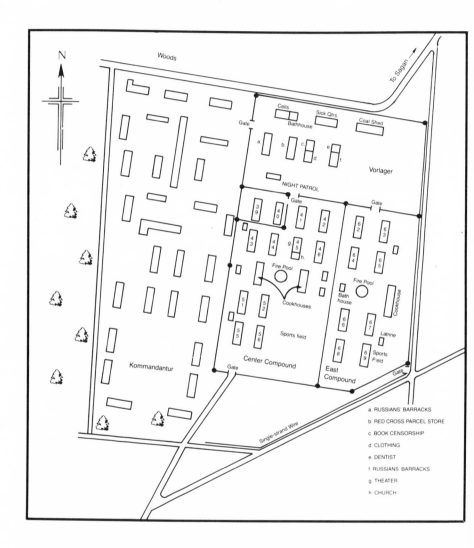

the majority of cases they appeared on statistical reports as members of the British contingent. The Polish, Czech, French, Belgian, Dutch, and Norwegian servicemen were primarily individuals who managed to flee their homeland and join in the fighting by becoming British subjects. At one time, the Germans viewed these individuals as traitors, but Wings Day argued in their behalf and apparently succeeded in convincing the authorities that these men could have joined the British military only if they had first become citizens, and that they therefore deserved to be treated as Englishmen.[3]

There were also some Americans in the British ranks at this time. Bill Hall was Stalag Luft III's oldest American prisoner in terms of time spent in captivity. Shot down on July 2, 1941, he may have joined the British at Barth, and he was apparently among the first to enter Stalag Luft III. A total of thirteen Americans were on the British and Canadian officer rolls—those who had joined the Canadian or British air forces before the United States entered the war. The honor of being the first United States Army Air Forces pilot to enter the camp went to Albert P. Clark. He became the first Senior American Officer (SAO) and served in that capacity from his arrival on August 15, 1942, until March, 1943, when a higher-ranking American, Colonel Charles G. Goodrich, arrived. By December, 1942, a total of 67 USAAF officers lived in East Compound along with the 13 other Americans and approximately 550 British and Commonwealth personnel.[4]

The compound was by then filled, and the Germans began juggling prisoners around until new quarters could be constructed. Actually, a purge of about one hundred officers from East Compound and a few NCOs from Center had been sent to Oflag XXI B near Schubin, Poland, in October, 1942, but this transfer seems to have been motivated more by the discovery that month of a large and well-engineered tunnel complex than by the need to relieve overcrowding. Those who were removed were primarily members of the escape

---

3. Report to State Department from J. E. Friedrich, representative of the International Red Cross, regarding a visit to Stalag Luft III on September 13, 1942, in File 740.00114 EW/3049, RG 59; Smith, *Mission Escape*, 41.

4. R. W. Kimball and O. M. Chiesl, *Clipped Wings* (N.p., n.d.), no pagination; Glenn A. Abbey, to Secretary of State, December 20, 1943, in File 711.62114 A/192, RG 59; Bern to Secretary of State, December 11, 1942, in File 740.00114 EW/2828, RG 59; Goodrich, "History of South Compound," Annex II. There were a few American enlisted men in Center Compound at the time, but no specific data on them could be found.

fraternity. But after January, 1943, with the exception of a few little groups from hospitals, virtually all the American and most of the British and Commonwealth fliers were sent to other camps, mostly to Schubin, until more space became available at Sagan.

The American contingent accordingly remained quite small throughout the first year of Stalag Luft III's existence. In East Compound the Germans segregated them for quartering purposes only, assigning the Americans to barracks 69. They otherwise mingled freely and participated in all camp activities, and thus the Americans learned quickly from the more experienced British. Furthermore, though a little mistrustful at first, the Americans and the British soon gained each other's confidence and shared leadership of the compound's internal administrative staff. The experience gained at this time prepared these men for key roles when the Americans began to arrive in large numbers and the compounds became almost totally segregated according to nationality.

East Compound was small compared to those that were built later. It contained eight barracks, one large cookhouse, a bathhouse, two pit-latrine huts, and a fire pool. The sports field was small, and activities there had to be carefully scheduled. Numerous stumps remained in the compound when it first opened, but the Russian workers removed most of them within a few months.

The single-story wood barracks varied in color from grayish green to brown, depending on the wood preservative used and the effects of aging.[5] Each barracks contained twelve large rooms equipped with six double-tier bunk beds and two rooms with two double-tier bunk beds each. Until the buildings became crowded, two large rooms were set aside, one as a library and reading room and the other as a recreation room. A large window in each room let in natural light and fresh air. At night when the shutters were closed, however, the air invariably became foul because of the ever-present and dense tobacco smoke. Each room also had a small stove to provide heat, but there was seldom sufficient fuel to keep it lit even a few hours a day. One entire barracks was set aside as a theater and gymnasium. This meant the remaining seven barracks could comfortably house about nine hundred men. More prisoners could be accommodated only if the bunks were converted to three tiers or if the reading and recreation rooms were used as regular living quarters.

5. Interview with Al LaChasse, October 13, 1975.

The wash huts contained cold-water spigots and wooden benches with plate basins.[6] The men shaved, washed their clothes, and often took cold baths or showers there.

There were two latrines in East Compound, and they became the focal point of much American concern. Each one contained twenty seats and an accumulation pit underneath. The pits were seldom emptied on schedule, and the latrine huts had never been properly sealed off on the outside. Consequently, a foul odor pervaded the area, millions of flies bred and swarmed about, and slugs crawled out of the latrines and all over the camp. The British preferred to stand on principle and insist the Germans do something about the problem rather than engage in such lowly tasks themselves.

When Clark arrived in August, 1942, he was shocked and disturbed by the unsanitary situation in East Compound. Impetigo and dysentery were rampant. When the prisoners sat down to eat, he recalls, they first had to conduct a "fly purge," which involved opening the window, shutting off the lights, closing the doors, getting shoulder to shoulder with bath towels and shooing all the flies out the window in a black cloud, and then slamming the window closed again before the flies could get back in.

6.   The difficulty of ascertaining the adequacy of certain facilities is revealed in a comment made about the washbasins. One report states that there was one basin for every four men in East Compound, implying that since this is "the proportion in the German Army," the Germans were treating the prisoners on a par with their own troops. A quick mathematical check suggests that an error exists somewhere in this equation, however. If the camp could accommodate nine hundred men, the wash huts should have contained 225 wash basins, or about 112 basins each. This obviously was not the case. It is probable that the prisoners' needs could have been adequately met even if more than four men had to use one basin, but that is not the issue. The question is whether or not the prisoners had the same sanitation facilities as did the German soldiers. If the soldiers did indeed enjoy such a favorable ratio of men per basin, it is clear that the prisoners were not given the same treatment. Thus, even though the inspectors often stated that the prisoners were treated the same as the German soldiers were, their statements must be scrutinized. There is an additional problem in comparing the care given the prisoners and that given the German soldiers. One cannot know how well the provisions specified on paper correlated with those the troops actually received. Resolving such problems would require extensive research into the conditions that prevailed in the German army at various times. See Protecting Power Report No. 1, concerning a visit made on December 9, 1942, by Mr. Gabriel Naville and Dr. Kurt Schaeffeler of the Swiss legation at Berlin, in "Stalag Luft III" Folder, "Camp Reports-Germany-Stalag Luft" File, American POW Information Bureau, Office of the Provost Marshal General, Record Group 389, Modern Military Branch, National Archives. Unless otherwise indicated, the descriptive information pertaining to East and Center compounds is taken from this report and from "A History of Stalag Luft III," Pts. I and II.

Clark's father was a doctor, and Clark had accompanied him on many of his trips to Civilian Conservation Corps camps in Colorado. He knew what a pit-latrine should look like and how it should be kept, so he went to the Senior British Officer and volunteered to lead a campaign to improve sanitary conditions. With the SBO's approval, Clark obtained the help of some South Africans and Australians who shared his concern and secured tools and the needed materials on parole from the Germans. The latrines were screened with mosquito net or burlap, and a stack was installed so that circulating air would take out some of the foul odors. The Germans were so pleased with the results that they adopted these measures wherever possible in the other compounds and camps in Germany.[7]

Center Compound was larger than East and could accommodate about sixteen hundred prisoners. It contained two cookhouses and twelve barracks, one of which (number 45) was set aside as a theater. It was described as "the finest seen in any prisoners' camp," its most notable features being a spacious stage and an orchestra pit. The remaining eleven barracks housed prisoners. They had double walls and floors and were about one hundred twenty feet long and thirty feet wide. Inside, there were two main rooms, each large enough to accommodate seventy men in relative comfort in terms of space but not, of course, with the same degree of privacy afforded in the barracks in East Compound. In addition, there were two small rooms at each end of each barracks: two contained little kitchen stoves; one was a night latrine, with plain buckets and a makeshift urinal for use after lockup in the evening; and one was used by members of the barracks staff. Each main room had a large slow-combustion heater, generally referred to as a Nuremberg stove, but there was seldom enough fuel to keep it lit. Five pit-latrines were eventually built in the compound, but it is not known how many of them were available for use when the camp first opened. Center also had a large sports field.[8] The same mixture of nationalities lived in

7.   Interview with LaChasse, October 13, 1975; interview with Clark, November 7, 1975; interview between Major General Albert P. Clark and Lieutenant Colonel Ben Pollard, former Vietnam prisoner of war, March 22, 1974 (Typewritten transcript in Clark Collection; copy in possession of the author).

8.   Interview with John Wells, January 26–27, 1975; Protecting Power Report No. 1, concerning the December 9, 1942, visit by Naville and Schaeffeler, in "Stalag Luft III" Folder, RG 389; "A History of Stalag Luft III," Pt. II, pp. 1–2.

Center Compound as in East Compound. Approximately twenty-six enlisted Americans lived in Center while it was occupied by NCOs.

The official representative or Man of Confidence among the enlisted men was chosen by popular vote rather than being automatically elevated by virtue of his rank, as was the senior man among the officers.[9] The American Man of Confidence was Sergeant G. A. Dillard. The British and Commonwealth prisoners chose Sergeant James ("Dixie") Deans. He had also served in this capacity at Barth. Dixie was the guiding spirit among the British NCOs, much as Wings was among the officers. Another man who became influential among the NCOs was Deans's assistant, Sergeant R. L. R. Mogg.[10]

Back in East Compound, Wings Day was SBO and Senior Allied Officer until a higher-ranking officer, Group Captain H. M. Massey, arrived in June, 1942. Massey was an old friend of Wings's. They had served together in Egypt, and they both approached their responsibilities with the same sense of professional commitment. Massey was somewhat handicapped, however, by injuries to his left leg that forced him to walk with a noticeable limp.[11] Like Wings, Massey was an experienced leader. He had been on a familiarization mission before going to America as an air commodore when he was shot down and captured. Upon his arrival in camp, Massey recognized the value of Wings's experience in prisoner affairs, saying that he wanted to be SBO in name only. Wings would continue to lead the prisoners and carry on official relations with the Germans. In actual practice, they seem to have shared these tasks—the prisoners were aware of Massey's influence in camp and often both Massey and Wings met with the Germans. In October, 1942, the Germans sent Wings to Oflag XXI B, and Massey remained at Stalag Luft III. He was SBO and Senior Allied Officer until the following spring when he left the camp

9. This is in accordance with the Geneva Convention, Section V, Chapter 2, Article 43.

10. "A History of Stalag Luft III," Pt. II, p. 3; report by Mr. Friedrich and Dr. Bubb, representatives of the International Red Cross, concerning a visit made on February 22, 1943, in File 740.00114 EW/3977, RG 59.

11. Disagreement exists over the exact nature of Massey's injury. Smith (*Mission Escape*, 90–91) states that he had been wounded in the legs in 1918 and had had trouble ever since, but that his use of a walking stick and his pronounced limp exhibited in World War II were the result of the heavy landing when his airplane was shot down. Brickhill (*The Great Escape*, 30) asserts that Massey smashed his foot when he was shot down in World War I, damaged it again in combat during the 1930s in Palestine, and hurt it a third time when he bailed out over the Ruhr in 1942.

to undergo treatment at Oberfmassfeld hospital. He was assisted by an adjutant and a complete staff that included, among others, the senior officers of the other nationalities in the camp.

Sometime during the fall of 1942, the Germans began work on a new compound situated on the west side of the Kommandantur. Because of that location, it was briefly referred to as West Compound. When it became evident that yet another compound would have to be built on the west side of the camp, the name was changed to North. This reflected the relationship between the first and second new compounds, the latter to be built south of and adjacent to North Compound. The second, accordingly, became known as South Compound (see Figure 2).[12] North Compound opened on March 27, 1943, but the majority of the 850 prisoners transferred from East Compound did not move there until April Fools' Day. Only about 20 prisoners (mostly Czechoslovakians) remained in East for a time, but soon prisoners were brought in from various camps throughout Germany and the compound began to fill up again.

The opening of North Compound marked the beginning of what is sometimes referred to as the Golden Era of Stalag Luft III's history. One prisoner recalls that in the following months "there was plenty of living space, plenty of food, [and] plenty of recreational and athletic activity," altogether almost everything a prisoner could want or expect under the circumstances.[13]

North Compound was larger than East and Center compounds put together. The Vorlager, on the north end, had a shower hut for North Compound prisoners only. The storage areas, a cooler, and sick quarters were for both North and South compounds, much like the Vorlager shared by East and Center compounds.

Inside the compound were fifteen barracks, a cookhouse, a large, well-designed theater (built by the prisoners), and a huge sports field. The Germans had planned to build ten additional huts in North, but for some reason never did, hence the unusually large playing field. With German approval, the prisoners began working on the theater

12.   The name change for North Compound was fortunate, for only a short time later a third new compound had to be built. It also was named West Compound, though this time the name truly reflected its location. Unfortunately, in many cases the name change is not self-evident in the documents pertaining to the camp, and care must be taken to ensure that references to "West" Compound do not in fact pertain to "North" Compound.

13.   Goodrich, "History of South Compound," Introduction.

and clearing the stumps out of the athletic area even before the compound opened for occupancy, though much remained to be done on these projects when the move from East to North Compound occurred in April. North offered a less barren appearance at first, since many trees were left among the barracks in the northern half. After a time, however, the Germans concluded the trees unduly hindered their efforts to detect escape activities, and all but a few of them were cut down.

The wood barracks of North Compound had a central corridor flanked by seventeen rooms, each designed to house four to eight officers. One room comfortably accommodated about eight men, the entire compound about twelve hundred. The barracks were more self-contained than those in East and Center. Each one had its own tea kitchen, washing and toilet facilities, dayroom, and a room for the orderlies. There were several wardrobes in each room, and the prisoners used them to store food and personal belongings.

The washroom in the center of each building had twelve to sixteen cold-water faucets. Here the prisoners took showers, apparently a stopgap measure that became necessary when all trips to the Vorlager for hot showers were stopped. Two escape attempts in June, 1943, involved two separate groups of prisoners being escorted to the showers by other prisoners disguised as German guards. The ban on hot showers in the Vorlager lasted for months, and the prisoners resorted to attaching hoses from faucets to a punched tin can. The latrines in the barracks were mainly for nighttime use. During the day the prisoners used large pit-latrines in the compound.[14]

Among those entering North Compound were several hundred prisoners gathered at Schubin to await the opening of the new facility at Stalag Luft III. One of them was an American colonel, Charles Goodrich. Wings spotted him one day while they were both at Schubin, Goodrich sitting quietly about three rows back listening to a briefing given newcomers on all aspects of life in a prisoner of war camp. A 1925 graduate of West Point, Goodrich hailed from the South. About thirty-five years of age, he was an unassuming, mature-

14. Protecting Power Report No. 3, concerning a visit made on July 6–7, 1943, by Mr. Gabriel Naville, representative of the Swiss legation at Berlin, in "Stalag Luft III" Folder, RG 389; report by Dr. Lehner, International Red Cross representative, concerning a visit made on July 26, 1943, in File 711.62114 A.I.R./3O, RG 59; "A History of Stalag Luft III," Pt. III, pp. 1–3; Goodrich, "History of South Compound," Introduction.

Figure 2.
The completed camp: Stalag Luft III (Sagan)

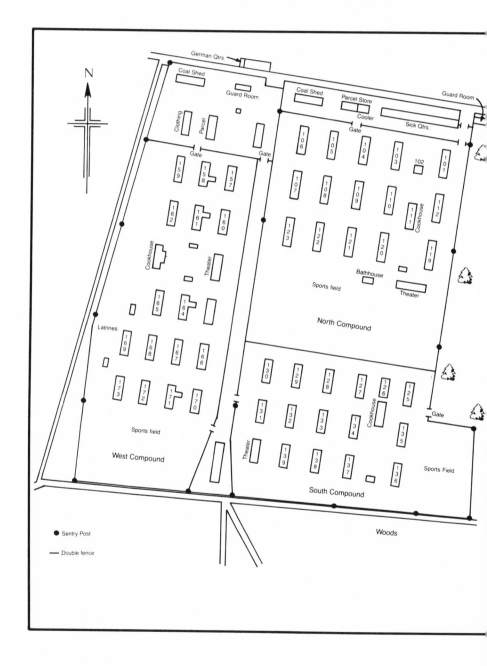

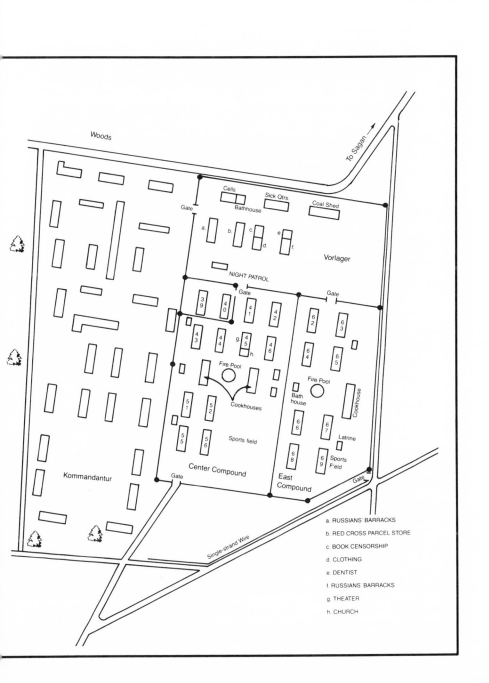

Woods

Gate

Cells

Sick Qtrs.

Bathhouse

Coal Shed

Vorlager

a.

b

c

d.

e

f.

NIGHT PATROL

Gate

Gate

39

40

41

42

62

63

43

44

g. 45

46

64

65

h.

Fire Pool

Fire Pool

Bath house

51

52

Cookhouses

66

Cookhouse

55

56

Sports field

67

Latrine

68

69

Sports Field

Kommandantur

Gate

Center Compound

East Compound

Gate

To Sagan

Single-strand Wire

a. RUSSIANS' BARRACKS

b. RED CROSS PARCEL STORE

c. BOOK CENSORSHIP

d. CLOTHING

e. DENTIST

f. RUSSIANS' BARRACKS

g. THEATER

h. CHURCH

Stalag Luft III   114

looking officer of medium height and stocky build, with wiry red hair and a complexion to match. Roho, as he was called, immediately became part of the senior staff at Schubin. Although he outranked Wings, Goodrich was content to spend his time finding out as much as possible about prison camp affairs in preparation for his duties as Senior American Officer, and Wings continued in his now well recognized role as camp leader. They became close personal friends, and before long Goodrich was privy to everything the British had learned about internal organization, camp administration, and clandestine activities. Goodrich was transferred from Schubin to Stalag Luft III before the others. He and one British officer arrived in East Compound in March, 1943, just before the prisoners in East moved to North. At that point he replaced Clark as the SAO.[15]

After the move to North Compound, Colonel Goodrich gathered all the Americans, a total of about three hundred men, into barracks 105 through 108. Other than this physical separation for housing, however, the entire compound functioned as a unit. Goodrich was consulted in matters of policy, and the Americans participated in every camp activity and organization.

When the Schubin group arrived in North Compound in late April, Massey remained in command as SBO but asked Wings to resume his active role in camp affairs. In late May, Massey went to Obermassfeld hospital, and Wings was SBO until the end of September when another higher-ranking officer, Group Captain D. E. L. Wilson, Royal Australian Air Force, arrived. Wilson held this position until Massey returned in November, and Massey served as SBO until May, 1944. He was then repatriated to England because of his injuries, and Group Captain Wilson was once again the SBO and remained in command until the end of the war.[16]

The summer of 1943 marked a turning point in the camp's development, for at that time the population began to grow rapidly and change in nationalities represented. The transformation was symbolically highlighted in a comic affair that took place in North Compound. One morning, just after the Germans had unlocked the barracks doors and while the sun was still edging up behind the pine trees, a sudden commotion caused a stir among the British prisoners

15.   Interviews with Charles G. Goodrich, February 25, November 18, 1975; Goodrich to the author, November 21, 1975; Smith, *Mission Escape*, 99.
16.   "A History of Stalag Luft III," Pt. III, p. 1; Smith, *Mission Escape*, 110.

and alerted the guards. The American contingent began a boisterous march toward the British barracks. Leading their ranks was a group of drummers and buglers, a man dressed like Paul Revere, and some forty whooping Indians. The British caught the spirit and joined the parade, many of them still in their pajamas. It was the Fourth of July, 1943, and the Americans had organized to share the festive occasion with their prison mates. Homemade brew flowed freely. The senior officers, among others, ended up in the pool of water kept on hand to fight fires. Although wary at first that the uproar might signal a general uprising, the Germans let the celebration run its course once they realized it was merely an Independence Day celebration. For that evening's roll call, one report indicates, the Germans counted the motionless forms in their bunks.[17]

The affair was more than a memorable celebration. It spoke volumes about conditions in the camp and the state of morale and cooperation between the American and British prisoners. It was also a microscopic replay of history, for the Americans were once again about to embark upon the path of independence. A few weeks earlier, the Germans had announced they were building a new compound on the south side of North Compound, one that would house only Americans. Thereafter, the Germans hoped, the Americans and the British could be strictly separated by nationality. This action was in full accordance with the Geneva Convention which stipulated that, whenever possible, prisoners of different races or nationalities were not to be assembled in the same compound.[18] The Germans never succeeded entirely, but they came close: by the time the camp was evacuated, all but about six hundred out of a total of ten thousand prisoners were in the respectively designated American and Commonwealth compounds.

Even before South Compound opened, the prisoners found themselves on the move. In June, 1943, all but fifty of the eighteen hundred NCOs who lived in Center Compound were transferred to Stalag Luft VI near Heydekrug, Lithuania, to make room for the Americans who were to be sent to Center. One report notes that the Germans openly stated their intention to make Center an American com-

---

17. Smith, *Mission Escape*, 119. Brickhill (*The Great Escape*, 85–87) also gives a vivid description of the celebration. Also see Goodrich, "History of South Compound," Annex II, who points out that no one dishonored himself by his conduct during the day's festivities.

18. Title III, Section II, Article 9.

pound. They nevertheless permitted British officers to move from East to Center for about six months to serve as advisors to the Americans being sent there. Most of them arrived directly from Dulag Luft and had no experience in compound administration.[19]

The NCOs had caused a great deal of damage in Center Compound. There were broken windows, torn-out wiring, and latrines half dismantled for firewood and for boards to shore up tunnels. Straw and dirt covered the floors. Many new arrivals were in poor health and could not undertake a major cleanup. Others were under the impression that they would be there only a short time until their transfer to another camp.[20] And the most capable group of men in the camp, the fifty NCOs who remained behind when the others moved to Stalag Luft VI, refused to do the work. Ostensibly they were to be orderlies for the incoming officers, but, in reality, they had a promising tunnel under construction. By September their tunnel had been discovered and the compound still had to be cleaned up.[21]

The cleanup campaign in Center finally got under way in September under the direction of Colonel Spivey when he became the new compound commander. Spivey, a West Point classmate of Colonel Goodrich, was also a southerner. Tall, slender, and balding, Spivey, like the other older men who arrived before and after him, brought badly needed experience into the compound. His West Point training, eighteen years of active service in the Regular Army and Army Air Forces, and command experience at large facilities in the States made him an excellent candidate to direct the tasks that lay ahead. The day after he arrived in camp he was taken into North Compound, where he stayed for two weeks, receiving a thorough and valuable introduction to prison camp life from Goodrich and other knowledgeable men there. He was briefed on all phases of camp operations and shown the tunnels and other escape activities under way in North Compound. Spivey took back with him to Center an experienced, capable group of men to serve on his staff. Spivey also had some

19.   "A History of Stalag Luft III," Pt. IV, p. 1.
20.   Protecting Power Report No. 3, concerning the July 6–7, 1943, visit by Naville, and report by YMCA Secretary Henry Soderberg on a visit made on July 14, 1943, both in "Stalag Luft III" Folder, RG 389; report of visit by Dr. Lehner, July 26, 1943, in File 711.62114 A.I.R./3O, RG 59; Thomas E. Mulligan, Lyman B. Burbank, and Robert R. Brunn, "History of Center Compound, Stalag Luft III, Sagan, Germany," 1945 (MS in Simpson Center), Pt. I, sec. l-a.
21.   "A History of Stalag Luft III," Pt. IV, p. 3; Spivey, POW Odyssey, 42–45.

definite ideas about what needed to be done to make life in Center more like what he had seen in North.

Back in Center, Spivey met with the other senior officers. The SBO since the officers began to occupy Center was Squadron Leader L. W. V. Jennens, but he was replaced in September by Squadron Leader S. G. Pritchard. The problems Jennens faced can well be imagined from conditions in the compound after the NCOs moved out. As for Pritchard, Spivey concluded that he possessed "the finest quality of manhood and integrity" and that he also wanted to put the compound "on a paying basis but more slowly and leisurely than . . . the senior Americans." Spivey also encountered the man who served as the SAO, Major MacMillan, a pilot from Texas who was "the type of American youth who won [the] war . . . smart, energetic, enthusiastic, and endowed with a world of precious humor and horse sense which pulled many an American through in the months to come." Spivey sat down with MacMillan and the members of his staff and worked out a program for cleaning up and organizing the compound.[22] Their methods and the organizational structure were by and large in conformity with those utilized in the other compounds. Within two months, Center Compound began to function normally and efficiently, and the prisoners achieved the sense of community so obviously lacking during the first month after the NCOs departed.

In spite of their best efforts, the prisoners in Center Compound were doomed to a lower standard of living than were those in the other compounds. Although the compound was only a little more than a year old when the officers began to move in, the buildings were so poorly constructed that the prisoners might as well have been living in very old facilities. The roofs leaked, the lights and heating fixtures were woefully inadequate, and general repairs had been consistently neglected. In addition, the large open bay rooms did not provide the privacy or the comfort of the enclosed rooms found in all the other compounds. The prisoners managed as best they could and grouped four to six beds around some room furniture. These arrangements became known as "combines." The men in each one shared their food and surroundings much as they would have if they had lived in an enclosed room. But the noise, drafts, and general confusion that often arises in large rooms were always present, and the prisoners could not compensate adequately for the lack of walls.

22. Spivey, *POW Odyssey*, 40–46; "A History of Stalag Luft III," Pt. IV, p. 2.

The long-awaited South Compound opened on September 8, 1943. Virtually all American prisoners previously detained in North Compound, plus a number of Americans from Center Compound and from the now German-controlled prisoner of war camps in Italy, moved into South. Thus from the beginning, South was occupied by experienced individuals capable of organizing themselves and operating in accordance with proven methods. The guiding spirit in the community-building effort in South Compound was Colonel Goodrich, commanding officer of the prisoners assigned to South from the time the compound opened until the end of the war.

South Compound was considerably smaller than North, but it contained the same number of buildings—sixteen. The sports field was about one-third as large as the one found in North. In the beginning, there were stumps all over the compound, and the prisoners removed them over a period of months. The work started in the area set aside for the athletic field. The buildings were constructed of prefabricated materials made of wood, and the fourteen barracks were self-contained. Each one had an indoor latrine with one urinal and two commodes, a washroom with six porcelain washbasins, and a kitchen with one cookstove. The indoor latrine was for use at night, and the pit-latrines were utilized during the day. The rooms varied in size and accommodated from two to ten people, the largest room measuring sixteen by twenty-eight feet. Each barracks could comfortably house 72 officers and 12 enlisted men, or a total of 84 people. The entire compound could thus hold about 1,175 men without overcrowding.[23] The Germans placed a shower hut in the compound, but for more than nine months failed to provide the equipment necessary for its operation. So the prisoners had no hot showers and had to settle for hose-and-punched-can devices. The compound also contained a large cookhouse and a theater built by the prisoners.

The heavy influx of prisoners throughout the summer and fall of 1943—the result of increased bombing activity—soon filled the barracks in every compound to capacity. In October the British began to put eight men in the six-man rooms and ten in the eight-man rooms. In November the same process was initiated in South Compound. Fortunately, crowding had not yet become a problem.

Some relief came in January and March, 1944, when the Germans opened Belaria and West compounds. Around January 10, 1944,

23. Goodrich, "History of South Compound," Pt. I, sec. 3A (4).

some 500 British prisoners from East and Center compounds were
sent to Belaria, where they immediately began the now familiar process of building another community in new surroundings. Belaria
was situated about three miles west of Stalag Luft III on a grassy hill
overlooking Sagan. The countryside consisted of flat agricultural
land with few trees and clay soil. The water table was only a few feet
below the surface. A strong wind blew through the camp because of
its exposed location, but that reportedly made the compound a
healthier place to live than it might otherwise have been. For a time
the site had been a training camp for German troops, and then a camp
for NCO air force prisoners, whereupon it was designated Stalag Luft
IV. Later Stalag Luft IV was moved north to Grosstychow, and Belaria
became an officers' compound for Stalag Luft III. It was in fact a semi-
independent camp, with its own commandant. For most of its goods
and services, however, it had to rely upon the facilities and personnel
located in or near the main camp south of Sagan. This divided existence was intended to be only temporary. The Germans planned to
build a new and separate complex around Belaria Compound that
would accommodate an estimated 5,000 prisoners. In July, 1944, the
Germans began construction on another compound at Belaria with a
projected completion date of October 1, but whether it was ever
finished and opened is not clear. Approximately 1,200 prisoners,
including at least 113 Americans but mostly British and Commonwealth fliers, lived in Belaria Compound by January, 1945, when it
too was evacuated. Group Captain J. C. MacDonald was SBO and
Lieutenant Colonel V. E. Warford was SAO.

At first the accommodations at Belaria consisted of six wood barracks built on brick supports. By September, 1944, four more barracks had been constructed. Each one was divided into rooms large
enough for eight to ten people. The rooms did not become overcrowded until early 1945, when as many as sixteen men had to live in
each room. Almost from the beginning, crowding was a real problem
in other respects because of the severe shortage of common rooms.
When the compound opened in January, six rooms (one room in each
barracks) were set aside as common rooms, libraries, and lecture
rooms. Already by the end of February, four had to be reclaimed as
living quarters. Of the remaining two rooms, one was a fiction library
and the other a reference library and reading room, and in the evenings they became common rooms for the occupants of the barracks
in which they were situated. To make matters worse, the sports field

was only large enough for playing basketball or volleyball. A barbed-wire enclosure adjacent to the compound later provided ample room for other sports, but the prisoners had limited access to the field, since guards had to accompany them, and frequently no one was available for this duty.

Belaria was about the same vintage as East and Center and had about the same kind of sanitation facilities. There were two wash huts with adequate provisions for cold running water, but no proper bathing facilities or hot showers. The necessary materials for hot showers were ordered, but it is not known if they were installed in time to be of use to the prisoners.[24]

West Compound was the last addition to Stalag Luft III, receiving its first large purge of prisoners on April 27, 1944, just two years to the month from the time the first prisoners walked into East and Center compounds.[25] It was the largest of the six compounds and contained seventeen barracks, a cookhouse, a theater, a shower building, and a laundry hut.

As in North and South compounds, the barracks in West were self-contained. There were thirteen rooms that could accommodate two to fifteen men, a washroom, a tiny kitchen, and a night latrine. Again, pit-latrines were provided for daytime use. Like the barracks in the other compounds, those in West were poorly constructed. The roofs leaked, and in winter the icy winds prevailing in that part of Germany found every crack in the floors and outer walls.[26]

24. Protecting Power Report No. 5, concerning a visit made on February 22–24, 1944, by Gabriel Naville, representative of the Swiss legation in Berlin, in File 711.62114 A.I.R./137, RG 59; report by Dr. Rossel and Dr. Thudichum of the International Red Cross, concerning a visit on November 24–25, 1944, in "Stalag Luft III" Folder, RG 389; American legation, Bern, to Secretary of State, June 19, 1944, in File 711.62114 A/669, RG 59; "A History of Stalag Luft III," Pt. V, pp. 1–2.

25. Different dates have been given for the opening of West Compound. April 1, 1944, is given in Goodrich, "History of South Compound," Pt. I, sec. 1, and April 27 is listed in Bob Neary, *Stalag Luft III: Sagan . . . Nurenberg . . . Moosburg. A Collection of German Prison Camp Sketches with Descriptive Text Based on Personal Experiences* (North Wales, Pa., 1946), 1. April 27 appears to be the correct date, however, since Appendix 6 of Goodrich's "History of South Compound" gives the names of fifty individuals who departed South Compound for West Compound on that day. It is possible, however, that a smaller contingent of prisoners was sent to West Compound on April 1, since Goodrich earlier comments that "in April of 1944, eleven officers and fourteen men were sent as a nucleus to open West Compound," and they do not seem to have been part of the larger group of fifty transferred to West on April 27.

26. Neary, *Stalag Luft III: Sagan*, 4.

Colonel Darr H. Alkire served as the commander of West Compound until the end of the war. He and a group of other experienced prisoners from South Compound undertook the task of organizing the new community, and by midsummer they had everything running smoothly.

By fall, 1944, the prisoners' comfort and well-being came to depend more and more on the success of their community efforts. In the six months from April to November, 1944, the population doubled from a little more than five thousand to more than ten thousand. Crowding became a serious problem. In most of the compounds, prisoners had to live in tents until a third tier could be added to all the bunks. Sleeping space could be provided through this expedient, but living space in the rooms could not be correspondingly enlarged, and all the available facilities, as well as the prisoners' nerves, began to be overtaxed. In addition, food became increasingly scarce, and the prisoners began to suffer from malnutrition. They were less able to withstand the cold and were more susceptible to respiratory infections and other diseases. Many tried to conserve their energy and body heat by remaining in bed as much as possible. And as the Russians closed in on the eastern front, the prisoners became restless and anxiety-ridden. And yet, when General Vanaman arrived in Stalag Luft III in August, 1944, he marveled at how well everything was organized and how smoothly and efficiently the prisoner community functioned.

Vanaman's arrival created quite a stir. The prisoners were well aware that as a group of trained and combat-experienced fliers, they represented a valuable resource for the Allies. Some anticipated a rescue attempt by means of a spearhead attack on the eastern front or a parachute drop to secure the immediate area long enough for them to be flown out. It seemed logical that if a rescue were in the works, someone would be sent into the camp to prepare the prisoners. Some felt confident that Vanaman had come for just that purpose—and the evidence seemed incontrovertible. An assistant air attaché in Berlin from July, 1937, to July, 1941, Vanaman was personally acquainted with Göring and other Nazi officials. He knew how they thought, he spoke German fluently, and he was familiar with the countryside. And since he was a general, the prisoners reasoned, he would not have been flying over enemy territory had he not been on a special mission. In fact, the plane Vanaman flew in had returned to England,

and he reportedly had turned down an opportunity to live in a camp especially for generals and had insisted instead on being sent to Stalag Luft III.[27]

All the pieces seemed to fit, but they did not yield the true reason for Vanaman's arrival in camp. Only a short time before, he had become Doolittle's chief of intelligence in the 8th Air Force. Observing that intelligence officers too often briefed air crews on conditions in enemy territory they themselves had never seen, Vanaman decided that they should go on orientation flights. He determined to set an example by being the first. Since he had been briefed on Ultra (the system whereby the Allies had broken and were exploiting the German cipher code), Vanaman had to obtain special permission from Doolittle before he could go on a mission. Doolittle did not like the idea but eventually acquiesced, and Vanaman soon found himself over enemy territory and in the midst of heavy anti-aircraft fire. The plane he was in carried the smoke bombs used to mark targets, and when the craft was hit the interior filled rapidly with smoke. Vanaman was in the nose with the navigator and the bombardier. They helped check his parachute pack, opened the hatch, and out he went along with five other crew members. Only seconds later the source of all the smoke was discovered, and the relieved pilot countermanded the bail-out order in favor of pressing for home.[28]

Vanaman evaded capture that night but was caught the following day and spent four weeks in the hospital at Frankfurt. He was treated well and given an aide who, he correctly concluded, was primarily interested in gathering anything of intelligence value that Vanaman might let slip. Vanaman knew he had to be extra careful not to divulge inadvertently information on Ultra, and he kept his guard up at all times. He even tore off a little of his bandages each night to tape his mouth shut so he would not talk in his sleep. He obviously succeeded in keeping the secret to himself.

The Germans repeatedly told him about a special camp they had near Dresden for generals and other dignitaries who became prisoners, and insisted on sending him there. Before doing so, however, they sent him to the Air Ministry in Berlin, where he encountered an

---

27.   Interview with Clark, April 7, 1973.

28.   Interview with John W. Houston, November 7, 1984. Houston, the navigator on the mission, remains convinced that what happened to Vanaman that day was purely one of the vagaries of war.

old German acquaintance. He realized that here was an opportunity to make his bid for going to an air force prison camp. Knowing German psychology, Vanaman confronted the unsuspecting officer, pounded on the table, and said, "You can't send me down there [to the special camp]. I am going to the largest place that we have. I don't know where it is, but that's where you're going to take me."[29]

But circumstances periodically continued to cast him in a suspicious light. Bob Hackwith, a recently captured prisoner who had been badly beaten by the SA, sat on the transport bus carrying him toward Brussels and watched warily out the window as it pulled over to the curb to pick up a passenger. His eyes quickly fixed upon the scene unfolding at the edge of the alley: a German officer gave some food and wine to a man decked out in American flying clothes, and then they shook hands. Wearing no insignia, the man boarded the bus and immediately walked down the aisle toward Bob. Cheerily, he said, "Hi. I'm General Vanaman. Where are you from?" Bob could hardly contain himself. "This S.O.B. must take me for a real fool," he thought to himself, "to think I'd fall for such a blatant fabrication. This guy is no more an American pilot than the man in the moon." Rebuffed by Bob's silence, General Vanaman stoically found another seat. Like many others, Bob was genuinely surprised to discover several days later that Vanaman indeed was who he claimed he was.[30]

Although not sent to Stalag Luft III as part of a giant rescue operation, Vanaman nevertheless had an important role to play when he arrived in August, 1944. It was reassuring to the prisoners to have someone of his rank and experience in camp. At a time when virtually all contact among the compounds had been cut off, Vanaman was one man who could still sign a parole and visit the three American compounds. And he did so. He recognized the splendid work done by the compound commanders and their staffs, in fact by virtually all the prisoners who had worked so hard to create communities that functioned well and met the basic needs of the majority of the men. As the Senior American Officer, he envisioned a twofold role for himself: to boost the prisoners' morale merely by sharing their hardships and making himself visible, and to negotiate with the Germans whenever possible on the prisoners' behalf. In this regard, he stood ready to use his rank for any task that might require the special force that rank

29. Interview with Arthur W. Vanaman, April 2–3, 1973.
30. Interview with Bob Hackwith, July 14, 1984.

carried in World War II Germany. He did not get around to see all the prisoners as much as he would have liked, but in Center Compound where he lived, the prisoners came to know and admire him. They were pleased when he refused a truckload of furnishings for his room that Göring had reportedly sent. And though most of the prisoners never knew the details of what happened, the time also came when Vanaman's rank was important to their safety and welfare.

6

The Price of Allegiance

At age sixty-one, Colonel Friedrich-Wilhelm von Lindeiner-Wildau was tormented by divided loyalties when he took over as commandant of Stalag Luft III in May, 1942. A staunch German to the marrow of his bones, von Lindeiner clearly had not shown the same affection for the new Nazi regime. He wanted to retire and simply fade from the scene, but the authorities would not let him go. As a professional soldier, he never gave a thought to insubordination. Somehow he would have to fulfill his assigned duties in this twilight world where the high ideals and values of the past were being subjugated to political and military expediencies, the full consequences of which few could yet guess. His independent actions would get him into trouble sooner or later, of that he was almost certain. The more important question for him, however, was whether he could remain true to his principles when such things no longer seemed to matter. He was proud to serve his beloved Germany, but he dreaded the thought of waking up some-day, no longer knowing who he was or what he stood for.

He had joined the army for the first time in 1908 and served six years in the colonial service. Severely wounded three times in World War I, he received two coveted Iron Cross awards. Unable to return to active combat, he then served as aide-de-camp to Prince Joachim, the emperor's youngest son, and became head of the guards at court.

Leaving the service in 1919, von Lindeiner spent the next several years engaged in business abroad, taking numerous trips to various countries in western Europe and North and South America. He also was attracted to politics, inspired in part by his brother, a respected member of the Reichstag. But he married a Dutch baroness and they took up residence in Holland. He was recalled to Germany for busi-ness reasons in 1932, but the situation there had changed so radi-cally, he backed away from any sort of political involvement, hoping for better times. They never came.

Already the die had been cast. Living in the Netherlands from 1919 to 1932, he had opposed Nazism's penetration of the clubs and societies to which he belonged. After returning to Germany, he refused every connection with the party and was removed from the upper German sports board on that account. Since his wife also was a staunch anti-Nazi, both of them were surprised when in 1937 he was suddenly notified that as a member of the central staff of Schenker and Co., an import-export company, which had been swallowed by the German government, he was considered an Anwärter (aspirant) for Nazi party membership. He never heard whether full membership followed. Wanting desperately to escape such entrapment, he left the firm at the end of 1937 and accepted an appointment in the Luftwaffe as a member of Göring's personal staff. For the next four years he immersed himself in the build-up of the Luftwaffe and the hectic activities that accompanied the attacks against Poland, the Low Countries and France, the Battle of Britain, and finally the attack against Russia. The strenuous duties wore him down both physically and emotionally. Applying for retirement three times and being turned down on each occasion, he found comparative relief only when his reassignment as commandant of Stalag Luft III came through in the spring of 1942.

The von Lindeiners moved to Sagan as a family, taking up residence at Jeschkendorf Manor, an estate just outside the town. He felt at home immediately. Silesia, he proudly proclaimed to anyone who would listen, was "a Germanic domain, and Sagan itself became a city in 1230 under German law." The town and the surrounding territory had a rich and varied history. In 1628 the Duchy of Sagan was given in fief to Sagan's most prominent citizen, Albrecht von Wallenstein, Duke of Friedland and Mecklenburg. It was he who constructed the remarkable castle at Sagan, for which the houses of sixty-five freemen had to be torn down. He worked hard for the growth of the city, ordered that the Bóbr River be made navigable, and called the famous astronomer and mathematician Johannes Kepler to Sagan. In 1742, Silesia became part of the Kingdom of Prussia and Sagan became a Prussian principality. By inheritance it was later part of the estate of Duchess Wilhelmina, known to the world as "The Sagan," the confidante of Prince Metternich. Her youngest sister, Countess Dorothea de Talleyrand-Périgord, the beautiful Dorothea, Duchess of Valençay and Dino, settled in Sagan and brought all her art treasures with her. With the help of Count Pückler-Muskau, she built the famous park of

Sagan, had a brilliant court, and was a friend of the Prussian royal family. After the death of her son Ludwik in 1898, the property, renamed Forest Dominion Sagan after the fall of the Prussian monarchy, went to members of the Talleyrand family living in France. But for von Lindeiner, the national identity of Silesia was clearly German. Inhabiting Silesia at the outbreak of World War II were 6.5 million people, 5.75 million of whom were Germans. Sagan, 80 percent Protestant and at least partly German, was a town the von Lindeiners could call home. [1]

But in wartime Germany, home did not necessarily mean peace. Von Lindeiner had traveled too much, seen too much, and experienced too much to think his tenure as commandant would be idyllic. His decision to join the Luftwaffe, the least Nazified of the services, was still paying dividends. As commandant of Stalag Luft III, he would be spared much of the moral and mental anguish he knew others involved with prisoners of war were experiencing. Much of the horror associated with life behind barbed wire in Germany did not become known to the outside world until the final days of the war. Even many involved in the prison camp system itself did not comprehend the magnitude of the suffering. The Nuremberg trials, however, put the story in grim terms that everyone could understand.

The prison system officials on trial made desperate efforts to show their organization in its best light, but the damning evidence left little room for explanations. The prosecution began its case against those accused of committing crimes against prisoners of war by asserting: "The defendants murdered and ill-treated prisoners of war by denying them adequate food, shelter, clothing and medical care and attention; by forcing them to labor in inhumane conditions; by torturing them and subjecting them to inhuman indignities and by killing them. The German Government and the German High Command imprisoned prisoners of war in various concentration camps, where they were killed and subjected to inhuman treatment by . . . various methods." In the list of particulars was the statement that "French

---

1. In addition to von Lindeiner's "Memoirs," see Colonel von Lindeiner-Waldau to Delmar T. Spivey, June 22, 1948, in Von Lindeiner Folder, Spivey Collection. Other letters from von Lindeiner and his wife to Spivey, including those dated July 31, 1948, and October 22, 1964, sources for most of the information on von Lindeiner's career, can be found in the Spivey Collection under von Lindeiner's name. Mention of von Lindeiner's political awareness and his brother's role in government is also in Simoleit, "Organization and Administration," in Simoleit Folder, Spivey Collection.

officers who escaped from Oflag X C were handed over to the Gestapo and disappeared; others were murdered by their guards; others sent to concentration camps and exterminated. Frequently, prisoners captured on the Western Front were obliged to march to the camps until they completely collapsed. Some of them walked more than 600 kilometers with hardly any food; they marched on for 48 hours running, without being fed; among them a certain number died of exhaustion or of hunger; stragglers were systematically murdered. . . . Many ill-treatments were inflicted without motive with rifle butts, and whipping." In Stalag XX B, the report went on, "the sick . . . were beaten many times by sentries; in Stalag III B and Stalag III C, worn-out prisoners were murdered or grievously wounded. . . . In May 1942, one loaf of bread only was distributed (daily) in Rava-Ruska to each group of 35 men. Orders were given to transfer French officers in chains to the camp of Mauthausen after they had tried to escape. At their arrival in camp they were murdered, either by shooting or by gas. . . . American prisoners . . . were murdered in Normandy during the summer of 1944, American prisoners were starved, beaten, and otherwise mistreated in numerous Stalags in Germany and in the occupied countries, particularly in 1943, 1944, and 1945." And in the eastern countries, at Orel for example, "prisoners of war were exterminated by starvation, shooting, exposure, and poisoning. Soviet prisoners of war were murdered en masse on orders from the High Command and the Headquarters of the SIPO and SD. Tens of thousands of Soviet prisoners of war were tortured and murdered at the 'Gross Lazarett' at Slavuta. Prisoners of war who escaped and were recaptured were handed over to SIPO and SD for shooting. In March 1944, fifty R.A.F. officers who escaped from Stalag Luft III at Sagan, when recaptured, were murdered."[2]

On the whole, these charges were later fully substantiated. By the time the verdicts were read in the autumn of 1946, the facts revealed a shameful record that cast a dark shadow over the entire German prisoner of war system.[3] But there were exceptions to the rule. In the broadest sense, the Germans developed two policies relating to prisoners of war—one of almost total disregard for humanity and law in dealing with prisoners from the East, and the other calling for correct,

2. *IMT*, I, 52–54.
3. The portion of the "Judgement" that pertains to prisoners of war is in *IMT*, XXII, 471–75.

if not always humane, treatment of prisoners from the West. The evidence suggests that the policies were based almost exclusively on criteria of race and ideology.

As Gordon Wright has pointed out, Nazi racial policy was clearly the decisive factor in explaining Germany's conduct on the Russian front, a gruesome chapter in the history of the war. He reveals the essence of the problem:

With the attack on Russia, the Germans embarked on a savage propaganda campaign designed to justify their conduct in the east. The word *Untermenschen* [brute, gangster], heretofore rarely used by the Nazis, now entered the common language; soldiers and civilians alike were deluged with pamphlets and periodicals that purported to demonstrate the subhuman character of the eastern peoples. Carefully selected photographs of Russian prisoners reinforced this message. That the Nazi leaders believed their own propaganda is clear. The Russians, noted Goebbels in his diary, 'are not people, but a conglomeration of animals.' And Hitler added, in an order of the day to the armed forces, 'This enemy consists not of soldiers but to a large extent only of beasts.'[4]

Given these racial attitudes as a foundation, Germany naturally developed brutal policies regarding the treatment of Russian prisoners of war.

Ideological considerations were also important. Erwin Lahousen, assistant to intelligence chief Admiral Canaris, testified at Nuremberg that the Red Army man was looked upon by the German High Command as an ideological enemy and was therefore subjected to "special measures." One was to divide Soviet prisoners into those to be shot and those to be interned. Theoretically, only those with the Bolshevist taint were to be shot. In reality, little effort was made to determine the prisoners' political leanings. The process was quite arbitrary, and protests by men such as Lahousen secured only the minor concession that the victims were moved some distance away before the executions were carried out.

Many of those interned in camps fared little better. Lahousen further testified that "enormous crowds of prisoners of war remained in the theater of operation, without proper care—care in the sense of prisoner of war conventions—with regard to housing, food, and med-

---

4. Gordon Wright, *The Ordeal of Total War, 1939-1945* (New York, 1968), 126. Strictly speaking, the Germans should not have referred to the Russians as a "race," but since the Nazis and others who have written on German policies adopted this usage, the word *race* is used in reference to the Russians here also.

ical care; and many of them died on the bare floor. Epidemics broke out, and cannibalism . . . manifested itself."[5]

Alfred Rosenberg, Reich minister for Occupied Eastern Territories, revealed more than he perhaps intended when he wrote to Field Marshal Wilhelm Keitel on February 28, 1942: "The fate of the Soviet prisoners of war in Germany is . . . a tragedy of the greatest extent. Of 3,600,000 prisoners of war, only several hundred thousand are still able to work fully. A large part of them has starved, or died, because of the hazards of the weather. Thousands also died from spotted fever. . . . The camp commanders have forbidden the civilian population to put food at the disposal of the prisoners, and they have rather let them starve to death."[6]

In time the treatment given to Russian prisoners changed somewhat for the better. General Adolf Westhoff, a high official in the German prisoner of war system, asserted that "until 1942, the Russian prisoners of war were treated on the basis of purely political considerations. After 1942 this was changed, and in 1943, as long as I was in the German High Command, prisoners of war were treated in accordance with the Geneva Convention, that is to say, in all points their treatment was adapted to that of the other prisoners of war. Their rations were the same as those of the others, and their employment and their treatment were in every detail in accordance with the treatment given prisoners of war of other powers, with certain exceptions."[7]

A great deal of emphasis must be placed upon the phrase "with certain exceptions," since further testimony at Nuremberg revealed that huge numbers of Russian prisoners continued to suffer. Furthermore, the reason for improving their treatment was to salvage a wasted work force, not to demonstrate a change of heart toward the Russians. The tragedy that Alfred Rosenberg saw was not, in his mind, the cost in human life, but rather the regrettable loss of laborers.

A report issued by a labor allocation office, dated February 19, 1942, again revealed the extent of the devastation: "There were 3,900,000 Russians at our disposal, of which at present there are only

5. Testimony of Erwin Lahousen, November 30, 1945, *IMT*, II, 471, 460.
6. Robert Houghwout Jackson, chief prosecutor for the United States at Nuremberg, read the letter aloud (*IMT*, II, 137).
7. Testimony of General Adolf Westhoff, April 10, 1946, *IMT*, XI, 184.

1,100,000 left. From November 1941 to January 1942 alone 500,000 Russians died." In this instance the Germans came to realize that transportation accounted for many of the deaths, as the report emphasized: "The utilization of these Russians is exclusively a question of transportation. It is senseless to transport this manpower in open or unheated closed boxcars and then to unload corpses at the place of destination." The military and economic realities of the situation forced the Germans to alter their treatment of prisoners of war. As Field Marshal Keitel recalled, the army alone needed 2 million to 2.5 million replacements every year—about 1 million came from normal recruiting and another .5 million from rehabilitated men. That still left over 1 million to be replaced annually, and the men taken from the work force had to be replaced by prisoners of war. But a policy evolved from necessity seldom bears fruit beyond the barest essentials. The original thrust Hitler gave to the direction of the war against Russia never lost its flavor. And as Keitel himself readily admitted, Hitler and his followers could never speak of Bolshevism as anything less than a deadly enemy. The war could not be viewed as a battle between two states to be waged in accordance with the rules of international law, but only as a conflict between two ideologies.[8]

Nazi racial attitudes and ideological concerns, which led to the development and merciless implementation of brutal policies pertaining to prisoners of war from the East, also determined the treatment of prisoners of war from the West. Nazi Germany had more esteem for the Commonwealth countries and the United States than for the countries of the East. One result was a policy that called for fairly strict observance of the Geneva Convention.

Germany had much to gain by being more lenient: a large number of German soldiers were held in captivity by the West. In the spring of 1945, Lieutenant General Gottlob Berger, the SS general in charge of all prisoner of war affairs in Germany at the time, reminded Hitler that the West had approximately 12 million Germans in custody.[9]

Moreover, Germany had every reason to believe that the Allies would adhere to the Geneva Convention of 1929 unless provoked into doing otherwise. All were signatories (while Russia was not), and

8. Labor report quoted by Colonel Pokrovsky, Russian prosecutor at Nuremberg, *IMT*, XI, 187, 186; testimony of Field Marshal Wilhelm Keitel, April 5, 1946, *IMT*, X, 561, 558.

9. General Gottlob Berger to General Delmar T. Spivey, August 6, 1964, in Berger Folder, Spivey Collection.

inspection reports from various sources supplied ample evidence that German soldiers were being treated well.[10] Germany had to reciprocate in some measure so there would be no reprisals against German soldiers in Allied hands. Observing the terms of the convention was the surest way of accomplishing that end.

Germany's policies toward prisoners of war were implemented with shocking disregard for the inconsistencies they contained, aided in large measure by the almost incomprehensible bureaucratic machinery. On paper, the German prisoner of war system was under the control of the Oberkommando der Wehrmacht (O.K.W.), the High Command of the German Armed Forces, throughout the war.[11] Hitler, Supreme Commander of the Wehrmacht, had the final word in all prisoner of war matters. Field Marshal Keitel, chief of O.K.W., served as his immediate subordinate in the chain of command. General Hermann Reinecke served below Keitel and administered the General Armed Forces Office, which, among other things, exercised control over prisoner of war affairs.[12] And finally, within the General Armed Forces Office, there existed one office the sole responsibility of

10.   The practice of allowing inspections by the protecting power was formalized in the 1929 convention. In addition, the right of inspection was granted to other organizations at this time, and by World War II the Red Cross and certain charitable organizations such as the YMCA conducted fairly regular inspections. See the Geneva Convention of 1929, especially Title III, Section IV, "Prisoners Relations with the Authorities," and Title VI, "Bureaus of Relief and Information Concerning Prisoners of War," *Treaty Series, No. 846: Prisoners of War. Convention between the United States of America and Other Powers* (Washington, D.C., 1932).

11.   Primarily five sources were relied upon for the organization of the German prisoner of war system: the various records of the Nuremberg trials, British Intelligence reports, a book entitled *Crimes Against POWs: Responsibility of the Wehrmacht* by Szymon Datner (Warsaw, 1964), and two German officials' personal observations. The British reports are part of a large series compiled by the Combined Services Detailed Interrogation Center. The ones used here are C.S.D.I.C. (U.K.) S.R.G.G. 1303 and 315. The S.R.G.G. 1303 report has no title, but may be located by its number among the records of the British War Ministry that are housed at the Simpson Center. The S.R.G.G. 315 report is titled "The Kriegsgefangenenwesen," and a copy may be found in File 100–411–23, Record Group 153, Records of the Office of the Judge Advocate General, Washington National Record Center, Suitland, Md. The two German officials, both of whom held posts in the prisoner of war system, wrote about their jobs and experiences in personal letters to Spivey. General Berger took charge of all prisoners of war in Germany on October 1, 1944. Dr. Major Gustav Simoleit served both as deputy commandant and commandant of Stalag Luft I and as deputy commandant of Stalag Luft III. Their correspondence is located in the Spivey Collection under their respective names.

12.   Testimony of General Gottlob Berger, *Trials of War Criminals before the Nurmberg Military Tribunals* (Washington, D.C., 1952), XIII, 58–61.

which was prisoners of war. [13] That office, in turn, delegated authority over the camps to the army, navy, and air force chiefs who assumed control of virtually all administrative matters in their respective camps. [14]

It is not possible to determine precisely how or why the three services were able to gain that administrative authority. However, the airmen believed that Göring was the man who secured this arrangement for the downed fliers. Göring did wield tremendous influence with Hitler, and it is logical to assume that he utilized his favored position to secure good treatment for his beloved fellow fliers. Göring apparently had been impressed by the sense of chivalry that prevailed in World War I and felt that there was a special bond among fliers of all nations. [15]

However, it is also possible that the entire arrangement resulted from practical concerns. During the early months of the war, the only German prisoners held by the British were airmen. Segregating captured airmen in Germany made it easier for the Germans to provide them with special care, all of which was carefully made known to the British so that captured German airmen would receive good treatment in England. Whatever the reason for assigning control of the camps to the individual services, the decision made it possible for the Luftwaffe to affect virtually every aspect of life in the camps under its

13. Abt Kriegsgefangenenwesen im O.K.W. (Office in Charge of Prisoners of War) was expanded in early 1943 into an Amtsgruppe. The two offices in the group, and their titles, respective sections, and assigned duties, were as follows. Allgemeine Abt (General Office)—Gruppe I: Discipline, punishment, and legal proceedings; Gruppe II: Liaison with the protecting powers and Foreign Office; Gruppe III: Exclusively concerned with German prisoners in Allied hands; Gruppe IV: Administration (stores, equipment, clothes, and food); Gruppe V: Welfare and liaison with Red Cross and YMCA organizations; Gruppe VI: Return or exchange of prisoners. Abt Organization (Organization Office)—Gruppe I: Responsible for all plans for new camps or changing of sites of camps and the planning of large transports of prisoners; Gruppe II: Personnel. Responsible for postings of the German officers holding such positions as a) Kommandeur of Kriegsgefangenenwesen (KGW) in each Wehrkreis (military district) or Luftgau (air district), b) Lager Kommandenten (camp commandant), c) Deputy Lager Kommandanten; Gruppe III: Camp security and investigation of escapes. The first office was primarily responsible for prisoner of war affairs and contacts with foreign governments and relief and welfare organizations. The second office was assigned the duties associated with camp construction, administration, and the appointment of personnel. "The Kriegsgefangenenwesen," 2–3.

14. *Trials*, XI, 649.

15. Gustav Simoleit to Delmar T. Spivey, March 17, 1948, in Simoleit Folder, Spivey Collection; *Nazi Conspiracy and Aggression*, Supp. B, p. 77.

control, to the almost total exclusion of the army or the O.K.W. Major Gustav Simoleit, deputy commandant of Stalag Luft III, explained how the arrangement worked in practice: "In each military district was a Commander of the Prisoners, an army general. Under his command were all the camps in the district. But except for the regular reports we had not very much contact with him. Göring had great influence and so the air force camps were a special section. In all matters [pertaining to German personnel] and all economic administration (construction of camps, food, accommodation, clothing, etc., of the prisoners) we were under the command of the air district (Luftgau)."[16]

The intelligence network set up by the Germans for use in the camps was associated with the Abwehr (Intelligence and Clandestine Warfare Service of the German High Command). Each camp had one or more Abwehr officers assigned to it. They were part of the camp commandant's staff but also reported directly to their superiors in the Abwehr. They were primarily concerned with security, searches, and escapes. Again, it is difficult to ascertain their exact relationship to the SS and the Gestapo in regard to these matters. The evidence suggests, however, that the Abwehr officers were responsible for security inside the camps and the SS and the Gestapo operated outside the camps. This arrangement was the source of much conflict within the German prisoner of war system.[17]

16.   Gustav Simoleit, "Prisoner of War Camps"; Simoleit to Spivey, March 17, 1948, in Simoleit Folder, Spivey Collection.

17.   There was one other command channel that affected life in the camps—an inspectorate. The Inspekteur des Kriegsgefangenenwesen (Office of the Inspector of Prisoners of War) was a part of O.K.W., but its place in the chain of command and its duties and powers changed from time to time. Its mission was to inspect the camps administered by all three services to ascertain whether the basic directives issued by the Prisoners of War Office in O.K.W. were being carried out. Testimony of Keitel, April 4–5, 1946, *IMT*, X, 554. Until its temporary demise in April, 1944, it had no power to issue orders. In June, 1943, however, a supplementary inspection system was established, the General Inspekteur des Kriegsgefangenenwesen, which was given authority to issue orders direct to camp commandants and others in the system and to take disciplinary measures on the spot against camp personnel (but not prisoners). "The Kriegsgefangenenwesen," 3; *Nazi Conspiracy and Aggression*, Supp. B, pp. 265–66. The general inspector reported directly to Keitel. In effect, an inspector could bypass two echelons of control (the chief of the Prisoners of War Office, who in turn would have reported to the chief of the General Armed Forces Office). In October, 1944, the Office of General Inspector was disbanded and the Inspekteur des Kriegsgefangenenwesen, which had been unoccupied from April, 1944, until October, 1944, again became the office primarily responsible for inspecting the camps. It is unclear whether this change meant the loss of direct access to Keitel. But from the beginning, and especially from

Although the Abwehr was responsible for thwarting escape attempts, the small number of Abwehr officers assigned to any one camp (three at Stalag Luft III)[18] meant that they had to rely in part upon other camp personnel in carrying out their duties. Accordingly, whenever successful escapes took place, the entire prisoner of war system came under indictment and pressure increased to devise a better security system.

Men like Himmler vigorously argued that only the SS and the Gestapo could do the job properly. Camp administrators and prisoners alike expressed anxiety that Himmler might have his way. The administrators spoke of this possibility as a means of discouraging escape activities. And the prisoners had to weigh carefully their duty to escape against the threat that their actions might hasten the day when the SS could gain control over their lives. In October, 1944, their worst fears seemed to materialize. On the first day of that month, the SS reportedly was placed in charge of the camps.

A great stir arose around the world when word got out that Himmler had been placed in charge of prisoner of war affairs. He had, in fact, been endeavoring to secure control of the system for some time. His primary interest was to tighten security in the Reich, and the issue that opened the door for him was the problem of escapes. During 1943, between 46,000 and 48,000 prisoners reportedly escaped, mainly in the East.[19] Although the number of successful escapes had been greatly reduced by late 1944, Hitler was concerned that the escapers might engage in sabotage or, worse yet, organize a revolt among the 6 million foreigners in Germany. Himmler openly accused Keitel of being too lax and convinced Hitler that only the SS could provide adequate security against escapes and the ensuing threat of sabotage and internal disorder. The escape of seventy-six airmen from Stalag Luft III served Himmler's purposes well; Hitler put the

---

June, 1943, on, the inspector and his staff were an important element in the command structure, and their presence in any camp warranted special care and attention from both the camp staff and the prisoners. *Trials*, XI, 650.

18. Simoleit to Spivey, March 17, 1948, in Simoleit Folder, Spivey Collection.

19. Testimony of Berger, *Trials*, XIII, 62; testimony of Keitel, April 4–5, 1946, *IMT*, X, 559–60; S.R.G.G. 1303, p. 2. Keitel stated that he was told (apparently by Hitler) that during the summer of 1942 the quartermaster general said that "thousands of Russian prisoners of war were escaping every month, that they disappeared among the population, immediately discarded their uniforms, and procured civilian clothes and could no longer be identified" (*IMT*, X, 564).

incident at the top of his list of reasons for making the command changes. He claimed that "everyone had lied to him and betrayed him" and that the Sagan affair would not have happened "if the commander there had acted and undertaken suitable measures, in accordance with his duties."[20]

Most observers at the time concluded that Himmler secured control over the entire prisoner of war system in the fall of 1944. Simoleit recalled the transfer of power, noting that "in the first years of the war neither the SS, the Gestapo, nor any other police had anything to do with our camps, and we did what we could to keep them apart. In 1944 Himmler was appointed Chief of all PW matters, so we were put under the command of the Higher SS and Police Leader of the district. That was a very unpleasant time and we always lived in fear and expectation of some dangerous regulations and measures."[21] In reality, Himmler's control was somewhat less than complete, though it was by no means insignificant.

The responsibility for the whole organization remained with Keitel as chief of the O.K.W., but the offices at his disposal were greatly reduced. He was, in fact, allowed to retain effective control over only the General Office. That portion of the system delegated to the individual services now came under the control of the SS.[22] Quirks in the bureaucratic framework, however, made the reorganization a relatively hollow gesture as far as the administration of camps housing primarily Commonwealth and American prisoners was concerned. Himmler was a busy man by this time and had to rely almost exclusively upon subordinates to do his bidding in matters pertaining to prisoners of war. The SS man he placed in charge was Waffen-SS Lieutenant General Gottlob Berger.

Colonel Spivey and General Vanaman later met Berger face to face during a secret conference in his command bunker just outside Berlin. A hail-fellow-well-met sort of character, Berger rushed forward to greet them with hearty handshakes and great backslaps. A complex man, he hated the Russians and most easterners with a

20. *Nazi Conspiracy and Aggression*, Supp. B, p. 71; Hitler's four reasons—the escape from Stalag Luft III; the discovery of a broadcasting station in the American prisoner of war camp at Fürstenberg; the revolt in Warsaw; and the Allied plan for landing airborne troops and parachutists in the vicinity of prisoner of war camps—and his claims are given in testimony of Berger, *Trials*, XIII, 60.
21. Simoleit to Spivey, March 17, 1948, in Simoleit Folder, Spivey Collection.
22. "The Kriegsgefangenenwesen," 4.

fierce passion, but repeatedly showed a willingness to risk his career, and if necessary perhaps even his life, on behalf of prisoners from the West.[23]

Berger told Hitler that he did not wish to take over the prisoner of war system since he had no ambitions to become such a custodian and felt that he was not a policeman by nature. Hitler sharply rebuked him, saying his generals did what he wished them to do. Berger dutifully acquiesced, but he decided to take some precautions that had surprising results. He learned from an acquaintance assigned to the Swiss legation in Berlin about the furor created abroad when Himmler's new role in prisoner of war affairs was announced. Realizing how negatively this could reflect on Germany and that reprisals against German soldiers in Allied hands were possible, Berger took extra pains to dissociate the SS from the prisoner of war system. First, even though he knew it would be a great administrative inconvenience, he moved the chief of the Prisoners of War Office some two miles away from his main SS office. Second, he refused to bring any SS members into the system. Rather, he brought into his office the entire existing structure with its full delineation of duties and its full complement of personnel. His main purpose in doing so was, in his words, "to break all enemy propaganda which might arise from such an act" as incorporating large numbers of SS personnel into the prisoner of war system.[24]

Ironically, he convinced very few people that the SS had not gained full control of prisoner of war affairs, but in the process he achieved much that was beneficial to the prisoners. On October 1, 1944, Himmler theoretically did gain full control of the prison camps and at that point could have robbed them of their separate army, navy, and air force identities by putting SS personnel into the prison camp system. Berger's precautions effectively prevented all such efforts and ensured that the respective service personnel would remain in control. Accordingly, when the prosecution at Nuremberg asked whether Himmler's takeover meant the systematic "inhuman treatment and destruction of Allied prisoners of war . . . by the SS," Friedrich Karl von Eberstein, a high SS official, was able to say no. The camp commandants continued to be responsible for the internal workings of the camps, and the task assigned to the SS was restricted

---

23. Testimony of Berger, *Trials*, XIII, 59; Spivey, *POW Odyssey*, 152.
24. Testimony of Berger, *Trials*, XIII, 59–62.

to security outside the camps.[25] These measures did not, however, entirely eradicate the danger for the prisoners. Prisoners who fell into the hands of the SS and the Gestapo outside the confines of the camps were still likely to be mistreated or even killed. And in the fall of 1944, Himmler transferred to the Higher SS and police leaders the responsibility for safeguarding prisoner of war camps against mass escapes and attempts from the outside to liberate prisoners. For this purpose, he made them the senior commanders of the prisoners of war in each defense area.[26]

Their assignment, however, was another largely hollow gesture. The individuals who held these posts were already heavily burdened with duties and in most cases were given only one extra officer to handle the new responsibilities. And he was usually an army man obtained from the existing staff of the commander for prisoner of war affairs in the military district. In the final analysis, British Intelligence concluded, this involvement of the SS and police leaders had little practical effect on the lives of the prisoners.[27]

Through such bureaucratic twists, most western prisoners were spared the SS and Gestapo brutalities so prevalent in the concentration camps. In fact, unless and until the system went totally awry, as in many respects it did near the end of the war, the bureaucracy secured more safety for the prisoners than it did for the German camp staff. If the administrators were unscrupulous and uncaring, they could use the bureaucracy to literally get away with murder. By contrast, there was great risk in upholding traditional values and basic human rights. The system simply was not designed to reward virtue.

Berger himself was in a difficult position. Both Hitler and Himmler led Berger to believe he was to assume authority over all prisoner of war affairs without limitations or restrictions. But in reality, things were not so clear-cut. The Prisoners of War Office in the O.K.W.

25. Testimony of Friedrich Karl von Eberstein, August 5, 1946, *IMT*, XX, 306.
26. An interesting and revealing maneuver took place in this regard. According to custom and international law, police officials are not supposed to be used to guard prisoners of war since the latter are not considered criminals. The Higher SS and police leaders were police officials, so Himmler took them over en masse into the Waffen-SS, where they were automatically appointed generals (testimony of von Eberstein, August 5, 1946, *IMT*, XX, 306). This is a classic example of what is meant when it is said that the Germans adhered to the letter if not the spirit of the law in caring for prisoners from the West.
27. "The Kriegsgefangenenwesen," 5. Escapers, however, still ran the great risk of encountering the SS and the Gestapo after they got away from the camps.

retained some control, as did the army commanders fighting at the various fronts.[28] He did not worry much about competition from these two sources. More important, he had to share his responsibilities with Oswald Pohl, a high-ranking economics and interior minister who naturally looked to the prison camps as a source of forced labor. There was also Dr. Ernst Kaltenbrunner, who carried such ominous titles as chief of security police and security services, chief of the Reich Security Main Office, and general of police. These two men were a source of constant concern for Berger and everyone below him in the prison system. And there was yet another element that affected everybody in the chain of command, the Parteikanzlei (Party Chancellery) of the Nazi party. Ordinarily party functionaries should have no part in prisoner of war affairs since such matters are essentially a military concern, but this was not the case in Nazi Germany. Officially the party was represented at the level of General Reinecke's General Armed Forces Office in the O.K.W. Any suggestions or orders that came up from lower levels to Reinecke's office for approval could be and frequently were vetoed or changed by the party chancellor. And orders and decisions affecting prisoners often originated in the Nazi party and were passed down through the chain of command where little could be done but comply with them. Both official and unofficial channels permitted party interference at all levels, beginning with Hitler and extending down to the smallest local office. References to unwanted interference appear frequently in the written record. Keitel said: "The Party-Chancellery, the German Labor Front and the Ministry of Propaganda likewise were included in this purely military question. The O.K.W. was engaged in a constant struggle with all these agencies, which for the most part had more influence on Hitler than the O.K.W."[29]

The shooting in the spring of 1944 of fifty of the seventy-six escaped

28. Testimony of Berger, *Trials*, XIII, 61. This, incidentally, had always been the case. The authority of the O.K.W., for example, did not even extend to the Russian front, and the army and the security services controlled prisoner affairs there. In the West the O.K.W. exercised control, but it was always understood that the system proper took the prisoners only after they had been evacuated from the operational areas. There was, of course, a system for processing the prisoners within the operational zones, but the methods of doing so varied greatly because of differing circumstances (Datner, *Crimes Against POWs*, 2–5; Final Defense Plea of Field Marshal Wilhelm Keitel, *Nazi Conspiracy and Aggression*, Supp. B, p. 273).

29. "The Kriegsgefangenenwesen," 7; Datner, *Crimes Against POWs*, xxvii; Final Defense Plea of Keitel, *Nazi Conspiracy and Aggression*, Supp. B, p. 266.

prisoners from Stalag Luft III serves as a prime example of the power and influence exercised over prisoners by forces outside the established prisoner of war system. The fate of these men involved only one individual in the prisoner of war chain of command, Hitler himself. The others were individuals, like Himmler, who were not yet legally associated with prisoners.

In short, the German prisoner of war system was directed by a complex and nebulous command structure. Ample provisions existed for observing the requirements of the Geneva Convention concerning such matters as inspections by neutral observers, food, health, and transportation.[30] Avenues were available as well for circumventing these offices. And circumvented they were, not only by party officials but also by numerous individuals and agencies both within and outside the O.K.W. who judged themselves above the law.

In addition to bureaucratic nightmares, the camp administrators had to compete mightily for available resources, a continuous task that added immeasurably to their worries. In April, 1945, General Berger boasted that Germany had more than 10 million prisoners of war within its borders.[31] That late in the war, his estimate may have been too high, and it is doubtful that the correct figure will ever be known.[32] But already in 1942, a set of statistics passed along by the American Red Cross to the State Department indicated that Ger-

---

30.   The Prisoners of War Office in O.K.W. served as the legislator and control organ for the entire prisoner of war apparatus. It published a basic directive applicable to all three services, KGB–38 (Prisoner of War Regulation 38), that contained all the clauses in the existing international agreements and the provisions for carrying them out. According to General Keitel, every department down to the smallest unit had this directive and every soldier, to a point, received instructions about its meaning and application. Furthermore, courses were instituted in Vienna to offer special training for those especially charged with the care of prisoners of war. And finally, every soldier had a leaflet in his paybook that instructed him on proper conduct toward prisoners of war. This information was offered to the Tribunal by Keitel and his attorney, Dr. Nelte, April 4, 1946, *IMT*, X, 553–54.

31.   This figure was recalled by General Spivey, one of the four men (including a translator) present at the meeting, and it was in a draft of an article prepared for *Air Force Magazine* that discusses the conference with Berger. The article, from which the figure was deleted, appeared in the September, 1975, issue (pp. 115–20).

32.   When the American legation in Bern, Switzerland, attempted to gather accurate statistics on the number of American prisoners of war held by the Germans, it was found that the indicated number in July, 1944, was less than that reported for June of the same year. The legation gave three possible reasons: the Germans only submitted figures readily available to them; they omitted figures because chaotic conditions led to the loss of records; and they did not judge accurate statistics to be important informa-

many then held approximately 4.75 million prisoners of war. Of these, 1,742,287 were British, Belgian, Polish, Yugoslavian, and French, and 3 million were Russian.[33]

The physical plant itself consisted of a far-flung empire of major base camps, hospitals, three civilian internee camps, and hundreds of small work detachments and detention points. The figures vary, but the impression they leave is unmistakable—Germany operated a gigantic prisoner of war system. Despite its great size, the system seldom kept pace with the demands placed upon it. Before the war, plans were made pertaining to the care of prisoners.[34] But it is unlikely that Germany anticipated the capture of such large numbers. Certain segments of the prisoner population fared better than others, and the first prisoners to enter a new camp usually found plenty of space for their use. In time, however, almost every camp became crowded and greatly exceeded its capacity. A random sampling of eight camps that on the average should have held no more than 4,725 prisoners each in actuality held an average of 24,666 men by the end of the war.[35]

It was into this boiling situation that von Lindeiner stepped in May, 1942.

---

tion. Bern to Department of State, May 15, 1944, in File 711.62114 A/539, RG 59. Berger's figure is questionable not because Germany had never dealt with such large numbers of Allied prisoners, for that many and more probably had been under German control at various times during the war, but because by April, 1945, Allied armies had overrun great expanses of German-occupied territory and liberated untold numbers of former prisoners.

33. C. E. MacEachran to Bernard Gufler, n.d., in File 740.00114 EW/2892, RG 59.

34. Datner, *Crimes Against POWs*, 1.

35. "Strengths of Prisoner of War Camps in Germany as Known to SHAEF-PWX on 1 February 1945," File 740.00114 EW/2-2645, pp. 1, 4, 7, 12, 17, RG 59.

7

Home Rule

With the exception of Colonel von Lindeiner and the Abwehr officer, virtually the entire German staff had accompanied the prisoners when they moved from Barth to Stalag Luft III. The Germans brought with them a thorough knowledge of the prisoners' crafty ways and many activities. The recent troubles with higher authorities were also fresh in their minds. The staff eventually grew from the seven officers and one hundred or so guards to approximately two thousand German soldiers pulling duty in May, 1944. The number of German personnel in the camp fluctuated but, according to one estimate, generally hovered around 10 percent of the number of prisoners.[1]

The same seven administrative departments that existed at Barth were incorporated into the system at Stalag Luft III. The commandant, of course, was the most important man in the chain of command and controlled virtually all affairs in the camp in accordance with rules and regulations imposed from above and by the influence of his own personality.

Altogether, four different commandants were assigned to Stalag Luft III. The first one, Colonel Stephani, did not speak English and had no experience with prisoners. He was replaced within a month by Colonel von Lindeiner.

1. Simoleit to Spivey, March 17, 1948, in Simoleit Folder, Spivey Collection. This estimate is considerably lower than one made by Aidan Crawley, who states that, even though the number of prisoners increased as the war went on, "at no time was there less than one guard to four prisoners" at Sagan (*Escape from Germany*, 15). This would have meant that there were approximately 2,500 guards alone in the camp. If he is correct, the prisoners obviously succeeded in making their point that the Germans could expect to achieve no economies in the guarding of Luftwaffe prisoners. On the other hand, Simoleit, who served as deputy commandant at Sagan from the time the camp opened until it closed, was certainly in a position to know how many German personnel were in the camp. Unfortunately, no independent data are readily available to reconcile the discrepancy in the figures.

Most observers have rated von Lindeiner very highly as a camp commandant. He was well educated, spoke English fluently, and was extremely capable. One report states that he was a man with whom "a shouting match was out of the question," but another source says that while von Lindeiner was usually courteous and considerate, he was also "liable to fits of uncontrolled rage," and at one point he personally threatened one of the prisoners with a pistol. The same source goes on to add, however, that "von Lindeiner was more friendly . . . to prisoner requests than any other commandant" and that "it was during his regime only that weekly conferences between the Senior Allied POWs and the German staff occurred." Perhaps the most telling comment on the man came from the prisoner who wrote: "No commandant, to a prisoner, is a good man, but I think von Lindeiner was." He served as commandant until shortly after the mass escape in March, 1944, when he was relieved of command, arrested, tried, and convicted by the German government on a variety of charges, most of which centered upon his having treated the prisoners too leniently.[2]

Von Lindeiner was replaced for a short time by Lieutenant Colonel Cordes, but he served only on an interim basis until Colonel Braune, the fourth and last commandant, could be appointed.[3] Colonel Braune reportedly was "exceedingly severe, but . . . quite fair." His great drawback was "his complete lack of knowledge of the English language and the American mentality." Although his manner was direct and businesslike, he was able to stop the misunderstandings that had been allowed to continue for some time. These had to do with guards who shot into the camp with increasing frequency during the spring and summer of 1944 in the wake of growing tensions.[4]

2. Smith, *Mission Escape*, 111; Goodrich, "History of South Compound," Pt. I, sec. 2B; Brickhill, *The Great Escape*, 168. For a good account of von Lindeiner's trial and subsequent difficulties first with the German government and then with the British for being implicated in the murder of fifty of the prisoners who escaped, see von Lindeiner to Spivey, July 31, 1948, in Von Lindeiner Folder, Spivey Collection; and von Lindeiner, "Memoirs," 248ff. Von Lindeiner was in fact totally innocent of the murders.

3. Colonel Braune's first name does not appear in any of the official reports or other sources that were examined. For the circumstances surrounding Cordes' assumption of command and his brief tenure, see von Lindeiner to Spivey, July 31, 1948, in Von Lindeiner Folder, Spivey Collection.

4. Protecting Power Report No. 7, concerning a visit made on July 19, 1944, by Gabriel Naville and Albert A. Kadler, representatives of the Swiss legation at Berlin, in File 711.62114 A.I.R./8–3044, RG 59; Goodrich, "A History of South Compound," Pt. I, sec. 2B.

The commandant had an experienced staff. The largest group under his command was the guards, most of whom were very young, very old, or otherwise unfit for duty at the front. They were constantly rotated out of camp. As with all the other German personnel in the camp, the guards understood that if they failed in their duties, they could expect to be sent to the Russian front, a fate most of them considered to be synonymous with death.

The camp adjutant, known as Department II, performed the functions of adjutants everywhere and took care of all the necessary military business and personnel matters pertaining to the German staff. Because of the nature of his duties, he had little contact with the prisoners.

Department III consisted of various Abwehr people whose duties were to maintain camp security and prevent escapes. It was Department III that searched the prisoners when they first entered the camp, searched the barracks on a routine basis, and probed every corner of the compounds in an effort to uncover escape activities. The men who worked inside the compounds were the ones the prisoners called "ferrets." They could be easily spotted because of their dark blue utility coveralls, designed to withstand their work under, around, and inside the barracks and other buildings. One officer and six NCO ferrets were assigned to each compound, and they paraded among the prisoners from dawn until dusk, probing anything and everywhere. They could enter rooms unannounced, listen at windows, hide under floors or inside the roofs, and search or arrest anyone they thought looked suspicious.[5]

The Verwaltung, or Department IV, was responsible for a variety of camp transactions and affairs. It handled the construction of new barracks, arranged for the repair of furniture, and provided the camp's food supply. This department also took care of the Russian prisoners who worked in Stalag Luft III.

The Lagerfuhrung, otherwise known as Department V, was still under Simoleit's control just as it had been at Barth. Composed of twelve officers and about fifty sergeants and privates by 1944, it was the largest administrative department in the camp. Almost all of its personnel understood and spoke English, which was an important

5. Von Lindeiner, "Memoirs," 121–211, provides the most thorough discussion of the various administrative departments. Also see Simoleit, "Organization and Administration"; and Crawley, *Escape from Germany*, 16.

qualification for their work, since they were in closer contact with the prisoners than was anyone else on the German staff. One of their duties was to maintain a large file of index cards on which was noted the personal history of every prisoner. Two Lagerfuhrung officers were assigned to each compound and were called "Lageroffiziers." They had several sergeants who helped them, and together they were responsible for much of what happened in the compounds. They spent almost their entire working day inside the compounds and knew most of the prisoners by sight. According to Simoleit, the camp officers were "ordered to act in good cooperation with the prisoners, to help them as much as possible and to accept their wishes and complaints." "Of course," Simoleit quickly adds, "they also had to care for the execution of all camp orders given by the commandant." One suspects that it is in this latter role and not the former one that most of the prisoners remember the Lager officers and men.

One of the most important duties assigned to Department V was the Appell. Simoleit recalls, "We had always great trouble if our final numbers did not correspond with our lists and if only one of our [thousands] of prisoners was missing. Often it took hours, and often a second roll call was necessary to detect the cause of our trouble. Perhaps one of the Lager officers had only made a mistake in his report, or the prisoners had hindered and deceived him when he was counting 'to keep the Germans busy'. Perhaps some prisoners had only hidden in the camp to prepare an escape, or they had already left the camp." In this last and worst case, Simoleit went on, "we had to inform immediately the police and the military authorities, and hunting for the escapers began first in all neighboring districts and later all over Germany, in which cases we were always severely blamed that we were not able to guard our prisoners and that we gave them too much freedom in our camp. . . . For me the roll call with the following examination, calculation, and evaluation was a real nerve strain every day. I could not relax before I had handed my report to the commandant." It was also the Lagerfuhrung personnel who had to organize burial for prisoners who died.[6]

But some in Department V helped the prisoners obtain special items for their education, theater, recreation, and athletic programs as well as unusual items such as manure for their gardens and sometimes (improperly, of course) materials needed in their clandestine

6. Simoleit, "Organization and Administration."

activities such as film, cameras, passes, and radio equipment. Department V also arranged for the occasional parole walks.

Department VI, the Postzensur, censored the mail and books that were sent to or from all Luftwaffe camps. This task had originally been the staff's at Dulag Luft, where the intent had been to collect information from the mail that might be helpful in interrogating new prisoners. Captain von Massow, the brother of a well-known Luftwaffe general, was in charge of the censoring office at Dulag Luft and remained as its chief when it was transferred to Stalag Luft III in the spring of 1942.[7] About one hundred censors, mostly women but also some soldiers, examined the prisoners' mail, trying as much as possible to concentrate on the mail of certain individuals. The censors were well prepared to screen all the letters and books written in English, but Simoleit was the only man in camp at times who could censor the mail of the Polish, Czech, and Russian prisoners. He often spent his evenings at this task, and though he found the Polish and Russian letters easy to read, for the Czech ones he needed a grammar and a dictionary.

The German medical or Lazarett staff was the seventh department. Simoleit indicates that there were three German officers assigned to medical duties. Since only two names appear in the camp inspection reports, however, the third probably attended to the Germans only. Dr. Keil served as the chief medical supervisor and Dr. Kremer supervised all dental work. Each man was assisted by prisoners, most of whom were fully qualified for the work they undertook in their respective fields.

The prisoners' main obligation was to look after their own interests, and to a large extent, under the provisions of the Geneva Convention, the Germans were obligated to help them. In this regard the German record was far from perfect, but the consensus is that the Germans who operated Stalag Luft III probably did all they could for the prisoners, in view of the exigencies of war and the conditions that prevailed under Nazi rule.

The meager German staff was neither designed for nor capable of ministering to all the prisoners' needs. Stalag Luft III attained the size of a small city, and if the prisoners had remained completely idle,

7.   Smith, *Mission Escape*, 30. Brickhill (*The Great Escape*, 27) gives his name as von-Masse. Both men agree that he was the brother of a Luftwaffe general but no information could be found to confirm the general's name.

their standard of living would have fallen drastically. With the fierce pride usually found in men accustomed to being self-sufficient, the prisoners desperately wanted the Germans to stay out of their business so they could find their own solutions to the internal communal problems that confronted them.

It is doubtful if the prisoners saved the Germans many man-hours by doing so much for themselves, since most of the tasks they undertook simply would not have been done. But the prisoners' efforts helped their captors in other ways. Because the prisoners had their internal affairs well in hand, the camp made a better impression on visitors than otherwise would have been the case. In addition, the prisoners' broad range of activities helped keep them occupied and reduced the risk of their becoming restless and unruly. But it can be assumed that any help the prisoners gave the Germans was only incidental: the prisoners had to organize and take on various duties and responsibilities in order to best protect and foster their own interests. The need to do so had become clear to them during the years at Dulag Luft and Barth and was reaffirmed on countless occasions during their stay in captivity.

Military customs and traditions were at the heart of the prisoners' administrative and organizational system. Although they often deviated from the norms of military life in matters of dress, courtesies, and personal appearance, they were reacting more to the privations of camp life than showing a willful desire to deny their military identity and heritage. There were some who felt that as captives they were beyond the control of their commanding officers. Overall, however, such men were a small minority, and most of them agreed to abide by the rules when they learned that the military chain of command did indeed function in the camp. It was based on date of rank and structured by duty title.

The highest ranking officer in the camp assumed the duties of Senior Allied Officer, a position the Germans recognized. A short time after the prisoners were separated according to nationality, the Germans acknowledged one man as the Senior American Officer and allowed him to speak for the prisoners in Center, South, and West compounds. The Senior British Officer, in turn, represented the prisoners in East, North, and Belaria compounds. Thus, even though General Vanaman was clearly the ranking man in Stalag Luft III after August, 1944, he was not allowed to visit any of the British compounds. When the American compounds became overcrowded in the fall months of 1944 and the new American arrivals had to be housed in Belaria and North compounds, they were represented by SAOs who resided in the respective compounds, but were otherwise considered to be under the control of the SBO, who was ultimately responsible for all the prisoners in the three British compounds.[8]

Next in the chain of command came the senior officers, of the various nationalities, who served as compound commanders. The senior officer of the nationality most widely represented in the compound usually became the compound commander, and the senior officers of the other nationalities then served in some capacity on the compound staff or were otherwise consulted in all matters that concerned the prisoners they represented.

The compound commanders were the cornerstone of the prisoners' administrative system, and their personalities strongly influenced events and conditions in the compounds. They led by exercising military authority blended with careful persuasion. They were expected to maintain discipline and order, but did not have court-martial authority in the camp. To cope with this delicate situation in Center Compound, Colonel Spivey set out at once to organize the camp as a military unit. He called all the Americans together and told them his plans, explaining that each one of them was still in the army and liable to the Articles of War, which he could and would invoke if necessary. On the whole, the reaction to this meeting was not good: "The advocates of the iron fist manner of control believed that the only way to get the Americans to band together for their own good was to be positive and ruthless, but those of us who were older and more experienced in dealing with men realized this was no place for harshness or unreasonableness." He and his staff held fast to their decision "to run the camp in a military manner, giving orders and demanding they be carried out. Our approach was firm but geared to an understanding of the situation. We determined to lead, guide, direct, and encourage instead of being arbitrary and unreasonable." Reflecting on the situation somewhat later, he admitted, "I do not know what I would have done if a group had steadfastly refused to cooperate."

Although Spivey was never confronted with large scale resistance, there were instances when individuals refused to cooperate: "Not all the men were willing to do their part and many believed the authority of the SAO was fictitious and could not be enforced. Some believed

8.   Charles G. Goodrich to the author, November 21, 1975.

they owed no allegiance to the will of the camp as a whole nor did they care to consider what inconvenience the camp suffered as a result of their individual actions. They maintained that their instructions to escape were the only ones they intended to obey." But again taking the pragmatic view, he stated, "These mavericks in our otherwise disciplined herd had to be treated as individuals and if the barracks commander couldn't take care of the situation the man was brought to me; if I couldn't reason with him he became the ward of the strong arm squad of his barracks. . . . They weren't averse to manhandling a boy who wouldn't obey camp orders nor were they beyond taking a lad who wouldn't bathe to the ice-cold shower and scrubbing him with a GI scrubbing brush and Octagon soap. These cases were few and as a general rule I could rely on the men carrying out any order given them."[9]

Colonel Goodrich agreed that discipline was of the greatest importance and sought to instill it in the prisoners in much the same manner as Spivey did. Both men and their staffs conducted orientation and indoctrination talks for newly arrived prisoners, pressured their subordinates to enforce directives and policies pertaining to conduct, and used the Appells to march the men in formation and enforce good order and military behavior. Men late for Appell were required to report early for several days, and some violations were punished by reprimand. In the more serious cases, the incidents were investigated as a prelude to possible court-martial action after the war. The results of the investigation were always announced to the compound as a warning.[10]

Although there was some discontent expressed, most prisoners realized that the military nature of the organizational structure and some of the rules and regulations were necessary. Typically, some men were shocked to learn that Spivey planned to hold Saturday-morning inspections in Center Compound, but most of them responded in traditional fashion. They spent long hours, the day and night before, cleaning their rooms, getting haircuts and shaves, polishing their shoes, and putting together the best pieces of their uniforms. And when the West Point colonel gave his approval to a room

9. Spivey, *POW Odyssey*, 44–45.
10. Goodrich, "History of South Compound," Pt. I, sec. 2C. No such cases were found in the documentary material. Some of the prisoners I interviewed recalled such cases but were understandably reluctant to give details.

and the men who occupied it, everyone exhibited a genuine sense of pride in their mutual achievement.[11]

The compound commanders were assisted by numerous people who served either in functional capacities or directly in the chain of command. Prominent among the former were the personnel assigned as intelligence, security, or operations (escape) officers, and those placed in charge of major camp departments such as the mail office, clothing store, Red Cross parcel and personal parcel stores, YMCA equipment office, compound kitchen, dispensary, libraries, and camp carpenters, electricians, and metalworkers. Also prominent were those who supervised such camp activities as the educational programs, publishing ventures, concerts and theatrical productions, sports events and religious services. The individuals who were part of the chain of command or who were considered members of the commander's personal staff included one or more interpreters, camp office personnel, an executive officer, an adjutant, and the barracks and room commanders, the latter often being called "room Führers."

The offices and living quarters of the compound commander, the executive officer, and the adjutant were the nerve center of daily camp life. These men carried on all official relations with the Germans, the protecting power, the YMCA and Red Cross representatives, as well as other compounds. Prisoners also visited those offices to make requests for supplies, register complaints, obtain clarification of policies, arrange schedules, and get help on personal problems. Domestic worries were the subject of many conversations. One prisoner complained because he had left his car and his power of attorney with his girlfriend. She married someone else and the happy couple were using his car and spending his money. Letters from home, or the absence of them, often motivated prisoners to talk with the "old man," to whom they would pour out their feelings, doubts, suspicions, and fears. Some prisoners had personal financial matters that required a power of attorney or other official correspondence that had to be processed by the clerical staff. In addition, there were unending requests for use of the office equipment to type news articles for the Newsrooms, compound newspapers, translations of

11. Mulligan, Burbank, and Brunn, "History of Center Compound," Pt. I, sec 1-a.

German communiqués, scripts of plays for the theater, and parcel and property lists.[12]

The barracks or "block" commanders were another link in the chain of command. To the prisoners, a block was the equivalent of a squadron in a regular installation, and they organized it in much the same way. Each block had a commander, and, as might be expected, the entire block benefited or suffered in accord with his abilities and efforts. One source goes so far as to state that it became apparent to the prisoners that "the Block Commander's job was the keystone for the effectiveness of the whole compound organization." The point could be argued, especially given the importance of the compound commander's role, but it highlights the extent to which the prisoners relied upon their designated leaders. Much of the block commander's time was taken up in supervising his people, cautioning them not to talk to the Germans without permission, maintaining good order at Appells, ensuring that basic sanitation practices were observed in the barracks, and restricting the liberties of the individual for the good of all. His was a demanding job, and persons suited to it were not easily found. Some officers who had performed brilliantly as fliers did not necessarily make good block commanders. Overall, however, the prisoners expressed general satisfaction with the men placed in charge of the blocks, and in many cases the block commanders earned reputations for attaining efficiency and cooperation in ways that impressed both the men and the senior officers.[13]

In each block, the staff largely duplicated the compound staff. Thus the compound sports officer was assisted by a sports officer in each of the blocks, as were the kitchen officer, education officer, operations officer, theater officer, and the like.

The lowest level in the echelon of command was the individual room. In Center Compound the large rooms were divided into six combines, each marked by arrangements of beds and lockers. The senior man in each room was the room Führer, and on a smaller scale his duties paralleled those of the block commander. Each room worked out in more or less democratic fashion the many details that have to be considered when men live in close quarters, but the room commander often cast the deciding vote. In addition, he served as a

12. Goodrich, "History of South Compound," Pt. I, sec. 3A (1).
13. *Ibid.*, Pt. I, sec. 2C.

major communication link. When something of special importance had to be communicated to the prisoners but could not be announced at Appell or at an assembly in the theater, the compound commander would give out the news to the block commanders, and they, in turn, would tell the room commanders, who then repeated the messages to the prisoners in their rooms. In short order, important matters that could have been badly distorted if left to the rumor factory were carefully cleared up. And when need be, the system worked well enough to prevent the Germans from learning anything that was not meant for their ears.

The prisoners might have organized their community in other ways, but none would have suited their purposes nearly so well as did the military chain of command and functional organization they developed and upon which they relied. To the present-day observer, the system might seem cumbersome and unnecessarily heavy-handed because everyone was accountable to someone higher in authority. But that organization answered some very basic needs. The commanding officers could direct and control the men in each compound in a way that everyone understood. At the same time, there were reliable channels through which the prisoners could express their opinions and have a voice in camp affairs. And the broad base of involvement helped a large proportion of the prisoners be constructively occupied. Finally, the system admirably complemented the German administrative system. The prisoners could look after their own interests with good prospects for success in instances where the German system proved inadequate.

8

The Essentials

When the German and prisoner administrative systems worked in tandem the prisoners obtained the essentials of life, though not without some difficulty. The captives and their captors, however, still represented opposing sides in a bitter war, and it would have been too much to expect continued cooperation in everything affecting the vital interests of either the prisoners or the Germans. The Germans often ignored the prisoners' urgent needs in order to devote more of their resources to the war. At times they also fell victim to their own propaganda about the terrible and vicious Luftgangsters: prisoners' relatively minor infractions prompted reprisals of unwarranted severity. At the same time, the prisoners never tired in their efforts to escape and to "keep the Germans busy." They understood the possible penalties if they were caught in their forbidden acts and were willing to accept the consequences as long as they were not too severe. But they would not accept unnecessary privations and looked to their organizational structure and sense of identity as a community to help fill the voids or overcome any unreasonableness in the German administrative system. In the final analysis, they fully grasped the importance of helping themselves and proceeded to do so on a routine basis in order to achieve the best possible living conditions and the most meaningful approach to life that circumstances permitted.

George Sweanor's first impressions of the camp were fairly typical. Looking at the camp for the first time, he was struck by the multiple high fences with the concertina wire between, a most effective barrier against escape. The tension among the prisoners broke when a Welsh wit remarked, "So this is where we are going to spend the best years of our wives."[1]

The routine of life in Stalag Luft III began the moment the pris-

1. Sweanor, *Pensionable Time*, 119.

oners passed through the gate into the Vorlager. The Germans, accustomed to receiving new purges almost daily, soon came to view each new group as being no different from the dozens of others that had entered this particular camp. The procedures for processing them were standardized. First, the prisoners were counted and thoroughly searched.

The fingerprinting and photographing were necessary since virtually every one of them was officially categorized as an "important prisoner," a designation given to every army and navy officer prisoner with the rank of colonel or above, and to every British or American flier, regardless of rank.[2] They also were given a prisoner of war number. By this time, the prisoners were tired, unshaven and dirty after their long train ride to the camp, and the pictures showed some rather grisly-looking characters. The photographs were useful in newspapers and posters for showing the nature of the terror fliers or "Chicago types" that were ravaging the countryside. In sequence, the men were then stripped of any flying clothes they might still have, were allowed quick showers, and were deloused. Finally, they were issued their bedding—two blankets,[3] one sheet, one mattress cover that held the wood shavings for the mattress and was a bottom sheet, one pillowcase, one pillow filled with straw, and one small face towel. In addition, they were usually given a two-quart heavy mixing bowl, a cup, a knife, a fork, and a spoon—these items, they were admonished, would not be replaced if lost or broken. The men were then sent into one of the compounds.[4]

The old and new prisoners quickly looked each other over in the hope of seeing the face of an old friend. Before the officers in Center Compound became organized in the fall of 1943, Spivey has observed, prisoners who recognized one of the new men showed him around the camp and helped him get settled, which aided him in adjusting to life in captivity. However, those who were not recognized were left to shift for themselves. Understandably, it took some of these less fortunate men two or three months to learn what was expected of them and how they might help themselves. By October the reception of new prisoners was far less haphazard.

2. Brickhill, *The Great Escape*, 72.
3. Most prisoners were later given one additional Red Cross blanket.
4. Spivey, *POW Odyssey*, 32–33. Different prisoners have noted variations in this routine and property issue, but this account can be considered fairly representative of what the prisoners encountered in the Vorlager during their first day in camp.

The new system provided for the orderly processing of the prisoners in a way that left little to chance. They were segregated from the old prisoners upon arrival in the compound and taken to the compound theater, where they were briefed by the camp staff on what would happen to them in the coming hours. One prisoner recalls, "When we were seated inside, a tall American colonel stepped through the front door, and the major called us to attention. He executed a snappy salute and the colonel returned it as he climbed the steps leading to the stage. Our groups remained silently at attention." In a dignified manner the colonel said, "At ease." He then went on, "I am Colonel——, Commanding Officer of——Compound. The next few days will be somewhat confusing for you new men. That has been the case with me and every older man who came through those prison gates before you. Being prisoners, we are forced through circumstances to do things we had never dreamed or conceived of doing before. We are called upon every single day to sacrifice, endure, and work together in the common struggle for our survival."

After explaining in broad terms how the compound was organized, the colonel emphasized, "We have learned that through organization we live better, eat better, and get along better, and in general, life is much more bearable for all of us." Pausing at this point and looking toward some old prisoners, he continued, "I call upon you to do your job to the best of your ability, and to do it good-naturedly. Listen to the older men for they can help you. Treat them with respect for they have earned it. Some of the older prisoners may bite your head off. I ask you to try to hold your temper. Some of these men have been prisoners at Sagan for over twenty months. Their nerves are strained; they are sometimes easily antagonized, and you must try to understand. You will find that the older prisoners have gained judgment and wisdom. Brotherhood, kindness, and understanding will take you a long way while you are here. Don't be a slacker, for you will find yourself without a single friend. Life will be only as pleasant as you make it yourself." Pausing once more, he cautioned, "We do not know who you are. We know that we have one hundred twenty-one men before us who are supposed to be Americans. We intend to make sure you are—to the last man. . . . You are probably Americans to the last man, but we have had German stooges in these groups before who speak perfect English and have every characteristic of being American. There are many things which the Germans would like to know. These men live among us as spies for the Germans. We have eliminated them to the last man. We do not intend to allow another stooge in this camp." Knowing what the men must be thinking by now, he provided a measure of reassurance, saying, "This identification will take only a few hours, but until you have been identified as an American, the old prisoners will not speak to you. You will be asked many questions, and you may be placed on exhibition so that someone can identify you. You must be identified by our Intelligence before any of us can accept you. The sooner this is over, the better. . . . We will have these talks from time to time."

After the colonel departed a member of the intelligence staff filled in the necessary details. "I am going to send you to the library for interviews with my staff. When each of you is identified you will be assigned to your barracks. If we have not identified you by noon you will remain in the library for the noon meal. We will feed all of you the meal; but starting tonight you will eat in your combine, unless you still have not been identified. If we have not identified you by five o'clock, you will be assigned to a special isolation ward until you are cleared with Intelligence." He also informed them that within the next two or three days, he would be sending men from Intelligence to interview them: "They will ask you questions about the war, its progress, your duties in the Air Force, news about the U.S., Dulag Luft, your trip here, and many other questions. You will answer any question they ask you, for this is a part of our system of information."[5]

The prisoners felt that their interrogation efforts were an essential aspect of their security program. And in at least one instance a German agent was exposed during an interrogation session. An Egyptian Air Force officer in North Compound did not give satisfactory answers to certain questions, and the prisoners put him under close arrest. After several days he broke down and admitted that the Germans had placed him in the compound. After representations by the Senior British Officer to the commandant, the agent was removed from the camp.[6]

The details varied, but basically the same procedures were followed in each compound. When George Sweanor finally entered North Compound, he was surprised by the reception he received. Two pris-

5. Kenneth W. Simmons, *Kriegie* (New York, 1960), 91–96; Sweanor, *Pensionable Time,* 119–20.
6. "A History of Stalag Luft III," Pt. I, p. 80.

oners in his group recognized old friends but could only exchange shouted greetings. Two RAF flight lieutenants asked them to remain in the group and not mingle. About an hour later he was taken into a separate room where he found himself facing a board consisting of a wing commander and two squadron leaders (a Briton, a New Zealander, and a Canadian). They proceeded to interrogate him, at one point asking him an operational question. Quite annoyed by the whole process, at this point, he declined to answer on the grounds that he did not know if they were genuine prisoners themselves.

Smiling, the wing commander replied, "Your caution is commendable, but we will not accept you unless we are certain of your identity. Do you know anyone in the compound?"

"I went to school with Flight Lieutenant Lewis who has been a prisoner of war for eighteen months. Is he here?"

"I know Mike well. He is in East Compound; you are in the North Compound; describe him to me."

George described Mike to the board's satisfaction, and they released him. He joined a group of other prisoners who had passed interrogation, and together they were taken to block 119. The room "Führer" welcomed and assigned them to their rooms.[7]

There were undoubtedly some new prisoners who were processed into the camp less smoothly, but the system worked well in the vast majority of cases. The prisoners were able to boast that after a compound had been fully organized, prisoners were adjusting as well in three or four days as they did under the old system in a month or two.[8]

The new prisoners were quickly exposed to the daily routine of collecting, preparing, and sharing their food. Experienced in problems associated with the frequent privations encountered by prisoners of war, Dr. Albert P. Clark, Sr. wrote to his son, revealing his deep concerns. "Don't worry about the Red Cross packages and nutrition," he stated, "for I have you covered if Carolyn's [Bub's wife] packages ever get there; you will have plenty of vitamins and minerals in each to outlast the period between." The packages were being sent at sixty-day intervals. He went on to say, "The tablets are to be taken 1–3 times a day, but if you have a little reserve you might well take one extra one-a-day. I have also sent powdered egg and powdered milk."

7. Sweanor, *Pensionable Time*, 119–20.
8. Mulligan, Burbank, and Brunn, "History of Center Compound," Pt. I, sec. 1-a.

Confessing that he intended to "make each letter a little lecture on survival," Dr. Clark cautioned:

The symptoms of even a slight lack of vitamins or minerals, or certain nitrogen foods, are so hard to see and find in the early stages that even most physicians can't diagnose them. One of the first is swollen, puffy gums near the edge or surface of the tooth—gums that bleed easily—due to lack of vitamin C which you get from citrus or tomatoes, or vegetables, potatoes, greens, cabbage—all preferably raw. . . . If each man in your outfit can find himself an old nail, iron or steel, and remove the rust, then with a stone file off a little iron filings every day or so and put it on the tongue and wash it down with water—the stomach will change it to iron chloride. This will keep up their iron reserve and prevent anemia.

Dr. Clark's advice was highly appropriate and his concerns well founded. One prisoner observed, "The German rations were just enough to insure starvation in its most prolonged and unpleasant form."[9]

The Allied doctors in camp agreed. A grown man who is fairly active should be nourished by about 3,000 calories a day, and the German rations that provided from 1,500 to 1,900 calories a day clearly were inadequate. Although the amount and quality of the food varied from time to time and deteriorated near the end of the war, a reasonably accurate impression of the deficiencies was presented in a 1944 protecting power report:

Item	Amount Allotted, Oct., 1944	Amount Necessary	Deficiency
Calories	1,900	3,000	1,100
Fats	35	100	65
Protein	45	100	55
Carbohydrates	340	400	60
Vitamin A	2,500	5,000	2,500
Vitamin B-1	240	600	360
Vitamin C	1,300	1,500	200[10]

9. Albert P. Clark, Sr., to Albert P. Clark, Jr., April 5, 1943, in Clark Collection; Brickhill, *The Great Escape*, 192.

10. Protecting Power Report No. 1, concerning the December 9, 1942, visit by Dr. Schaeffeler, in "Stalag Luft III" Folder, RG 389. The data given in the chart were compiled by the American and British doctors in Stalag Luft III and given to Dr. Rossel and Dr. Thudichum, International Red Cross representatives who visited the camp on November 24–25, 1944.

The shortages of food often were quite serious. Theoretically, the prisoners were supposed to be receiving the same rations the German troops were. The meat given them should have contained no more than an average of 25 percent bone—in reality, it often contained as much as 40 to 50 percent. Vegetables were frequently scarce or nonexistent. The Germans used potatoes as one of the staples in the prisoners' diet but often provided spoiled potatoes or none at all, as was the case during the fall, 1943, potato famine in eastern Germany. Appropriate substitutes were seldom available. John Wells, for example, thought some sauerkraut was far too bitter. He examined it closely and found some of it was nothing more than fermented weeds. The kohlrabi distributed in place of potatoes was a coarse vegetable (a cabbage-like plant with bulbed stems that resembled turnips when prepared) that many prisoners could not stomach. On at least one occasion, the prisoners went for several months without any green vegetables.[11]

It would have been little comfort to the prisoners if they had known that the German troops were not eating any better than they. But in all fairness to the German camp staff, it should be pointed out that the prisoners were getting an average of 300 grams of bread per day, but Simoleit and the other German officers were receiving only 180 grams. For a long period of time, he reports, the German officers were getting less to eat than the privates were; in addition to the 180 grams of bread, the German camp officers were allotted only a tiny piece of butter, some cheese or sausage, and a plate of thin vegetable soup for dinner. Only after they had lost a great deal of weight did the commandant send a sharp protest to higher authorities, and then the officers were given permission to eat the better food and larger rations the privates had. He does not state how this inequity came about in the first place or what the privates were given to eat.[12] But it appears that at least the general populace in Germany, if not the German soldiers, probably ate less than the prisoners, especially near the end of the war.

One staple that the prisoners did receive on a regular basis was bread. One prisoner recalls, "Bread, which was issued several times a

11. Interview with Wells, January 26–27, 1975; Protecting Power Report No. 5, concerning the February 22–24, 1944, visit by Naville, in File 711.62114 A.I.R./137, RG 59; report of visit made on May 22, 1944, by Dr. Rossel and Mr. Paul Wyss, representatives of the International Red Cross, in "Stalag Luft III" Folder, RG 389.
12. Simoleit, "Organization and Administration," n.p.

week, was the most essential and sought after item. The average prisoner had to cultivate a taste for this heavy black loaf, as it was a repulsive, soggy mixture of questionable ingredients with a definite sour taste. I can recall my incredulity on the evening of capture when I was given several slabs of this bread to eat with some cheese and bologna. At first I couldn't believe that I was expected to eat it." After several months, he overcame his distaste for it and, at the end of a year, had almost developed a liking for this German army ration. The sogginess and sour taste, he learned, could be counteracted somewhat by toasting, which was done on the tiny room stoves when fuel was available. The five-pound loaves, in batches of thirty or forty for each barracks, were carried from the cookhouse on a door from a food locker or an upturned bench. Two men then laboriously carried it on their shoulders. At Sagan, the bread ration approximated a loaf per person per week. Other items that were issued fairly regularly included a dish of cooked and hot pea or barley soup every other day at noon, occasionally some cooked millet, cooked potatoes nearly every day in fair quantities (but sometimes uncooked), some sugar, margarine, jam, cheese, fresh meat, token amounts of fresh vegetables such as cucumbers, lettuce, and kohlrabi, and German blood sausage, never popular in camp since it consisted of nothing more than congealed blood with a few slices of onion added.[13]

The freshness of the meat also was open to question. Sergeant Raymond Orozco worked in the South Compound kitchen, and it was his job to divide up the meat so that each man would receive about four ounces each week, enough to make one small hamburger. "Without exception," he vividly recalls, "the meat arrived in the kitchen covered with white maggots." The first thing he did was clean off the maggots and soak the meat in salt water to kill the germs and the smell.[14]

Kohlrabi did not set well with the prisoners. Clifford Hopewell described his reaction to it: "I well remember this vegetable as it had absolutely no taste at all. We fried it, baked it, boiled it and still no taste. Best of all we tried to eat it raw laced with salt—still no taste. It was very hard and grainy, and we rarely ate it and then only as filler. Most of the time we threw it up and down the block halls, as one would throw bowling balls. Then we would throw them in the aborts

13. Neary, *Stalag Luft III: Sagan*, 14.
14. Interview with Raymond Orozco, April 15, 1983.

[latrines], but finally the goons started complaining about that."[15]

The prisoners considered themselves fortunate to have access to the Red Cross food parcels. Although some camps did not receive these parcels regularly or in sufficient quantities, Stalag Luft III almost always carried enough Canadian, British, or American Red Cross parcels to supply each prisoner with about one parcel a week. The contents varied, but a typical parcel contained a well-thought-out selection of items. When issued at the rate of one per man each week, the parcels added about one thousand calories per day to the prisoners' diet. Thus the prisoners could not have survived for extended periods of time on either the German rations or the Red Cross food, but the combination provided an adequate, though by no means tasty, diet.[16]

During and after the war, the vast majority of prisoners in Stalag Luft III gave endless praise to the Red Cross for the life-saving food and other items it provided. Some prisoners did not know the source of some of the food they ate: when special Christmas food parcels were sent in 1943, they wrote home that the Germans had been extra generous in issuing food. But most knew the food was paid for by their governments and assembled, packaged, and shipped by the respective Red Cross units through International Red Cross channels. And they expressed their gratitude for the tremendous efforts of the Red Cross workers.

Serious difficulties were encountered in shipping parcels for prisoners. The American Red Cross was unable to make its contribution widely felt until late 1943 because shipping space could not be obtained for the rapidly accumulating stocks. Reflecting the misunderstandings that sometimes occurred as a result, one prisoner wrote home on May 23, 1943: "The American Red Cross isn't coming thru with the boxes. It's funny the British and Canadian Red Cross can get anything thru to the prisoners, but the Americans can't. So far, we have had three times as many boxes from the British and Canadians

---

15. Clifford Hopewell to the author, July 29, 1982.

16. British embassy in Washington to George S. Brandt, March 13, 1943, in File 740.00114 EW/3316 3/13, RG 59. For a brief but excellent discussion of the Red Cross program for prisoners of war, see Foster Rhea Dulles, *The American Red Cross: A History* (New York, 1950), 489–506. A more comprehensive account is given in Arthur W. Robinson, "Relief to Prisoners of War in World War II," 1950, Vol. XXII, "The History of the American Red Cross" (MS in Archives Division, American Red Cross Headquarters, Washington, D.C.).

as we have from Americans." And again on July 10 he reported, "Most of the fellows are wearing British Army uniforms, so you can figure for yourself how much help we are receiving. Don't let those grafting pigs hand you a line."[17]

Records indicate that American Red Cross officials spared no effort in trying to ship the quantities of goods they had ready for the prisoners. British and Canadian goods were getting through simply because those countries had already established reliable channels for delivering the parcels. By mid-1943 the Americans succeeded in working out the necessary details, but within less than a year the problem of getting the food from the coast to the camps in Germany became acute. The breakdown of rail service between Marseille and Switzerland, first because of partisan activity and then because of the invasion of France, prevented the movement of supplies by that route from late May, 1944, and it took about eight months to open up new routes through Sweden. When a northern route was found, thirty ships made the round trip from Sweden to Germany. While the Allies daily sowed the Baltic Sea with mines, the Germans provided minesweepers for the Red Cross ships. One report asserted that there must have been several German minesweepers performing just this one operation for about six months.[18] Because the southern route through France was closed, however, few new parcels were put ashore in Europe from May through December, 1944. From September 4, 1944, until January 17, 1945, the prisoners in Stalag Luft III received only "half-rations," or one-half parcel per man per week.[19]

Ever since the early years of the war, the Germans had faithfully punctured the tins of Red Cross food when they were handed out to the prisoners so they could not be used as escape rations. But the prisoners found they could keep the meat several days until the tin began to turn blue.[20] In addition, they saved other food items from

17. Stella M. Mills to Senator H. Lodge, October 29, 1943, in File 711.62114 A/155, RG 59.

18. Robinson, "Relief to Prisoners," 111. For a fuller discussion of the American Red Cross's efforts to ship the parcels, see Robinson, "Relief to Prisoners," 95–116; and Cordell Hull to U.S. embassy, London, September 30, 1944, in File 740.00114 EW/9–3044, RG 59.

19. Mulligan, Burbank, and Brunn, "History of Center Compound," Pt. III (Diary), September 4, 1944, January 17, 1945.

20. Interview with Clark, November 7, 1975. The color change in the tin indicated that the meat was about to spoil and had already undergone some chemical change that affected the tin.

Red Cross issues until they had enough to prepare special dishes. The prisoners ate in small groups rather than individually, and only by saving food could they prepare a group mess. They were understandably alarmed when they heard about a new German order that came out in September, 1944, directing that all Red Cross parcels be opened and the tins punctured immediately upon arrival in camp. If fully observed, this practice would have meant no more parcels would be stockpiled in the camp, an especially serious threat since transportation in Germany was becoming increasingly difficult. And the restriction to a single day's ration would have required that food be distributed from centralized kitchens rather than the individual room messes.

The Red Cross vigorously protested: even though the Geneva Convention did not guarantee the right to receive parcels, agreements had been reached between the belligerents in Europe that called for their distribution, and the agreements included a de facto right to store reserves in or near the camps. The Germans argued that they merely wanted to keep large quantities of tinned goods from falling into the hands of partisan groups. One unidentified Allied source interpreted this statement as a sign that the Germans were becoming afraid that the millions of prisoners held in Germany would be armed by weapons dropped from the air or released by Allied paratroops and would attack the German armies from the rear.[21]

The prisoners were already apprehensive about the impending food crisis when yet another incident occurred concerning the Red Cross parcels. One day in early October, a Luftgau inspector toured the museum set up in the Kommandantur by the German staff to help train ferrets and to impress visitors with their skill in confiscating the prisoners' escape equipment. The inspector noted that most of the

21. Unless otherwise noted, the information pertaining to the Red Cross food reserves was extracted from "Copy of memorandum prepared in the Department of State regarding the German prohibition against the accumulation of reserves of food parcels at prisoner of war camps in Germany," January 22, 1945, in File 619.2/43 "Food and Subsistence, American and Allied Internees and POW," Archives Division, American Red Cross Headquarters, and "Minutes of the 40th Meeting of Sub-Committee B of the Imperial Prisoners of War Committee," December 21, 1944, in File 740.00114 EW/1–2045, RG 59. The comment by the unidentified Allied source is included in a two-page summary of Red Cross activities, "Prisoners of War in World War II." The document is filed under the heading "Red Cross, U.S., ANRC, Prisoners of War Activities (Miscellaneous-European)," in the Archives Division, American Red Cross Headquarters.

escape aids had been made out of tin taken from the cans of Klim (milk spelled backwards) powdered milk that came in the Red Cross parcels. He dug up a 1940 regulation that prohibited retaining tins of any kind in the compounds and insisted that it be implemented immediately. The commandant amended the order, allowing each prisoner six cans for keeping his various food items separate, but otherwise required that by noon on October 5 all the tins in camp be turned in at the gate. The order was given on October 4, and the prisoners complied on schedule. It was a serious loss for them. In addition to using the tins for making escape aids, they had also fabricated coffeepots, baking pans, eggbeaters, and a host of needed items that the Germans did not provide. When several inspectors arrived a short time later, General Vanaman showed them some of the tinware made by the prisoners, and they were sufficiently impressed to ask for samples to take to headquarters in a bid to have some of the tins restored. But the order stood, and thereafter the prisoners had to return the tins from one Red Cross parcel before they could receive another.[22]

In the meantime, the prisoners' attention was drawn back to the more serious problem of the one-day-food-supply order. It appears the original German order was not as severe as originally thought, since individual camp commandants could retain a two-month supply of food as long as the reserves were stored outside the camp under special lock and key. At Sagan this had always been done anyway, so there was no visible change in the system. The parcels were controlled from the Red Cross parcel store in the Vorlager shared by East and Center compounds and sent as needed to the Vorlagers of West Compound, Belaria Compound, and the North Compound sick quarters. When these facilities were filled, additional stocks were kept in a nearby granary.[23] But the problem remained concerning the one-day supply of food inside the camp. The prisoners were told that after November 20 the Abwehr would confiscate any extra food in the camp and that henceforth all food in Red Cross and personal parcels would be emptied into large containers and delivered to the cook-

22. Mulligan, Burbank, and Brunn, "History of Center Compound," Pt. I, sec. 1-h, Pt. III (Diary), October 4, 7, 1944.
23. Report of visit by Dr. Rossel and Dr. Thudichum, November 24–25, 1944, in "Stalag Luft III" Folder, RG 389; Mulligan, Burbank, and Brunn, "History of Center Compound," Pt. III (Diary), January 1, 1945. The granary appears in the background as the only building rising above the tree line in photographs of the camp.

houses, where it would be cooked and then distributed. The problems had already been spelled out by Colonel Spivey in March, when the question of issuing Red Cross food in bulk had come up. The idea was highly impractical since the parcels were designed for consumption over a one-week period, the food would spoil if emptied into large containers, and the cookhouses were not equipped to provide for the entire camp. Perhaps equally important, he concluded with the telling statement that "the preparing of food in barracks has been the greatest single thing to bring contentment and happiness to the prisoners of war. It occupies one-fourth of the prisoners' . . . time during each day and affords much pleasure in enjoying better food."[24]

The prisoners had won their case in March, and after the November order became known, General Vanaman wrote a persuasive letter to the commandant, protesting the most recent attempt to interfere with the prisoners' use of Red Cross food. The order would also remove food that the prisoners received from home. Such items, though unimportant in terms of quantity, were of great value. The food not only helped vary the diet but also assumed "significance [of] huge proportions" in the prisoner's mind "because it [came] from his wife and mother." In addition, he reminded the Germans, it took four or five days to assemble enough food of certain varieties to prepare a satisfactory meal. If the order were carried out, the entire system of preparing meals would at once disappear. Furthermore, he argued, every ounce of the prisoners' meager food savings would be used during "the two approaching great National Holidays, our Harvest Thanksgiving Day and Christmas, both of which are celebrated by nearly every civilized nation." He concluded by saying that it would be considered an injustice to every prisoner of war in the camp if these traditional holidays could not be appropriately remembered by using the food they had saved for this purpose. It is not known what effect Vanaman's letter had on the Germans, but they never instituted the one-day supply order in Stalag Luft III.[25]

The prisoners did have several other sources of food that allowed them to change their diet somewhat. Although the soil was too sandy

---

24. Mulligan, Burbank, and Brunn, "History of Center Compound," Pt. III (Diary), November 16, 1944; Delmar T. Spivey to the Camp Commandant, Stalag Luft III, March 27, 1944, *ibid.*, Pt. I, sec. 1h.
25. Arthur W. Vanaman to O.K.W. through Commandant, Stalag Luft III, November 20, 1944, *ibid.*

to sustain good growth, many of the prisoners planted and cultivated vegetable gardens. With his constant hunger for food, Cy Widen, pilot of the Great Gut, lavished much attention on his garden. He obtained seeds from the Red Cross, the YMCA, and home. They were far easier to come by than was the fertilizer needed to make them grow. When it came to collecting animal droppings—horses pulled the honey wagons used to clean out the latrines—Cy faced tough competition. He and Lieutenant Rivers, in particular, often collided trying to scrape up the same pile of fresh manure. In time, however, he discovered a secret that seemed to give him the edge: horses, he observed, usually defecate when turning corners. Years later, Cy pointed out with a bright twinkle in his eye, "When a horse is moving on the straight-away, it will sometimes lift its tail, but most times it's a false alarm, with just a little *ppsssttt*, you know, to show for it. But when he slows down for the corners—that's when the black gold is most likely to materialize." Furthermore, each gardener sort of staked out his own territory. Cy claimed the area around the cookhouse and barracks 131, where he lived. He watched his ground closely, fully aware that Rivers was apt to come sneaking out from behind a building and scoop up deposits right in Cy's own backyard. Anything on the commonly used camp roads was fair game for everyone, of course. But even there, Cy did well. Using a sturdy wood Canadian Red Cross box cut at an angle like a dustpan and a small paddle fashioned out of sticks, he could, without stopping, reach down and scoop up droppings while on a dead run.

Cy "put a few of those road apples in a bucket of water and let them set a bit, and then poured it on the plants near the roots, early in the morning." Tomatoes in particular produced well, and Cy harvested several hundred from his small plot. He also had great success with onions, a highly sought after seasoning for the prisoners' notoriously bland diet. It gave Cy great pleasure to be able to share a few of his zwiebel with his buddies. He also was pleased that nobody ever stole any of his carefully nurtured produce. In addition, his flower garden became the most colorful spot in the compound. Situated at the edge of the sports field, it became quite a showpiece.[26]

Another source of food was the next-of-kin or personal parcels, which could be sent by relatives every two months postage free and

26. Interview with Widen, April 11, 1979.

could range up to eleven pounds in weight. The contents varied, but the most commonly recommended items were cigarettes, crackers, canned fish and meat, bouillon cubes for broth, chocolate, cheese, condensed milk, and dried fruits and vegetables. As happened with the Red Cross parcels, the food from home was usually shared equally by everyone in a room. These items enabled the prisoners to prepare special dishes and at the same time reminded them of their families.[27] George Sweanor retains fond memories of the first parcel he received from home. It arrived six months after he had been shot down and was the first box received by anyone in his room. By the time he shared its contents with his roommates, not much was left. As one might expect, some things were more important to him than others. "Like a child at Christmas going for the ten-cent toy and ignoring the expensive gifts, I shouted with joy at the sight of a pair of shoe laces," he recalls. "I had been walking around for two months without laces, and these were most welcome." Commenting on the rest of the contents, he stated, "That towel in the corner of the box—instinctively I knew what it hid, and that was something I was not going to share with the five vultures hanging over me. I left the towel in the box as not being too important. Later, I retrieved Mother's fudge, and rationed myself to one piece per day."[28]

An additional source to which prisoners could turn for food was an institution in the camp that became known as Foodaco. Another product of the formative years, Foodaco (originally Food Acco, which stood for "food account") was a Canadian institution that originated at Warburg, a joint army-RAF camp in Silesia. Although running the establishment with utmost integrity, the two individuals who set up Foodaco realized a sizable profit. At Stalag Luft III, Wings Day "nationalized" the business and sent the profits to the kitchen and the messes after a certain amount of the food, cigarettes, and other valuable items traded there were set aside for bribing the Germans. At Foodaco, those with a surplus of one type of food could trade on a

27. For a complete list of items that could be sent by next of kin, as well as the detailed mailing instructions, see James L. Fieser to Chapter Chairman, July 30, 1940, and "Next-of-Kin Prisoner of War Parcels," both in File 619.2/43, Archives Division, American Red Cross Headquarters; Mulligan, Burbank, and Brunn, "History of Center Compound," Pt. I, sec. 1.

28. Sweanor, *Pensionable Time*, 132–33.

point-value system for other types of food. It soon became the center of legitimate camp trading for cigarettes, pipes, cigars, and tobacco.[29]

And there was also the canteen. Food items for the canteen were purchased in bulk from the Germans whenever possible and included vinegar, mustard, pickled vegetables, and, on rare occasions, an unpalatable beer from which all alcohol had been removed. Reportedly the brew was so bad that even the liquor-starved prisoners could not stomach more than a cup or so at one time.[30]

The prisoners put as much effort into preparing the food as they did into obtaining it. The personnel in the compound kitchens handled primarily the German rations and either cooked them in large vats and ovens or distributed them among the prisoners. The kitchens offered very few pieces of equipment for such a large task. In South Compound, for example, the kitchen equipment consisted of ten boilers, two ovens, three cooking pots, fourteen milk cans and fourteen pails (for distributing soup to each of the barracks), four ladles, and five wood pails for washing potatoes. Since this equipment was entirely inadequate for anything approaching a camp mess, almost all the food received in personal and Red Cross parcels, and some of the German rations, were prepared by the prisoners in the barracks. The vats in the kitchens were used mostly to supply hot water for coffee and other "brews" and for washing. Each room could obtain two jugs of hot water each morning, one at noon, and two each afternoon. However, soup made of potatoes, barley, dried vegetables, and meat stock was cooked in the kitchens four times a week and issued at the noon meal. Ground meat was also partially baked in the kitchen ovens before being issued to the blocks.

Within the blocks, the men in each room ran their own mess. The kitchen stoves inside the blocks were woefully inadequate. They offered a heating surface of about three square feet and an oven that could hold two flat pans at a time. Since every room in the block had to rely on the same stove, the cooking times were rotated. The cook for the day from each room had to prepare an entire meal for twelve to sixteen men in about one-half hour. Two rooms shared the stove at one time, and in order to allow everyone time on the stove, some

29. For a fuller account of Foodaco, especially as it was set up and operated in Center Compound, see Mulligan, Burbank, and Brunn, "History of Center Compound," Pt. I, sec. 1-h; Smith, *Mission Escape*, 83.

30. Goodrich, "History of South Compound," Pt. I, sec. 3A (2).

rooms had to eat their evening meal as early as two-thirty in the afternoon while others ate at the fashionably late hour of eight o'clock in the evening.

The prisoners had to rely mostly on handmade cooking and eating utensils. The Germans claimed that the prisoners willfully destroyed what was issued them and refused to replace lost or broken items. The prisoners do admit that many eating utensils were damaged or lost in tunneling and gardening work, but it is also true that the German issue was not adequate. The men had to make special baking pans, eggbeaters, grinders, scrapers, pots, and percolators out of tin. Every compound had its own tinsmiths, who mastered the art of making watertight containers. A surprising amount of effort went into the construction of timesaving devices, such as grinders and crushers.[31]

Chef duty was usually decided by rotation unless someone was a particularly bad cook, in which case the less adept individual "hired" a replacement and offered to do some other chores in his turn. The cook's job was difficult primarily because of the limited time available on the stoves. The communal spirit frequently broke down in the kitchen, and if a cook did not finish in his allotted time, the next man on the schedule usually just removed the uncooked food from the top of the stove and put on his own pots and pans. The unfortunate victim might then spend an hour or more simply scrounging space in which to heat a pot of water. But any cook who was skillful at camouflaging the daily cuisine and making something new out of what was always essentially old usually found the trials at the stove a small price to pay for the hearty appreciation and thanks he received from his roommates. Virtually every prisoner learned something about home economics, and new recipes were constantly invented and passed around. The prisoners usually adopted standard names for their makeshift concoctions. A few of the more popular were Grape-nuts (German bread crumbs roasted in the oven, served as a cereal); noodles or macaroni (Canadian hardtack soaked in water and heated, with cheese, diced Spam, and seasoning); lemon custard pie (condensed milk, Klim, and lemon powder, whipped until smooth); caramel pie (burnt sugar and milk, with cracker crumbs for thickening); snow ice-cream (childhood recipe of snow, condensed milk, sugar, and chocolate); freezer ice-cream (regular recipe, prepared in a freezer constructed of a large German jam can, three Klim cans soldered together, wood or tin paddles, and a bow or wood gears for turning). The ice-cream industry was limited to those periods when the fire pools were frozen. Pulverized crackers were the primary source of "flour" for thickening and for making piecrusts, cakes, and cookies. Baking powder was scarce since it was never issued and few were lucky enough to get some from home. Most cooks used a tooth powder that contained a hint of soda or else had to aerate the batter by tiresome beating—hence the great demand for tin eggbeaters. One source comments, "Occasionally the finished product was light and fluffy. The other extreme was well illustrated by the solid mass which held its shape when a prankster fastened it to the wall with a single nail."[32]

By drawing on all the available food sources and using everything in the best way they knew how, the prisoners had a daily menu that resembled the following:

Breakfast—9:00 A.M.
  Two slices of German bread with spread
  Coffee or tea during lean periods (for the
  Americans—the reverse was true for the
  British)

Lunch—noon
  Soup (3–4 days a week from the camp kitchens)
  Slice of German bread
  Coffee or tea

Supper—2:30–8:30 P.M.
  Potatoes
  $\frac{1}{3}$ can of meat (Spam, corned beef, etc.)
  Vegetables (possibly twice a week)
  Slice of German bread
  Coffee or tea

Evening snack—10:00 P.M.
  Dessert (pie, cake, etc.)
  Coffee or cocoa

32. Goodrich, "History of South Compound," Pt. I, sec. 3A (2).

The prisoners often saved up for a big "bash" on a special occasion such as a birthday or holiday. Elaborate menus were drawn up for such events and usually carried the notice "Due to unforeseen events, Spam has been substituted for the scheduled turkey." In 1943 and 1944 the prisoners received specially prepared Red Cross Christmas parcels and these added greatly to the festivities.

Few manners were displayed at mealtime, and there was never a second helping. But great care was always given to the equal sharing of food, especially when it came to cutting cakes and pies. Usually the man who cut the dessert had to take the last piece as an incentive for him to be judicious in the cutting. Everyone else in the room drew straws to determine who would be first, second, third, and on down the line—just in case some pieces might still be a shade larger than the others.

Everything considered, the prisoners obtained enough food to sustain their health until the fall of 1944. Thereafter they began to lose weight and strength. Because they had been on meager diets all along, their stomachs shrank, and the rare bashes often caused sickness. But if their stomachs were sometimes satisfied, it seems that the same cannot be said for their palates. The pies and cakes were relished, not because they were good by normal standards, but because everything else in their diet was so bland. It is doubtful if a former prisoner would care to eat any of his room-cooked meals today. In Stalag Luft III, as one might well expect, the philosophy the prisoners had to adopt was "eat to live" rather than "live to eat."

It did not take long for new prisoners to learn that the Germans had no intention of observing that part of the Geneva Convention that required the detaining power to furnish clothing and footwear. They also knew that clothing, like food, stood very high on the list of necessities in a prison camp. There were times when the lack of clothing became a serious matter, and again it was the Red Cross that helped the prisoners most.

The prisoners' search for clothes began at Dulag Luft, for it was there that they often had their leather jackets, flying boots, and electrically wired flying suits taken away by the Germans. The Germans refused to permit the prisoners to use their air force uniforms until the spring of 1943, claiming that they were too mufti-looking. To replace the confiscated clothing, the new prisoners were given a sweater, a pair of socks, and a pair of long winter underwear, usually supplied by the British Red Cross. Dulag Luft was supposed to be the main issue point for clothes, but the amounts available there were seldom sufficient. Thus the prisoners usually arrived at Stalag Luft III poorly clothed. Their plight was not serious during the summer, but at the onset of winter the search for adequate clothing became intense. The Germans provided little clothing. The prisoners and the protecting power repeatedly asked the Germans to supply clothes, but the latter's only significant contribution came in the early autumn of 1943. They issued boots and overcoats that were mainly plunder from France and Belgium. In addition, they provided each barracks with about twelve pairs of trousers, which the prisoners could borrow and wear while they washed and dried the one pair they owned. The two blankets they provided each prisoner were thin and inadequate for a northern climate. When pressed, the Germans replied that they would be happy to supply more booty clothes on condition that they be clearly marked and that the prisoners turn in all their other clothes. They adamantly refused to let the prisoners have two sets of clothing, claiming that too often one set was converted to civilian clothes for escape.[33]

Prior to the fall of 1943, the Americans had to rely primarily upon the British Red Cross for clothes. As was the case with food, the British and Commonwealth countries already had a cooperative supply system in operation when the Americans arrived. The clothing store, situated in the Vorlager shared by East and Center, was supervised by Germans and operated by British and American prisoners. The prisoners could put their names on a list for items they needed, and usually when a shipment of clothes arrived it had already been entirely spoken for. Eventually every man in camp acquired a fairly complete set of clothes either through the Red Cross or through gifts from home in next-of-kin parcels. Some men dressed extremely well, some were neat but not well dressed, and some were quite unpresentable.

33.   See Protecting Power Report No. 1, concerning the December 9, 1942, visit by Naville and Schæffeler; Protecting Power Report No. 2, concerning a visit made on March 22–23, 1944, by Gabriel Naville and Dr. Aloys Schnieper, representatives of the Swiss legation at Berlin, and Protecting Power Report No. 3, concerning the July 6–7, 1943, visit by Naville, all in "Stalag Luft III" Folder, RG 389. Also see, in RG 59, report of visit by J. E. Friedrich, September 13, 1942, in File 740.00114 EW/3049; report of visit by Mr. Friedrich and Dr. Bubb, February 22, 1943, in File 740.00114 EW/3977; report of visit by Dr. Lehner, July 26, 1943, in File 711.62114 A.I.R./30; Protecting Power Report No. 4, concerning a visit made on October 25–26, 1943, by Gabriel Naville, representative of the Swiss legation at Berlin, in File 711.62114 A.I.R./53; and Protecting Power Report No. 5, concerning the February 22–24, 1944, visit by Naville, in File 711.62114 A.I.R./137.

The camp goal was to provide everyone with at least an overcoat, a blouse or jacket, three pairs of socks, a pair of wool trousers, three shirts, three pairs of winter underwear, one sweater, one pair of high shoes, a scarf, a pair of gloves, one belt or suspenders, a cap, four handkerchiefs, and one blanket. Since the Red Cross clothes were considered only a loan rather than a gift, the prisoners had to be reminded continually not to modify them. Nevertheless, many of them made cut-offs for the summer rather than putting patches over patches, or converted greatcoats into sports jackets, removing the linings to make athletic shorts, or cut them to obtain materials for hoods and mittens. Part of Spivey's cleanup campaign was directed against slovenly dress and unmended clothes, as well as against the tendency of some men to appear at Appell dressed only in a "ball-bag," a loincloth made out of an old sock and worn for sunbathing.

The military clothing received through the Red Cross was regular enlisted army stock and quite durable, as it needed to be, since a pair of trousers that was worn every day was expected to last one year. However, the American officers felt self-conscious about the fact that they were the only ones in camp who did not receive insignia and proper dress uniforms. A special request was sent, asking for dress uniforms for the compound staff so that they might appear in proper attire before the commandant and at formal gatherings, such as funerals or when acting as escorts for visiting dignitaries. The special uniforms never came, but by borrowing uniform items from various prisoners, they could create several good and complete uniforms for special occasions.

The prisoners also complained that the clothing sent them through official channels was often too small. Out of one shipment of more than one thousand coats, only about 10 percent were size thirty-eight or larger. Another report indicates that a stock of one thousand pajamas offered nothing larger than what a five-year-old child would wear. Shoes also were frequently too small. One survey showed that the average shoe needed in camp was a size nine-C, but that until the summer of 1944 the average available was about a size seven. A special order was filled in Berlin for a man who wore a size thirteen and one-half. [34]

34.   John J. Lee to Delmar T. Spivey, February 27, 1948, in "Red Cross Clothing Store" Folder, Spivey Collection; Mulligan, Burbank, and Brunn, "History of Center Compound," Pt. I, sec. 1-h; Goodrich, "History of South Compound," Pt. I, sec. 3A (3); Delmar T. Spivey to Maurice Pate, May 13, 1944, in File 619.2, "American and Allied POWs-Europe-Germany," Archives Division, American Red Cross Headquarters.

When Cy Widen arrived in Stalag Luft III, he was struck by how remarkably different the prisoners appeared—some were sharp and spiffy, but most were disheveled and scruffy. He decided he would do everything in his power to be one of the spiffy ones. While still in England awaiting transfer to the African theater of operations, Cy met and dated a young lady named Bea West. He wrote to her from Stalag Luft III to ask a favor: "Bea, I'd sure like to get an American uniform—I mean the whole thing. I don't want the pinks; I want a forest green solid looking suit, the insignia, the propellers that designate the Air Corps, the First Lieutenant bars, a couple of shirts if you can do it, and a belt." Bea generously complied, paying for the entire outfit out of her own money. Cy replied immediately, thanking her. He would repay her as soon as he got home, he said, and if for some reason he did not make it, his father would see that she was duly compensated. It arrived in 1943, and he wore it proudly at Appells and on Sunday mornings.[35]

35. Interview with Widen, April 11, 1979.

9

Health and Welfare

Visitors to Stalag Luft III frequently commented on the good state of the prisoners' health. The prisoners, too, were surprised they stayed so healthy. But once again the primary credit belongs not to the Germans but to the Red Cross and to the prisoners themselves.

One Red Cross inspector made note of the "very healthful" climate around Sagan and asserted that the class of prisoners he saw "evidently represent[ed] an elite from the physical point of view."[1] In all important respects, his observations were correct. The camp was located well away from all combat zones, slum districts, and industrial areas. The prisoners complained about the damp rainy spring and cold winter weather, but the climate at Sagan was not unusually harsh. And it is true that the prisoners represented a physical elite, since the physical requirements for fliers have always been among the strictest found in any of the services. But the presence of these two favorable factors did not eliminate the prisoners' worries. They were concerned about their physical well-being and had good reason to be, for the medical care provided in Stalag Luft III was inadequate.

Dr. Clark gave Bub more good advice, saying, "You look in good health, but don't assume you are or will continue to be unless you take special precautions and use every bit of health and nutritional knowledge I have been able to give you in the past, or can give you in the future. Get every minute of sunlight you can on as much of the body as possible. Exercise enough to keep your muscles hard and your circulation in good shape, but not enough to burn up too much food, and fat especially."[2]

The prisoners required health care in several broad areas. Injuries

1. Report of visit by J. E. Friedrich, September 13, 1942, in File 740.00114 EW/3049, RG 59.
2. Albert P. Clark, Sr., to Albert P. Clark, Jr., April 5, 1943, in Clark Collection.

were one of their greatest problems. Many crewmen arrived in camp with combat wounds that either had not been properly dressed or still needed extensive medical attention. The heavy emphasis on sports also added to the number of injuries. The danger of epidemics was another major concern. Large groups settled in one location for an extended period of time have always meant difficulties for armies, and Stalag Luft III was no exception. When crowding occurred, it became increasingly important to combat infectious diseases before they could reach epidemic proportions. Of course, there were the unexpected medical emergencies, as well as the everyday colds and viruses. Dental problems were yet another area of concern. The unbalanced diet contributed to eventual tooth decay, and some of the men had received jaw wounds or other damage to their teeth when they were shot down or later when engaged in sports. Perhaps the area of greatest concern, however, pertained to the treatment of mental cases, usually referred to as victims of barbed wire psychosis.

The Germans made a variety of arrangements for the prisoners' medical and dental care. When the camp opened in 1942, one hut in the Vorlager served as the Revier (infirmary) and the dental office. The Revier contained around forty beds, with about five or six beds in each room. A German doctor supervised the Revier, and two English doctors took care of the patients. Surgical cases were sent to the large French-operated hospital located about one mile away in Stalag VIII C, and X-rays were taken in the local hospital in Sagan. There were two dentists, one German and one British, and about twenty patients a day asked for treatment. Both the facilities and the staff were too small—the capacity of the Revier was less than 2 percent of the prisoner population, and an average of eighty men reported for sick call each day. Medicine was in short supply, and the Red Cross medical parcels were the only adequate source. The Red Cross also supplied invalid-food parcels, which contained white bread and other items needed by those who had to be put on special diets.[3]

Conditions improved briefly in the spring and summer of 1943. In East Vorlager the dental office was moved into a separate building, and the space was filled with more hospital beds until accommodations were completed for about sixty patients. Medical supplies were

3. Protecting Power Report No. 1, concerning the December 9, 1942, visit by Naville and Schaeffeler, in "Stalag Luft III" Folder, RG 389.

increased—the Germans contributed too—and in July a dental prosthetic laboratory was opened in the camp.

The prisoners in the new North Compound received medical care in a seventeen-bed Revier in the Vorlager located just north of the compound. The facilities were shared by North, South, and West compounds. The Revier was manned by two British doctors who were assisted by a number of French and Serbian medical orderlies. The British medical officers asked for and received a large table and blankets for the massage room to help them take care of the patients undergoing therapy.

Despite these improvements, the health care provided the prisoners was still inadequate at times. When inquiries were made on behalf of seven prisoners who needed surgery, the Germans granted permission for only two, saying the others could wait a year or more. In strict terms, they may have been correct, but one patient suffered from repeated tonsillitis, and the German decision in his case hardly seemed justified. In another case, the British medical staff said Sub-Lieutenant John Kiddell needed to be transferred to a private mental hospital. The German authorities, however, refused because their own "experts" found that his problems were not serious or recurrent. Kiddell was killed on July 1, 1943, during "an attempt to escape while at the height of his mania." Endeavoring to flee from the infirmary, he was caught under the barbed wire, and the sentinel, who did not know the prisoner, killed him.[4]

There were some complaints about the non-English-speaking orderlies, but the Germans were reluctant to put British personnel in these jobs because of the constant fear that they might help the prisoners escape. Finally in early 1944, British and American orderlies were admitted in the Reviers. About this time also the first American medical officers arrived. The American prisoners had been cared for by British medical personnel.

The addition of British and Americans to the hospital staffs was one of the few bright spots on an otherwise rather dismal medical scene in

4. The Kiddell case is discussed in report of visit by Dr. Lehner, July 26, 1943, in File 711.62114 A.I.R./30, and report of visit by Mr. Friedrich and Dr. Bubb, February 22, 1943, in File 740.00114 EW/3977, both RG 59. The other information pertaining to the care provided in the spring and summer of 1943 is extracted from those reports and Protecting Power Report No. 3, concerning the July 6–7, 1943, visit by Naville, in "Stalag Luft III" Folder, RG 389.

1944. It is true that on July 1, 1944, the Germans opened a new 60-bed facility in West Vorlager and continued to add to it, with the aim of eventually providing 150 beds, but the influx of new prisoners was so great that the facilities were never adequate. Medicine again became scarce. Dental parades were reduced from three to two per week because of the shortage of guards, and the waiting time for dental work increased from only a few days in the summer of 1943 to several months by the end of 1944. East Revier had deteriorated and was badly in need of repair. The beds were basically the same hard mattresses used in the barracks, and consequently the patients developed bedsores. As overcrowding became widespread among the compounds, the danger of epidemics grew. And as some of the older prisoners began to mark off their fourth and fifth years in captivity, the number of mental cases increased. The only chance of reducing the instances of barbed-wire psychosis would have been to increase the number of parole walks or begin a program of repatriating prisoners after they had been in captivity a certain length of time. Both these sources of relief were sought, but to no avail. The only prisoners who were repatriated were a few individuals who went before a mixed medical commission and were judged medically unsuited for further incarceration.[5]

Ralph Saltsman, a prisoner in Center Compound, remembers one insanity case in particular. One of Saltsman's jobs was to evaluate escape ideas and intelligence plans. One day a flier by the name of Robin E. Tabor came to him with the proposal that the prisoners establish a weather station to tell the Allies what the weather was like in that part of Germany. Tabor did not address the question of how the information could be gotten to the Allies without the Germans knowing about it. Saltsman thought Tabor's shortsightedness a little unusual but said nothing about it.

5. No figures are available on how many prisoners were repatriated from Stalag Luft III, but it is known that at least three groups of various sizes left the camp for home. For accounts of how the repatriation system worked, as well as the deteriorating medical conditions after the fall of 1943, see Goodrich, "History of South Compound," Pt. I, sec. 3B (2); Mulligan, Burbank, and Brunn, "History of Center Compound," Pt. I, sec. 1-i; Protecting Power Report No. 4, concerning the October 25–26, 1943, visit by Navalle, in File 711.62114 A.I.R./53, RG 59; Protecting Power Report No. 5, concerning the February 22–24, 1944, visit by Naville, in File 711.62114 A.I.R./137, RG 59; Protecting Power Report No. 8, concerning a visit made on November 7, 1944, by Albert A. Kadler, representative of the Swiss legation at Berlin, in "Stalag Luft III" Folder, RG 389.

Later Tabor came to Ralph with a substance he called ersatz rubber that supposedly could be used for making forgery stamps. Ralph found that it would indeed stretch and resume its place. Approached by two German ferrets at that point, Saltsman stuck the substance in his pocket. When the Germans left about twenty minutes later, he reached into his pocket and discovered a gooey mess. It turned out to be fatty meat that had had all the water boiled out of it and then been allowed to cool. However, when put next to moisture and heat, it returned to its original fatty form.

Tabor then exhibited a series of frustrations about which the doctors became concerned. When they took him out to be examined by the German medical staff, he showed all the signs of going berserk. The Germans recommended his repatriation for reasons of mental instability, and he left in the summer of 1944. About two or three months later, Ralph recalls, a postcard arrived in camp from their friend Tabor with the short comment, "Who's crazy now!"[6]

The Americans suffered less from barbed-wire psychosis than the British did, primarily because they were not in captivity as long and because their families and homes were not being subjected to bombing raids. One doctor who spent considerable time in Center Compound stated that there were fewer mental abnormalities among the prisoners in Center than there were in any civilian group of comparable size. The prisoners attributed this to the thorough screening crew members received before they were ever allowed to fly. In addition, fliers were carefully watched by their fellows to ensure that shaky individuals were taken off the flight rosters before each mission so as not to jeopardize the mission and other crew members.[7]

The prisoners set up first-aid stations in each compound to screen patients asking to go to the Revier and to take care of minor medical matters and physical therapy cases. Usually the first-aid stations were manned by individuals who had had medical experience before capture. Every effort was made to obtain medical books so that they might increase their knowledge both to help them do a better job while in camp and to prepare them for further training, if they desired, after they returned home. In some instances, a fully qualified medical doctor also served in the first-aid stations. The work load here was also very heavy, the records showing that in South Com-

6. Interview with Ralph Saltsman, July 17, 1979.
7. Mulligan, Burbank, and Brunn, "History of Center Compound," Pt. I, sec. 1-i.

pound alone more than twenty thousand requests for medical assistance were answered in a one-year period.[8]

Upon arrival at Stalag Luft III, the new prisoners were often shocked and dismayed by the sight of those already in residence, many of whom were unshaven, had long dirty-looking hair or haircuts of weird design, and wore unkempt clothes. The new prisoners were themselves tired, unshaven, and dirty, but were usually filled with resolve that they would never "let themselves go." They were soon to learn, however, that this was easier said than done.

Most of the new men were deloused and allowed to shower before they entered a compound. After that they were on their own and quickly discovered that the authorized one hot shower per week was seldom forthcoming. Cy Widen recalls:

You'd go down to the shower house and strip together. Two or three were apportioned to each shower head. You'd grab the soap and get ready, and then they'd turn the shower on for a brief time, two or three minutes. After they turned the shower off you'd lather up, and if the shower dripped you might get a few more drops of water to help the sudsing along. They'd then turn the water back on for two or three minutes so we could rinse off. But being there were two or three of us per shower head, we'd each get barely a minute to get all the soap out of our hair and off our bodies. And that was the end of our long-awaited shower.[9]

In spite of the brevity of the showers, long lines assembled for the shower parades into the Vorlager, and in cold weather the rewards hardly seemed worth the effort. The shower huts in North and South compounds could not be used for months on end because the proper pipe fittings or boilers were missing. In North Compound the prisoners were not allowed to go on shower parades for several months because of an attempted escape by men who left the compound on a fictitious delousing parade in July, 1943. In South Compound it took so long to get the shower hut working that many men went more than a year without a hot shower. Colonel Goodrich, in fact, cannot recall ever having taken a hot shower during the entire thirty-four-month period he was at Sagan.[10]

The alternative was to take sponge baths or cold showers. Since the water table at Sagan was about three hundred feet below the surface,

8.   *Ibid.*; Goodrich, "History of South Compound," Pt. I, sec. 3B (2).
9.   Interview with Widen, April 11, 1979.
10.   Interview with Goodrich, November 18, 1975.

the water was extremely cold. Few men stayed under the sprinkler buckets attached to the spigots for more than a minute or two. In winter, cold showers were understandably forsaken altogether. Sponge baths were preferred, but here too water was a problem. It had to be heated on the busy kitchen stoves, which became free, if at all, only late at night. Soap was extremely scarce in Germany, but the prisoners received ample amounts from the Red Cross and from home. All in all, bathing was possible but easily postponed.

Shaving was another unusually difficult chore. There were very few razor blades available, obtaining hot water was always a problem, and shaving facilities in the washrooms were limited. One prisoner recalls, "The luxuries of an early morning shave in the washroom were enjoyed only by those who got up before Appell. Sweating out a basin and mirror after Appell, a man could stand there all morning, awaiting his turn, watching his lukewarm water getting colder." When one of the basins was empty, a waiting Kriegie placed his can on the sink and lathered up his face, using the Klim tin of water for steaming up his face, softening his beard, and brushing up the suds. Once the actual shaving began, the razor was sloshed in the can to rinse free soap and beard. Ice-cold water from the taps served as an astringent and skin conditioner. Often a couple of "buddies" would lean over the same basin, sharing the same hard-to-come-by water.[11] Because of these difficulties, men often shaved in their rooms, hunched over small mirrors propped up on tables or in front of the windows.

Haircuts were largely a matter of personal taste and convenience. At first, there was a shortage of barber's instruments, and in a few of the compounds enlisted men used whatever was available to cut their own and their comrades' hair. In time the YMCA supplied enough clippers for nearly every block. But when these wore out, the prisoners had to rely on the services of a few individuals who had gotten implements in their personal parcels and had set up barbershops. The most frequent solution, however, was for the prisoners to borrow the scissors and clippers and cut each other's hair.

Many prisoners chose to wear their hair long, but in the summer months it was not unusual to see numerous shaved heads. Novel designs sometimes appeared, either as personal experimentation or

11.   Kimball and Chiesl, *Clipped Wings,* n.p.

as the price of a lost wager. Mohawk cuts were seen quite frequently, but the ones that caught the most attention had one side of the head shaved and the other side untrimmed. Colonel Spivey stirred some controversy soon after he arrived when he proclaimed, "I hate hairy people," he himself being partially bald. Soon almost all the beards and handlebar moustaches in Center Compound disappeared. The compound historians noted in their log: "After his announcement, the appearance of the men improved, and we realized definitely that ours was not a prison camp in the old traditional sense of the word. Anyhow we could afford to leave the growing of beards and handlebars to the British. They were better at it than we."[12]

When East and Center compounds first opened, clothes were sent out to a laundry shop in Sagan. As the prisoner population increased, the shop could not handle the work load, and sometimes two months passed before the prisoners got their clothes back. By the time North Compound opened, the prisoners were doing most of their own laundry, and nearly all of it was done in camp by early 1944.

It was hard to keep one's clothes clean when the same ones had to be worn virtually every day. As noted earlier, the Germans distributed to each barracks some trousers for the prisoners to wear while they washed their own. Again, obtaining hot water took time and the washhouse was usually crowded. In South Compound, for example, an average of two hundred men used the cement basins and troughs every day. An alternative method was the bucket washer, which was nothing more than a large tin can with a smaller can inside that was attached and could be worked up and down by a broom handle to agitate the soapy water.

Fortunately, the prisoners received a bar in every Red Cross parcel, and later GI soap began to arrive in large quantities. There was no reason why a prisoner could not keep clean, but washing clothes, like taking showers, was an easy task to postpone, and many men accordingly never did look neat and clean.[13]

The individual rooms were cleaned by the occupants, usually on a rotational basis. Cleaning supplies were hard to come by, but the task

12.   Goodrich, "History of South Compound," Pt. I, sec. 3B (11); Mulligan, Burbank, and Brunn, "History of Center Compound," Pt. I, sec. 1-g.

13.   Kimball and Chiesl, *Clipped Wings*, n.p.; Goodrich, "History of South Compound," Pt. 1, sec. 3B (5); Mulligan, Burbank, and Brunn, "History of Center Compound," Pt. I, sec. 1-f.

had to be undertaken regularly in order to keep the bedbugs and lice under control. A typical monthly issue of cleaning materials for the entire camp included eighteen brooms, twenty deck scrubs, fifteen hand scrubs, three to four kilograms Carbolineum, and twenty-five kilograms chlorical.

The brooms were of especially poor quality and the supply wore out quickly. So before a prisoner could sweep out his room, he had to go to considerable lengths to get "next" on the broom. The rooms often received a very thorough cleansing in the spring just after the cold weather broke. One prisoner describes the process: "Furniture was removed from the rooms. Walls, ceilings and floors were completely swabbed down. Men of one room would form a bucket brigade from the kitchen, slosh bucket after bucket onto the walls and floors and scrub and clean away the winter's grime and soot. Windows were washed and shined sparkling clean with newspapers."[14]

Another account adds that in an effort to get rid of the bedbugs and lice the same procedure was followed, only with a little more thoroughness. It involved "removal of all furniture, dissembl[ing] of wall and ceiling panels and wooden bedsteads as well as the removal and changing of wood ticking in paliasses (mattress)[sic] and airing of bedclothes and linen. All suspected or confirmed hiding places of the offenders were swabbed and soaked with creosote or strong soap solutions. . . . The above duty accomplished by nightfall, weary prisoners tossed their last chair through the open window, followed it, and crept into their beds—with a silent prayer on each pair of lips for a few nights uninterrupted sleep."[15]

In addition to bedbugs and lice, the prisoners had to combat the sanitation problems created by the appearance of common houseflies, bluebottle and greenbottle flies, and mosquitoes. Screens were unavailable, so the prisoners' efforts were bent toward eliminating the insects' breeding and feeding grounds and preventing the bugs from carrying disease to the mess table.

Following the practice Clark started in East Compound, all the latrines were ventilated and sealed off with burlap as much as possible. Springs from exercise machines sent by the YMCA were attached to the latrine doors to keep them closed, and flytraps were installed. In South Compound, at least, a crew thoroughly scrubbed

14.   Kimball and Chiesl, *Clipped Wings*, n.p.
15.   Goodrich, "History of South Compound," Pt. I, sec. 3B (3).

and cleaned the aborts daily while others attended to the garbage disposal areas and incinerators.[16]

South Compound benefited from Clark's continual emphasis on such matters, based in part, it seems, on his father's earnest prompting. In April, 1943, Dr. Clark advised: "Fight flies at source—they breed in warm, moist, contaminated spots and look like tiny white or gray worms (maggots). They take the color of wet muck in which they develop from eggs so small you can't see them. It takes seven to ten days from egg to fly. Keep flies out of warm, moist places by killing all adults. Keep them from hatching by burning the warm, moist places if you can't dry them up. Build fly traps and bait them with scraps of wet smelly food. Flies can't stand being dried. Fly larvae can't stand heat. Wood and coal ashes contain lye and kill flies while breeding."[17]

Von Lindeiner genuinely appreciated Clark's contribution to improving the latrines but noted that here again the shortage of material made it almost impossible to procure screens for the windows. Von Lindeiner felt somewhat trapped. Between Stalag Luft III and the nearby Stalag VIII C, there were about 35,000 persons in the area, and the waste extracted from the latrines was hauled less than two miles into the woods and dumped there. After about a year of concerted effort he felt that a somewhat more suitable sewer system had been devised. But this accomplishment did not sit well with the town of Sagan, which had no sewer system either. The best he could do was to appease their tempers by pointing out that the system built for Stalag Luft III reduced the risk of sickness for the townspeople.[18]

The prisoners had to keep after the Germans to ensure that the pit-latrines were emptied on schedule. When the honey wagon finally came, the men were both pleased and displeased, for the odor stirred up was truly nauseating. The prisoners always marveled at the seeming indifference of the German civilians contracted to do this unpleasant task, especially when they noticed the workers eating their lunches without leaving the pump.

One last sanitation item that deserves mention had to do with the barracks area. The Europeans objected to the filthy American habit of spitting on the ground. The Americans in turn objected to the

16. *Ibid.*
17. Albert P. Clark, Sr., to Albert P. Clark, Jr., April 5, 1943, in Clark Collection.
18. Von Lindeiner, "Memoirs," 198.

guards' promiscuous urinating, especially in the same places where the Americans were not supposed to spit. Another difference between German and American habits surfaced when the Germans volunteered to let the prisoners put the contents of the aborts on the camp gardens. The offer was declined, and the prisoners let their requests for horse manure stand.[19]

The prisoners' internal administrative system, the food they ate, the clothes they wore, the medical treatment they received, and the measures they undertook to maintain their health and observe the basic rules of good sanitation were all affected by several incidentals in the supply system with which the new prisoner had to acquaint himself.

The Red Cross clothing store, for example, handled more than simply clothes. Through this facility passed most of the toilet articles and other miscellaneous items which the men used—toothpaste, toothbrushes, soap, combs, shaving cream, razor blades and razors, toilet paper, shoelaces, shoe repair materials and tools. On one occasion, some twelve tons of toilet tissue were received in one shipment. One of the store workers reports that the shipment completely filled two freight cars and that when it was unloaded in the store, the floors sagged as much as six inches. The paper was extremely welcome since the Germans daily supplied only one small sheet (about four by four inches). Colonel Spivey recalls that when a much smaller quantity had earlier arrived by train, the staff in Center decided to issue four sheets a day to each man. In order to be fair about the matter, one of the store workers brought a whole roll to Spivey's office, where the

19.   Goodrich, "History of South Compound," Pt. I, sec. 3A (1). The spitting problem became so serious that General Vanaman felt compelled to have Colonel Spivey issue the following memorandum on December 8, 1944: "It is desired to bring to the attention of all concerned the filthy and vulgar habit of spitting. Many contagious diseases are transferable by this means and if for no other reason it should be cut to the minimum. It is the duty of each individual in this compound to carefully consider the health, comfort and welfare of every other individual and to never wantonly or willfully, by act or word, do or say anything that will make this already miserable life more intolerable. You are therefore urged to carefully consider the low and uncouth habit of expectorating at random and if you must hawk or spit have the decency to cover it or spit over the guard rail. Under no circumstances are you to commit this vile act within doors or on public walks" (Mulligan, Burbank, and Brunn, "History of Center Compound," Pt. III [Diary], December 8, 1944). The Germans did use the prisoners' "night soil" in a large cabbage and potato garden situated in East Vorlager. The prisoners objected to eating the produce from it but their protests were ignored (interview with Clark, April 15, 1976).

worker and three full colonels painstakingly unrolled it and counted the sheets. Somewhat beside himself, Spivey grumbled, "The blamed stuff was all over our room and when we finally rerolled it, it was as big as a nail keg. I think I caught as much hell from the boys for rationing TP as I did for any other thing I ever did in camp."[20]

Toilet articles could also be obtained through the canteen. The canteen offered quite a variety of items during the early years of the war, but by the time the Americans arrived, the large stocks of meerschaum pipes, straight razors, fine china, wooden shoes, and other luxuries bought on the German market were exhausted. All supplies were ordered through a central purchasing office that was run by the British until June, 1944, and thereafter by the Americans. When the goods arrived, they were distributed to each compound according to its strength. Every compound had its own canteen, and each block had its own canteen officer to whom toothbrushes, tooth powder, shaving equipment, and other items were given as requested. When special shipments came in, issues again were made to each of the blocks according to strength. Sometimes the canteen benefited prisoners indirectly and made their lives brighter by providing items such as paint for the theater interior and sets, varied music supplies, sanitation aids, and some of the spices and seasonings used in the cookhouses.[21]

Items in large quantities and of every description came to the prisoners through the YMCA store in the Vorlager. Although concerned primarily with providing religious, athletic, educational, and entertainment materials, the YMCA answered innumerable miscellaneous requests for items ranging all the way from medical supplies, such as crutches and prescription eyeglasses, to wristwatches and model kits.[22] All incoming goods were carefully inventoried and distributed according to everybody's needs. As far as possible, the British and Americans each received the materials sent by their respective countries, but there were exceptions to this rule, espe-

20.   Lee to Spivey, February 27, 1948, in "Red Cross Clothing Store" Folder, Spivey Collection; Spivey, *POW Odyssey*, 56.

21.   Goodrich, "History of South Compound," Pt. I, sec. 3B (8).

22.   An extensive collection of order forms for miscellaneous items requested through YMCA channels is found in several uncataloged folders contained in the "Prisoners of War" Drawer, in the Research Division, Air Force Museum, Wright-Patterson Air Force Base, Ohio.

cially when a new compound opened and everyone contributed items to help the prisoners assigned there get started with their many tasks.

Other incidentals that affected camp life from day to day can be viewed through the unending battles between the prisoners and the Germans over the use and abuse of items listed on individual and group property accounts. The Germans were most reluctant to replace broken items and were extremely slow when it came to completing needed repairs. These were battles that the prisoners, through no fault of their own, almost always lost.

Poor lighting was one of the worst features of Stalag Luft III. Each sleeping room had either one 60- or two 40-watt bulbs, and the indoor washrooms, latrines, and kitchens had mostly 15-watt bulbs. For a long time, the electricity was shut off completely during daylight hours, but after the prisoners promised not to use the lights in the barracks, the electricity was left on all day so that artificial lighting would be available in the libraries, reading rooms, and classrooms.

The low wattage was in itself a problem, but the real difficulty came in obtaining replacements for burned-out bulbs and getting faulty wiring fixed. According to one report, "With an average German issue of 22 bulbs per month and a monthly shortage of 75 to 100 bulbs, many rooms that should have burned 80 watts could get only a single 15-watt bulb issue."[23] In most compounds, lights were taken out of the hallways and latrines for use in the rooms. The Germans charged that the prisoners were abusing the lighting system either through carelessness or by tapping into the wiring for tunnel lights. Colonel von Lindeiner complained that in East Compound, where there were 160 sockets, the prisoners obtained during one period, mostly without his approval, 167 bulbs, which represented a 120 percent yearly use rate. No wonder he was upset—the Germans estimated that a light bulb should normally last three years! In this case, most of the evidence seems to favor the prisoners' argument that they were not to blame. In July, 1943, a Red Cross inspector reported that the lighting was below standard because the current was weak. Tunnel wiring might have had something to do with it, but the wiring problems the prisoners detected in the existing system were the more likely answer. The list included electric leads into blocks not properly

23.   Goodrich, "History of South Compound," Pt. I, sec. 3A (4).

joined, junction boxes that were broken and caused much shorting, inside wires that became wet because of leaking roofs, loose barracks flooring and construction that caused constant jarring of light fixtures, thus weakening filaments. Thirty fuses burned out from overloading, and questionable voltage control resulted in unsteady and flickering lights. Fortunately, the YMCA was able to send a large quantity of bulbs into the camp. The number was never sufficient, but the addition from the YMCA did improve matters greatly.[24]

Window panes were another item that was seldom replaced. The prisoners admit to breaking some with carelessly thrown balls, and in Center Compound a regulation prohibited all activities in and around the barracks that endangered the windows. What they did not accept, however, was the reluctance on the part of the German staff to supply adequate amounts of wood to cover the openings left by the broken panes. In Center Compound alone, there were 281 broken panes by January, 1945.[25]

The prisoners did as much of their own repair work as possible, organizing compound utility crews and repair shops staffed with competent electricians, carpenters, and tinsmiths. They repaired bedsteads, built extra tables, shelves, and other furniture, cleaned the indoor latrines (often clogged by newspapers used in the absence of toilet tissue), replaced sections of roofing torn off by high winds, repaired faucets, rigged and maintained the tin-can showers, and served as troubleshooters for minor electrical failures in the blocks. Tools for these various tasks were usually obtained from the Germans on parole, but a few items also were sent by the YMCA or in personal parcels.[26]

Tools were also acquired on parole from the Germans to clear stumps from the athletic fields and procure wood for fuel. The shortage of coal was constantly reported to the protecting-power representatives who, in this instance, seemed inclined to take the German side of the argument. During the winter of 1942–1943, they acknowl-

24. Report of visit by Dr. Lehner, July 26, 1943, in File 711.62114 A.I.R./30, and report of visit by Mr. Friedrich and Dr. Bubb, February 22, 1943, in File 740.00114 EW/3977, RG 59; Goodrich, "History of South Compound," Pt. I, sec. 3A (4); Mulligan, Burbank, and Brunn, "History of Center Compound," Pt. I, sec. 1-c.

25. Mulligan, Burbank, and Brunn, "History of Center Compound," Pt. I, sec. 1-c; Goodrich, "History of South Compound," Pt. I, sec. 3A (4).

26. Goodrich, "History of South Compound," Pt. I, sec. 3A (4); Spivey, POW Odyssey, 63.

edged that "the coal ration cannot have been sufficient" in Center Compound, but stated that the situation was not as serious as it was in the internees' or repatriables' camps. In any case no representation would be made to the German authorities, as the coal supply was the same for German troops. On one occasion when the matter was discussed with the camp authorities, they defended their actions by pointing to the findings of a recent commission. The conclusions were that 26.4 pounds of coal would be sufficient as a daily supply, that the 33 pounds given to the prisoners each day (at the time) was a liberal ration, and that the prisoners "had any amount of wood at their disposal would they only be prepared to collect it."[27]

The prisoners in turn questioned the quality of the coal. What they received was the final product of the great coal-conversion plants in Germany after the ingredients to produce synthetic oil, margarine, and countless other items were extracted. The one-pound bricks retained little of their original qualities outside of color, and they lacked heating power, especially when used in small quantities.

The stumps augmented the coal supply, and the Germans asserted that prisoners could go out on parole to collect wood. There is nothing in the available records to verify that such trips were in fact allowed, but there are numerous accounts of the difficulty of pulling the stumps. One prisoner recalled:

The Germans provided a large stump puller for this bulldozer task. Monstrous and grotesque, the stump puller, a tall wooden derrick, was operated and moved about by sheer bodily force. . . . The derrick stood ten feet high and had two twelve foot long wooden lever arms extending from the top. They were connected to . . . [a] long iron lifting rod that ran down the center of the derrick; at the end of this rod, a heavy iron chain and a clasp hook . . . was used to fasten around and under the roots of the stump. A ditch about two to three feet deep was dug all around the stump down to the larger roots, allowing enough room to work in. The thicker roots were sawed through before trying to lift out the stump.

Then the serious work began.

With the chain fastened snugly around the stump, five men at each lever arm on either side alternately raised and lowered their levers. To get the gripping irons to bite firmly on the iron lifting rod, the men at one arm stood on tip toe

27. Protecting Power Report No. 3 concerning the July 6–7, 1943, visit by Naville, in "Stalag Luft III" Folder, RG 389; report of visit by Mr. Friedrich and Dr. Bubb, February 22, 1943, in File 740.00114 EW/3977, and report of visit by J. E. Friedrich, September 13, 1942, in File 740.00114 EW/3049, both RG 59.

and threw the arm upward. Then they jumped up, grabbed hold of the arm and with their combined weight, pulled it down to the ground. This applied force to the lifting rod and caused the stump to be pulled slightly upward. While they held their arm down to the ground, the five men at the other arm, tossed theirs up into the air and repeated the procedure. The chain had to be readjusted several times before the stump was lifted cleanly from the hole. If a room averaged two stumps during their morning session with the stump puller, Kriegies' aching backs, blistered hands and tired muscles screamed to let them know they'd had a workout.[28]

Once the stumps were out of the ground, the prisoners dragged them over to the barracks. Then, whenever a room's turn on the axes and saws came around, two or three men at a time hacked away at the roots and the base of the stumps.

The prisoners found other ways to keep warm. Uniforms were remodeled for warmth; lower halves of overcoats were cut off and fashioned into hoods, paper was sewn into linings, and large gloves were tailored out of scraps of material.[29]

Clark was one of the "cold sleepers" who found it worthwhile to prepare a sleeping bag. Shredding many issues of the *Völkischer Beobachter*, he placed the paper between his two blankets, sewed up the edges, quilted the puffy bag to keep the paper in place, folded the blankets over, and sewed the bottom and one side. Getting into the bag was a bit of a problem for someone with Clark's long torso. But he did not want his flannel pajama bottoms to come out of the sweat socks holding them in place or his pajama top to be pulled out of the bottoms where it was properly cinched. But when he finally settled in, he undoubtedly slept more comfortably than most.[30]

Colonel von Lindeiner repeatedly told the Red Cross and protecting-power inspectors that the prisoners were entirely unreasonable in their requests for supplies: he was being asked to give them five times as much as German troops would normally receive.[31] There is no indication whether he meant that figure to be taken literally or figuratively. At any rate, it would be difficult to substantiate or to deny his claim without conducting extensive research on the German military supply system. But it is easy to understand the prisoners'

28. Kimball and Chiesl, *Clipped Wings*, n.p.
29. *Ibid.*; Spivey, *POW Odyssey*, 59–60.
30. Bob Stillman to Alfred F. Hurley, July 3, 1974, in Clark Collection.
31. See, for example, report of visit by Dr. Lehner, July 26, 1943, in File 711.62114 A.I.R./30, RG 59.

point of view that they were only asking for what the Germans should have provided if they wished to boast that they were observing all the provisions of the Geneva Convention. The prisoners in Stalag Luft III did not suffer from material want as much as did many prisoners in Germany. But they were quite correct in saying that when it came to responding to their physical needs, the Germans did not live up to their usual reputation for efficiency. With regard to obtaining the necessities, as well as the normal comforts of life, Spivey spoke for all the prisoners when he confessed that "the inability to get anything accomplished by the Germans or to get their permission to do it ourselves nearly drove me to distraction at times."[32]

32.   Spivey, *POW Odyssey*, 50.

10

Man to Man

A wide range of factors affected relations between the prisoners and their captors. Perhaps the most important was their attitude toward each other. The prisoners were surprisingly frank in this matter, admitting that "the attitude of the German authorities always depended directly upon whether or not the prisoners were giving trouble.... As long as there was no escape activity apparent and camp regulations were being followed the Germans were prepared to grant privileges and relax restrictions." No wonder, then, that the Germans earned a reputation for granting few privileges and imposing numerous restrictions on the prisoners. In Colonel Spivey's words, the prisoners loved nothing better than to "start a fight with the German administration." Referring to the times he had to rely on the men in Center Compound to support him in his frequent battles with the German administration, Spivey continued, "I never had any difficulties with the prisoners in this respect. It was only when I ordered them to do something which seemed to them to be cooperating with the Germans that I had grave problems."[1] Colonel Goodrich found the same attitude among the prisoners under his command: "It was found that encouragement by the Senior Officer of anti-German activity had value as a morale booster. The POW always derived great satisfaction in knowing that he had, or anybody had, put something over on the Germans." Speaking with the voice of experience, he added, "It was a delicate matter for the Seniors, however, to align policies that would not bring on too many reprisals from the Germans and yet leave the POW with the feeling of active opposition."[2]

Escape was the most potent form of anti-German activity, but there

1. Goodrich, "History of South Compound," Pt. I, sec. 2B; Spivey, *POW Odyssey*, 64.
2. Goodrich, "History of South Compound," Pt. I, sec. 2B.

were many less dramatic, but nevertheless effective, ways of being noncooperative. By far the favorite was goon baiting, that is, doing whatever one could to upset the German routine and general sense of composure. The forms of activity ranged from humorous to barbaric. On the humorous side was an incident inspired by Jerry Sage, an American who gained a reputation as an avid escaper. A short distance from Stalag Luft III was an Arbeitskorps (German work camp similar to those associated with the Civilian Conservation Corps in the United States), and every morning the young Nazis tramped to their work along the road just outside the camp, shovels over their shoulders, smartly in step, and singing Nazi marching songs. Sage gathered together about two hundred men every morning. They all stood near the fence, smirked offensively, and noisily sang "Heigh-ho, heigh-ho, it's off to work we go." After four days the Germans changed their route.[3]

One of the prisoners' favorite goon-baiting practices was to get everyone in a room busily engaged in some activity after the lights were turned off at night but just before the German guards came through the barracks on their nightly bed check. Several prisoners sat around the table playing cards, another mended his clothes, one was reading a book, and the rest were occupied with various tasks. His curiosity aroused by seeing the prisoners so busy in the pitch-dark room, the guard invariably flashed his light on the scene. The prisoners squinted, shading their eyes, and rebuked him for making it so bright that nobody could work. The guard would wonder even more about those "crazy Americans" or, even better yet, would worry that something was going on—something to do with escape—that he obviously was missing.[4]

The prisoners recognized early that the Germans generally were a proud people, and many were downright vain. One day an especially haughty sergeant strutted through South Compound. Knowing how much German soldiers loved American cigarettes, an American one day lit up a Camel. Chaplain Daniel tells how the prisoner "took one or two draws and then flipped it out of his window into the path of the haughty Oberfeldwebel. The battle was on between the sergeant's appetite for nicotine and his enormous pride. Would he ignore the delicious aroma of the smoking cigarette or would he humble him-

3. Brickhill, *The Great Escape*, 49.
4. Interview with John M. Storer, April 19, 1975.

self, bend over to the ground in the presence of the prisoners and pick up a 'duck' which had already been smoked by a lowly American 'Luftgangster'?" The prisoners watched with glee as he fidgeted and squirmed and then finally bent down and picked up "the fag" and put it to his own lips. As might be expected, the story was related throughout the camp, with all sorts of embellishments, for days.[5]

One of the more serious forms of goon baiting was harassing the ferrets as they probed their way around the compounds looking for tunnels. A few weeks after his arrival, Spivey looked out his window and saw five or six men scurrying between the kitchen and their barracks, carrying pitchers full of boiling water.

It was unusual since it was not teatime nor mealtime, so I concluded they were carrying water to scrub the barracks. About five minutes later, the German Abwehr (guard) sergeant who was in charge of the ferrets . . . came tearing into my room in the greatest possible state of excitement. I had had several conversations with this man, and as with the commandant, had reached an agreement as to procedure in dealing with men in trouble in my camp. In all cases other than escapes I would be consulted before he took any direct action. So in keeping with this understanding he had to come to find me. Only a German would have kept his word under similar circumstances. At his urgent request I followed him at a dead run to the barracks into which the hot water had been flowing so rapidly from the hot-water kitchen.

There Spivey found the source of the commotion. "The barracks, which was built on pillars about three feet tall to allow searching parties to go under it, was practically empty except for eight or ten Americans madly dashing boiling water on the floor and yelling such incoherent clauses as 'Here's the SOB,' 'more water,' 'teach the bastard a lesson,' 'scald the SOB,' 'don't let the skunk escape,' and 'watch the exit.'" Seeing that the German sergeant was too excited and angry to talk, Spivey called a halt. The men responded, "Why in hell do you have to appear just when we are having a little fun?" The prisoners explained that they had caught a ferret eavesdropping under the barracks and were merely teaching him to mind his own business. Having a somewhat broader perspective, Spivey said that "the poor ferret was in agony since he couldn't escape without exposing himself to a full pitcher of scalding water, and he couldn't defend himself since he wasn't allowed to carry arms in the camp, so he was trying to change his position under the barracks often enough to

5. Daniel, *In the Presence*, 72.

avoid the hot water." Spivey ended his narrative with the revealing comment, "This incident and many to follow could have resulted in severe action being taken had it not been for the good relations we had with the German administration at this time [summer 1943]."[6]

Those good relations were jeopardized by the worst kind of goon baiting, such as the time the prisoners put broken razor blades into the garbage to make sure that it could not be fed to the neighboring farmers' pigs. Virtually none of the senior prisoners condoned this type of goon baiting and even took the German side whenever it was discovered. As Spivey pointed out, in addition to being barbaric, such actions served no good purpose and only put the prisoners' few privileges at risk. If provoked sufficiently, the Germans could cut off the prisoners' rations altogether, and in this respect they held the trump card.

However, the prisoners were not the only ones whose actions created strained relations between the captors and their captives. In many instances the prisoners' hostile attitudes clearly stemmed less from the Germans' being the enemy than from how certain German personnel acted in camp. And the captives were angered not so much by new rules as by the German practice of enforcing such rules before they had been announced to the prisoners. Too often it was a case of the guards being told to shoot prisoners for doing something the prisoners did not know was a punishable offense.

The worst German aggression was to shoot into the compound either at random or with the intent to kill. The prisoners understood and accepted the Germans' shooting at anyone who got too close to the wire, though they understandably protested the Germans' refusal to fire a warning shot first. The men shot near the wire were usually there during escape attempts and they knew the risks involved. But there also were instances where the Germans fired at prisoners who were retrieving a ball that rolled beyond the warning wire, and sometimes this occurred even after an individual had secured permission to cross the wire. And in at least one case a prisoner was shot through the hand while walking with his hand on the wire.[7]

Far more serious were the acts of firing directly into the compound. The shooting usually came in conjunction with air-raid alerts. When

6. Spivey, *POW Odyssey*, 46.
7. Interview with Clark, April 15, 1976; Clark and Schrupp interview with Glemnitz, April 9–10, 1984 (MS in Clark Collection).

the siren sounded, the prisoners were supposed to move indoors immediately and remain there until the all clear sounded. If the men did not seem to be moving fast enough, or even if they peered out the doors or windows and the Germans saw them, a hail of bullets would likely as not be directed into the barracks. There were three such incidents in South Compound alone, the first resulting in a severe wound, the second causing no injuries, and the third killing a man.

Around 8:30 P.M. on December 29, 1943, Lieutenant Colonel John D. Stevenson was seriously wounded while sitting in his room. When an air-raid alarm sounded at night, a warning signal was supposed to be given before the lights were extinguished. On this particular night the warning was not given, and after the lights were shut off, a German guard shot into the barracks area, reportedly at "some figures" moving outside the barracks in which Stevenson was sitting. The evidence suggests that there were no prisoners outside at that time, and especially not in the area in question, since it was definitely in a no-trespass zone at that time of night—prisoners spotted there would have been shot at whether or not an alarm had sounded. Two shots were fired into the barracks. One passed through both of Stevenson's legs above the knee and broke the bone in the left leg. The prisoners gathered evidence and presented it to the protecting power, but the only action seems to have been asking the Germans for an official explanation.[8]

In the aftermath of the Great Escape, tension between the prisoners and Germans reached unprecedented levels, and shootings into the compound became all too frequent. In late March, 1944, two shots were fired into block 130 late at night. Fortunately, though the bullets went directly through two rooms crowded with men, no one was hit. The prisoners asserted that again there was no plausible justification. The Germans alleged that a disturbance had been taking place at the window of one of the rooms in question. However, the prisoners insisted that nothing of the sort had occurred.[9]

On April 6, 1944, the prisoners in Stalag Luft III were told about the murders of fifty of the seventy-six men who escaped from North Compound on the night of March 24–25, 1944. They were stunned

8.   For pertinent documents outlining both the prisoners' and the Germans' views on this incident, see Goodrich, "History of South Compound," Annex III, "Protecting Power File."

9.   *Ibid.*, Pt. I, sec. 2B.

and dismayed beyond belief by the news. To the best of their knowledge, the punishment for escaping had always been a sentence to solitary confinement. It took the men some time to grasp the full meaning of what had happened.

On Easter Sunday, April 9, 1944, Corporal C. C. Miles, U.S. Army, was shot and killed inside South Compound. There was not even a remote possibility of his being engaged in an escape attempt. The report filed by the Senior American Officer described the tragic event. "An air-raid alarm had been sounded at about 1330 hours in the afternoon. The prisoners had returned to their barracks according to the German order. Those working in the cookhouse, of which Corporal Miles was one, remained in that building. About twenty minutes elapsed after the Compound had thus been cleared. The day was clear and warm, windows and doors were open, prisoners standing near the openings." One German guard pointed his gun at several of those prisoners, though no provocative act had been committed. The report continues:

Corporal Miles, talking with two other prisoners, was leaning against the doorway of the cookhouse, about 200 yards inside the barbed wire fence. He had stood thus for several minutes when, without warning, the guard was seen to aim and fire the shot that killed him. The local German authorities have stated that it was the duty of the guard to shoot Corporal Miles because his body was not entirely inside the building. No warning whatever was given that such a minor infringement of the rules would be punishable by shooting. In the past, during air raids in daylight, no notice at all was taken of prisoners standing in doorways or leaning out of windows."[10]

Bub Clark happened to be looking toward the cookhouse at the moment Miles was killed and saw the entire sequence of events. From his vantage point, he also saw something not observed by the others—the bullet, fired by a guard outside the fence and not in the tower, hit the ground first and ricocheted into Miles. Clark saw the dirt kicked up by the bullet and examined the direction the bullet then traveled. It entered Miles's spine, came out through his neck, and lodged in the ceiling. Later the prisoners dug the bullet out of the wood and it indeed had a flat spot. The prisoners did not mention the ricocheting bullet in their letter of protest to the protecting power, however, in

10. Darr H. Alkire to Secretary, Swiss legation, Berlin, April 10, 1944, *ibid.*, Annex III, "Protecting Power File."

part perhaps because they felt strongly that the guard should not have shot so close to Miles in the first place.[11]

There is nothing in the available records to explain precisely why the Germans felt so strongly about keeping the prisoners tucked tightly inside the barracks during air raids. It is possible that the German administration feared an arms airlift and locked the prisoners in to make it more difficult for them to gain effective control of the weapons. It is also possible that they simply did not want the prisoners outside where they could gloat over the increasing strength of the Allied Air Force. There might have been a question of safety, but the only target in the immediate vicinity was the relatively small railroad yard. Perhaps the most plausible explanation comes from the prisoners themselves. They concluded that they had better exercise extreme caution during the air raids since "some of the guards in the 'goon boxes' had lost relatives and friends in air raids and, therefore, might be 'trigger happy.'"[12]

Fortunately, the majority of the disagreements and misunderstandings between the prisoners and their jailers did not end in shooting incidents. Usually the battle was verbal, though the disputed issues themselves were important enough to warrant keen interest in the outcome. The Germans posted copies of the Geneva Convention all around the compounds, and the prisoners relied heavily upon that information when arguing their case. The senior officers especially came to look upon the convention as their Bible, and could quote its articles chapter and verse. Sometimes it helped, sometimes it did not, but the mere existence of the convention was comfort to the prisoners.

Colonel Spivey aptly summarized the attitudes of the prisoners and the Germans toward the Geneva Convention.

As I read over the letters which I wrote to the commandant concerning the German violations of this treaty I marvel that the old man didn't put me in solitary confinement for the language used in them. Sometimes they caused some action to be taken, most of the time nothing happened. I am sure that most of the Germans to whom I talked took great pride in the fact that American POWs were being treated in accordance with the provisions of the Convention. And I am even more certain that the treatment the German POWs in America received influenced them in their treatment of us. I had a

11. Interview with Clark, April 15, 1976.
12. Mulligan, Burbank, and Brunn, "History of Center Compound," Pt. I, sec. 3-a.

faint recollection of what was in the treaty when I arrived in camp but I knew it by heart within two months after I arrived. There isn't the slightest doubt in my mind that we would have perished otherwise.

Speculating on why the treaty gave the prisoners so much leverage, Spivey continued. "I know of no other nationality, including Americans, so concerned with being regarded as honest (inherently honest) in all things as the Germans. If I ever wanted to taunt and anger any of my captors all I had to do was to refer in an off-hand manner to his dishonesty. Immediately he would flare up and down with a gush of German reminiscent of Hitler's tirades." Then, balancing the German sense of honor against the political realities in Nazi Germany, he concluded that the Germans were

honest in all things except those pertaining to the Fatherland. Anything was excusable if committed in its name. It made no difference whether it was the breaking of a solemn treaty or the liquidation of all the Jews or the starving of a couple of million Russians or denying a lowly POW a replacement of his one and only eating utensil which he had accidentally broken. These same people, who could do all the above things without batting an eye, delivered Red Cross food and supplies to us when they themselves were hungry and when their transportation system was taxed to the breaking point to sustain their war effort, all because it was a part of their code of honor and because an order said to do it. [13]

These attitudes influenced German actions, mannerisms, and practices around camp that related directly, indirectly, or not at all to the convention. For example, most prisoners were favorably impressed by the high state of discipline among the Germans who worked in and around the camp. They were also struck by the will power demonstrated by those Germans who had opportunities to steal but did not. One of the prisoners who worked in the Red Cross clothing store wrote:

It has always been amazing to me that there we were with all that clothing in the midst of an area where the people had no opportunity to get new clothing or soap for several years, yet despite the obvious temptation, I know of no instance in which there was any thievery by any of the Germans. Whether this was due to any moral compulsion or was prompted by fear of punishment I do not know. Many a time in taking inventory I would see old Heindricks [a German] almost lovingly handle the toilet soap or shaving cream. The Lord only knows what the Germans used.

13. Spivey, *POW Odyssey*, 50.

There were times when property belonging to the prisoners was stolen, but in many instances it could not be proven that the Germans were the thieves. Nor did the losses occur frequently enough to warrant much concern.[14]

The Germans were also punctilious when it came to observing military customs and traditions. The Geneva Convention states that prisoners must salute all officers of higher rank that belong to the armed forces of the detaining power, and the Germans became upset when the prisoners ignored this custom. Actually, the prisoners had an alibi: it is considered improper for a soldier to salute outdoors unless he is wearing a hat. And they seldom failed to take advantage, obviously enjoying their small victories wherever they could. One prisoner recalls, "Whenever von Lindeiner came into the compound, the bare-headed prisoners who passed him would nod politely, and the impeccable Prussian would salute the scruffy prisoner who, like as not, had a great hole in the seat of his pants and a two days' stubble because he'd been using the same razor blade for a month."[15]

Saluting became a potential bombshell right after the July, 1944, attempt on Hitler's life. Shortly thereafter the Heil Hitler became mandatory in Germany and replaced the regular military salute. When the camp staff at Sagan tried to force the prisoners to recognize the salute, trouble followed. After much discussion the senior American officers decided that discretion was the better part of valor and agreed to acknowledge it. The British flatly refused and after three days were greeted by a military salute from their Lager officers. The Germans apparently concluded that the party salute was compulsory between Germans but that it was an individual matter when saluting prisoners of war.[16]

There was always the question of what the Germans could or would do when the prisoners misbehaved. The prisoners most feared the possibility that the Gestapo would be brought into the camp. And whenever the atmosphere became too tense, the senior officers cautioned the prisoners to exercise extreme care at all times. After the fifty prisoners from North Compound were killed, Colonel Spivey

14.   Lee to Spivey, February 27, 1948, in "Red Cross Clothing Store" Folder, Spivey Collection. See Mulligan, Burbank, and Brunn, "History of Center Compound," Pt. I, sec. 1-h, for examples of thievery by the Germans.
15.   Brickhill, *The Great Escape*, 56.
16.   Mulligan, Burbank, and Brunn, "History of Center Compound," Pt. III (Diary), July 25, 1944.

sent word around to all his men: "We are approaching a critical period in our captivity and the first signs are already evident that the Geneva Convention may mean far less than it has so far, and may possibly be totally disregarded." Correctly perceiving the mood among Nazi officials, he warned:

From all the information available, it seems clear that the Gestapo will be inclined to assume greater control over all POW activities, probably in a supervisory capacity at first, but tending gradually to increase to the extent of taking over entire control of the camp. In order to insure, as far as is within our power, the safety of the personnel in this camp from the consequences of Gestapo control, it is absolutely essential that every possibility of an incident be avoided. I want everyone to realize the fact that one individual, through momentary lack of self-control or disobedience to orders, may be responsible for bringing the full Gestapo attention to these camps with all that that entails.[17]

Short of bringing in the Gestapo, the Germans were not above initiating reprisals. The most frequent was to deprive all the prisoners in a compound, or even in the entire camp, of certain "privileges," such as entering the Vorlager to take showers. Or the prisoners would be denied access to their theaters, or intercompound visits and sports competition would be prohibited. The prisoners also felt that the Germans punished them by curtailing their parole walks. In reality, the Germans simply did not have the manpower. As von Lindeiner pointed out, a population of only 3,000 prisoners with a goal of 1 parole walk each week would have meant 200 walks in a six-day week or 36 walks a day. This would have necessitated 72 escorts daily for 540 POWs, dispersed over a three-mile radius around the camp. Aside from the logistic concerns, von Lindeiner feared hostile actions against the prisoners by the local populace. Nonetheless, the pris-. oners felt that the Germans were cruel for not granting them strolls outside the barbed-wire fence more often. When a walk was announced, the prisoners themselves decided who would go. Men were chosen according to the date on which they were shot down, so that those who had been confined the longest would be granted walks first. The list grew longer and longer until by September, 1944, there was an eighteen-month waiting list.[18]

Prisoners could also be punished individually, either as a result of

17. *Ibid.*, Pt. I, sec. 3B.
18. Von Lindeiner, "Memoirs," 202; Goodrich, "History of South Compound," Pt. I, sec. 2C.

court-martial or merely by order of the commandant. Actions for which prisoners could be court-martialed included: all acts directed against the body or life of men or harming the war effort; damaging or destroying buildings or barracks (*i.e.*, breaking walls, floors, etc.); destroying, damaging, or stealing barracks installations, (*i.e.*, bed boards for tunneling purposes, damaging the lighting system, cutting blankets, bedclothes, and towels, etc.); altering uniforms not their personal property, theft of tools, raw materials, and unauthorized use of electric light for building tunnels, etc.; forging or stealing passes, etc.; and disguising oneself as a member of the German army or in civilian clothes in an attempt to escape.[19] Courts-martial were seldom carried out, however; when they were, the sentences were usually postponed.

Most often the disciplinary action consisted of assigning the offender to the cooler for a limited time (rarely more than two weeks). One might suspect that ordinarily the prisoners would dread being sent into the cells because of the close confinement and relative isolation. According to Simoleit, however, frequently the opposite was true. In discussing the problems faced by the German administrators at Sagan, he noted:

According to the Geneva Convention, our commandant had disciplinary power over all prisoners. For disobedience, disorderly behavior or violation of camp orders he could put them under arrest. But this system of punishment did not work at all. Prisoners who were tired of the uneasy life in the overcrowded barracks were often happy to pass a few peaceful, undisturbed days alone in the arrest room. Others regarded such "punishment" as an honour. It was a proof that they had been active in some way against the German "enemies". The demand for arrest became so urgent and numerous that the arrest rooms were sold out for many months in advance. At last we were forced to declare that no "bad boys" could hope to be put under arrest.[20]

There were times when the prisoners and the Germans got along very well. The meetings in the commandant's office were often friendly, with mutual concern for the state of affairs in the compounds binding the participants together. And on many occasions members of the German staff were invited into the compounds by the prisoners to attend opening-night presentations of plays and concerts as well as major sports events. But relations at this level were still considered

19. Mulligan, Burbank, and Brunn, "History of Center Compound," Pt. I, sec. 3B.
20. Simoleit, "Organization and Administration."

"official" and were purposely open and aboveboard. Furthermore, they involved only the senior staff on both sides. Something of quite a different nature occurred in "unofficial" relations between the prisoners and the German rank and file.

To most of the men in camp, the guards and the Germans who worked in the compounds were a curiosity and a nuisance in an exclusively British and American environment. Established policy dictated that the prisoners were not to converse with the Germans and vice versa. However, there were violations of this rule on both sides, particularly among those Germans who spoke fluent English. Sometimes they would stop to visit with a prisoner "friend" or two, usually just for conversation or to pick up a cigarette or drink some coffee. The senior officers frowned upon prisoners who encouraged Germans to visit them unless the prisoner was acting as a "contact," one who was able to obtain information and forbidden goods from certain Germans.

It should perhaps be pointed out that these meetings could be dangerous for both parties, and one must assume that the Germans seeking contact with the prisoners were often interested in far more than personal gratification. The conversations provided an excellent opportunity for the German administration to obtain information that might give them clues about escape activities or simply keep them up to date about what was going on inside the compounds. Because so much could be said or transpire in a few unguarded moments, uncontrolled fraternization was discouraged at all times by both sides.

Relations among the prisoners themselves were also important. The prisoners' feelings and attitudes toward one another were exhibited in many ways, such as the manner in which they dealt with their food, clothing, and medical needs. Equally revealing was their approach to financial affairs in general.

There was an obvious inequity among prisoners of war in World War II: officers received monthly payments from the detaining power while the NCOs and enlisted men did not. This disparity had its origin in earlier times when an officer was expected to pay for his own living expenses while he was a prisoner of war. Since he usually relied upon a monthly salary to help him meet his obligations, arrangements were generally made for an officer prisoner to receive pay from his own government. The difficulty of getting funds to an officer in enemy hands led to provisions in international law that permitted private arrangements between belligerents whereby the detaining power would pay the prisoner as if he were one of their own soldiers and be reimbursed by the prisoner's government after the war. The Geneva Convention of 1929 endorsed this system, and the belligerents in World War II concluded separate agreements providing for payments to officers by the detaining power with the understanding that the necessary reimbursements would be made when hostilities ended.[21] The inequity developed when the detaining power assumed the major burden of support for both officers and men. Thus the officers had surplus funds with which to buy on the local market such goods as additional tobacco products, toiletries, and any other items the detaining power would allow them to have in the camps to make their lives more comfortable.

The disparity would not have been so pronounced if all the other ranks had worked outside the camps and received pay for their labor (as is allowed by the Geneva Convention), for at least then they would have had some money for their own use. As it was, NCOs, like officers, could not be forced to work except in supervisory capacities, and their opportunities to earn money thus depended upon the availability of enlisted men who could be sent out on work details. Since air force personnel could not fly combat missions until they had attained NCO rank, however, there were no enlisted prisoners for the air force NCOs to supervise. There was thus little or no chance for them to acquire funds for their own personal use.

The Allied Air Force officers were keenly aware of the opportunities this inequity provided the Germans in terms of inciting discontent among the air force NCOs who lived in the vicinity of the officers. The officers also felt a moral obligation to aid their less fortunate subordinates. While still at Barth the officers donated one-third of their monthly pay to a communal fund, part of which was made available to the NCOs through periodic grants to the NCO Man of Confidence for the prisoners' general needs as well as through loans to individual NCOs.[22]

The communal fund was continued when the prisoners moved to

21. Herbert C. Fooks, *Prisoners of War* (Federalsburg, Md., 1924), 206; Article 23, Geneva Convention of July 27, 1929.

22. C. G. Goodrich to the Chief of the Army Air Forces, Washington, through George Tait to Secretary of State, August 2, 1943, in File 711.62114 A/21, and "Financial Policy of Stalag Luft III," enclosed in Howard Buckness, Jr., to Secretary of State, May 30, 1944, in File 711.62114 A/637, both RG 59.

Stalag Luft III. The money raised there —$375,951.38—was used to help various groups of prisoners, among them the NCOs at thirteen prison camps and medical facilities, as well as families of Allied officers and sergeants, the French-run hospital near Stalag Luft III, and Russian POWs being held at Sagan. At the time these funds were donated, first and second lieutenants received 50 RM per month, captains 75 RM, and majors and up 100 RM. At the time, one Reichsmark was equal to forty cents in American money (the exchange rate was two and one-half Reichsmarks to one American dollar).[23]

Money from the communal fund also was used to purchase numerous items on the German market for the officer prisoners, to pay for damage to German property, and to meet other miscellaneous costs. Among the categories were services of orderlies, entertainment supplies, sports equipment, library materials, education supplies, sundries (plaques, ashtrays for sports awards, etc.), office and administration costs, medical supplies, damages to Reich property and Air Ministry property, newspapers and periodicals, church supplies, photographs, mail letter forms, beer, matches, cigarettes, tobacco, toothbrushes, razor blades, cleaning and washing materials, food, seeds, plants, crockery, clothing, insoles for shoes, and shoe polish. The damage charges were always disputed by the prisoners—they objected to the German practice of adding 50 percent to each bill as a "willful damage" charge—but the Germans consistently deducted the disputed amount from the prisoners' monthly pay.

Many of these items went into the compound canteens and were distributed to the prisoners without charge through the block canteen officers. This practice worked especially well in Stalag Luft III, where there were always a number of NCOs and enlisted men in the same compounds with the officers (in addition to those who were housed separately in Center when it was an NCO compound). The communal fund rounded out the community sharing system adopted by the prisoners. It admirably complemented the automatic distribution of supplies through the Red Cross parcel store, the Red Cross clothing store, and the YMCA store.

The canteen in particular illustrated the extent to which the community spirit prevailed in Stalag Luft III. The officers donated to the

23. "Pay and Correspondence of American Prisoners of War," in "Dulag Luft" Folder, "Camp Reports-Germany-Air Force Transit Camps" File, RG 389.

communal fund on a voluntary basis with the hope, but without any assurance, that they would someday be reimbursed.[24] When queries were sent to the respective Allied governments, the prisoners were told that all Americans who became prisoners still had their full pay (minus allotments) sent directly to their bank in the States. British prisoners, however, had an amount equivalent to the German monthly payments deducted from their checks before the money was sent to the bank for them. Again an inequity in the system became apparent, and again the prisoners responded by juggling their finances. The Americans agreed to pay for all canteen purchases so that the British would not have to lose part of their money.[25]

With several important exceptions, the relationship between the officers and men in Stalag Luft III was about the same as that found in most military organizations. The primary differences were that at Sagan the officers greatly outnumbered the men and that the issue of physical labor created some difficulties. NCOs were usually the lowest air force rank in the camps and traditionally they were responsible for supervisory and not manual labor.[26]

Article 22 of the Geneva Convention authorized the presence of orderlies in officers' camps, and the officers in Stalag Luft III asked for their services. But the British expected their orderlies to take good care of them, make their beds, launder their clothes, and do the necessary cleanup work around the camp.[27] The Americans demanded much less, assigning duties primarily in the compound kitchens and on general cleanup details. It appears that each com-

24. All Americans contributed, but about a dozen British prisoners exercised their option not to donate funds. American legation, Bern, May 3, 1944, transmitting Stalag Luft III financial records for six months ending November 30, 1943, Enclosure 3, in File 711.62114 A/562, RG 59.

25. In the documents researched for this study, no information was available concerning the final settlements between the United States and Germany in regard to the payments made to the prisoners. For more information on money owed the prisoners in spring, 1945, see Goodrich, "History of South Compound," Pt. I, sec. 3B (7). See also Walter Rundell, Jr., "Paying the POW in World War II," *Military Affairs*, XXII (Fall, 1958), 121–34.

26. Sometimes, men of lower rank were captured when airfields were overrun and in other unusual circumstances.

27. Interview with Clark, November 7, 1975; Smith, *Mission Escape*, 68. Smith says that the British orderlies were known as batmen until Wings ordered a name change at Barth, specifying that henceforth they would be called orderlies. He also directed that the officers make their own beds. The orderlies' duties are not known to me, but Clark states that they were very busy men in East Compound when he arrived in August, 1942.

pound differed somewhat in this regard. For example, in North Compound, where about 500 Americans were housed again during the fall of 1944, the orderlies who worked in the kitchen were expected to carry water to the officers in their barracks, whereas in Center and South compounds this task appears to have been done by the officers themselves.[28] In Center and South compounds the orderlies were expected to clean the night latrines each day. This task incited the one known case of insubordination in Center. The night latrines were particularly inadequate, consisting of only two buckets. Eighty to 120 men had to use them, and there were always some who were sick. By morning the rooms gave off a choking odor and displayed a stomach-churning mess. A few NCOs took the position that the officers made the mess and they should clean it up. Colonel Spivey decided that more was involved than merely the cleaning of latrines. So he ordered some of the officers to do their part in keeping the night latrines halfway clean and at the same time dealt sternly with the NCOs. On July 6, 1944, the issue of enlisted men's work details blew wide open: a sergeant told Colonel Spivey he would not work because the officers did not work. He made the statement shortly after Appell, and by 1100 hours the colonel had ordered all enlisted men and the camp staff to meet in the camp theater. The enlisted men joked and made unsoldierly comment on the "no work" strike, wondering how far they could get with it. The men stood at attention when the colonel entered. Spivey said, "Be seated, gentlemen," and as soon as the squeaking of chairs had stopped, he continued. "Is there any man in this auditorium who is not a citizen of the United States and has not pledged allegiance to the United States and obedience to his commanding officer? Until someone replaces me and as long as I am Senior Officer of this camp, my orders will be obeyed. If there is any man in this auditorium who believes differently he will keep his seat. The rest are dismissed." In twenty seconds the theater was empty. Four days later, the enlisted men proposed to work for 200 RM for eight-man rooms and 100 RM for four-man rooms. Spivey denied their request.[29]

Such discontent seems to have been unusual because most NCOs were only too happy to be in a camp where they could share in the

28.   Donald G. Charland to the author, May 8, 1975.
29.   Mulligan, Burbank, and Brunn, "History of Center Compound," Pt. III (Diary), July 6, 1944.

relatively better conditions enjoyed by the officers.[30] Their presence was not to be taken for granted, for the officers had to go through considerable trouble to obtain orderlies in the first place. Until October, 1943, only British orderlies were available, and a number of them offered their services to the Americans. In October the British orderlies were reassigned to the British compounds as a result of the arrival of several hundred American ground force orderlies. The ground force personnel were allowed to remain until the fall of 1944 when they too were transferred out and in a few weeks replaced by American air force NCOs.

An incident involving the army personnel again reveals the ability of the prisoners to join forces to frustrate the wishes of the enemy. At one point the Germans threatened to remove more than half the army orderlies from Center Compound, claiming that they were in fact privates and should therefore be on work details outside the camp. Spivey interviewed the orderlies and found that at least a third and probably more were in fact privates who had pinned on higher rank just prior to capture precisely to avoid the work camps. He then took their identification cards and initialed them in the proper space, thereby promoting all of them on the spot. It also says something about German-prisoner relations in Stalag Luft III that the commandant seemed perfectly satisfied with this procedure and did not remove any of the army personnel because of their rank.[31]

In Center Compound the orderlies lived in a separate barracks and were supervised by an officer who had served in the enlisted ranks before receiving his commission. In North, South, and West compounds the orderlies were divided up, a group living in one room in each of the barracks. In all other respects the orderlies and officers shared their facilities. The NCOs played in the officers' sports league, and their team usually performed well in all major competitions. They also participated on an equal basis in all theater, music, religious, and education programs. Their work details required only about three hours a day and thus left them plenty of time for such activities.

Contrary to the impression given in one of the novels written about life in Stalag Luft III, there appears to have been little if any racial

30. Goodrich, "History of South Compound," Pt. I, sec. 3B (18); and Mulligan, Burbank, and Brunn, "History of Center Compound," Pt. I, sec. 3-c.
31. Spivey, *POW Odyssey*, 48.

strife. No statistics are available on how many blacks or Jews there were in Stalag Luft III. The Center Compound diary indicates that on July 9, 1944, two blacks arrived from Italy, the entry ending with the cryptic comment, "Good impression on camp." Again, they were fliers, which meant that they were well educated and highly trained. And so perhaps they were accepted more readily than might have been the case under other circumstances.[32]

As for the Jews, there seems to have been a concerted effort to help them conceal their identity and make their presence as inconspicuous as possible. Either this effort was successful or else the Germans simply decided not to bother the Jews in Stalag Luft III, for the records indicate that none was ever removed from the camp. In fact, other than the Jew who died as a result of injuries when he tried to escape from a train, the only Jew who died in the camp was a man suffering from pneumonia who, at the time of his death, was in a German hospital under an oxygen tent.[33]

There were, however, numerous times when the community spirit and the veneer of civilization wore thin. It would be too much to expect a total absence of familial strife. Some examples were immediately visible in the block kitchens when men removed others' half-cooked food and placed their own pots on the stove, as well as in the problems with a few of the orderlies. Another frequent source of discontent was the supply-distribution system, and charges of "rackets" came ever more frequently as fewer goods were available to be divided among more and more men.

After months of grumbling by the prisoners of Center Compound, Spivey called a special meeting in July, 1944, to determine if there was negligence in performing camp duties, if there was profiteering in jobs dealing with communal property, and if any effective measures could be taken to ease the men's minds on these matters. The chief complaints were that meat from the kitchen was not distributed equally, that parole walks were often taken by a "certain few," and that some blocks had not received communal phonographs in many

32. Len Giovannitti, *The Prisoners of Combine D* (New York, 1957), *passim*. This book has many strong points, especially in portraying what it must have been like to live in one room for an extended period of time, all the while searching for relief from the monotony of seeing the same faces and hearing the same voices and following the same routine. But it appears the author did a grave disservice to the men who lived in Stalag Luft III by representing them as southern "Nigger haters" and "Jew baiters."
33. Confidential interviews with former prisoners, April 19, 1975.

months. The editor of the compound newspaper was asked to be more specific about certain insinuations made in the paper. The conclusion drawn at the meeting was that most complaints arose from the men becoming restless and short-tempered.[34]

Yet another source of irritation was the differing attitudes of the old and new prisoners. The former felt that since they had done most of the work to set up the community, they should be able to enjoy the fruits of their labor. The latter often criticized the way things were done and thought they knew the best way. The older men were less optimistic about the future since they had been captured when Germany was riding the tide of victory. The new men were brash and insolent and, at first, infinitely confident about the outcome of the war. They felt that it would end quickly and did not understand why the older prisoners were so concerned about setting food aside for emergencies. The old and new prisoners could hardly communicate at times. Talk of Halifaxes and B-24 Liberators meant little to the older prisoners—they had never seen either one. The more recent arrivals talked about new hit songs and movies and battle fronts that were all unfamiliar to the older men. The entry in the Center Compound diary for July 7, 1944, noted, "New men immature, seem spoiled, unappreciative for the most part."

Even the new prisoners, however, soon realized that things had to be done a certain way in prison camps. Furthermore, most tried hard to be tolerant of each other's peculiar habits and personality traits. There seemed to be a common understanding that as long as everyone had to live so close together for an undetermined length of time, they should be as civil and compassionate toward one another as possible.

But sometimes the unending routine, crowded conditions, scarcity of materials, and overfamiliarity with one's roommates got on the prisoners' nerves. A man usually lived in one room for the duration, and that was enough in itself to tax even the most patient prisoners. As one observer put it, "Each room was kitchen, mess hall, lounge, library, and bedroom, all in one, and all at once!"[35] Then there were the uncertainties about the future to contend with—would there be enough food, would the Gestapo take over the camp, would the inva-

34. Mulligan, Burbank, and Brunn, "History of Center Compound," Pt. III (Diary), July 25, 1944.

35. Goodrich, "History of South Compound," Pt. I, sec. 3B (3).

sion of the Continent ever come, would the latest offensive get bogged down, did the Germans really have a new secret weapon, how much mail would come tomorrow, was the family getting along all right, and would the war ever come to an end? These and other thoughts continually gnawed at the prisoners' peace of mind and added to their general irritability.[36]

As might be expected, the boredom of it all, the worries, the doubts, and the fears made men in their early twenties grow old before their time. One prisoner captured the essence of their daily existence: "The bed boards groaned as Lawton rolled over on his back. The noise of more than a hundred voices talking simultaneously had roused him from his early evening nap. Out of habit, he raised himself and looked around the barracks with an appraising eye. . . . Below, to his right, the members of his own combine were sitting at the bare, rectangular table playing pinochle. Cigarette smoke hung above their heads like a dead cloud. On his left, Fernandez was standing over the wooden sink drying the last of the dinner dishes. All six cups were neatly lined up on the shelf. So far everything was in order." After describing the general arrangement of the combines, the author continued:

In most of the combines card games were in progress and the slap of the cards added to the noise of conversation. Some men were lying on their bunks reading pocket books or sleeping; others were gathered in small groups intently discussing food, sex, and the war—the only topics of interest to the prisoners. Lawton relaxed again on his back. The thick, smoky air irritated his eyes. He wondered how long it was until lights out. If they didn't shut the lights off and open the [blackout] shutters he felt he'd suffocate. What time was it anyway? He wished he had a watch. The nights were so damn long in Germany, much longer than in the States or Italy. It was always night in this country.

The thought of another night in Stalag Luft III reminded Lawton that he yet had an important duty to perform:

How many nights had he been a prisoner? He looked up at the ceiling four feet above his bunk. A square section of the ceiling was covered with red

36. It is in regard to the men's daily routine and inner thoughts that the novels about life in Stalag Luft III prove far superior to the image fostered in the "Hogan's Heroes" stereotype. There are two novels published in America (known to me) that use Stalag Luft III as the primary setting. They are Giovannitti's *Prisoners of Combine D* and Simmons' *Kriegie*. A third novel, *Maybe I'm Dead* by Joe Klaas (New York, 1955), makes many references to what life was like in the camp, but deals primarily with the march westward in late January, 1945.

pencil marks. He counted them, his lips forming the numbers. He took a red pencil from his pocket and marked a new line. May 13, 1944. Two hundred and nineteen nights. Long German nights. He wondered if he would be free before the entire ceiling was covered with red marks. The thought made him smile. At least he would know the day. A man had to know his place in time or he might as well be dead. The last red mark was Lawton's place.

Finally came the long-awaited notice from the block commander— the lights would be extinguished in five minutes.

Instantly the large room was filled with the sounds of one hundred and fifty men scurrying to undress and get into bed. Lawton listened to the bed boards creak as their bodies sank onto the hard paillasses. Did the beds at home creak so loudly? After the lights went out, the prisoners slammed open the window shutters and fastened them to the outside wall of the barracks. The cigarette smoke drifted out into the night. A breeze blew through the room, rustling the cards and papers on the tables. Does there always have to be noise? A few men still stumbled clumsily about in the dark, swearing from time to time as they collided with a chair or table.

Along with the fresh breeze that swept through the building came the putrid odor of the latrine:

Lawton leaned over the edge of his bunk and looked out the window. The barbed wire fence reflected the light of the tower searchlight as it swept over the compound. When the beam flashed past the window, Lawton began counting to himself . . . one, two, three, four, five . . . the beam flashed again. Five seconds. Right on schedule. Every five seconds, twelve hours a night for two hundred and nineteen nights. He began to calculate the number of flashes since he became a prisoner. After a moment he stopped. *Jesus Christ!* He clenched his hands. He wanted a gun to shoot out the search-light. Anything to stop the endless routine.[37]

The routine took its toll. But in most cases the men managed to keep their sense of humor about what was happening to them, even to the point of joking about their short tempers. There were the "old Kriegie arguments," which one observant prisoner described as "a positive statement of fact, followed by a categorical denial, followed by a personal insult, followed by complete silence."[38] If the disagreement continued, it would not be long before someone would cry out, "Big flap in room fourteen," and like a bunch of schoolboys looking for an excuse not to study, the prisoners in the block would go thronging

37. Giovannitti, *The Prisoners*, 8–10.
38. Mulligan, Burbank, and Brunn, "History of Center Compound," Pt. I, sec. 1-a.

down to the room and join in the commotion. There was little enough diversion in their dull lives.[39]

The prisoners seem to have recognized various stages of barbed-wire psychosis in themselves and others. The mildest forms consisted of nothing more than an increasing inability to concentrate; the worst cases were actual insanity. When someone began to act strangely, the others said he was "going around the bend." Most prisoners had little difficulty recognizing the symptoms—in someone else. They got tired of seeing the "same damn faces" every morning and every night. Men who had been very good friends quarreled or fought over small matters that later seemed meaningless. Men either became sullen or "blew their top" in an effort to relieve the pressure. They often lost their perspective and failed to understand ordinary procedures. They developed a mild mania for talk or endless chatter about anything. One of the most common symptoms at this stage was the daily complaint of "brain fag" and the inability to concentrate for any length of time. It somtimes manifested itself as a constant getting up and sitting down in the midst of a meal, a theatrical production, or group discussions. Every prisoner found his memory failing him in some way. He could not remember dates, names, streets, addresses, or his own home telephone number. The past seemed to fade and there was only the present. Often one prisoner, bantering, asked another if he knew his first or middle name in the morning. The usual reply was, "Well, as long as I know my first name, I'll get by another day." These tests for "stir craze" assumed many forms and varieties. Connected with brain fag was a feeling of physical exhaustion and a need for more sleep. Prisoners were often more tired when they woke up in the morning than when they went to sleep. Some complained of defective eyesight, hearing, and smell. At this point they were often likely to misinterpret their actions. Unless the tension was relieved, the prisoners now began to develop an intense hatred for another prisoner or the guards.[40]

Although very few individuals suffered complete insanity while in the camp, the conditions that brought it on undoubtedly worked

39. For more details on such incidents, see Kimball and Chiesl, *Clipped Wings*, *passim*.

40. Walter A. Lunden, "Captivity Psychosis Among Prisoners of War," *Journal of Criminal Law and Criminology*, XXXIX (March-April 1949), 721–33.

havoc in the lives of everyone, and the prisoners were wary of even the lesser degrees of barbed-wire psychosis. If only one man in a room began to go around the bend, everybody in the room suffered. Everything possible had to be done to prevent abnormal behavior. An article in the September 3, 1944, edition of the *Kriegie Klarion*, a newspaper published in West Compound, listed ways for keeping oneself mentally fit:

Set a study program that you will follow each day for at least two weeks, regardless—and what better way could you find to get a head start on that career you had to interrupt because of war?

Take part in all sports you possibly can—volleyball, softball, swimming, the bar, boxing, weight lifting (Kriegie brew is verboten).

If you get the blues, get out and try to cheer someone else up. You'll find it's very easy to laugh.

If mechanically minded, invent a "Kriegie Klim Kan Kontraption" that will help make your housework easier. Why have a tired back after a big day's wash?

Meet and talk to someone new each day. "Monkeys is the craziest people."

Most of the prisoners instinctively followed this advice. Perhaps that is why the instances of barbed-wire psychosis were so few. Whatever the reasons, the strain in prisoner relations brought on by this disease or by anything was never sufficient to overshadow the sense of cooperation and sharing that prevailed among the vast majority of prisoners. Spivey noted, "It was extraordinary for people to be generous when they had so little and didn't know where they were going to get the next meal."[41]

41. *Klarian* quoted in Kimball and Chiesl, *Clipped Wings*, n.p.; Spivey, *POW Odyssey*, 54.

11

Sustaining Mind and Spirit

There was also a bright side to life in Stalag Luft III. A wide range of activities and pursuits was available to the prisoners, and most of the men took advantage of the opportunities. Visitors to the camp were impressed by the extensive religious, educational, cultural, and athletic programs found in each of the compounds. All this existed for several reasons. The prisoners were mostly officers, and, according to the Geneva Convention, they could not be forced to work. Thus it was possible and even necessary for them to arrange numerous leisure-time activities. Further, the prisoners were able to develop their resources to the fullest. The prisoners themselves frequently expressed surprise at the talent and initiative displayed in the camp. Many of them were college graduates, most had traveled widely, and a number of them had practiced one or more professions.

The materials the prisoners needed for their activities came primarily from the YMCA, and the Germans contributed little more than the buildings already described. Nevertheless, the Germans again deserve credit for giving the prisoners a certain amount of latitude in developing their own programs and for allowing others to lend material aid that would not have been available from German sources.

After his capture in North Africa, Chaplain Daniel was sent to numerous locations but spent most of his time serving as chaplain to the American enlisted men in Stalag VII A near Moosburg in southern Germany. In January, 1944, he was transferred to Stalag Luft III and assigned to Center Compound.

To the best of Daniel's knowledge, there were no Air Corps chaplains in Germany and he was the only Protestant army chaplain until after the Normandy landings. Colonel Spivey welcomed him with open arms, saying that wherever he had been in command, the chaplains had a good place to live and work. He showed Daniel the large room being used as the theater and chapel and told him religious services would have priority. Thereafter Spivey, Vanaman, and most of the other senior officers attended virtually every church service, sitting in the front row and often taking an active part in the reading of the service.[1]

In time of danger or great need, people frequently express a renewed interest in religion and matters of faith and morals. The record clearly suggests that this was the case at Sagan. Many prisoners found the atmosphere conducive to religious growth and moral development. They had plenty of time to think about themselves—how they had lived, and what they might do with their lives during and after their release from captivity. Those who held strong beliefs before capture were relieved to find that services were held for Roman Catholics, Protestants, Christian Scientists, and Mormons. Others for whom religion had not been important found their interest kindled. Whatever the origin or basis for their beliefs, many prisoners found that religion had a significant role in their lives. The particular circumstances in which they lived and worshiped seemed to deepen the experience.[2]

Church services and religion classes were usually held in the compound theaters or in classrooms where public gatherings took place. The YMCA offered to send the necessary materials from Sweden for a chapel, but the project never reached fruition. Most of the accoutrements were contributed either by the YMCA or by other religious organizations outside Germany. The furnishings were simple, but invariably included altars, altar cloths, candles, and stations of the cross. The clergymen wore the customary vestments. Frequently, a harmonium was available. Hymnals, prayer books, and rosaries were scarce, as were Bibles, but efforts were made to obtain a copy for anyone who desired a Bible for his own use.[3]

The chaplains ministered to large congregations. There were seven or eight clergymen in the camp by late 1944, and they represented numerous denominations. Whenever possible they served

1. Interview with Daniel, April 15, 1983. Also see Daniel, *In the Presence,* 55ff.

2. For a revealing account of a similar experience in the Vietnam War, see Robinson Risner, *The Passing of the Night: My Seven Years as a Prisoner of the North Vietnamese* (New York, 1975), *passim.*

3. See Chaplain's Reports, especially those dated January 11, 1943, June 9, July 7, July 18, September 29, and December 4, 1944, all in "History" Folder, AF Museum, Wright-Patterson AFB; Goodrich, "History of South Compound," Pt. I, sec. 3A (5); Mulligan, Burbank, and Brunn, "History of Center Compound," Pt. I, sec. 2-a.

members of their respective churches in more than one compound. In referring to the active pace imposed upon the clergymen, Spivey noted that one priest "used to preach in East before reveille, in Center right after breakfast, in North at eleven, in East in the afternoon, and Center again at night." Until the early summer of 1944, the chaplains were able to visit the various compounds almost at will. After that time, however, their movements were closely controlled. One American chaplain in Center Compound was refused a pass because he was considered "politically unreliable." He could go to South and West compounds only when accompanied by a guard.[4]

Attendance at services seems to have varied widely. One report indicates that in May, 1943, attendance was "very low." A more specific account states that in East Compound in January, 1943, about 150 officers out of a total of 650 regularly attended Church of England services and that an additional 60 men attended Roman Catholic services. In Center Compound, attendance was reported to be good— it was limited only by the small size of the auditorium.[5] Padre Murdo Ewen MacDonald, a Church of Scotland minister who first served the British and then volunteered to serve the Americans in South Compound, won a devoted following. He is said to have been a man of obvious sincerity who spoke with a rich Scottish accent. One report noted that on Sunday mornings after Appell, "it was quite a sight to see a thousand men running pell-mell for six hundred seats at Padre Mac's service." It is quite clear that the minister's popularity noticeably boosted the attendance figures in South Compound. Sometimes allowed to visit other compounds as well, he always drew large crowds.[6]

In addition to Sunday-morning services, many other activities were offered. There were church choirs in each compound, and Chaplain Daniel was pleased with the twenty men in the Center Compound choir. Lieutenant Bevins, "a splendid organist and choir director," led

4. Spivey, *POW Odyssey*, 77; Protecting Power Report No. 8, concerning the November 7, 1944, visit by Kadler, in "Stalag Luft III" Folder, RG 389.
5. Report of visit made on May 27, 1943, by an unnamed YMCA representative, RG 389; report by Alexander G. Robinson, Senior Chaplain, East Compound, February 12, 1943, in "Religious Activities" Folder, AF Museum, Wright-Patterson AFB; report prepared by the YMCA at Geneva regarding the religious activities, the library, and the athletic recreation at the Central Compound of Stalag Luft III, based on information received from the camp at the end of September, 1944, transmitted from American legation, Bern, to Special War Problems Division, Department of State, in File 711.62114 A.I.R./11–1644, RG 59.
6. Kimball and Chiesl, *Clipped Wings*, n.p.; interview with Daniel, April 15, 1983.

the group. In time another man who had majored in choral music came into the compound. He played the organ while Bevins directed exclusively. "Having plenty of time to practice," Daniel recalls, "they always came up with a beautiful number for the worship service. During part of the year we held two identical services to accommodate all the men who wanted to attend. Often music lovers would attend one service and return to hear the music in the first part of the second service. For some reason, they seldom stayed to hear the same sermon again."[7] Bible and confirmation classes, religious instruction, lectures on church history and various topics in religion, and opportunities for personal counseling were also offered. Special services were prepared for Christmas and Easter, including nativity readings and repeated renderings of Handel's *Messiah*. Evening and midweek services were held regularly, and the stations of the cross were said during Lent.

Spivey undoubtedly spoke for many when he said, "The place where I found time and the desire to pray was while I was locked in solitary confinement [at Dulag Luft] and had time to reflect on what my family must be suffering, knowing of my MIA status but not knowing whether I was safe or not. I prayed for them, and throughout the entire time I was a prisoner a day never went by but that I had a little session with God on many problems, and I received a great deal of solace that way. I know that many others fell back on their religion and developed their religious lives more than ever before."[8]

Chaplain Daniel spent much time counseling prisoners. One case he remembers involved a young man engaged to marry a Presbyterian girl. He earnestly pursued the required course of instruction to become a member of her denomination. One day, however, Daniel noticed that the man no longer seemed interested. He explained that he had been ill in the hospital for a while but, more important, had received a "Dear John" letter that had "thrown" him. Daniel sympathized and tried to point out some lines of thought that would help him through his disappointment. He seemed grateful. Daniel did not tell him that he, too, had received a Dear John shortly before arriving at Stalag Luft III. In fact, he never told anyone in Germany about it,

7. Daniel, *In the Presence*, 60.
8. Delmar T. Spivey, "History of Center Compound," 1946 (Copy of MS in possession of the author), 76.

but the German censor who read the letter and stamped it sent his sympathy.[9]

In their views on morals, the prisoners in Stalag Luft III represented a cross section of humanity. Sex, of course, was a frequent topic of conversation. Spivey wrote, shortly after the war:

Many of the men spent many of their waking hours bemoaning the fact that they had no female companionship and that they had not completely explored and exploited all their possibilities before being shot down. Contrary to the British custom that women were never mentioned in the club, all of the Kriegies whiled away long hours telling lies of their conquests and what they were going to do when they got home. The censors picked up one letter which a boy had written to his wife in which he advised her to paint their bedroom ceiling her favorite color before he returned home since she would spend many hours looking at it when he got back.

The British officers seemed to have more wife and sweetheart trouble than the Americans did, Spivey noticed, but attributed their increased woes to their having been away from them longer. Besides, he noted, "the dashing men of the American army of occupation in England had so much money and were such gay blades bent on adventure that some of the poor British women just couldn't remain faithful any longer. It all led to the decision on the part of one British wife who wrote her longtime POW husband that the Americans were overpaid, overfed, oversexed, and over here. Since the first two didn't apply to us Kriegies, the latter [two] worried us a great deal." Then he addressed a sensitive subject:

I had anticipated that I would run into trouble with the men and that homosexual tendencies would appear from time to time. So many articles and stories have been printed concerning such activities among prisoners and even the general public here in the USA that one of the first things I did was to have my squadron [block] commanders keep a special lookout for any queer activities. The long hours of close confinement with overcrowded conditions prevailing nearly all the time offered possibilities for such activities, but they never occurred, or, if they did, they were never brought to the attention of any of my commanders or to me. It is to the everlasting credit of the American officers that they were men and acted in a rational manner concerning sex at all times while POWs.[10]

9. Daniel, *In the Presence*, 63.
10. Spivey, *POW Odyssey*, 74–75.

Sometimes the men were given unexpectedly vivid reminders of their plight. Spivey mentions two instances in particular. In the first, a young man received pictures from his best girl displaying practically all her charms along with assurances that she was saving them all for him. In the second instance, about two hundred prisoners lined up to gaze at a sunbather some forty feet away just across the fence who was enjoying their admiration and longing. The commandant tried to keep women from appearing near the camp, but some of the young German mail censors would walk by from time to time, Spivey surmised, "for the purpose of being mentally raped by a thousand men." No women ever came into the camp, however, and the warnings the men received in England about the Germans' using lewd women to break down the soldier's will to fight were unnecessary as far as the prisoners were concerned. Spivey expressed relief: "I can imagine the discord, suffering, and mischief a few women could have caused in our camp and I shall always be grateful they were not there."[11]

Liquor, or brew, did not pose a serious problem in Stalag Luft III, primarily because it was scarce. Almost everyone in camp, and especially the senior officers and German camp staff, realized the special dangers even a little innocent drinking could pose. An intoxicated prisoner could too easily get himself killed and bring down a spray of bullets on other prisoners as well. In spite of the various efforts to discourage the consumption of alcohol, some prisoners always managed to procure it from somewhere, often from their own stills.

Experiments among the prisoners in making brew dated back to Barth. Wings Day discovered the men there using the most primitive method known—chewing up potato peelings and spitting them into mess cans in an effort to get the starch to turn into sugar. He immediately forbade that practice. A more successful approach was to use the dried fruit in Red Cross parcels and yeast obtained from one of the Germans. After fermentation, this brew was distilled in a large milk tin with half a football bladder wired to the top and the neck of the bladder attached to the mouthpiece of a trombone, the latter then being placed under running cold water. According to Wings's biographer, "The first bottle of pure alcohol from this remarkable contrap-

11. *Ibid.*, 74–76.

tion was ceremoniously presented to Wings, who declared it horrible but nevertheless a major breakthrough in prisoner-of-war *Kultur*."[12]

The British prisoners in particular made the brewing and drinking of liquor a part of camp life. When Spivey reached Sagan in the summer of 1943, he found that the British

had saved their brew so they could put on a grand farewell party for the Americans before we left for our own compounds. Two large rooms were fitted up as bars and several of the boys who took feminine roles in the local POW productions dressed up as barmaids and painted their cheeks like hussies. Colonel Goodrich and the other older POW colonels were especially honored guests and I, as a newcomer, went along with them. There was much conviviality and some close harmony, a few bawdy songs by Wings Day and several others, and a couple of farewell speeches by hosts and guests.

Screwing up his courage, Spivey had a couple of cups of brew. Almost immediately feeling a little uneasy in his stomach, he went out of the barracks and sat on the sunny side right under a window where he could hear the singing. Unfortunately, "that was a mistake, because I had no more than got comfortably seated when one of the boys on the inside became violently ill and regurgitated the brew and cookies all over my rather bald head. I was a mess and the senior British officers were very apologetic." His reaction to the party was one of revulsion for the most part. "Some of the older POWs became very maudlin and wept and then disappeared to sleep off the effects of drunkenness in their bunks. Others wanted to fight and there was much horseplay around the barmaids which didn't sit too well at the time. My overall impression of the drunks was that they were frustrated from one cause or another and the alcohol acted to release the pent-up feelings which they had been so carefully concealing. I was determined I would not allow brews in my camp."[13] The making of brew in fact was limited in both Center and South compounds.

One other aspect of prisoner morality, or lack of it, that disturbed Spivey was the use of profanities and obscenities. Recalling some of the measures the compound staff adopted in an effort to clean up the men's language, he stated, "We had several conferences on the subject after the British and Canadians left [in January, 1944]. The Canadians, like Americans, were super foul-mouthed and it was decided it

---

12. Smith, *Mission Escape*, 76–77.
13. Spivey, *POW Odyssey*, 80.

would be easier to begin our drive with them gone. We strove with might and main to remember George Washington's classic order pertaining to swearing and I believe we came up with a fairly good replica of it. We published it along with several editorials on the subject, had meetings and devised penalties which each combine enforced to a degree consistent with their wishes. Our efforts helped, but the habit remained."[14]

The prisoners endeavored to re-create as closely as possible the way of life they had known and loved. One of the ways they kept their memories alive was to celebrate birthdays, the Fourth of July, Memorial Day, Thanksgiving, Christmas, Good Friday, and Easter. For Colonel Spivey, the Christmas of 1943 was particularly memorable:

Feeling sorry for us in Center [because we did not have any brew] the group captains in east sent over to the colonels in my room enough to make up quite a shaker full of "orange blossoms." The Germans must have felt sorry for us because our chief censor, von Massow, sent me a bottle of the finest French brandy, and the lager officer, Hauptmann Shultz, brought me another bottle of brandy. I think the British padre got the wrong impression of me because he brought over from his room a bottle of sacramental wine which he said he never [would] need since the war would be over long before he could use it in the church. We drank the drinks at an official reception in my room for the camp staff and the squadron commanders and then I made a speech before several hundred in which I promised them all that none of us would be there for Christmas 1944, as all of us would be home.

Perhaps trying to convince himself as much as the others, Spivey was only too well aware of the façade. "My, how wrong I was! We sang songs and tried to be gay but in our hearts not one of us was happy and each of us wondered what the future would bring and what our families were doing at that very moment. I felt particularly sentimental on this first Christmas because that day I had received my first word from home since July 1943 and I had to bite my lip until it bled to keep from crying when I saw my wife's handwriting and the childish note from my young son." The commandant had granted them permission to visit each of the camps to wish one another a Merry Christmas.

About ten of us senior officers were allowed to go after duly signing our parole. My group met east camp group and we chatted on our way over to north where we joined a group celebrating the yuletide in a truly festive manner. They had the barracks decorated and bars set up to get rid of the

14. *Ibid.*, 76.

verboten grog. We all had several drinks and then moved on to south where we were to have dinner with Colonel Goodrich, more grog, and then a kriegie banquet. There was some good singing and quite a little buffoonery and when the German guards were ready to take us back they couldn't find part of us and no one seemed to care whether we left or not.

That night was hectic because several of the British from East climbed the barbed-wire fence between the camps for the purpose of paying a visit. Spivey was afraid they would be shot, but the senior Abwehr sergeant saw the humor in the horseplay and had instructed his guards not to shoot. He pleaded with Spivey to round up the boys from East so he could march them back. The Americans hurried up the process and took them over. But less than ten minutes later one of them appeared in Spivey's room to say he had forgotten to wish the colonel a Merry Christmas. Before Spivey could stop him, the prisoner dashed for the barbed wire and back over he went, the German guard waving his rifle in the full glare of a powerful searchlight. But he did not shoot. There were many repercussions. Spivey recalled: "Some of the men were sick, others morose and all had that terrible indescribable feeling of loneliness and uncertainty which held us after any little excitement. The commandant had other feelings and he gave a stern warning as to what would happen if anything like that ever happened again. His wrath didn't descend on Center Compound because nearly all had remained sober through necessity. He even praised us a bit and said we could be excused from roll call on New Year's Day! The boys got quite a kick out of that and proceeded to call all Germans an extra special kind of S.O.B."[15]

Two other prisoners recalled how special the Christmas of 1944 was for them. The first man, from West Compound, wrote:

Christmas day, 1944, proved to be much happier than any homesick Kriegie had reason to hope for because of a beautiful gesture by the Mail Officer and a few others in his confidence. At evening roll call on December 24, the men were waiting in orderly formation for dismissal after the count had been taken when sleigh bells and general clatter announced the arrival of a small wagon carrying Santa Claus, resplendent in a red and white suit, and an assistant. The wagon was pulled by two men dressed as reindeer. As the assembled men watched hopefully, Santa made the rounds tossing out bundles of mail to each group as he passed. Faces were a little brighter as the men returned to the barracks. Santa had brought the Spirit of Christmas to this lonely camp in the wilderness where the ever-burning light of hope at times

15. *Ibid.*, 79–82.

grew dim. Mail had been allowed to accumulate over a period to permit Santa's visit.

Loren E. Jackson described an equally memorable moment in Center Compound.

Normally, the Germans locked us up as soon as it became dark. On Christmas Eve 1944, they made a special concession and let us visit in the various blocks until well after dark. Then, after we had all been confined, I remember a brass ensemble—a couple of trumpets, an alto horn, a trombone or two, and a baritone—played "Silent Night." In the still bitter cold of that lonely, dark night, the music, played by American prisoners in the middle of the compound, had a great impact on all of us. It became deathly quiet in the cell blocks as everyone paused to hear the clear, mellow strains of this beautiful, traditional Christmas carol. And there were some misty eyes here and there. I can remember that some of our German guards were as touched as we were. I suspect that this auditory impression will remain with me always; in fact, I never hear "Silent Night" without recalling that night in Sagan.[16]

The educational programs in Stalag Luft III were plagued by difficulties, and yet they represent one of the prisoners' most successful endeavors. "Sagan U," or "Kriegie College," as the prisoners affectionately called their educational system, offered poor facilities, suffered from a lack of textbooks and teaching materials, and experienced slumps in student performance at times when the war news was exceptionally good or bad. But it offered a wide range of courses, enjoyed large enrollment, and achieved recognition from examining boards in England and Canada and from many universities in the United States, thereby allowing the prisoners to earn full credit for courses completed while in the prison camp.

In Stalag Luft III, equipment and classroom space were inadequate. The classes were held in small rooms set aside for such purposes, but the rooms were frequently in undesirable locations. In Center Compound, for example, classes were held in three small rooms, two of them in one end of the theater building and the third next to the potato room in the kitchen. The rooms were crowded and were cold in the winter. Students near the kitchen had to contend with the smell of rotting food while those in the theater found themselves in competition with the band, the orchestra, and the choral groups that practiced there. For equipment the prisoners turned to the YMCA and obtained books, large blackboards, and other educa-

16. Neary, *Stalag Luft III: Sagan*, 19; Loren E. Jackson to the author, February 2, 1975.

tional materials. The Germans provided tables and benches but frequently took them away for use in the barracks. In early 1944, East Compound reported that there were neither tables nor benches available for use in the classrooms. North Compound made a similar complaint.[17]

An even bigger problem was how to maintain student interest in academic work. The enrollments were usually large enough at the beginning of each semester, often 50 percent of the prisoners. But as time went on, only about 40 to 60 percent of those who originally signed up still attended class. There were, of course, the usual reasons for declining interest, such as lack of aptitude or inadequate educational background. More important, however, were factors such as the weather and the war situation. During the winter months when the prisoners had to remain inside most of the time, the courses were avidly pursued. When spring and summer weather arrived, the students tended to become restless and turned their attention to outdoor activities. The men were highly sensitive to the current war situation, and being young and unsure of their future vocations, they did not need much distraction to miss classes and forget to prepare lessons. The education staff tried with little success to maintain attendance rates and student interest by calling roll, administering exams, and awarding proper recognition to those who finished the required work.

In addition to consuming time and occupying the students' attention, many courses offered opportunities to acquire college credit. Credit was given only for those courses that had adequate facilities and qualified instructors, and only after the students' performance was comparable to what one might expect to find at an average college. Thus, no credit was given for science courses that required laboratory work, but full credit could be earned for courses in business, social science, and the humanities. The British also had to pass exams at various levels of difficulty administered by agencies in England, a few of which were the Associated Board of the Royal Schools of Music, Institute of Civil Engineers, Institute of Bankers, Institute of Chartered Accountants, and Cambridge of London Cer-

17. See Education Reports, "History" Folder, and Education Reports, "Education and Entertainment" Folder, both in AF Museum, Wright-Patterson AFB; report of visit by Mr. Friedrich and Dr. Bubb, February 22, 1943, in File 740.00114 EW/3977, RG 59; Mulligan, Burbank, and Brunn, "History of Center Compound," Pt. I, sec. 2-d; Goodrich, "History of South Compound," Pt. I, sec. 3A (5).

tificates of Proficiency in German, Russian, and French. The Americans received certificates signed by the compound commanders, and in Center Compound, 350 prisoners received certificates of completion. Although statistics are not available, one source indicates that after the war, colleges in the United States granted credit to many of the former prisoners on the basis of those certificates.[18]

A surprisingly long list of courses was offered in the various compounds. Understandably, the British prisoners developed the most extensive programs since they were in camp longer. During the spring semester of 1944, East Compound offered seventy different classes in forty-five subjects. Since West Compound was just opening then, the prisoners there were able to enjoy courses for only a short time before the camp was evacuated. Here again, however, the prisoners' transferring their communities almost intact proved to be remarkably successful. Although Belaria Compound opened only in January, 1944, by May the education program there offered thirty-five courses in twenty-seven subjects. No statistics are available on West and South compounds, but Center Compound consistently offered between twenty-five and thirty-five classes and maintained an average enrollment of about five hundred. The courses offered most frequently included: arithmetic, basic and advanced algebra, basic and advanced trigonometry, integral and differential calculus, agriculture, zoology, meteorology, accounting, sociology, speech, music, grammar, history, shorthand, English literature, photography, debating, geology, chemistry, body building, French, Spanish, and German.

In addition to the formal classes, there were special programs and lectures designed to meet specific needs and interests. In South Compound, law students were able to complete more than one year of study. Future attorney general Nicholas Katzenbach was among those who studied law while in Stalag Luft III. At least thirteen men studied for the ministry. Courses in military subjects were taught for those who wanted to apply for permanent commissions after the war. When the senior officers teaching the military course in Center Compound needed some organizational charts depicting the command structure of the American military forces, a German Lager officer graciously supplied them along with the names of key personnel.[19]

---

18. David R. Porter to Delmar T. Spivey, February 19, 1946, in "POW Letters-General" Folder, Spivey Collection.

19. Interview with Wells, January 26–27, 1975.

One biology student even offered to teach a course in human sexuality in an effort to raise the sex discussions in camp to an academic level. Special courses were also offered in mountaineering, gardening, handicrafts, journalism, and broadcasting, to mention only a few.

There were also discussion and debating groups, and the latter sometimes held intercompound tournaments. Some of the topics discussed in Center Compound were Business and Business Opportunities, The World at Peace, War Aims, The Negro Problem, The Treaties of Paris and Their Consequences (Versailles), Labor in the United States, Religion, Modern Education, Opportunities in the Western Hemisphere, and The Farm and Its Problems.

Each compound had at least two libraries, one for reference materials and one that served as a general lending library for works of fiction and nonfiction. The libraries were a necessary component of the education program, but their overall importance was even greater. The fiction library especially was "probably the greatest morale factor in the camp next to the Red Army."[20]

The titles and quantities of books found in the libraries varied from time to time, but the holdings were impressive by prison camp standards. Within the first year after the camp opened, the prisoners in East and Center compounds alone had access to 8,500 volumes, about two-thirds of which were literary works and one-third scientific works. Not included in these figures are some 20,000 volumes that the prisoners had received in personal parcels and circulated among themselves. A breakdown by category indicates that the Center Compound lending library at one time held 1,128 works of general fiction, 75 westerns, 342 detective novels, 28 biographies, and about 371 miscellaneous books, a total of 1,944 volumes. The reference libraries contained fewer books, averaging about 500 volumes in each compound.[21] In addition, many of the books in the reference libraries in

20. Mulligan, Burbank, and Brunn, "History of Center Compound," Pt. I, sec. 2-d.

21. As of March 4, 1943, German regulations prohibited the following books and materials in camp: navigational charts, plans, wharf and code maps or parts thereof; meteorological charts; charts of currents; navigational reference books, including sailing instructions; lists of lights; lists of wireless signals; tide tables; distance tables; nautical and air almanacs, directories, and calendars; information of any nature about ports, harbors, anchorages, and inland waterways; military, naval, or air force subjects; chemistry; espionage; explosives; geography and mapmaking; lithography; politics; weapons and armaments; wireless and radio; enemy propaganda; any subject that might be considered doubtful or of a technical or scientific nature, including patents, inventions, and discoveries ("Summary of Regulations pertaining to Book Programs for Prisoners of War," March 3, 1943, File 740.00114 EW/3227, RG 59). On October 14,

the American compounds were British and therefore of somewhat lesser value in the eyes of the Americans: notable differences existed in their respective approaches to topics ranging from accounting and agriculture to literature and law practice. The reference libraries, however, were used extensively. Students had to share many textbooks for their course work, and the rooms were usually larger than those that housed the lending libraries and therefore provided one of the few places where the prisoners could study and keep warm in the winter. The reference library in Center Compound could seat sixty and was generally full from ten o'clock in the morning until ten at night. Unfortunately, the libraries, like the rest of the camp, lacked sufficient lighting. The reference library in Center, for example, had only two 60-watt bulbs.

The condition of the books worsened rapidly because of frequent use and the absence of materials to repair them. It was noted in Center Compound that the more popular novels began to show signs of wear after about thirty or forty readings, and from that point on deteriorated rapidly. This was a serious problem. Records kept by the libraries in Center Compound indicated that books changed hands about every ten days.[22]

American magazines were also available in the reference library and eagerly read and reread. The issues most frequently received in the American compounds included *National Geographic, McCall's,*

1943, the Germans proposed to liberalize the regulations to allow the prisoners to receive books on technology, physics, chemistry, optics, wireless telegraphy, aeronautics, navigation, shipbuilding, astronomy, meteorology, geography, and the like. They reasoned that "instructions contained in textbooks relating to the manufacture of articles which could serve as a means of escape or sabotage, as well as details regarding the manufacture of radio apparatus, etc., do not constitute a reason to withhold these books, the prisoners of war lacking the possibilities of putting the acquired knowledge to practical use *because the necessary material is not available to them*" (Memorandum on German Proposal regarding Reading Materials for Prisoners of War, from the Legation of Switzerland, Washington, D.C., to the Department of German Interests, October 14, 1943, in File 711.62114 A/71, RG 59, emphasis added). It is unlikely that any knowledgeable Germans really believed that the materials required to make radios, etc., were unavailable to the prisoners, and so it is possible that the proposal was primarily a propaganda measure. Another possible explanation is that they believed the materials were less available to Allied prisoners in Germany than they were to Axis prisoners in Allied hands, and that the liberalized regulations would therefore benefit the latter far more than the former. In any event, the proposal does not seem to have received serious consideration in the United States.

22.   Delmar T. Spivey, "Report of Center Compound Activities," February 3, 1944, in "Education and Entertainment" Folder, AF Museum, Wright-Patterson AFB.

Yale Review, Harper's, Atlantic Monthly, and *The New Yorker.* German pictorial magazines were also sent into the camp.

The prisoners received their books and magazines from several sources. Large quantities of books arrived in personal parcels, and these were willingly passed around or donated to the libraries after the recipient had read them. The magazines were usually paid for out of communal funds. In addition, organizations such as the International Red Cross, the Canadian Legion Educational Services, the European Student Relief Fund, the International Bureau of Education, and the YMCA were all instrumental in collecting and sending book donations.

Closely associated with both the education programs and the libraries were the compound Newsrooms, for they too offered the prisoners much-needed diversion and a means of enhancing their knowledge of and perspective on what was occurring in the camp and in the world beyond the barbed wire. Almost every man in Stalag Luft III, including most of the Germans who worked inside the compounds, stopped at least once a day to check the latest news as depicted on large wall maps and carefully printed or typed briefs. The Newsrooms were usually located in or near the cookhouses or theaters, primarily because those were the places the Germans installed their loudspeaker system through which news communiqués transmitted from Radio Breslau were broadcast to the prisoners throughout the day.

The news was gathered from many sources and was posted in several different formats. Volunteers translated the news in the communiqués and either wrote it out in longhand or typed it on the adjutant's typewriter. In addition, the German newspapers and magazines that were sent into the camp provided numerous items that were translated and posted.[23]

23. The list of daily papers and magazines delivered to Center Compound included: *Das Reich, Simplicissimus* (Munich), *Wiener Illustrierte, Die Wehrmacht, Leipzig Illustrierte, Koeln Illustrierte, Illustrata Camerata, Deutsche Kraftfahrt, Signal, VB, Berliner Borsen Zeitung, Krakauer Zeitung, Die Woche, Münchener Illustrierte, Stuttgart Illustrierte, Hamburg Illustrierte, Der Adler, Der Adler* (English), *Der Adler* (French), *The Camp* (as issued), *Hamburger Fremdenblatt, Pommersche Zeitung, Paustian Lustige,* and *Enlace.* The *Illustrierte* were German pictorial magazines. The magazine *Simplicissimus* was a "savage Jew-baiting propaganda organ replete with sadistic cartoons." The English-language propaganda material consisted of three periodicals, two newspapers and one pictorial. One newspaper, the *O.K.* (*Overseas Kid*), was printed exclusively for American prisoners. Its counter-

The volunteers who did the translating and the posting usually had a specialized knowledge either of the language or of the topic under discussion. Each compound boasted a staff of twelve to fifteen individuals who together posted about five thousand to eight thousand words daily in South Compound and approximately fifty typewritten pages along with photographs each week in Center Compound. In Center the postings were organized into such categories as the East Front, West Front, Italy, United States, Occupied Countries, Neutral Countries, Inside Germany, Balkans, and British Commonwealth.

The topic that usually drew the most attention was the war, and considerable effort was expended to keep the prisoners fully informed on the latest developments. Large maps were obtained from the canteens and mounted on the walls. When those maps were not available, carefully hand-drawn ones were used. As the Allies closed in on all sides during 1944, the men diligently scrutinized the situation maps, and it became quite a task to keep the battle-line strings on the right towns and the flags on the proper Pacific islands. At the end of each month the area specialists in South Compound also wrote a summary of events in their respective theaters of operations. Having carefully studied the communiqués and articles, they were in a better position than anyone else was to present an unbiased survey of developments. Their summaries gave not only a coherent picture over a month's time but also, by a discerning separation of fact from propaganda, a somewhat truer picture of events as they actually happened than a cursory reading of the papers could give. Special charts posted in South Compound depicted all the USAAF and RAF raids, including the announced aircraft losses, and a log of Allied aircraft sightings over Germany as reported on the radio broadcasts.

Compound newspapers were also posted in the Newsrooms, primarily because the shortage of paper meant that there was only one copy, and everyone had to share it. Printed on one side of the page, the papers were spread out on the wall so that a number of individuals could read them. The publishing endeavors undertaken in Stalag Luft III reflected much of the free-enterprise spirit and penchant for

---

part for the British was *The Camp*. The pictorial *Signal*, printed in many different languages, was "a rather crude attempt to copy *Life* magazine," but the photographs were good (Mulligan, Burbank, and Brunn, "History of Center Compound," Pt. I, sec. 2-e). For more information on the Newsroom in South Compound, see Goodrich, "History of South Compound," Pt. I, sec. 3B (17).

freedom of the press usually associated with the United States, England, and the Commonwealth countries. Within weeks after each compound opened, energetic individuals organized staffs of reporters, artists, and layout men who devoted their efforts to producing newspapers that resembled as closely as possible those in the United States.[24] Even the spirit of competitiveness was present: at times, there was more than one newspaper in each compound, and the papers tried to provide interesting coverage of the scarce news in an effort to win the largest readership. The newsmen were convinced that a need existed for their services and diligently strove to meet the expectations of the prisoners. They sought to expose the men to ideas and news items that would give them a better perspective on the problems they faced as prisoners, and perhaps even help them forget for a moment or two that they were prisoners. The newspapers provided numerous outlets for the prisoners' need for recognition, self-expression, and emotional release. Individual feats were publicized and group efforts were noted and applauded. Generally, the entire community's sense of identity was enhanced through the pages of those publications. Official pronouncements, sports reports, entertainment notices, critical reviews and essays, poetry, song lyrics, advertisements, and news from around the camp and from the home front were all put into print. In addition, certain topics were aired before the rumor factory distorted the facts of the case beyond recognition.[25]

Virtually all the publishing efforts were successful in capturing the prisoners' interests and meeting their needs. Only four of the seven ventures, however, managed to sustain an unbroken record of publication from the time they were launched until the camp was evacuated in January, 1945. From October 27, 1943, until the day of evacuation, Center Compound was kept well informed by one and, for a time, two newspapers. The *Gefangenen Gazette* was in existence

24.   Only the newspapers published in the American compounds will be discussed here, since little information is available in the United States on those published in the British compounds.

25.   Arthur Dreyer, editor of the *Kriegie Klarion*, a West Compound newspaper, states that he was more satisfied with his job and exhibited more professionalism in the performance of his duties during the time he served as the paper's editor than at any other time in his military career. He was convinced that his job was important, and his convictions were confirmed by the large group of men who gathered around the bulletin board to read the news each time an edition came out. After the war, he continued to feel that the value of an adequate communications program in a prisoner of war camp is inestimable. Interview with Arthur Dreyer, February 25, 1976.

throughout that time. Its competitor, the *Kriegie Times*, published thirty editions between January 1, 1944, and August 27, 1944, when the demands of other camp duties upon its editor and staff became too great.[26] An article written in the *Gazette* when the *Kriegie Times* ceased publication included this comment:

Begun as a source of entertainment and background for future enterprises, the scene has changed considerably, applicable to both newspapers. Even though the *Gazette* was started several months prior to the founding of the *Times*, the need for newspapers was [imperative]. News was scarce. The papers gathered bits from all outlying sources and wove them into clarified and readable matter.

Rumor and conjecture were in full bloom in the fall of 1943. No news was ever given from an authoritative source. With the beginning of the camp newspapers, rumors were gathered, sifted and clarified and the papers acted as the only source of authoritative news, a much needed ramification of the administration. Until a few months ago, no official bulletin boards were present and then but little official information was released. Carrying the burden from the start, the papers shaped the kriegie reading public, and to this day are still looked to for official releases.

The compound commanders decided which official information would be released. The reporters, however, were not remiss in their duty to keep the administration honest. Whenever access was granted, a reporter attended the staff meetings and pressed camp leaders for information about negotiations with the Germans, the state of camp supply, and any controversial issues that might have arisen. Colonel Spivey, Center compound commander, sometimes became irritated at the reporters' persistence and was perhaps more than a little chagrined that even in a prison camp a commander could not get away from the nosy members of the press. At the same time he was wise enough to appreciate the public service being performed by the newspapers and gave them unstinting official support as well as considerable personal attention and praise.[27] One suspects that his

26. The information available today about the compound newspapers comes primarily from individuals who either worked on them or read them rather than from the newspapers themselves, most of which were left behind and presumably destroyed when the camp was evacuated in January, 1945. Certain editions were sent to the families of the various editors during the war through the Red Cross, but only a few of them arrived intact. The one exception is the *Gefangenen Gazette*. A complete set of this paper's editions safely reached the home of its editor, Ronald Delaney, and he has generously granted me free use of the entire set, which now resides in the Special Collections Room, USAF Academy Library.

27. *Gefangenen Gazette*, August 30, 1944; interview with Spivey, April 19, 1975.

experience and reaction were typical of those found among the other compound commanders.

In South Compound, two newspapers and a magazine flourished within two months after the compound opened. The first to be published, the *Circuit*, appeared regularly from October, 1943, until the end of the war. Its competitor, the *Shaft*, was well received but had a short life. A satirical news sheet that poked fun at the *Circuit* and Kriegie life in general, the *Shaft* was reportedly full of good humor, witty articles, and scathing diatribes. One headline read: "A Prisoner's Day." Fifteen lines of white blankness followed. Much to the disappointment of the prisoners in South Compound, the *Shaft* ceased publication after its fifth issue. Perhaps the most ambitious publishing venture in Stalag Luft III was *The New Yorker*. Also published in South Compound, the magazine attempted to imitate, in every detail, the original *New Yorker*. The writing was said to be superb, exhibiting a matter-of-fact style in columns entitled "Profiles," "Talk of the Town," and "Goings on About Town" that had the well-known frank and saucy touch. Expert cover illustrations, cartoons, and hand-lettered headlines added authenticity to the eight-page editions that appeared on the Newsroom wall. After two excellent productions, one at Thanksgiving and the other at Christmas, *The New Yorker* also ceased to exist. Again, the prisoners regretted the loss, but readily understood that the venture simply required too much work.[28]

The two competitors in West Compound were the *Stalag Stump* and the *Kriegie Klarion*. Issued each Sunday, these two papers "looked like little more than glorified notice sheets compared to civilian standards, but to the prisoners they looked like the *Sunday Times*."[29] Local news of front-page significance included a new musical show to be put on by the Kriegies, the arrival of sports or musical equipment, an interview with General Vanaman during one of his visits to West Compound, or the opening of a new school semester. The *Klarion* featured a "news and views" page that contained poetry, drawings of airplanes and girls, comic verse, and the results of a weekly poll on various topics. One of the prisoners in West Com-

28. Goodrich, "History of South Compound," Pt. I, sec. 3B (15).
29. Arthur Dreyer, "The 'Kriegie' Press," *Air Force*, XXIX (March-April, 1946), 47. The information presented here on the newspapers in West Compound is extracted from Dreyer's article and from the February 25, 1976, interview with Dreyer.

pound, Sam Northcross, had been associated with George Gallup and his Institute of American Opinion.[30] Northcross supervised the block correspondents who sought to obtain the prisoners' opinions, which were considered valuable though often marked by cynicism. A poll taken in November, 1944, showed that the men thought the war would be over by April 1, 1945. In another poll, an overwhelming majority wanted to join a new veterans' organization that had no ties to World War I groups. The polls could sometimes be useful. One was taken in January, 1945, for example, about the distribution of the dwindling Red Cross food parcels. The commander of West Compound, Colonel Darr Alkire, wanted to find out if the men would rather go from their half rations to quarter rations or continue to consume the parcels at the current rate. Quarter parcels would have assured the men of something to eat for a longer time but would have lowered morale and weakened them to a point they apparently were unwilling to accept. The *Klarion* pollsters covered the entire compound and had the results to Colonel Alkire in slightly over two hours. The men decided, by a wide margin, to stay on half parcels, and Colonel Alkire respected their wishes.

During the summer sports season, the *Klarion* came out every morning with a small daily, listing games to be played that day, scores and summaries of games played the day before, and new standings in the compound's two softball leagues. In addition, midweek news was published in a *Klarion* supplement that appeared every Thursday. During the winter when there was little to report on the sports page of the supplement, features were written by the sports experts among the prisoners. They included Hal Van Every, former Minnesota football great; Bud Elrod, All-American end from Mississippi State; Fay Frink, center and captain of Penn's gridiron team; and Lou Zaris, a New Jersey amateur boxing champ.

The newspapers even ran advertisements. They not only added to the American image but also served a purpose. One encouraged Kriegies to use the tooth powder given to them: "Use Dr. Vierling's Zahnpulver—why take a paste in the mouth if you can take a

---

30. Center Compound also had a polling organization, Pulse, which copied models used in the British compounds (Mulligan, Burbank, and Brunn, "History of Center Compound," Pt. I, sec. 2-f.

powder." Another exemplified the competitive spirit that existed between the two compound newspapers:

> *Kriegie Klarion* hits the spot
> Six full pages, that's a lot
> Twice as much as the *Stump* gives you
> *Kriegie Klarion*'s the paper for you.[31]

The competition between the various compound newspapers was keen and healthy. It encouraged the editors to be bold in placing heavy demands upon their volunteer workers, who worked to meet deadlines that otherwise might have slipped by all too easily because of adversity and the scarcity of news. Arthur Dreyer, who graduated from the University of Missouri School of Journalism just before joining the service, insisted that the *Klarion* be posted each week after church. In order to meet this self-imposed deadline, he often passed through the barracks and urged his reporters "with a cane" to get out and finish their work, a task they were often reluctant to do, especially in the winter when they preferred to remain inside where it was warm.[32]

Even the pressure of getting the scoop was nourished by the presence of two newspapers. The compound commanders had to censor the papers before they were published. The search for news often brought out into the open topics that needed widespread discussion, but at times the reporting ruffled feathers and caused unnecessary alarm. The repeated references to apparently nonexistent "rackets" are the classic example of the latter.

The news printed in the papers came from several sources. Each block was covered by a *Klarion* reporter and a *Stump* reporter. This competition ensured that virtually everything newsworthy was reported and, when space permitted, duly printed. The most highly sought-after news came from the new prisoners. Whenever a new purge arrived in a compound, the recent arrivals were barraged with questions. The *Klarion* sometimes ran a full page on the stories obtained in this way, and accordingly was able to inform the older prisoners about the adoption of the GI Bill of Rights, the creation of the combat infantry badge, and Dinah Shore, who was "wowing" the boys in France.

31. Dreyer, "The 'Kriegie' Press," 47.
32. *Ibid.*

One of the most popular features in all the newspapers was a variation of something called "Out of the Mailbag." From these columns, the prisoners learned about recent trends, political events, and fads and shows currently in the public eye back home. Especially noted were the excerpts from Dear John letters and ironic comments exhibiting the home folks' rosy misconceptions about life in a prison camp. Concerning the latter, the prisoners flew into a rage when they read "Hope you can get to Bayreuth for the opera season" or "The Red Cross bulletin shows a picture of your swimming pool and the cabins in the pines. We hear you are living four in a room."[33]

The Dear John letters that found their way into the newspapers were usually classic examples of tactlessness and insensitivity. The prisoners took sincere Dear John letters to heart but those that portrayed callousness or blatant infidelity were often posted on the bulletin board or in the newspaper so that others could express their contempt for the author or laugh at the irony that was so often visible in them. The January 10, 1944, issue of the *Gefangenen Gazette* offered these gems—first letter from a fiancée: "You were posted missing a month ago, so I got married." And from a fiancée: "Darling, I have just married your father. Love, Mother."

The prisoners managed to keep fairly well informed about entertainment and sports back home. The pages of their newspapers are filled with brief notations such as:

Perhaps you left the states before it became Sinatra conscious. As a lean, unprepossessing young man, he croons, and the teenage girls hit the floor in a swoon. Now, as a psychological question mark, this Lucky Strike singer has every other radio program on the air taking potshots at him, as the man with big ears and a bedroom voice.

Bob Hope, as usual, never is the one to miss a target. Sinatra and family had an eight pound baby boy a while ago, and Hope said it was the first time a man ever had a son bigger than he was.[34]

A follow-up story on January 24, 1945, reported: "Sinatra Retires: The 'Voice,' Sinatra, has retired from motion pictures. He said, 'Pictures stink, most of the people in them do too,' is one statement that arrived here by mail. He plans, however, to continue living in Hollywood."

The reporters were always looking for the unusual, and they often found it in the form of crazes or in the exhibition of a particular talent.

33.   Goodrich, "History of South Compound," Pt. I, sec. 3B (15).
34.   *Gefangenen Gazette*, April 26, 1944.

For a time in Center Compound, hypnosis became a fad. One prisoner was a student of medical hypnotic therapy, and he volunteered to teach others his mysterious skills. On another occasion ventriloquists created quite a stir. An article in the *Gefangenen Gazette* on August 20, 1944, was headlined: "Ventriloquism: Latest Prank Threatens Camp Sanity."

For preservation of the remaining fragments of sanity in the Center Camp, the beckoning and bewildering voices that have plagued kriegies for the past weeks, come out of Block 43. It all dates back, as does most of America's deviltry, to Texas. This overworked phrase of ventriloquism was dropped on Germany in the person of "Tex" Shackleford.

When the monotony of the barracks grew on, Tex resorted to this odd prank, but the blase old timers refused the bait. Unabashed, Tex waited patiently—summer and new purges came in together.

Tex's initial success was the roping in of a naive novice—one Lt. G——. It was after lights out—a voice from the outside requested Lt. G—— on the outside. Still new and unnerved, fellow pranksters abetting, Lt. G—— started to go out. With the immediate risk of a shooting coming up, the pranksters called the hastily dressed newcomer back.

This success brought to Tex a veritable throng of students. Art Pilley [and] Junior Wolfram, became the outstanding grads—but never appreciated by a few beleaguered innocents.

Pilley, still hysterical, [related] the anecdote about a new kriegie utilizing a stall in the midwest abort. Caught at his calling, the newcomer was perplexed at a call, apparently from beneath, "Hey, up there—"

When the newcomer jumped to his feet very agitated and startled and looked down the gap—observers said Pilley became hysterical beyond control and had to utilize a box himself!

Incidents come to the surface daily, but the mental pressure must be avoided—so thanks Tex, Art and Junior for the unselfish disclosures—and the subsequent offers to teach anyone in camp the novel knack of ventriloquism.

"That's right [Tex, Art and Junior], no one was calling you!"

The favorable impact such articles had upon the prisoners' morale can well be imagined.

On March 27, 1943, two thousand sacks of mail bound for GIs in Europe were lost when Nazi submarines torpedoed a U.S. cargo ship. To the GIs, including the men in Stalag Luft III, such losses were incalculable. According to Colonel Goodrich, mail was "probably the most important single factor in [the prisoner's existence]." Another source said: "Mail and personal parcels were our spiritual reminder that we still lived in the future and that somewhere, somehow, there were persons who had not forgotten us entirely."[35] The presence or absence of mail could bolster or depress the entire camp, and the uncertainties surrounding its arrival were the focal point of much of the prisoners' discontent and the subject of many complaints to the protecting power.

Prisoners could send certain quantities of mail each month. Generals were allowed to send five letters and five postcards, other officers three letters and four postcards, and NCOs and other ranks two letters and four postcards. Sanitary (medical) personnel and the clergy were allowed to send double the number permitted their corresponding rank in the services.[36] The prisoners' outgoing mail had to pass two censors. First, the mail was screened by a designated prisoner in each block to ensure that the writer was not revealing any important information to the Germans or stating something that would be useful to the German propaganda effort or disheartening to relatives and friends back home. Then the German censors struck out anything that cast Germany in a negative light or that appeared to be passing coded information. The block censors in Center Compound returned an average of twenty letters a day to the writers because the tone was sour or self-pitying. Such letters often were responses to mail from home. In November, 1943, for example, numerous letters from the United States revealed very negative impressions of American prisoners of war. One wife wrote to her prisoner husband, "I still love you darling although you are a coward." Another prisoner received a pair of wool socks in a Red Cross parcel. There was a note bearing the name and address of the contributor. He wrote a letter thanking the woman for knitting the socks, and she replied, "Sorry, but I made the socks for a member of the armed forces, not a prisoner of war." In return, the prisoners wrote a barrage of stinging replies. The letters were intercepted by block censors, and the prisoners were reminded once again of the need to write cheerful letters to their next of kin.[37]

There were no restrictions on the number of letters prisoners could receive from home. Since that was the case, the prisoners were

35. *Stars and Stripes*, March 27, 1983, p. 5; Charles G. Goodrich to Maurice Pate, March 22, 1944, in "Stalag Luft III" Folder, RG 389; Mulligan, Burbank, and Brunn, "History of Center Compound," Pt. I, sec. 2-b.

36.   George Tait to Secretary of State, May 11, 1943, in File 740.00114 EW/3604, RG 59.

37.   Mulligan, Burbank, and Brunn, "History of Center Compound," Pt. I, sec. 2-b, Pt. III (Diary), November 28, December 2–3, 1943.

extremely suspicious when month after month they received little or no mail. Many men waited six months to receive their first letter, and the average time en route for letters varied greatly, ranging from three or four weeks to many months.[38] The anxieties created by these delays profoundly influenced the tenor of life in the camp and added tremendously to the hostile feelings the prisoners held toward the Germans. It was clear, the prisoners concluded, that the censors or other personnel in the German administration were intentionally holding the mail. Some prisoners received letters regularly. Others suffered through lengthy "dry spells," only to be suddenly deluged. One officer received 112 letters in two days. Clifford Hopewell, on the other hand, had quite a different experience:

For me personally, the worst thing about it was that I received so very, very little mail and from November 15, 1943, on I never received one damned postcard while others received mail up until just a few days before liberation. I don't know where mine went, but plenty of it was sent to me because when I got home my father gave me a lot of letters he had written that were returned. So did many other friends, and they were all correctly addressed. You just don't know the mental torture it is not to receive mail day after day while all your roommates are getting theirs. I was bitter then about it and I still am, and the day I die I will be bitter about it.[39]

The frequency of the prisoners' complaints suggests that the Germans must have taken some liberties with the mail, but there were other reasons for the delays. It must be remembered that virtually all the mail for the Luftwaffe camps was censored at Stalag Luft III, and the work load at times became overwhelming. The Germans noted that some of the correspondence from home tended to ramble, often about inconsequential matters, which slowed the censoring process. And while the letters to Hopewell were addressed correctly, many were not and therefore remained en route for great lengths of time. There was ample publicity in the United States about the proper address:

Kriegsgefangenenpost
1 First Lieutenant GEORGE WEBSTER
Kriegsgefangenennummer 1391
Germany, Stalag Luft III

38. Letters from the United Kingdom took an average of sixty-one days to arrive in Center Compound; from Canada, thirteen weeks; from the United States, fourteen weeks; from Australia, sixteen weeks; from New Zealand, fifteen weeks; and from South Africa, eleven weeks (*ibid.*, Pt. I, sec. 2-b).
39. *Gefangenen Gazette*, December 19, 1943; Hopewell to the author, July 29, 1982.

And yet, the mail addressed to prisoners in Stalag Luft III often revealed errors in the address block with such variations as:

Krigsfangen NO. 3 D. L. Inpostlager
M—Stammalger Lutz
Saglet Luff
Ftenlager
Kriegsgenen Nr. der Luftwaffe
Stammlar Luft
Stagjug 4
Stall A. G.[40]

In addition, transportation across the ocean and in Germany itself was often disrupted. These possible explanations in no way diminish the prisoners' anguish. They merely serve to put the mail controversy into context. The prisoners might have gained an even better perspective on the problem if they had known that German prisoners in America often had to wait one year for their mail because of the "poor censoring set-up in the States."[41]

40. American Chargé d'Affaires at Bern to Secretary of State, January 5, 1945, in File 711.62114 Mail/1–545, RG 59.

41. The report was made by an unnamed Red Cross representative who visited Center Compound on May 22, 1944 (Mulligan, Burbank, and Brunn, "History of Center Compound," Pt. III [Diary], May 22, 1944). Although this information was obviously available to the camp leaders who talked to the representative, there is no indication that the average prisoner was aware of this assertion. Even if they had been told, it is unlikely that they would have believed it, since the prevailing view in Stalag Luft III was that the prisoners in America were pampered.

12

The Brighter Side of Life

The prisoners in Stalag Luft III created and enjoyed numerous entertainments, fine performances in theatrical productions, concerts, radio programs, and a wide range of hobbies and crafts. They constructed their own theaters, either from the foundation up or by modifying existing buildings, and spent considerable time in them. As in so many other facets of life in Stalag Luft III, the prisoners were surprised by the talent that existed within their ranks. Individuals with experience as professional actors and musicians led and participated in the entertainment programs in virtually every compound. The programs served several purposes. Long hours of practice consumed time that otherwise would have weighed heavily. The various performances gave the prisoners innumerable outlets for constructive self-expression. And the entire entertainment program diverted the prisoners' attention for varying lengths of time and added important features of "normal" community life to their environment.

Music was very important to the prisoners, and it absorbed a great deal of their time and attention as both individual and group efforts. They tried to become familiar with the latest songs through the new prisoners. They also received recordings through the YMCA and played them at concerts in the theater, out of doors, and in their rooms. The gramophones also came from the YMCA and though there never seemed to be enough (the limited number was further reduced by mainsprings breaking and needles wearing down), they were widely circulated. Each room enjoyed its own private record session about once a month. Records would be played well into the evening and even after lights-out. Usually one of the men in the bottom bunks would tend the machine so the others could go to sleep to the sound of their favorite tunes.

The YMCA supplied enough instruments to permit each compound to form its own band, and by means of careful scheduling, most compounds were able to support a dance or jazz band, a concert orchestra, and a junior band or orchestra.[1] Sheet music came from the same source, though the prisoners themselves wrote a considerable amount of music. In many cases they sat down with an instrument and worked out familiar songs note by note; at other times they composed their own renditions or wrote entirely new orchestrations. If the men could acquire one copy of anything, they recopied it by hand until everyone in the band was supplied.

Henry ("Nick") Negorka was one of many prisoners who devoted endless efforts and talent to musical pursuits. A graduate of the Warsaw Conservatory as well as the Juilliard School of Music, he could play any instrument and he arranged and composed music. Nick was particularly adept at listening to a tune hummed by a new prisoner and translating it into a full musical score. In time the lyrics were pieced together as well, and before long he had the compound bands playing the latest tune, an achievement of intense interest to the older prisoners. Ralph Saltsman remembers Nick's work fondly: "Not only did he have the ability to copy tunes; he often would be in the kitchen by himself at two or three o'clock in the morning with his accordian, writing out music for the orchestra."[2]

Each compound took great pride in its musical groups, most of which had names such as the Sagan Serenaders, the Luftbandsters, and the Flying Syncopaters. Concerts were often presented in other compounds, thus increasing the amount of exposure given each group and allowing longer runs for particular shows. In November, 1943, Major C. R. Diamond, a past member of the Philadelphia Philharmonics, was allowed to take his Glenn Miller Band to North Compound, where it performed on four successive days. Following a huge success there, the band moved to Center Compound, where they played three or four scheduled programs to a wildly enthusiastic audience of Americans and British. After the third performance, while walking back to South Compound, the band played "America"

---

1.   A typical orchestra comprised of first and second violins, viola, clarinets, trombones, saxophones (playing horn parts), cello, bass, trumpets, bassoon, flute, piano, and drums. Agenda for Meeting with YMCA Representative in Stalag Luft III on July 14, 1943, in "Education and Entertainment" Folder, AF Museum, Wright-Patterson AFB.

2.   Interview with Ralph Saltsman, November 28, 1979.

in front of the Kommandantur and all the prisoners within hearing distance cheered loudly. The commandant promptly canceled the remaining performance and banned all practice in South Compound for four weeks, saying that the men were not very tactful in their sudden burst of patriotism.[3]

There were also numerous choirs for church and general entertainment. Organized and spontaneous sing-alongs were held, and were especially frequent when the compounds first opened and more formal presentations had not yet been arranged.

The compound theaters were the focal point of the prisoners' formal entertainment world, and no effort was spared in making the facilities and equipment as authentic as possible. Canadian Red Cross boxes provided the wood for the approximately three hundred seats built by the prisoners for each of the theaters. German blankets served as the basic material for the curtains, which were often decorated with tassels made from unwoven socks. Carefully preserved wrapping paper was the background for stage sets constructed on wood slats that were reused again and again. Nails were often used ten or twenty times before being discarded. Spotlights with tin reflectors were rigged into the ceiling. Oleomargarine was used for grease paint. Costumes were either handmade or rented from Berlin at extravagant prices. The general policy was for the prisoners to offer some form of entertainment in the theater every night. But each prisoner could not attend every night. Most performances had to be given three or four times in order to accommodate everyone in the compound. Among the offerings were classical, jazz, swing, and popular music concerts, public debates and lectures, record concerts, mock radio programs, variety shows, and theatrical productions.

The radio shows resembled Stateside broadcasts in every possible detail, even to the point of including advertisements. The call sign was WPOW in Center Compound and KRGY in South Compound, and the shows were aired over public-address systems supplied by the YMCA. An article in the October 23, 1944, edition of the *Circuit*

---

3. Some prisoners said the song played that day was "God Save the King"; others called it "America." But they all agree that the Germans overreacted since German prisoners in the States were allowed to sing patriotic songs while marching down American streets. See Mulligan, Burbank, and Brunn, "History of Center Compound," Pt. III (Diary), November 26, 29, 1943, for accounts that differ slightly from the one given here.

was headlined "South Camp's Station KRGY Features Familiar to POWs":

It's 4,000 miles as the "Big Ones" fly from Sagan, Germany to the throbbing heart of the entertainment world which feeds "all four" radio networks of America from studios high above Manhattan.

But here "Behind the wire," standard American broadcasts have spanned the miles to bring music, drama, news and education to POWs who are thereby transported from South Theatre to the familiar haunts of home.

It's amazing what can be done with a few Y.M.C.A. records, a baby upright piano, an assortment of camp talent, and the day's German communique.

These are skillfully built into the day's program structure by Director Jim Aubele of WHK-WCLE, Cleveland, whipped into shape by Continuity Chief Dick "Ross" Rossignol of Mutual Hollywood and produced by voices coached by Chief Announcer Ted Brown of Roanoke's WSLS.

Technical problems involving the Y.M.C.A. sound equipment were worked out by D. H. Carey and Don Murchie.

The staff includes such capables as Bill Nance, Jack Mann, Kirt Langberg, Ray Rahner, Joe Rose, Lee Pilert, Jim Roberts, and John Torland, all voices behind the scenes of that familiar ringing phrase:

"KRGY, an overseas division of the American Broadcasting System."[4]

The many theatrical productions given in Stalag Luft III ranged from the very amateurish to some that most observers classified as strictly professional in spite of the total absence of women playing female roles. Most of the compounds produced one or more Shakespearean plays that featured excellent portrayals, elaborate props, and fine costumes from Berlin, all of which amazed and thrilled the initially skeptical audiences.

Renting the historical costumes, armor, and weapons for *Macbeth* cost the POWs more than 2,000 RM, according to von Lindeiner's records.[5] At the other extreme were the original one-act plays put on by each barracks in Center Compound in a series of competitions inspired by the wish to keep the prisoners busy and to encourage interest and participation in theater productions. Even the latter presentations, wherein most of the actors had never set foot on a stage before, were labeled "highly successful." Some of the plays produced in the various compounds were *Dover Road, The First Mrs. Fraser, Juno and the Paycock, The Bishop's Candlesticks, The Man Who Came to Dinner, The Invisible Duke, Front Page, Petrified Forest, Philadelphia Story, Midnight at the Mermaid, As You Like It,*

---

4. As reprinted in Kimball and Chiesl, *Clipped Wings*, n.p.
5. Von Lindeiner, "Memoirs," 149.

Charley's Aunt, Arsenic and Old Lace, The Amazing Dr. Critter-house, Strictly from Hunger, Veni, Vidi, Vici, Boy Meets Girl, Kiss and Tell, The Monkey's Paw, and *Hamlet.*

Variety and comedy shows were the most popular with the prisoners. According to the program, a variety show presented in West Compound included:

```
Theme—"The Prisoner's Song" ...................Band
"Sunday" .......................................Band
Master of Ceremonies ......................Mike Wyse
"Solitude" .....................................Band
"Harvard Square" ..............................Band
"Uncle Sam Gets the Blame" ...............Harmaniacs
"Trains in the Night" ..........................Band
"Impressionistic Dance" ...................Zip Zapinski
"White Christmas"—Vocal ..............Johnny Murphy
"Moonlight Sonata" .............................Band
"Rockin the Blues" ............................Band
"They're Never Too Young" .................Harmaniacs
"They'll Never Believe Me"—Vocal ..........John Palmer
"Siboney" ......................................Band
"Albert"—M.C. .............................Mike Wyse
"You Made Me Love You" .........Mot Williams and Band
"Night and Day" ...............................Band
"El Rancho Grande" .........Jerry "Miranda" Leichtman
"Sleep" ........................................Band
"Mexican Hat Dance" ...........................Band
"Sweet Tender Act"—M.C. ..................Mike Wyse
"Sugar Blues" ...................Tex Newton and Band
"The Earl" .....................................Band
"St. Louis Blues" .............................Band.[6]
```

The prevalence of the "airman's language" often gave these performances a flavor all their own. A January 5, 1944, article in the *Gefangenen Gazette* described an upcoming extravaganza:

"Flieger Frolic", piloted by Jack Wade, "taxis out to take off" the end of this month. This big vehicle clears the runway wing tanks abrim with laughing gas and full bomb load of music, horse play and dancing.

A full crew of comedians and musicians will handle the "gagantic" aircraft. Wally Kinnan and his boys control musical communication, sending a Johnny Ward "jiveocycle" frequency, as Gen Blue and the Three Stooges, White, Jerome, and Morris, "let go" with detonation dialogue and evasive vocal action. Master of Ceremonies, Robert Reginer, lays down a steady fire of

---

6. George Wenthe Diary (Copy in possession of the author; original held by Mr. Wenthe).

dum dum chatter, Bill Couhihan raises manifold pressure with a "taxi-strip-tease." Costumes by Lt. Tabor and stage settings by Sgt. Elliot complete the leadship lineup for a riotous rendezvous and a mirthful mission.

Entertainment was one facet of prisoner life that was perhaps enhanced by the separation of the Americans and British into different compounds. The Americans did not always seem to appreciate British humor, and one suspects that the reverse was also true. At one point the British and Americans in Center Compound came close to blows as a result of an argument over the use of the theater. The problem and the manner in which it was resolved were described in the December 1, 1943, entry in the Center Compound diary: "Highly strained Anglo-American relations in the camp theater staff were diplomatically solved today by Colonel Spivey when the American and British theater managers agreed that they would work together and forget past differences. The men were very persistent and headstrong in the ideas they had concerning Center Compound productions. Once they were on speaking and working terms there was much joking and wise-cracking as each unearthed 'tons' of equipment and material including costumes and paints, which each buried and hid when the feud over the theater management started."[7]

A few movies also were shown in camp from time to time. Some of them were German, but the prisoners attentively watched them anyway. Approximately six or seven American or British films were viewed by the men, among which were *The Spoilers, Shall We Dance?*, and *Bringing Up Baby.*

The prisoners were immensely enthusiastic when it came time to go to the theater. It marked an occasion in their lives when they consciously or unconsciously shined their shoes and dressed in their best clothes in preparation for the few moments in which they could mentally transport themselves outside the wire. Tickets were given out by allotment, and front-row seats were reserved for the brass and visiting dignitaries, many of whom were German, YMCA, and Red Cross officials. They were seated by ushers. After each major performance the prisoners avidly read the reviews in the compound newspapers. Such ingredients created a festive environment, one that the prisoners valued highly, and the success of the entertainment programs went far toward easing the discomforts of captivity.

7. Mulligan, Burbank, and Brunn, "History of Center Compound," Pt. III (Diary), December 1, 1943.

Perhaps no other camp activity matched sports in stimulating mass participation and widespread interest. One observer noted when he visited Stalag Luft III, "The men are young and spend most of their time at games."[8] The prisoners were wise to devote so much attention to athletics, for in addition to occupying their time and taking their minds off the everyday hardships encountered in camp, sports accounted in large part for their remarkably good health. The prisoners in Stalag Luft III were fully aware they were more fortunate than were prisoners in other camps. Indeed, they could hardly help it, since they were constantly reminded that "with regard to sports [Stalag Luft III] is the best equipped [camp] in Germany."[9] And the men repeatedly expressed their gratitude for the generous aid given them by the YMCA and the Red Cross. What did raise their ire, however, was the mistaken image many people had of the camp.

Explanations for the public's erroneous impressions are not hard to find. In keeping with the policy of writing cheerful letters home, few really negative reports got beyond the military and the State Department. A Red Cross bulletin published monthly for the benefit of next of kin printed pictures of one or two swimming pools, and the public assumed that every camp had one. The bulletin sought to allay the fears most families had and tried to highlight the most positive aspects of life in captivity. And finally, most people did not understand that prisoners often boosted their own morale by pretending their makeshift facilities were in fact the real thing. Thus a small and sometimes dirty fire-pool became a swimming pool, and a twisted path in the sand became a nine-hole golf course. Such misunderstandings aside, however, the athletic program in Stalag Luft III was indeed something to be marveled at and appreciated.

The sports the prisoners engaged in varied with the season. Among the British and Commonwealth troops, cricket, rugby, and soccer were popular. The Americans preferred softball and football. In the winter, ice-skating and hockey attracted much attention, though the winter of 1943–1944 was so mild that maintaining a rink was difficult. And the skates were the strap-on kind and very few in number since the Germans were afraid the prisoners would remove the blades to make wire cutters. In addition to these major sports, there were volleyball

    8.   Report of Gunnar Jansson, May 27, 1943, in RG 389.
    9.   Report of visit by Mr. Friedrich and Dr. Bubb, February 22, 1943, in File 740.00114 EW/3977, RG 59.

and basketball, track events, and boxing, wrestling, weight lifting, and fencing. And there were, in fact, several golf courses laid out in the sand between the barracks. It is doubtful, however, if one complete set of clubs existed in the entire camp, and the balls were usually made out of tightly wound leather taken from old shoes or other old balls. In spite of these handicaps, golf was a very popular sport and the limited facilities were almost always in steady use. East Compound alone reported more than three hundred players on the waiting list.[10]

The large number of participants made good use of their equipment and playing areas. When good weather prevailed, scheduled games kept the sports fields busy from morning until dark. Each of the compounds had highly organized clubs and divided the players into leagues for the major sports, each barracks supplying one or more teams. South Compound boasted three softball leagues—a major league, a minor league, and a beginners sandlot league. Among them they played five games a day, six days a week, and involved more than four hundred players. Sunday afternoons featured games—usually the participants wore uniforms received from the YMCA—by the outstanding players in camp. Many teams took on vocational images, such as Crack Pilots versus Bombardiers, and Fighter Pilots versus Bomber Pilots. There was a great deal of competitive interest in the major league: the better players were encouraged to move from one barracks to another to strengthen a ball club, and new arrivals were eagerly recruited.[11] Numerous bets were staked on the outcomes. In West Compound, barracks 163 became the champions in the summer of 1944, and as a result of their final victory over barracks 158, they collected 62 D-bars (army ration chocolate), 61 packs of U.S. cigarettes, and 2 cigars for the loyal rooters of barracks 163. In September they got 82 D-bars and 120 packs of cigarettes from the occupants of barracks 165, who had sponsored a team in a challenge match. Sometimes the Americans would make so much noise during the games that the British would climb on top of their huts to watch from afar. The Germans also found the competition interesting, and von Lindeiner often came to the games, applauding vigorously by beating his cane on his leather boot.

10. Report of Wing Commander Ryder, East Compound Sports Officer, in the agenda for the September 30, 1943, YMCA conference, in "Education and Entertainment" Folder, AF Museum, Wright-Patterson AFB.

11. Goodrich, "History of South Compound," Pt. I, sec. 3A (5).

Individuals decided for themselves whether they wanted to participate in organized sports, but in Center Compound, and one suspects
that this might have been true in the other compounds too, everyone
was required to take some form of exercise each day unless he was ill
or injured. A mandatory fifteen-minute calisthenics session was held
each morning, and sometime during the day most of the men took several walks around the "circuit," the beaten path that ran the perimeter
of each compound just inside the warning wire. Near the end of the
war, Colonel Spivey calculated that he had walked the circuit more
than two thousand times for a total distance well in excess of twelve
hundred miles, not to mention the three or four miles a day he normally walked in the performance of his duties.[12]

It is not surprising, then, that the men managed to stay in good
physical condition in spite of their confinement. A measure of their
fitness can be seen in the outcome of a track meet held in East
Compound on July 24, 1943:

100 yards	10.6 sec.
220 yards	24.8 sec.
440 yards	55.3 sec.
880 yards	2 min. 6 sec.
1 mile	5 min. 1 sec.
Cricket ball	104 yards
Discus	114 ft. $11\frac{1}{2}$ in.
Weight (11-lb. shot put)	42 ft.
High jump	5 ft. 4 in.
Long jump	18 ft. 10 in.

B. A. James, a prisoner in North Compound, commented that the
figures in fact were exceptional. In 1943 he ran in the mile race at a
track meet and barely managed to finish. Furthermore, he felt weak
for days afterward. He concluded that their diet was simply too sparse
to allow for the expenditure of the extra energy required for strenuous
physical activity.[13]

When food rations were decreased in the latter half of 1944, the
prisoners' stamina diminished even more. The emphasis on physical
conditioning remained, however, as the men realized that they had to
stay as fit as possible in the event they had to march to a new location

12.   Neary, *Stalag Luft III: Sagan*, 11; Spivey, *POW Odyssey*, 71, 72.
13.   R. Kellet to Sir Richard Howard Vyse, August 25, 1943, in File 619.2/08,
"Reports and Statistics, American and Allied Internees and POW," Archives Division,
American Red Cross Headquarters; B. A. James to the author, August 6, 1982.

or were faced with the danger of extermination by the Germans, who were becoming increasingly desperate as the war drew to a close. The prisoners' diligence paid rich dividends when they were forced to march westward in January, 1945. Even without those stimuli, however, the athletic programs and physical conditioning would have been worthwhile. They constituted another important ingredient in the brighter side of the men's lives, and contributed immeasurably to a general sense of well-being.

A host of unorganized activities also brightened the prisoners' lives. Various forms of gambling enticed the men to wager portions of their meager resources. Card games occupied the prisoners throughout the long winter months. Numerous hobbies and arts and crafts projects also found adherents.

Gambling and assorted schemes repeatedly appeared in spite of the fact that they were officially banned. In November, 1943, an officer from the Bronx introduced a numbers racket in Center Compound. The camp administration, Foodaco, and the camp newspapers all frowned on his scheme because it threatened to monopolize the medium of exchange—chocolate bars and cigarettes—and the first immediate result would have been the end of Foodaco. The Bronx promoter planned to net 10 percent of all the cigarettes and D-bars in the lottery, which would be run daily. Statisticians in the compound figured that the whole market, including the reserve held by Foodaco, would be in his hands within a month.[14]

Colonel Spivey repeatedly reminded the prisoners of the unique circumstances existing in a prison camp. And even though money had little value behind barbed wire, there were some unscrupulous men who would not hesitate to take every cent a fellow officer had earned while a prisoner. He stated that checks written against future deposits should not be given—there was no guarantee that they would be honored once the men returned home. He urged the men to use their common sense and keep all card games on a friendly basis.[15]

The men generally heeded his advice. There were exceptions, however. One man ran up a debt of five million cigarettes. Another example involved money but, if anything, it reflects the prisoners'

14. Mulligan, Burbank, and Brunn, "History of Center Compound," Pt. III (Diary), November 13, 1943.
15. *Ibid.*, December 20, 1944.

basic sense of honor. As the end of the war approached, numerous pools were begun based on who could come closest to guessing the actual date. One such pool organized in Center Compound called for fifty individuals to put up twenty dollars each in the form of checks written on banks in the United States. The checks were handwritten, many times on old scraps of paper. The officer who won the lottery was able to cash all but two of them, netting him $960.00 out of the $1,000.00 pot. In fact, most debts incurred in camp seem to have been honored after the war.[16]

In spite of the scarcity of materials and tools with which to work, hobbies and handicraft projects abounded in Stalag Luft III. Ingenuity was exercised in turning the crudest materials into fine finished products. Lead from the beads of tin cans was patiently gathered, melted, and poured into carefully carved molds to make military insignia. Old socks were unraveled to obtain yarn for making stocking caps or new socks. Model cars, boats, and airplanes were constructed. Flying model airplanes provided opportunities for men to exhibit their skills in mock air-to-air combat, and bystanders threw sand and pebbles to simulate anti-aircraft fire. Major Simoleit was especially impressed with a little steamboat that one of the prisoners made. It actually steamed across the water with its paddle wheel churning and a little puff of smoke coming from its stacks.[17] Many of the prisoners learned to play musical instruments or draw and paint while in captivity. A favorite pastime was for a prisoner to draw squares across a pin-up picture or some photograph or scene that he was particularly fond of and do the same on a blank wall in preparation for painting a mural. Most of the prisoners also had logbooks, which they kept with diligence, and more than a few tried writing essays and poetry. The quality of their work varied greatly, but enough good items appeared to warrant periodic craft shows. Emmett Dedmon's poem, "Willie Green and His Flying Machine," quickly won well-deserved acclaim:

> This is the fable of Willie Green
> Who invented a Kriegie flying machine.
> 'Tis as weird a tale as ever you heard
> Yet I'll swear by the truth of every word.

16. Interviews with Broach, winner of the lottery, April 19, 1975, and Royal D. Frey, former prisoner in Stalag Luft I, February 25, 1975.
17. "Kriegsgefangenenlager nr. III der Luftwaffe," enclosed in Simoleit to Spivey, December 19, 1968, Simoleit Folder, Spivey Collection.

The man who first heard it, suspicious as I,
Swore by his chocolate 'twas all a great lie.
But imagine his surprise, the gleam in his eyes,
When Willie's machine was seen to fly.

The parts were gathered—'tis no secret now—
But Willie alone knows the secret how.
They were hidden away in corners and places
While he carved away on the spars and braces.

The tin can piles were low indeed
When W. G. performed his deed.
There still is talk of that famous day
As the last Klim-tin was hidden away.

The engine was the first of the plane to be made
With crankshaft of steel from the missing spade.
While in Klim-can cylinders with mighty sound
The butter can pistons went up and down.

The flashy propeller so aerodynamic
Was carved from a board in the barracks attic.
While the peculiar strand that made the ignition
Was a length of barbed-wire from the compound partition.

Fuel was no problem to a man with a head
And Willie got gas from cabbage and bread.
In case of emergency, Willie held,
The thing could easily be Rocket-propelled.

The side of the bed the fuselage made
The stick, the handle of the fore-mentioned spade.
The instruments, it could be seen at a glance
Was none other than the seat of Willie's pants.

Two locker doors the wings did make
With dihedral taper and negative rake.
And a Red Cross box from a racket source
Served as the tail for his flying horse.

The question of wheels was mighty hot
Till Willie remembered the communal pot.
While Kriegies were wondering how it disappeared
Willie's machine became tricycle geared.

There were no guns on Willie's steed
Its only defense was its excessive speed.
To weight down the tail our hero used
A size "12" pair of British shoes.

And when it was done our Willie cried
"Enough, enough, I'm satisfied."
And one dark night when conditions were best
Willie's machine was put to the test.

The prop turned over, the engine caught
"Aha," said Willie, "twas not for naught."
The plane jumped forward, started to fly
And was over the fence in the wink of an eye.

The guard yelled "Verboten" and started to shoot
But all his efforts were as good as "Kapoot."
Willie flew on and into the dark
Toward Ellis Island and Battery Park.

The plane flew on until Willie spied
The lights that marked the other side.
He felt so good and oh so free
His Red Cross box fell into the sea.

A crowd was there when he landed his crate
"Where am I?" he asked. "It sure looks great."
"Why where," they cried, "were you headed for?"
"This my boy————is STALAG LUFT IV."[18]

The YMCA provided the bulk of the equipment the men used in their numerous "leisure time" pursuits, and the prisoners expressed their gratitude at every opportunity. The wide range of religious, educational, entertainment, and athletic activities available in Stalag Luft III earned for that camp the reputation of being the "country club" of the prison camps. It may have appeared that way in comparison to some of the more poorly run camps, but in terms of what a prisoner of war camp is supposed to offer captives, as specified in the Geneva Convention of 1929, Stalag Luft III was only the norm and not the exception. The convention fully recognized that prisoners of war needed to be active in the normal human pursuits. The absence of other employment made leisure-time activities both possible and necessary. The prisoners in Stalag Luft III made such excellent use of the limited diversions available to them that many people gained erroneous impressions about the camp, impressions that obscured the dismal and unpleasant realities of life in a prisoner of war camp.

18.   Emmett Dedmon quoted in Kimball and Chiesl, *Clipped Wings*, n.p.

13

Covert Activities and German
Countermeasures

The covert activities undertaken in Stalag Luft III fell primarily into two categories—intelligence and escape. The hope of regaining one's personal freedom undoubtedly provided the initial impetus for escape, but could not have remained the prisoners' only consideration since the odds against success were so overwhelming. Most of the prisoners in Stalag Luft III were able to see that other worthwhile objectives might be achieved as a result of their escape activities. While still at Barth, the prisoners had come to the conclusion that escape was the one operational mission still available to them. Whether anyone made a home run to his native land or not, the mere attempt to do so caused the Germans no end of trouble and expense. As a group, the prisoners followed President Lincoln's admonition to his Civil War generals that if they could not do the skinning, they could at least hold a leg. They accepted as their operational mission the task of holding one leg of Germany, hoping that diverting manpower to guarding prisoners might handicap Germany on the battlefield.

In order to translate this concept into reality, the prisoners organized their efforts and made escape their number-one priority. In this sense, everything that went on in camp, whether it pertained to education, entertainment, allocation of Red Cross and YMCA goods, or strictly following the chain of command, had to do with escape, at least partially.

The task of gathering and disseminating intelligence was as important to the prisoners as escape work was. Because of the dangers involved, however, only a few were allowed to engage in intelligence activities or learn the extent of such operations in the camp. Reliable intelligence was essential to the success of the escape program. And in a very real sense, it was a second operational mission—the German war effort was in fact hurt as a result of information obtained in Stalag Luft III and covertly transmitted back to England. Most important, however, the apparatus provided the information the men needed to assess accurately their precarious situation as captives of the Nazis. As accounts of German atrocities became known to the prisoners, they became convinced that survival itself depended upon being able to anticipate actions by the Germans that could endanger their lives. Thus the prisoners had to probe for clues and information that might indicate what the Germans were thinking and planning. In short, the prisoners engaged in espionage in an effort to aid the Allied cause and to protect themselves in the event the Germans threatened their safety or their very lives. Under international law, espionage is an offense punishable by death. So intelligence gathering was not in the same category as escape: it never acquired the "game" aura, and only a fraction of the prisoner population participated. But when it came to influencing the tenor of life in camp, escape and intelligence either affected or were affected by everything that went on.

The Luftwaffe personnel guarded the prisoners carefully in order to keep them from escaping or engaging in undercover activities. Like the prisoners, the German administrators and guards learned from experience. The security measures in force at Stalag Luft III when it opened in April, 1942, were notably stricter than those at Barth up to that time. And since the Germans continued to learn from their mistakes, intelligence and escape activities became increasingly difficult in succeeding years. The prisoners and their guards exercised considerable ingenuity and imagination in the pursuit of their respective goals.

Over the years the Luftwaffe developed a highly sophisticated system for guarding their captives and detecting secret activities. Whenever possible, people performed the same duty over a long period of time so their accumulated knowledge and experience would be fully used. The ferrets were specially selected and trained. The museum at Sagan was to assist them in their efforts to learn every subterfuge and technique the prisoners had devised. The usual precautionary measures were diligently observed, and the Germans exercised care in their roll calls and barracks and compound searches and vigilance over the prisoners' daily activities.

Appell was usually held twice a day, but when an escape had occurred or the Germans thought one was about to occur, three and sometimes four Appells were held throughout the day and during the night. Unless the weather was extremely inclement, the daytime Appells were held outdoors. During especially bad weather and at night, the count was taken in the barracks by room.

In theory, the Appells provided the Germans with an accurate count of the prisoners. The men fell out by barracks and either marched or walked onto the sports field where they lined up in five files arranged in a large, hollow square. The German Lager officer walked around the inner side, counting the men as he walked by. An Unteroffizier (equivalent to a sergeant) assisted him, simultaneously passing to the rear of the blocks and comparing his count with the officer's. The blocks came to attention one at a time while being counted, and the block commanders exchanged salutes with the German Lager officer when he approached. There was a space of several yards between each block of men representing a barracks, and a smaller space between the occupants of each room. Armed guards were posted to intercept any prisoner who attempted to move from one group to another during the count. Each barracks commander had to prepare a list or "chit" about the men assigned to his barracks: the number on parade from each room, the number sick in each room, names of personnel working in sick quarters, the Vorlager, and the theater, and the total number of personnel in the barracks. These chits were given to the compound adjutant, who then presented them to the German Lager officer. If the figures derived from the count did not match those on the chits and those in the official camp roster, a recount was taken.

After the British and Americans were placed in separate compounds, the Americans gradually adopted an attitude toward the Appells that differed from the one in the British compounds. The Americans concluded that since it was impossible to avoid having Appells, they would comply with the Germans' wish for an orderly assembly and use Appells to further their own ends in maintaining a high standard of discipline. They therefore marched to Appell in formation and stayed in relatively good order. The British, on the other hand, tended to be haphazard. While one group was being counted, the others milled about within their assigned area, talked to their neighbors, or engaged in horseplay. The conduct of the British was not a matter of lack of discipline, though it did perhaps reflect the boredom these men felt at having to attend two or more Appells a day for weeks, months, and years on end. Rather, their approach was an integral part of their escape program. When a prisoner escaped, the first few hours were crucial because his chances of success increased in proportion to the distance he traveled from camp before the alarm was sent out. By milling about, the British made it easier for a man from one group to slide over to another and be counted twice, thus concealing the absence of the escaped prisoner during one and sometimes several Appells.[1]

There were times when the Americans, too, were uncooperative. Upon arrival in Center Compound in the summer of 1943, Colonel Spivey discovered that during Appells prisoners sometimes hid in various locations around the camp in an effort to confuse and inconvenience the Germans. Spivey put a stop to this practice since it only prolonged the time the other men had to stand on the field.[2]

In another case the Americans staged a minor rebellion to protest the frequency of Appells. After the mass escape from North Compound in March, 1944, the Germans instituted a third Appell each day. It was called without warning sometime between the two regular Appells, and the object was to make undercover work more difficult. The prisoners in South Compound considered this an unjust nuisance since nobody there had been involved in the escape. So they decided upon passive resistance and disorderly conduct during the extra Appell held on March 27. The assembled men stood about casually, smoked cigarettes, and failed to come to attention for the Lager officer, who found counting an impossible task and gave it up temporarily. Shortly thereafter the prisoners were summoned for another Appell, and this time the parade ground was lined with German soldiers holding rifles and machine guns at the ready. The prisoners wisely chose to cooperate, and the Appell was completed without further incident. The protest was not without effect, however. The extra Appell was soon discontinued, and several Germans referred to the affair as being the sort of thing they wished to avoid if possible.

The Germans made bed checks routinely. One prisoner from South Compound recalled almost with a twinge of nostalgia the sound of German boots echoing in the night and the familiar "sing-songing"

1. Goodrich, "History of South Compound," Pt. I, sec. 2B; "A History of Stalag Luft III," Pt. I, pp. 3–5.
2. Spivey, *POW Odyssey*, 36.

voice of a guard saying, "Appell in zee night—eviryzing is awright—gudnight, gentlemen."[3]

The Germans also conducted frequent and thorough searches of the barracks. Sometimes a particular barracks seems to have been chosen at random, but usually the search was the obvious result of someone or something having aroused the Germans' suspicions. Generally, the Abwehr men entered the block in question during the morning Appell. When the prisoners returned, they found guards posted and could not enter their block until midafternoon when the search was completed. The searches were conducted with additional vigor if the Germans had reason to believe that there were escape aids or other forbidden items such as a radio or camera. Then they would tear open mattresses, remove sections of the walls, floors, and ceiling, clean out lockers and stoves, take books off shelves, and leave the rooms in a state of total disarray. It took the prisoners considerable time to clean up afterward, and they angrily protested the searchers' methods, but to no avail.

The Germans also had a variety of other ways of keeping track of the prisoners and curtailing their covert activities. One common practice was to station men with field glasses behind brush piles in the woods outside the wire in an effort to detect suspicious actions. They studied the traffic patterns within the camp. If the number of people entering or leaving a particular barracks seemed to be too large, for example, the Germans immediately suspected that the prisoners were dispersing sand from that building or using it for other forbidden purposes and it was soon searched. After a successful escape through the perimeter fence in September, 1942, sentries patrolled outside the fence, and other sentries were placed in the woods at night. During the hours of darkness, Hundführer, armed guards with specially trained dogs, patrolled inside and outside the compounds. Von Lindeiner felt that his twenty-four dog handlers and thirty-two dogs did a superb job. A watchdog could cover at least a 1,000-foot-wide area of the woods surrounding the camp, whereas a guard could only control an area about 35 feet wide. The guards stationed in the towers watched the prisoners from above, looking out upon the camp's 58.7 acres with its 5 miles of perimeter fence.[4] At the same time, ferrets observed the prisoners. The ferrets routinely probed underneath the

3.   Kimball and Chiesl, *Clipped Wings*, n.p.
4.   Von Lindeiner, "Memoirs," 183, 98.

barracks and sometimes left twigs in certain positions so they could easily tell whether the ground had been disturbed. At all times they looked for fresh earth in the cracks of floors or in the seams of prisoners' clothes and constantly checked the whole surface of a compound in order to discover whether earth from underground was being deposited aboveground. Seismographs were buried by the fence to detect tunneling work, and many of the prisoners believed that some of the rooms used for meetings were electronically bugged. Altogether, the Germans kept a close watch over the prisoners, and their persistent efforts were rewarded. In all likelihood, however, no matter how hard they tried, it would not have been enough. One prisoner noted, "No soldier has ever had so strong an incentive to keep prisoners in as prisoners have to get out. If a prisoner of war devoted all his time and energy to making his plans he was likely to find a way out in the end. That did not mean that he reached home, but to some prisoners of war a few days freedom were worth the effort of years."[5] This certainly held true for the prisoners in Stalag Luft III, and it applied to more than just escape, for the prisoners approached almost all their covert activities with the purpose and dedication normally associated with escape. To them, their few, but by no means insignificant, successes seemed worth the years of effort.

Intelligence operations in Stalag Luft III, though organized somewhat differently in each compound, were designed to achieve similar results through proven techniques. The prisoners sought any information that would assist them in their escape work as well as military information that might help them assess their own situation or possibly be useful to their respective home governments. In order to obtain and properly disseminate this information, the men in each compound set up staffs capable of handling radio work, code messages, interrogations, contacts with the Germans, internal security, intercompound and intercamp communications, and escape intelligence.

The interrogation of new prisoners did more than merely check identity. It yielded details for casualty reports, such as how the victim had been shot down (by flak or fighter), the type of attack, altitude when shot down, location, whether the plane caught fire in the air, whether the pilot had been killed or the casualty was due to fire, loss of control, weather, engine failure, or being hit by their own bombs. Other questions dealt with whether the crew succeeded in reaching

5. Crawley, *Escape from Germany*, 18–19.

and bombing the target or had to jettison their bombs, whether the aircraft was destroyed, difficulties with escape hatches, and the name of any secret equipment not destroyed. Anything of a military nature that the prisoner saw or heard between the crash and imprisonment—airfields, factories, state of railways and rail traffic, morale, etc.—also was collected, as were descriptions of the prisoner's interrogation by the Germans and especially how the Germans knew of his unit, mission, and secret equipment. Equally important were messages from Allied agents in civilian jails and what conditions were like there and in concentration camps.[6]

Members of the intelligence staff also chose some men, prior to escape attempts, to pay special attention to matters that could be of importance to the prisoners, such as train timetables, bomb damage, the attitudes of the German people toward prisoners, the state of German morale, and anything else that might possibly be significant. The practice of alerting the escapers in advance was necessary since the staff discovered that recaptured men who had not been briefed were able to provide very little useful information. But those who had been asked for specific comments usually made valuable contributions. The same was true of men who traveled outside the camp on official business. Prisoners who attended burials in the nearby cemetery, who went into Sagan to load Red Cross parcels, or who spent time in neighboring medical facilities were often able to bring back military information and special communications from foreign workers.

Perhaps the most important information came from the Germans themselves who revealed much to observant contact men. Prisoners who spoke German fluently were given extra food and other valuable items to bribe camp personnel. If a particular member of the camp staff held anti-Nazi sentiments, the bribes were hardly necessary, as was the case with "Corporal Harry." Harry was a genuine democrat who was prepared to take considerable risks to do anything he felt might bring an end to the Nazi regime. Once his confidence had been gained, he supplied a great deal of information and also made suggestions about British propaganda, which he listened to on the radio. The lack of an Allied policy toward postwar Germany, he said, was having a bad effect upon the increasing number of Germans who, from the time of Stalingrad onward, realized that the war was lost. His

6. "A History of Stalag Luft III," Pt. I, p. 66.

access to various offices enabled him to keep the prisoners well informed about orders from Berlin and about camp administration in general, and he regularly reported on changes in the regulations governing access to or exit from the compounds, alterations in passes, and changes in German personnel.[7]

Getting help and information from other Germans was more difficult. Usually a contact man was assigned to only one person, and it was his job to gain that individual's confidence over a period of time. To do this, the prisoner invited the German in for coffee or tea, offered him cigarettes and food, and talked to him at length about such subjects as his family or the problems and fears he encountered on his job. Once a good rapport was established, the contact man asked the German for a small favor and, if this was forthcoming, increasingly larger ones. At some point the German was likely to refuse, at which time the prisoners were not above blackmailing him, since by this time he had clearly compromised himself. Germans who cooperated in this manner were called "tamed" Germans. Information obtained from such individuals included: details of troop movements, locations, and strengths; locations of factories, the war matériel produced, output, and the number of workers; locations of airfields, the strength of their ground and air defense, and the number and types of aircraft; experiments with new weapons and the locations of the test sites and their defenses; the importance of local railways for transporting troops and matériel; German reactions to different types of warfare, methods of attack and strategies, new weapons, and the effects of all these things on morale; the extent of the bomb damage and its effect on production of matériel and on morale; and internal economics, details of the cost of the war, the shortage of food, raw materials, fuel, etc., and their effect on morale.[8]

The information gathered from these and other sources, such as German newspapers and radio broadcasts, was collated, evaluated, and disseminated. Data that might be helpful to the prisoners' home governments were transmitted through coded letters, in casualty reports, inside pictures, and by personnel who visited the camp or by prisoners who were repatriated.

The coding effort that began in the early years of the war at Dulag Luft and Barth was continued and expanded at Stalag Luft III. About

7. Crawley, *Escape from Germany*, 42–43.
8. *Ibid.*, 64.

15 men coded letters at Barth; the number of people involved at Sagan ranged from 40 in South Compound to more than 170 in the British compounds.[9] Those in South sent out several hundred messages and received as many in return. Until 1943 the United States government evinced little interest in this work, and the American prisoners obtained authorization to use the British system. In 1943 the U.S. War Department developed its own system, but it proved to be inferior, and the prisoners decided to continue to use the British system, though the incoming messages were still in the American code.[10] The work was carefully administered by the senior officers in each compound. They received reports, determined what information was worth transmitting, and then gave it to the coding section, which condensed the data into messages that never exceeded seventy-five letters in length. The same staff prepared the work for the letter writers by encoding the information and disguising it on card game scorecards. The letter writer himself did not know what information he was transmitting, nor did he know the identity of the other writers. When he received a letter, he gave it to the coding staff, who decoded it and reported to the senior officer.[11]

The other methods used to send information home were less sophisticated, but no less important. In the spring of 1943, the prisoners discovered that the Germans allowed casualty reports to go through with details uncensored. The prisoners immediately began including considerable information in them, all written in plain language. Another technique was to split the backing paper from a photograph, insert a piece of tissue paper on which data had been written, glue the picture back together again, and mail it through normal channels. The prisoners also transmitted information through individuals who were being repatriated. They memorized detailed reports word for word and were thoroughly tested by the intelligence staff to ensure that all the facts were straight. And finally, on rare occasions, opportunities arose for getting information home through people who visited the camp.[12]

9.   Goodrich, "History of South Compound," Pt. III, secs. 2, 3; "A History of Stalag Luft III," Pt. I, pp. 67–69. Figures are not available for Center and West compounds, and it is not known in which of the three British compounds the 170 men worked.
10.   Goodrich, "History of South Compound," Pt. III, sec. 3.
11.   Bob Stark, "Intelligence Operations in Air Force Officer Prisoner-of-War Camps in Germany, 1939–1945," n.d. (MS in Spivey Collection).
12.   "A History of Stalag Luft III," Pt. I, pp. 79–80; Stark, "Intelligence Operations," 7.

The effectiveness of the prisoners' intelligence system is clearly demonstrated by two incidents. While the men were still at Barth, a young German corporal became friendly with an American and one day in casual conversation disclosed that he would shortly be one of four hundred NCOs to take a two-month special officers' course at a camp in the village of Werel, near Frankfurt. Wings Day, the Senior British Officer at the time, reported this information home in a brief message that ended with "Suggest blitz." Nearly a year later the same German was at Stalag Luft III and told his prisoner friend that the RAF had bombed the camp at Werel, that thirty candidate officers had been killed, and that the camp had been reduced to ruins. His final comment was "I cannot understand why they should have bombed a little place like Werel." In the second instance, a German corporal deliberately gave details about a twenty-five-mile-long war factory that ran along the railway line near his hometown of Oplin. In return, he received a number of pills that the British camp doctor guaranteed would induce the symptoms of incipient ophthalmic goiter and ensure his rejection in a medical review for front-line duty. He gave pertinent details about the factory's layout and pointed out its exact position on one of the prisoners' maps. This information also was sent home, and three months later the American 12th Bomber Group, operating from Italy, pulverized the Oplin factory network.[13]

In terms of the prisoners' morale, the most important intelligence operation in camp had to do with receiving BBC newscasts. The prisoners relied upon these broadcasts to balance the information given in the German news communiqués. Radios were strictly forbidden in camp, and extreme caution had to be exercised in using them and in telling the prisoners what was said.

The first radio brought into Stalag Luft III was carried by the NCOs who were transferred from Barth to Center Compound in April, 1942. The parts had apparently been obtained through bribery—that is how new pieces were secured when elements of the existing radio were found and confiscated. The radio was put together and hidden in an accordion that could still be played. One evening in January, 1943, while one of the prisoners was working on the radio, the Abwehr NCO walked into the barracks without any warning and covered the man with his pistol. Another prisoner quickly pulled the fuses, and in the darkness the prisoners hid most of the parts before

13. Smith, *Mission Escape*, 113–14.

the German could get a flashlight out of his pocket. The men were able to replace what was confiscated, but less than two weeks later the Germans surrounded the same barracks at five o'clock in the morning and conducted a very thorough search. This time the entire radio, with the exception of the earphone and several parts, was found and confiscated. The prisoners later learned that the search had been carried out at the suggestion of the German who had originally supplied the radio parts. He was given leave as a reward. He later supplied new parts to replace those that had been found. The reconstructed radio was hidden in a wall panel and remained undetected throughout the remainder of the time the NCOs stayed in Center Compound. When they left for another camp in June, 1943, they took the set with them.[14]

There is some doubt how the officers in East Compound obtained their first radio. One account says it was smuggled in by the prisoners when they were transferred from Barth. Another report says the British prisoners who came from Warburg brought the radio with them.[15] Both accounts agree, however, that only one radio existed in East Compound in the first months after the compound was opened and that it was discovered and confiscated in July, 1942. They were unable to obtain another one until December, 1942, when a contact man acquired a German People's Set. Unfortunately, it was broken and needed parts. Before they could be obtained, the essential parts of another receiver were smuggled into the camp by the men who returned from Schubin in April, 1943. The pieces were put in individual luggage, a biscuit tin, and a medicine ball. By the end of April, they were assembled and hidden in a wall of barracks 69. In December, 1943, the receiver was rebuilt into the top of a desk. By June, 1943, another set had been made from spare parts and placed in a

14. "A History of Stalag Luft III," Pt. II, pp. 55–56. The same source reveals that leave was offered to any German who succeeded in finding the earphone. The same man who had previously betrayed the prisoners suggested that the earphone should be left in a certain cupboard so that he could make sure the Abwehr found it. He brought a new set, and they arranged the time for the "discovery" of the old earphone. The German's story to the Abwehr was that he had learned of the hiding place by overhearing a conversation. The earphone was duly found, and the German got an additional fourteen days' leave. This kind of jockeying between the prisoners and their contacts was apparently quite common.

15. The account of the radio being transferred from Barth is found in Albert P. Clark, "Radio and News Service," 1945 (MS in Clark Collection), 1–2. The prisoners from Warburg are given credit in "A History of Stalag Luft III," Pt. I, p. 72.

false side of a box in which a prisoner kept his clothes. Spare parts were continuously collected from contacts and some arrived in parcels from the United States and England.

When the prisoners were transferred from East to North Compound, Captain Pieber, the German Abwehr officer who had helped the prisoners at Barth and had accompanied them to Stalag Luft III, carried one of the radios for them in his bulging briefcase.[16] In June, 1943, a contact secured a large radio from which the prisoners obtained enough parts to build a small set. The pieces left over were donated to the Americans who would be transferred to South Compound.

The prisoners in South Compound sought to add to their collection, but the lack of critical pieces kept them from constructing a set of their own. However, on January 10, 1944, a specially built radio was received in a parcel sent by the United States government. Occupying a space no larger than that required for a carton of cigarettes, the radio had been smuggled past the censors in a large container. During the late spring and summer of 1944, prisoners in South Compound obtained several radios from various sources and either gave them to other compounds in Stalag Luft III or kept them hidden as reserves.[17]

The officers in Center Compound got their first radio by stealing it from the infirmary in the Vorlager. One of the American pre-med students who was allowed to accompany patients to and from the infirmary spotted the radio, smuggled it under his large coat, and managed to get it into the compound, where several men quickly disassembled it and hid the parts. A few days later, it was reassembled in the shape of a long tube and placed in a hollowed-out table leg. Four nails in the tabletop directly above that leg were connected to the lead-in wire and the earphones. The drop cord over the table was attached to two of the nails to provide power. Earphones were hooked to the other two nails. The earphones were made from the parts of the

16. Smith, *Mission Escape*, 112. According to this same source, Pieber also carried in his briefcase that day two pamphlets giving the takeoff, landing, and general flying instructions for the Messerschmitt 109 fighter and the twin-engine Dornier DOX, which the prisoners studied in case they might someday be in a position to steal one of these aircraft and fly home.

17. Interview with Albert P. Clark, March 8, 1976; Clark, "Radio and News Service," 2.

loudspeaker plus the thin diaphragm from the hermetically sealed tins of English cigarettes.[18]

Perhaps even more difficult than obtaining the radios was the continuing task of keeping them hidden from the Germans and disseminating the news without being detected. Again, only a few men in each compound actually listened to the broadcasts or even knew where the radios were. At night, after prisoners had been posted around the barracks so they could observe the approach of any Germans, the intelligence personnel responsible for radio operations listened to the newscast and wrote out brief summaries. Usually, one man in each barracks got a copy the next morning, read it to the assembled members of his barracks, and then destroyed the paper on which it was written. As with all such secret materials, the summaries were written on tissue paper so that they could be eaten easily if discovery appeared imminent.

The radios assumed special importance in the spring of 1944 when the prisoners worked out a system to speed up communication between the prisoners and their home governments. Months often elapsed between the time a message or inquiry in a coded letter was sent to the authorities at home and the time an answer was received in Sagan. They rightly concluded that if a special radio code could be devised, answers to those letters could be received in camp the same day that a reply was formulated in England. Two intelligence workers in East Compound developed a code suitable for radio transmission. Based on the letter code, it was far more elaborate and contained provisions for frequent changes since the Germans obviously would try to break it. Details were then sent home in duplicate, a process that involved about twenty different letters. In addition, the prisoners took advantage of an unusual opportunity. A high-ranking official from Geneva known personally to an officer on the intelligence staff visited the camp and agreed to take a cable to the man's wife and dispatch it from Sweden, not knowing, of course, what it really contained. As there was no limit on space, the entire wireless code was given in this long cable, which was devoted to advice on family investments and the education of their children.[19]

18.   "A History of Stalag Luft III," Pt. I, p. 103; Spivey, *POW Odyssey*, 103–104. I found no information on radios used in West and Belaria compounds.

19.   The men who knew about the contents of the cable were amused some time later when a coded message was received, asking on behalf of the officer's wife whether she was to follow this advice on investments. Stark, "Intelligence Operations," 7.

Seven weeks later the prisoners received word that the intelligence authorities in England had accepted the wireless code. Thereafter, replies were normally received in camp within twenty-four hours after they had been framed in England. This procedure was also used in the American compounds. One report indicates that on July 4, 1944, the home governments began sending special instructions to the prisoners over the radio, and that from then on, official instructions and information were received regularly. The report also notes that receiving the messages entailed considerable inconvenience, loss of sleep, and nervous strain for the individuals involved. Consequently, in South Compound at least, two teams worked alternately—four days on and four days off.[20]

The prisoners also devised covert ways of communicating between compounds. Two methods used in adjacent compounds were to place a message in a weighted object, or "bird," such as a tin can or hollowed-out rock and throw it over the fence, or to spell out messages in semaphore. The idea of throwing messages over the fence was not popular at first. It was difficult to coordinate the effort since the object had to be thrown when it would not be seen by the guards or the Germans working in both compounds. In addition, there was the problem of finding qualified "hurlers." Through trial and error, however, the prisoners perfected this method, and messages flew back and forth over an average distance of sixty yards with surprising frequency. The semaphore method called for a person standing in a room that was visible from another compound to send Morse code with a small paddle. A dip to one side was a dot, to the other was a dash. It was simple and effective but time-consuming, and could be utilized only when the two stations were close together. The simplest method was to have a person who could move from one compound to another carry messages. Father Coates, the British Catholic chaplain who worked in Center Compound, often brought verbal messages back to Center after his visits to other compounds. Much information also was exchanged when workers or leaders from the various compounds got together to conduct such official business as allocating Red Cross parcels, YMCA equipment, or canteen supplies. After the mass escape in March, 1944, the Germans did everything in their power to keep the prisoners in the different compounds apart. Even

20. Clark, "Radio and News Service," 2.

then the men were able to get important messages back and forth. Perhaps the most sophisticated approach involved the accountants who managed the prisoners' communal fund. They, along with the German accounting staff, met once each month in the Kommandantur to audit the records. At these meetings the prisoners naturally had many papers, among which were coded messages. During the meeting, papers would be strewn all over the table, and afterward the prisoner accountants would include each other's coded figures among their own papers. Once each man was back in his own compound, he would decode the messages at leisure.[21]

The prisoners placed tremendous emphasis upon their ability to establish and maintain secret intercompound communications. For day-to-day business, as well as undercover activity, proper communication between compounds was essential. In the normal course of events, weeks might pass before a routine financial matter could be handled through official channels, and such channels could not be used at all for covert work. Finally, the Germans were only too eager to play one compound off against another, and it was only by means of secret communications that the prisoners were able to achieve a high standard of coordination and maintain a unified front against the common enemy.

Yet another area of intelligence involved photographic work. The prisoners needed cameras to take mug shots for the forged passports carried by escapers, to document certain aspects of camp life and conditions in camp that they felt violated the Geneva Convention, and to secure photographs of certain Germans who might be sought by the Allies after the war.

Prior to the summer of 1943 the prisoners possessed only "pinhole" cameras, homemade devices without true lenses. During that summer, however, contact men in North Compound obtained excellent German equipment through bribery. Alexander MacArthur, a former photographer for the Chicago *Times*, was assigned duties in the Vorlager and had frequent contact with German workers. In addition, the West Compound intelligence staff officially asked him to cultivate a contact among the Germans. MacArthur selected a Corporal Fischer, a former trapeze artist. The Escape Committee kept Mac-

21. Stark, "Intelligence Operations," 5; Mulligan, Burbank, and Brunn, "History of Center Compound," Pt. V; Albert P. Clark, "Signals," 1945 (MS in Clark Collection), 1–2.

Arthur supplied with trade goods, and he used them well. After some time he approached Fischer and asked if a camera might be procured. Fischer said such an item would be hard to get—he did not even know where he might begin to look for one. About a month later he called Alex aside and gave him a package. MacArthur smuggled it into the compound and was surprised to find an F-1 Leica. A couple of days later, Alex asked Fischer where he got the camera, and was politely reminded that it was none of his business, an answer that MacArthur fully expected to hear.[22]

At first the photographs were clandestinely developed by commercial black-market studios, and bribed German camp personnel took the film in and out of the camp. In early 1944, South Compound obtained three cameras along with quantities of film and developing equipment. Passport photographs were given priority, and as many as thirty-two mug shots were taken during the course of one afternoon. Each man posed in front of a canvas backdrop with artificial lighting. The subject was dressed in civilian clothes and had a European haircut. Since the standard size for German passport photographs was larger than those made by the thirty-five-millimeter cameras the prisoners had, they built enlargers out of the extra camera lenses. All necessary darkroom equipment over and above what was obtained through bribery or in parcels from home was constructed inside the camp. Selected Germans were lured to prearranged spots where pictures could be taken through knotholes or attic windows in the barracks. In some cases, photographs were taken from roofs of buildings, and the only protection was diversion.[23]

A final responsibility assigned to the intelligence staff was emergency planning. From the winter of 1943–1944 onward, the prisoners learned more and more about the atrocities occurring in Germany, through eyewitness accounts. Some prisoners entering the camp had been beaten by the Germans, and some had been mistakenly sent to concentration camps before being redirected to Stalag Luft III.

Bill Powell was among 165 fliers who had been routed to Buchenwald by mistake. Shot down on January 29, 1944, he evaded capture with the help of the Dutch underground until August 16. With the invading Allied forces only miles away, the Germans began to close in,

22. Interview with MacArthur, September 7, 1979.
23. Albert P. Clark, "Photographic Work," 1945 (MS in Clark Collection), 1–2.

forcing Bill to attempt an escape through France. Captured there in civilian clothes and without military identification, he spent one week at Fresnes prison before boarding a train for what he thought would be further interrogation at Dulag Luft. Instead he ended up at Buchenwald, where he joined a number of others still listed as saboteurs. With no warning of what to expect, Powell stared in disbelief as he witnessed the terrible machinations of life and death in one of Germany's worst concentration camps. He had every reason to believe that he and his fellow Allied inmates would be sucked into the vortex as well. Wearing prisoner number 78162, he slept outside most of the time and worked at gathering undetonated incendiary bombs that had been dropped on the camp. With shaven head, dressed in clothes that had been worn by fifty others, and wearing no shoes, he felt totally humiliated. Weighing 185 pounds when he was captured, he emerged six weeks later weighing barely 118.

Stalag Luft III looked to him like a real haven. There he found people who spoke English, he received more adequate clothing, enjoyed an extra ration of Klim milk, and regained twenty pounds. Somewhat puzzled at first why few prisoners seemed interested in what happened to him in Buchenwald, he concluded that they were no more prepared to grasp what was happening elsewhere in Germany than he had been. What he did not know, however, was that the senior officers and intelligence staffs did indeed take note of the condition of the men from Buchenwald. It coincided all too well with the murder of the fifty men who participated in the Great Escape. The camp leaders thereafter felt they had no choice but to try to prepare for almost any eventuality.[24]

The prisoners concluded that there were several contingencies for which they should be prepared: a German withdrawal that would

---

24. Interview with Bill Powell, November 7, 1984. He noticed that people frequently questioned the idea that an Allied Air Force officer spent time in Buchenwald. When applying for aid in a veterans' hospital many years later, he encountered yet another doubting Thomas, this one being the examining physician who skeptically scribbled in Powell's medical record: "Claims he was in Buchenwald." For more information the prisoners obtained about atrocities then occurring in German concentration camps, see E. R. McCright, "Urkunden Stalag 3 fur die altesten offiziere (Record for the Senior Officer), giving names and addresses of dead flying comrades," in Manuscripts Division, Library of Congress. This report, written in pencil in South Compound, relates the eyewitness accounts of several fliers who were mistakenly sent to Buchenwald, where they saw many of the horrors associated with that camp. The prisoners collected such information in anticipation of a postwar crimes report and, in the process of doing so, kept themselves well informed on the state of affairs in Germany.

leave the prisoners on their own; an attempt by the Germans to move them into cities to discourage Allied bombing or into a redoubt, after which the Germans would bargain for peace terms, using the prisoners as hostages; a move westward before the advancing Russian army; a rescue attempt by Allied forces or envelopment by advancing Russians; and finally, an attempt by the Germans to liquidate the prisoners en masse. The prisoners devised several plans, which varied somewhat in each compound, but generally fell into the following patterns.

In the event the Germans decided to move the prisoners westward, the men were determined that every effort should be made to escape in large numbers. In South Compound, for example, the Escape Committee was charged with the responsibility of providing 25 percent of the people in the compound with articles of civilian clothing, maps, papers, money, and the necessary information to make an escape attempt if the opportunity should arise. If, on the other hand, the Germans should suddenly pull out of the area, the prisoners would have to shift for themselves until rescued by the Russians. This entailed more dangers than one might suspect. If the situation became bad enough to warrant such a move on the part of the Germans, the prisoners realized that the possibility existed of the country being thrown into chaos. Under such circumstances, all utilities would likely be shut off and the camp itself would be raided. Hence the prisoners laid plans for their own defense and established procedures for getting along with minimal resources as well as for giving the Russians the camp's location and the identity of its inhabitants.

What most worried the prisoners was the possibility that the Germans might attempt to liquidate them en masse. The plans they devised to meet this threat called for extreme measures that would have been inappropriate in any other situation. In essence, suicide squads would try to overpower the attacking forces. Meanwhile, the other prisoners would rush the guard towers and the fence along only one side of the compound according to a prearranged plan. In certain cases, tunnels that were virtually completed were left unopened so they could be used at the last moment, if necessary, to get specially trained teams of prisoners outside the wire, where they could neutralize some of the attackers and perhaps secure arms for the prisoners still inside.[25]

25. For more details on the prisoners' contingency plans, see Goodrich, "History of South Compound," Pt. III, sec. 6; and Spivey, *POW Odyssey*, 114.

All the prisoners' intelligence operations required strict security measures. In safeguarding intelligence activities, as well as escape work, the prisoners found that they could easily be their own worst enemy. New prisoners especially tended to be overly curious about certain activities in camp, and it took only a few of them gathered in one place to arouse the Germans' suspicions. Hence, the first step was to instruct new prisoners to ignore—or pretend to ignore— much of what they saw going on about them. Second, elaborate procedures were established to ensure that sentries, normally called "stooges," were strategically placed so that the whereabouts of every German insiαe a compound could be known at all times. In addition, normal precautions were observed, such as limiting the number of people who knew about certain projects, concealing the identity of the people who worked on the different staffs, prohibiting loose talk, and keeping records to a minimum or writing them on cigarette paper so they could be chewed up and swallowed with relative ease if necessary.

The stooging system was thorough and effective. The main stooge, the duty pilot, sat at the front gate and logged the Germans into the compound, a practice used and perfected at Barth. George Sweanor pulled the duty often and was interested in the German reaction to it. One day the German ferret, Corporal Griese (called Rubberneck by the prisoners because of his long neck), tried to hide in the compound at the end of his shift. All other Germans gradually left, and the compound looked clean. George's log, however, showed Rubberneck still in. A thorough search revealed that the door to the cookhouse had been locked from the inside. Suspecting that Rubberneck was in there, the searchers closed the outside shutters. An hour later he stomped out, red-faced and mad, glaring at George and his partner as he passed by the duty pilot's post. Rushing to find Glemnitz, he demanded that the duty pilots be thrown in the cooler. Glemnitz refused. He was philosophical about the post and each time he entered the compound he made a humorous remark about atten- dance records. Late one afternoon he came in, walked right up to George, saluted, and barked, "I'm in. Mark me down." Then he added, "Who else is in?" Taking George's log, he stared in disbelief: no other German was booked in. Rubberneck and another ferret, Adolf, had been in but had left a few minutes before Glemnitz entered. Glemnitz's smile faded. "Book me out," he said grimly. Later the prisoners learned from a tame ferret that Glemnitz had gone straight

Figure 3.
Fields of view covering tunnel Harry

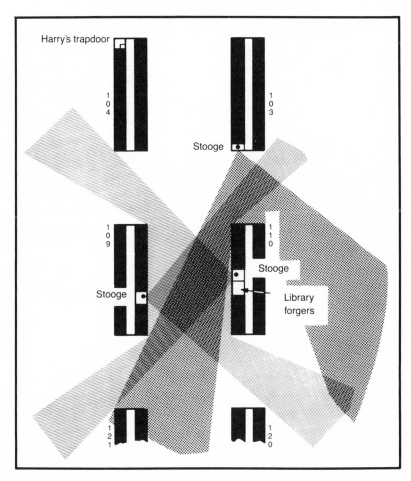

to the German barracks, where he found Rubberneck and Adolf getting ready to go into town. Both had been listed for duty in the compound until 5:00, and the log showed they had left at 3:50 P.M. Adolf got four days in the cooler; Rubberneck was given extra duties and was confined to the camp area for two weeks.[26]

26. Sweanor, *Pensionable Time*, 126–27.

Stooges also took up positions in various parts of each compound to keep track of the ferrets. Figure 3 shows how the prisoners positioned themselves in order to provide overlapping views of every access to a point where covert activities were under way. If by some chance a German should get close to the workers before the alarm could be given, additional prisoners were posted nearby to intercept the intruder. If the situation was not critical, a prisoner would ask the German a question or otherwise divert his attention. If the German's approach was determined, indicating he knew what he was looking for, the prisoners took drastic measures, such as engaging in a brawl so one of them would be flung against the unwanted visitor. This disruptive exercise would be followed by extended apologies, all of which consumed sufficient time so the work could be hidden and everyone could assume an air of innocence. The need for such precautions can readily be appreciated in view of the prisoners' many intelligence activities. The importance of security measures becomes even more obvious when one adds the numerous escape efforts and the large amount of covert work that was carried on in support of the escape program.

Acting in a Shakespearean play, North Compound
Courtesy of U.S. Air Force Academy Library

North Compound theater
Courtesy of U.S. Air Force Academy Library

The air pump used in tunnel Harry for the Great Escape
Courtesy of Richard Kimball

Trolley car, track, and shoring boards as reconstructed for the escape museum
Courtesy of Richard Kimball

Vertical shaft of tunnel Harry
Courtesy of Richard Kimball

A German inspects the exit opening of tunnel Harry
Courtesy of Richard Kimball

Makeshift shelters at Moosburg
Courtesy of Richard Kimball

The American flag rasied at Moosburg at the moment of liberation
Courtesy of U.S. Air Force Academy Library

Glemnitz, Simoleit, and Day at the 1965 Stalag Luft III reunion
Courtesy of U.S. Air Force Academy Library

14

Escape: The Binding Thread

Paul Brickhill's book, *The Great Escape*, and the movie based on his book have made the name Stalag Luft III synonymous with escape. Although this image unfortunately overshadows the prisoners' numerous other achievements, it is essentially accurate and fitting. No other camp activity so exhibited the prisoners' ingenuity, dedication, and sense of community spirit and purpose.

Under the leadership of Wings Day, escape activities grew from a fragmented effort in 1939 and 1940 to a highly organized aspect of camp life in 1941. By the time the prisoners were transferred from Barth to Stalag Luft III in April, 1942, they had adopted escape as an operational mission, had formed their Escape Committee or X Organization, and had gained diverse practical experience. Jimmy Buckley (the man appointed by Day to head the X Organization), Squadron Leader Roger Bushell, Flight Lieutenant John Gilles, Flight Lieutenant Harvey Vivian, and an American serving in the British army, Major Johnnie Dodge, and three men selected from each barracks were on the original committee. Under their experienced leadership, escape work became a highly coordinated and sophisticated art which absorbed the energies and talents of a considerable percentage of the prisoner population. Roger Bushell escaped before the prisoners arrived at Stalag Luft III. He subsequently was recaptured and later rejoined the escape effort, serving as the mastermind. But the X Organization otherwise remained intact and immediately went into operation at Sagan, the prisoners' "new battlefield."

In time the escape program at Stalag Luft III took on an even more serious complexion than it had possessed at Barth. The change at first was inspired largely by Wings Day, who again, as Senior British Officer in camp, found himself having to formulate policy in light of the prisoners' environment. As the years went by and the Germans continued to ride the tide of victory, Wings concluded in the spring and summer of 1942 that too many of the prisoners (and he apparently included himself) still thought of escape in terms that were inadequate to the situation confronting them. For Wings, "the time had come to change into higher gear, to interpret the motives for the existence of his escape, intelligence and security organization in terms of the war effort rather than as a sort of fairly safe game with the International Red Cross as referee." His feelings coincided with those of most activists in that "prisoners of war, just because they had brushed with death and fallen into enemy hands, should not be thought of as semi-neutrals."

Earlier he had thought of escape as a way to maintain the prisoners' pride, for through such activities the prisoners felt they were still waging war against the Germans. Now escape was to be pursued primarily to hinder the German war effort, and there would be less concern for its impact upon the prisoners' morale. At Barth, Wings had been nervous about letting a man take suicidal risks while attempting escape because he had not yet convinced himself that the likely outcome was worth the added danger. He altered his thinking on this issue while at Sagan. On distant battlefronts, operations were not calculated on the basis of discomfort or loss of life but solely on their contribution to winning the war. Combatants were seldom justified in curtailing their efforts merely because the probable results appeared microscopic, and he felt that the same philosophy should dictate the actions of prisoners of war. Besides, it was well known that escapes sometimes had a considerable effect upon the enemy. Every escaped prisoner caused the Nazis to mobilize hundreds of soldiers, and a mass escape (five or more people) meant that thousands of police, troops, and civilian volunteers had to turn their attention toward recapturing the escaped men. Escape alarms created havoc at all echelons of the enemy's command structure and upset the local populace. In short, virtually every escape made the enemy divert attention from the war zone to the home front.

Wings knew he had the resources to transform this idea into reality. To compensate for the loss of Bushell, who remained at large for some months, Wings had acquired new talent—a group of prisoners who came from Warburg. They were all hardened and experienced prisoners who brought with them a mass of new ideas and techniques, including the art of extremely skillful forgery and some handy tips on transforming RAF uniforms and battle dress into whatever might be needed, civilian or military. Jimmy Buckley incorporated these men into his X Organization, and full-scale escape work began.[1]

In the following weeks and months, the prisoners in East Compound made a variety of escape attempts, which included using disguises for walking out through the gates, sneaking off while on sick call parades, filing through the bars on the cooler, cutting through the wire fence, and tunneling. That last activity was the most feverish. During the spring and summer of 1942, the prisoners started some sixty or seventy tunnels. Most of them were poorly concealed, only a few men got out of the camp, and virtually all the escapers were recaptured.

The Germans and the prisoners now engaged in their duel in earnest. When the Germans dug a seven-foot trench around the compound, the prisoners crawled into it and began to tunnel from there. The Germans filled in the trench and planted microphones in the ground around the fence; the prisoners set about digging deeper tunnels beyond the range of the listening devices. When the Germans discovered and destroyed the tunnels with regularity, the prisoners adopted an idea brought over from Warburg. First, two trapdoors were cut in the floors of two barracks, and two shallow "camouflage" tunnels were dug. Each went down about four feet and then went about thirty feet toward the fence. Halfway along the horizontal part of each of these tunnels, the prisoners made a second trapdoor. They dug down another twenty feet before again going toward the fence. The Germans seldom crawled through a tunnel when they found it, usually being satisfied to cave it in with water. The prisoners thought that if the Germans discovered and destroyed the shallow tunnels, the deeper ones could be tapped from a different direction and continued without much delay. One of the entire tunnel complexes, along with its second trap, was uncovered and destroyed; but the other one, which originated in barracks 67, went forward. When the sand began to build up under there, the prisoners dug a short tunnel back to the adjoining hut and started putting sand there. The main tunnel itself was then channeled under the cookhouse, but to their dismay, they found no space under it.

Again the Germans struck, found the shallow dummy tunnel, and caved it in. As the prisoners had anticipated, the main tunnel was not

1.   Smith, *Mission Escape*, 81–82.

found, so they dug a new dummy tunnel from another room in barracks 67 and sank a secret shaft to link once again with the main tunnel. Unfortunately, all the burrowing had undermined the barracks' foundations, and the weight collapsed the new dummy tunnel, bringing down a ten-foot stretch of sand on one of the tunnelers. He miraculously had his face just over the trapdoor to the secret shaft and could breathe. Disregarding their own safety, the other tunnelers dug frantically for an hour before pulling him out. Another shallow dummy tunnel had to be dug, along with another deep shaft, before contact could again be made with the main tunnel. From then on, the tunnels were fully shored.

Months passed, and the engineering feat progressed well, reaching three hundred feet by autumn. With only about one hundred feet to go, the Germans launched an intensive search of the building from which the tunnel started. Underneath they found fresh sand over the exit of the dispersal tunnel, dug down to the trapdoor, and traced the hole all the way back to the deep shaft. They then destroyed the entire complex of burrows.[2]

To no one's surprise, a major purge out of the camp followed the discovery of the tunnel in October, 1942. About one hundred men, mostly from the escaping fraternity, were sent to Oflag XXI B at Schubin within that same month. Although not originally included in the group, Wings asked permission to go along, and his request was granted. Many of his closest friends and associates were going, and he wanted to be with them. Besides, a higher-ranking officer, Group Captain Martin Massey, had arrived, and the camp would be in good hands. And Roger Bushell, who had been returned to Sagan after evading capture for six months, could handle anything undertaken by the remaining members of the escape organization.

The night before they left, Wings and Buckley had a long talk with Bushell and recommended that he shut down all escape activities for a time. He had been rescued from the Gestapo only through the intercession of prominent persons, including Captain von Massow. Although Bushell was now back in prison, he was a marked man, and certain death awaited him if he was caught outside the camp again.[3]

2. "A History of Stalag Luft III," Pt. I, pp. 37–38; Brickhill, *The Great Escape*, 24–27; Smith, *Mission Escape*, 88.
3. Smith, *Mission Escape*, 89–91.

The tempo of escape activity in East Compound did not pick up again for several months after the October, 1942, bust. Tunneling usually slowed in the winter months anyway, and the ranks of the original escape organization had been badly depleted by the Schubin purge. As the Germans soon came to realize, however, transferring of the prisoners solved nothing; it merely moved the battlefield to another location. Before winter set in at Schubin, an attempt to scale the wire while the perimeter lights were momentarily fused out had been tried, and, with Buckley again at the helm, six tunnels had been started.

One of the tunnels at Schubin proved to be an unqualified success. On March 3, 1943, forty men crawled out the opening beyond the wire and scattered themselves throughout the Reich. Within two weeks, everyone but Buckley and his traveling companion had been recaptured. These two men reached the Danish coast and set out in a small boat to cross the remaining three miles to Sweden. No one knows for sure what happened, but a heavy fog settled in during the night, and it is suspected they were accidentally run down by a ship. His companion's body washed ashore sometime later, but no trace of Buckley was ever found. An invaluable member of the escape organization had disappeared from the scene forever, but not without exacting a price from the Germans. The escape diverted more than four thousand German troops to the area and, for a period of a week or more, held the full attention of at least one thousand policemen and home guardsmen.[4] Another purge followed. It did not come for almost two months, but several hundred men were involved, and they were all sent back to Sagan.

When the Schubin men arrived back at Stalag Luft III in May, 1943, they discovered many changes and anything but the quiet that had prevailed when they had left the previous October. During the intervening months the new North Compound had been built. The prisoners who had remained in East Compound over the winter became aware of the construction work on North Compound in early 1943 and learned that they would be transferred there when it opened. Bushell had taken Wings's and Buckley's advice and kept escape activities to an absolute minimum throughout the final months of 1942 and into the early months of 1943. The lack of activity had lulled the Germans, and by the turn of the year they had con-

---

4. *Ibid.*, 95–97, 103–109; Brickhill, *The Great Escape*, 27.

cluded that the prisoners had resigned themselves to captivity. Consequently, when the Germans announced the pending move to North Compound, they did not suspect an ulterior motive on the part of the prisoners who volunteered to help build the camp because they wanted to be kept occupied.

The Germans gave the prisoners permission to work in the new camp, and Bushell set the Escape Committee to work. Before his return in October, 1942, while he was still making his way through Germany and hiding out with Czech partisans, Bushell conceived an intense hatred for the Nazis. He thus had arrived independently at Wings's conclusions about escape and had committed himself totally to the idea of turning Stalag Luft III into a hornet's nest for the Germans. Bushell thought primarily of causing maximum harm to the Reich by arranging mass escapes on a scale never before imagined by the Luftwaffe, and set about getting two hundred or more men beyond the wire at one time.

The Escape Committee met and began to lay their plans. Bushell's requisitions astounded the men: shoring boards for three tunnels, each descending thirty feet and extending out toward the woods three hundred feet or more; underground railways and workshops; two hundred forged passes; two hundred civilian outfits; two hundred compasses; and one thousand maps. When the chief forger, Tim Waleen, heard the request for two hundred passes, all properly dated, his only reply was "Jesus." Bushell reportedly answered, "Maybe he'll help you."[5]

The volunteer workers were busy. They surveyed and stepped off the new camp with great precision. The men also gathered and hid materials left by the workmen—nails, cement, electrical wiring, pieces of lumber, metal, and anything else that might prove useful later on. Because of the relative ease with which these items were obtained and the numerous prospects for escape the prisoners now envisioned, the opening of North Compound became known to many as the Golden Era. On April Fools' Day the prisoners scheduled to be moved from East Compound to North transferred their belongings,

5. Brickhill, *The Great Escape*, 31. Brickhill's account of these efforts and their culmination in the mass escape on the night of March 24–25, 1944, provides detailed coverage of all aspects of the episode, and I have relied upon it heavily. The information provided here mentions little that has not already received widespread public attention, but is included because the events were important in the overall history of Stalag Luft III.

among which were detailed plans for three large tunnels. Tom, Dick, and Harry, as the tunnels were named, originated from barracks 123, 122, and 104, respectively (see Figure 4). All three tunnels were well under way when the men from Schubin arrived. Relations between the Americans and British had been good. And although the Americans were a minority in the North Compound, they were fully integrated into the camp's administrative and escape machinery. Until Colonel Goodrich entered their ranks a short time before the purge from Schubin, Lieutenant Colonel Clark had remained the Senior American Officer. He and other Americans had distinguished themselves in every camp activity. Americans worked in each of the "factories" that manufactured escape materials. Jerry Sage proved to be a genius at the seemingly impossible task of "destroying" sand from the underground tunnels. Clark had established a fine security system.

Clark served as Big S in the escape organization in North Compound. His mannerisms and physique gave him the perfect cover. In fact, most prisoners were unaware of the key role he played. And Clark knew instinctively the advantages of perpetuating his low-profile innocent image. Among other things, Clark divided the compound into two sections: the "S" or safety zone was the east portion of the camp where the gate was situated; the remaining area was in the "D" or danger zone. As soon as a German went into D he was followed, and if he got within fifty feet of an exposed tunnel or factory, warnings were issued and the work put away until the intruder moved out of the area. In time the prisoners developed techniques and practiced drills so they needed only minutes to pack everything away and conceal all activities.

Protecting all the work in the numerous factories was a major undertaking, but so was the labor that went on there. The methods used to produce escape materials were developed largely by the prisoners in East and North compounds and were used in the other compounds as well.

Clothing used in escapes was obtained from several sources, including the Red Cross clothing store in the Vorlager, the Abwehr store of confiscated clothing, parcels from prisoners' next of kin, successful trading by contact men, and through clandestine shipments from the American and British intelligence services. Cloth of all kinds was used, such as blankets, sheets, quilts, towels, kit bags, and wool comforters. The prisoners who worked in the clothing store were especially helpful since they were sometimes able to appropriate con-

Figure 4.
Tunnels Tom, Dick, and Harry

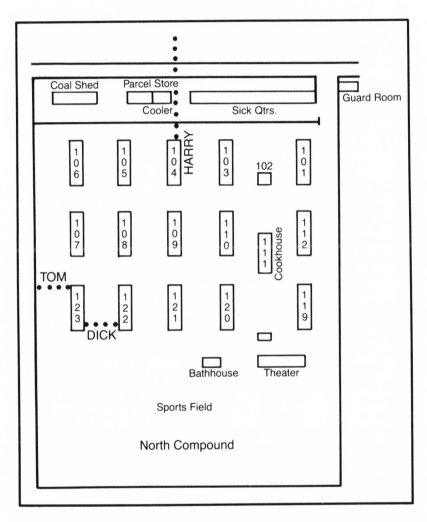

siderable quantities of clothing and other materials. In East Compound, for instance, the German officer in charge of the store removed all the civilian buttons on the greatcoats. He absentmindedly left them on a shelf, and one prisoner carefully took them. The items sent by the home government were cleverly concealed. Blankets were sent with concealed markings that, when rubbed with a damp cloth, provided detailed patterns for men's suits. One RAF officer's uniform received in North Compound proved, on close inspection, to be a cleverly disguised Luftwaffe uniform.

Dyes were indispensable and were needed in considerable quantities. Permanganate of potash and gentian violet were stolen from sick quarters. Chloride of lime left by the Germans in the washhouses for cleaning purposes was used for bleaching. Tea and coffee were used especially for dyeing khaki trousers. Coloring was also obtained by boiling bookbindings. Contact men secured some dye, and in late 1943, British and American sources began supplying dye that could be used with cold water. This was particularly useful since all the others needed boiling water, which had to be fetched in jugs, ostensibly for making brew, and boiled up again on room stoves. All dyeing took place in the barracks at night, and every article had to be dried in time to be hidden in the morning. Records from East and North compounds indicate that many varieties of escape clothes were prepared. Forty-six overalls like those the ferrets wore were made from sheets dyed dark blue; those worn by German and foreign workmen were made from white unstriped pajamas dyed dark blue. Forty-two German uniforms were put together, including caps, belts, buckles, and insignia. The prisoners remodeled their field service caps, and the roundel and badge were embroidered on; the buckles, buttons, and badges were created by pouring molten silver paper from cigarette packages or lead from the beads of tin cans into casts made out of soap or plaster of paris taken from sick quarters. Contacts secured the loan of buckles, buttons, and badges long enough for craftsmen to make impressions for the casts. Belts were made of black paper from barracks walls, by altering existing belts, or from leather boots. Two hundred sixty civilian jackets were made from uniform tunics dyed after pockets and belts were removed and corners were rounded off. Uniform trousers and blankets were tailored into 230 pairs of civilian trousers. Officers' greatcoats, with shoulder straps removed and civilian buttons substituted, became 140 overcoats.

With altered lapels, substitute buttons, and modified pockets, military uniforms were transformed into 100 civilian suits. Altogether, 300 civilian caps emerged from blankets, including ski caps made from officers' hats with cardboard-stiffened peaks. Uniform ties with patterns worked in colored threads became 90 civilian neckties. From kit bags and the mackintosh covers in which game boards were sometimes sent came 60 haversacks. Shirts and waistcoats were modified with pockets to carry a ten-day supply of food concentrates.[6]

Forged papers were as important to the escaper as was his specially designed clothing. The materials needed for this arduous task included pens, brushes, inks, paper, tracing paper, and copies of the original documents, all of which were procured from a variety of sources. Contact men provided these items in limited quantities. The prisoners used toilet paper and the flyleaves of books and Bibles for tracing paper. Linoleum and rubber from boots were used to make stamps. Pens, inks, and paper were obtained from the education office and in parcels from home. A few Germans provided the original documents for copying and often warned the prisoners, through the contact men, when the passes were changed. Some documents were also received from home governments, but these were usually outdated before they arrived. The prisoners produced such documents as the *Dienstausweise* (a brown card entitling the holder to be on Wehrmacht property); *Urlaubsscheine* (a yellow form used as a leave chit for foreign and domestic workers and soldiers); *Rückkehrscheine* (a pink form for foreign workers being sent back to their own country); *Kennkarte* (a light gray form that served as an identity card); *Carte d'Identité* (identity card issued in France that bore a fifty-centime stamp); *Sichtvermerk* (a visa); *Ausweise* and *Vorläufige Ausweise* (passes and temporary passes); *Polizeitliche Bescheinigung* (a police permit authorizing the presence of foreign workers in given areas); and letters from firms for which the holder was supposedly working, with the firm's heading on the notepaper.

Some of these documents were covered with closely printed lines, and others had a background of fine whirled lines. Some took one man a month to produce, working five hours a day. Mistakes were sometimes removed by means of a lit cigarette. Almost all the work

6. "A History of Stalag Luft III," Pt. I, pp. 21–24, and Pt. III, pp. 14–15.

was done by hand. A few items were typed, however, and at least one German took things home and had his wife type them for the prisoners.[7]

A special food concentrate was made for the escapers that could be stored indefinitely. It consisted of Red Cross food with high nutritional value, such as milk powder, Morlicks powder or tablets, vitamin pills, oatmeal, crushed biscuits, Ovaltine, raisins, glucose, and chocolate. These items were boiled together until they formed a fudgelike substance. During 1942 the prisoners also developed two white powders that reportedly quenched thirst.

Maps were drawn to various scales for every probable escape route from Germany. The originals were secured from contacts or borrowed from the Newsrooms. Copies were either hand drawn or reproduced by means of jelly crystals from Red Cross food parcels combined with ink from indelible pencil leads that had been boiled down. Toilet paper was used for tracing paper. Several prisoners in East Compound worked every day for one month to produce a large-scale, detailed map that was used for briefing escapers.[8]

Compasses were acquired from prisoners who managed to retain them until they arrived in camp and from a manufacturing process that enabled the prisoners to turn out hundreds with relative ease. Australian Flight Lieutenant Albert Hake and Captain John Bennett, an American B-17 pilot shot down in September, 1942, developed the technique for making compass cases out of old phonograph records and glass. He also adopted the practice of putting "Made in Stalag Luft III" on them. To make the compasses, a circular piece about the size of a nickle was stamped out of heated records, molded into the shape of a cup, and beveled around the top edge. Cardboard was then placed inside the cup to act as a cushion for the glass cover and to absorb moisture. A phonograph or sewing needle was mounted in the center to serve as the post upon which a magnetized strip of razor blade could rotate. Directional markings were inscribed on the cardboard with phosphorous paint.[9]

A variety of miscellaneous escape equipment also was constructed in the camp or obtained from diverse sources. Rifles, carved from

7. *Ibid.*, Pt. III, pp. 17–18.
8. *Ibid.*, Pt. I, pp. 26, 27.
9. Mulligan, Burbank, and Brunn, "History of Center Compound," Pt. V; interview with Clark, April 15, 1976.

hunks of wood, had stocks stained with brown shoe polish. The "metal" parts were lead pencil markings polished until they appeared to have been blued. Holsters were made out of stiff cardboard stained with shoe polish. Tools left lying around by workmen when the compound first opened were collected by the prisoners and hidden. Others were stolen from workers and electricians who entered the camp from time to time. Such things as bolts from wagon wheels became hammers and picks, and table knives became saws and chisels. Gramophone springs also were made into saws. Parts for wire cutters were taken from stoves. Wood for shoring up tunnels was obtained by removing wall sections from obscure parts of buildings, by disassembling tables, benches, and other camp equipment, and by taking several of the eight or so boards that supported the mattresses in the bunks.

Finally, numerous gadgets were devised to aid in the construction of tunnels. Air pumps were made out of two kit bags distended with wood hoops. The valves were worked in part by springs taken from chest expanders provided by the YMCA for physical conditioning. The air lines consisted of dried-milk tins connected end to end. Digging tools were made from tin cans and wood. Tin tunnel lamps were filled with margarine that had been boiled and strained to get rid of the water. Wicks were made from pajama cords.[10]

Many hiding places were found for all these materials. The tunneling equipment was usually stored where work was being done; other items were stowed in "inactive" tunnels. The carpentry shop installed special wall cupboards and built false bottoms and backs into closets and footlockers. In addition, numerous items were buried in the gardens and elsewhere.

The factories were located throughout the camp. Forging documents and mapmaking had to be done close to windows where there was good light. The prisoners tried to perform noisy labor in the tunnels or near band or choir practices. Much activity took place in the classrooms, theaters, and church rooms, where they could easily work on clandestine projects while appearing to be occupied with approved tasks.

In addition, many escape-related chores required the cooperation and labor of almost everyone in camp—stooging, for example, and disposing of tons of sand. Right under the eyes of the Germans,

10. These miscellaneous items are discussed in numerous sources, but see especially "A History of Stalag Luft III." Pt. I, pp. 32–36.

hundreds of cubic yards of whitish yellow sand were dumped in the compound and dispersed without leaving any telltale signs for the ferrets to detect. This was done primarily in authorized digging projects such as gardens, and then small quantities of sand were worked into the existing soil over a long period of time. The sand was usually carried out of the tunnel area in small elongated cloth bags concealed in the carrier's pant legs or under his coat. A string attached to a pin opened the bottom of the bag, and the sand gradually drained out. On the sports fields, players dispersed the sand during the normal course of play.

Given American participation in these wide-ranging activities, the prisoners in North Compound had to make a difficult decision when they learned that the Americans were to be placed in a separate compound during the summer of 1943. If work on the three tunnels then under construction continued, the Americans would be long gone before any of them could be finished. After weighing the pros and cons, the Escape Committee decided to concentrate solely on Tom. The effort produced a tunnel that extended 260 feet toward the woods, and the projected exit was about 140 feet outside the fence. Only the upward shaft remained to be dug when the Germans discovered the tunnel and destroyed it. The German explosives' engineer, unfamiliar with such a long tunnel, overloaded the charge: the tunnel caved in, but so did the framework and roof of barracks 123.[11]

The Americans in North Compound moved into South Compound one week later. About the same time, American prisoners were being placed in Center Compound, from which the NCOs had recently been transferred. The Americans in Center and South compounds generally succeeded in duplicating the British effort to manufacture escape equipment and devise sophisticated and complex escape schemes. The Americans, however, never achieved fame as escapers, primarily because they arrived in large numbers at a time when escape, for reasons that will be explained, was becoming increasingly difficult and extremely dangerous.

Americans in Center Compound found upon their arrival in August, 1943, that the few British officers sent to help them get established had already formed an escape committee and undertaken numerous escape projects. The Americans were accepted into the organization, but disagreements frequently arose. In this instance,

11. Brickhill, *The Great Escape*, 100.

the British felt that the Americans were too individualistic, and with regard to the early arrivals in Center Compound, they appear to have been right. The British, for example, shared the labor of digging tunnels and did not question that certain men would escape first when the tunnel was finished. The Americans in Center were initially unwilling to admit that one person was any more qualified to escape than another was.

In time the Americans in Center adopted most of the British attitudes toward escape and made progress in their own efforts. Colonel Spivey had been shown the three tunnels under way in North Compound during his short visit there in August before he became the SAO in Center. Rather than attempt anything so ambitious, however, the Escape Committee in Center decided to try a rush job and take the Germans by surprise since they would undoubtedly think that the new prisoners were still too disorganized to do much tunneling. Several long tunnels were constructed, one of which reached a length of about one hundred feet before it ran into a cesspool and was abandoned. At least four other tunnels were dug, and there were numerous attempts to fool the Germans into letting prisoners out through the gate or over the fence. Between August, 1943, and March, 1944, however, only one man from Center succeeded in getting outside the wire. The British flier planned to imitate one of the well-known ferrets who had a habit of walking slowly around the camp with his hands clasped behind his back. For weeks, the escaper practiced the German's distinctive gait and posture. A ladder was constructed the night before the escape and stored in a barracks attic. At the appointed time, during lunch hour when most of the Germans were eating, the escaper donned his specially made clothes, took the ladder, and stalked slowly across the warning wire toward the fence. He yelled in German to a guard in the nearest tower that he was going to climb the fence to repair the barbed wire. The guard let him proceed. The prisoner climbed the ladder to the top of the fence, lowered himself down the other side, climbed the other fence, and casually walked into the woods. But the only German he encountered was a man he had been trying to "tame." The German was therefore readily able to identify him. Within minutes the prisoner was led back through the gate and placed in solitary confinement.[12]

12. Spivey, "History of Center Compound," 144–46, 151–52, 155–56; "A History of Stalag Luft III," Pt. IV, pp. 3–7.

The prisoners in South Compound experienced even more difficulties with their escape program than did the men in Center Compound. When Colonel Goodrich assumed command as SAO in South, he took with him from North a number of Americans who had worked closely with the British. These men were optimistic about the possibilities for escape because opening a compound always seemed to present new opportunities. The Germans, however, had learned much between March, when North Compound opened, and September, when the prisoners marched into South.

The earlier move to North had marked the beginning of the Golden Era of escape in Stalag Luft III. When the Germans had opened that compound in March, the prisoners found materials that could be used in escape work and hid them away with relative ease. Furthermore, the Germans had not taken careful note of the appearance of the facilities before the prisoners moved in, and so found it difficult to determine when something had been altered. For a time trees were left standing in the northern half of the compound, which made close observation of escape activities all but impossible. All these oversights were remedied before the prisoners moved into South Compound.

South Compound was neat and clean when it opened. The sand under the barracks was raked smooth, all the trees were cleared, and all loose articles were removed. As an extra security measure, the Germans put a shadow on Clark. For two weeks he could not even go to the latrine without somebody following him. Although Clark was never able to confirm his suspicions, he is convinced that Bushell was responsible, at least indirectly, for the Germans' precautions. Clark felt that, in an effort to divert the Germans' attention from the two tunnels still under construction in North, Bushell secretly gave them the impression that the British were happy to see the Americans go, that they, not the British, were the fanatic tunnelers who achieved the wonders underground that were revealed when tunnel Tom was discovered. The implication plainly was that the British would be causing no more trouble now that the bloody Yanks were gone, and the Germans would do well to concentrate on South rather than North Compound. The Germans apparently took the bait, for they sent their most diligent and successful anti-escape expert, Glemnitz, to South Compound, where he continued to be a keen opponent. Thus, escape attempts were made in South Compound, but the efforts proved unsuccessful, and the escape team there never achieved the fame it deserved. Many members of South Compound's

X Organization had worked on tunnels in North, which their un-
timely move meant they could not use. These same men served as
decoys in South while work eventually met with success in North
Compound. The members of the Escape Committee in South Compound seemingly were the unsung heroes of Stalag Luft III's escape
organization.

The last two compounds to be opened in Stalag Luft III, West and
Belaria, did not gain reputations for escapes. Both were opened in the
winter and spring of 1944, and the prisoners simply did not have time
to get organized before the mass escape from North Compound in
March, 1944, ended in tragedy and put a damper on further escape
efforts.

The men in the older communities had better luck. Several escape
attempts in East and North compounds that occurred between April,
1943, and the end of March, 1944, deserve special attention. The
first, in East Compound in October, 1943, used a modern-day version
of the Trojan horse. A vaulting horse, a large hollow wood box open on
the bottom, was carried to the same spot on the playing field every
day, and the prisoners took turns jumping over it in the course of their
exercise drills. Inside, a tunneler put a trapdoor in the sand that could
be covered over with dirt each day. Underneath the trap door he dug a
shallow tunnel. The sand was placed in twelve bags that hung on
hooks in the horse. When these were full, the trap was shut and the
horse, with the sand and the prisoner inside, was carried back to the
barracks, where the sand was quickly dispersed. The work, begun in
July, was necessarily slow, but by October 29 the tunnel was completed. Three prisoners used it to escape, and they reached England
by ship from Sweden.[13]

The success of the Trojan horse encouraged the prisoners to try
tunnels with similar traps. In the winter of 1943–1944, Margaret was
started in East Compound. The trap for this tunnel was sunk, of all
places, right on the parade ground. During an Appell, two cubic feet
of sand were dug away, the trap was put in and covered with sand.
During each roll call the trap was raised while work progressed on the
sinking of the vertical shaft. That this project could be carried on
during the Appells is ample testimony to the British boast that they

13. "A History of Stalag Luft III," Pt. I, p. 38. Two books written about this escape
by two of the participants are Eric Williams, *The Wooden Horse* (New York, 1949); and
Oliver Philpot, *Stolen Journey* (New York, 1952).

could indeed confuse the German count anytime they wanted. At the bottom of the four-foot shaft the prisoners built a chamber large enough for two men, who usually went down together during the morning Appell and stayed there until evening roll call. During this time the trap was in position, and prisoners stamped and shuffled their feet to make the replaced earth over the trap look the same as the surrounding soil. For ventilation, there were air holes that the men punched up to the surface. To get the tunnelers up in time for the evening count, the prisoners who formed the squadron covering the trap went out to the parade ground early. They were accompanied by two or three other squadrons so that the consistent early arrival of one would not alert the Germans. Since it was winter when the tunnel was dug, the prisoners could hide the bags of sand under their great-coats as they walked off the field. They could also carry shoring boards, which were handed down to the tunnelers. When the weather became so bad that the Appell was taken inside, the prisoners organized a rugby game over the trap while the tunnelers got out. Tunnelers did not go down if the weather was bad, but when the weather deteriorated in the afternoon after the men were already in the tunnel, the rugby games had to be played since the prisoners would not have survived the night. Furthermore, they sometimes played rugby in the worst weather simply to get the Germans used to the idea.

The tunnel was almost completed when the mass escape from North Compound occurred in March, 1944. When the prisoners in East Compound learned that fifty of the escapers had been shot, they decided not to use Margaret. The tunnel was completed, however, and set aside for the special defense teams organized as part of the contingency plans.[14]

The prisoners in North Compound were ingenious in other ways as well. In May, 1943, for example, plans were laid for a mass escape by several groups of prisoners who were to go be deloused in the Vorlager shared by East and Center. Two of these groups, escorted by prisoners disguised as German guards, were to march toward the Vorlager, and while the first turned off into the woods bordering the road between the Vorlagers of North and East compounds, the second was to occupy the guards and sentries. The escape took place on June 12, 1943. The first group, with two German-speaking prisoners acting as guards and twenty-five other prisoners, got through the

14. "A History of Stalag Luft III," Pt. I, pp. 40–41.

gates and into the woods. The second group of seven prisoners, including Lieutenant Colonel Clark and Colonel Goodrich, were stopped at the second gate by a German who did not recognize the "guard" leading the party. Everyone in both groups was recaptured, but not before one man had traveled to within several hundred yards of the Swiss border and two others had made their way to a local airfield where they were caught trying to start a plane.[15]

Many other escapes were tried from North Compound, but the center of attention undoubtedly remained the three major tunnels, Tom, Dick, and Harry. The magnitude and complexity of these engineering feats were truly astonishing.

The entrances to all three tunnels were cut out of concrete since the barracks in North Compound were on concrete piers several feet high, and only those made contact with the ground. Tom originated in barracks 123 and ran westward. Its trap, in the concrete floor of a small annex to one of the rooms, was bounded on two sides by walls and on the third by a chimney. The trap itself, made from concrete left lying around by the Germans, was so well disguised that workers reporting for duty had to have it pointed out to them. Dick originated in barracks 122 and ran westward. The trap was inside a drain in the washroom floor. The concrete drain was eighteen inches square by two feet deep and was covered by a metal grating. The prisoners chipped out one side of the drain and replaced it with a slab of concrete that could be slid up and down. When the trap was in place, the drain functioned normally. Harry emerged from barracks 104 and ran northward. Its trap was built under a stove that sat upon a tile-covered concrete foundation.

The shafts directly beneath the traps extended thirty feet straight down and were in themselves complex structures. They were completely shored up with boards. At the bottom of each one were three separate chambers: one to house the air pump, one to store sand temporarily, and one to serve as a general workroom and storage area for tunneling equipment and escape aids.

The tunnels themselves were all similarly constructed. As soon as they were long enough, rails were attached to the floor boards. Wood trolley cars, with ropes of plaited string, carried sand from the tunnel face back to the shaft. The air-line ran under the flooring and was extended as the tunnel progressed.

Dispersing or "destroying" the sand took enormous effort. Digging

15. *Ibid.*, Pt. III, pp. 43–44.

the vertical shaft and three chambers produced twelve tons of sand from each tunnel. Where the tunnels ran horizontally, one ton of sand was excavated for each three and a half feet of forward progress. Approximately eighteen thousand individual trips were made by the "penguins," the men who carried the sand from the traps to the dispersal areas. The maximum amount of sand dispersed in one day's work from any one tunnel was sixty pounds per minute for a period of one hour. During the winter, when it was impossible to camouflage the sand in the snow or work it into the frozen ground, the sand was placed under the floor of the theater, which, unlike the other buildings, was enclosed all the way down to the ground. The prisoners had built the theater, and the Germans assumed that there was no space under the floor. The trapdoor was beneath one of the seats. Sixty-eight tons of sand were put under the theater. Tunnel Dick, though well along, had been left alone in favor of Harry and then was used to store twelve tons of sand.

Constructing the tunnels required massive quantities of wood and other materials. Fifty bed boards were supplied daily for shoring; tunnel Harry took about two thousand. Boards from the barracks' double floors were also used. Hardwood for trolleys, railway tracks, and ladders came from chairs, tables, benches, and stools. Thirty Klim cans were needed each day for the air lines. The trolley wheels were wrapped with tin from Klim cans. Axles for the trolleys were made out of bars taken from barracks stoves. Each week the parcels officer had three hundred feet of string, which was braided into rope for hauling the trolleys. The prisoners stole four hundred feet of manila rope that the Germans brought into the compound to make a boxing ring. They used it in the mass escape because the plaited string was not strong enough to pull the men down the tunnel on the trolley. Eight hundred feet of single-strand, insulated, dampproof electric wire was stolen from German workmen who were wiring a building in North. Contact men provided electric lamps. To power the tunnel lights, the prisoners tapped into the lines that supplied the barracks. Screws and nails were stolen from workmen or removed from buildings in the compounds.[16]

On the night of March 24–25, 1944, eighty prisoners managed to get through tunnel Harry before the Germans discovered the hole

16. These details and a great many others pertaining to the tunnels and the escape are revealed in "A History of Stalag Luft III," Pt. III, pp. 33–99.

outside the wire. The number was far below Bushell's two hundred, but the men who did escape succeeded in creating massive turmoil within the Reich.[17] Four of the eighty were captured at the mouth of the tunnel, but seventy-six cleared the camp area. The Germans issued a *Grossfahndung*, the most extensive and highest-priority search order in the land. And the man-hours, the embarrassment, and the danger of coordinated sabotage caused Hitler to issue the famous Sagan Order, which led to the death, by shooting, of fifty of the seventy-six escapers. Bushell was among the fifty. Wings was captured and later escaped again, but he spent agonizing months, enduring uncertainty, starvation, and ill-treatment in several concentration camps. Ironically, what helped save his life was his status as one of the "prominent prisoners" whom Reich leaders intended to hold hostage for bargaining purposes until the end of the war. Three of the seventy-six men made it home to England.[18]

On April 6 the prisoners in Stalag Luft III were told that fifty escapers had been shot. Neither the German camp staff nor the prisoners ever had quite the same attitude toward escape again. The prisoners were numbed by the news and believed the camp administrators when they said the Luftwaffe could not ensure the prisoners' safety outside the wire and that the men must realize that escape was no longer a game. News of the Normandy invasion, in turn, caused the prisoners to hope that Germany would soon be defeated. In light of these developments, many prisoners became more conservative and questioned whether the possible rewards of escaping were worth the added and perhaps unnecessary risks. In August, 1944, General Vanaman spread the word that he would not order the men to give up further attempts at escape. He did ask that they carefully weigh the obvious dangers against the gains at this late stage of the war. Finally, in October, London announced that escape was no longer considered a duty, and shortly thereafter the Americans received the same information.

Not all activity ceased, however. In most compounds, the prisoners

17. Two hundred men were in fact prepared to escape that night. They were in barracks 104, awaiting their turn. Because of unexpected delays in getting the men through the tunnel, however, only eighty actually emerged through the opening. The others destroyed their forged papers and maps when they heard the shooting outside the wire. They also took off their escape clothing, which could not be readily destroyed and so was found and confiscated by the Germans.

18. Brickhill, *The Great Escape*, 172–223; Smith, *Mission Escape*, 137–235.

kept on making escape aids and preparing tunnels. In June, 1944, the British in North Compound began yet another tunnel named "George," from the theater. Although it was never opened, it was reserved for possible use as part of the contingency plans. The escape aids might serve if the prisoners were marched westward, a move that they correctly anticipated would offer them numerous opportunities to slip away.[19] The importance of this work became increasingly clear to the prisoners in the fall and winter months of 1944–1945 as they watched conditions in Germany deteriorate and pondered what might lie ahead for them in the closing months of the war.

19. Goodrich, "History of South Compound," Pt. III; "A History of Stalag Luft III," Pt. III, p. 32; Mulligan, Burbank, and Brunn, "History of Center Compound," Pt. III (Diary), August 23, 1944.

15

On the Outside Looking In

The prisoners in Stalag Luft III tried to keep everything in perspective, an all but impossible task in a prison camp. To understand the events that influenced camp life, to appreciate more fully the motives and actions of the Germans and others with whom the prisoners came in contact, one must view the prisoners' world through the thoughts and actions of those who were outside the barbed wire, looking in.

Members of the German camp staff, though themselves an integral part of the prison environment, had an interesting vantage point. They found, for example, that they had to adjust their thinking and ways of doing business with the prisoners almost on a nationality-by-nationality basis because of the variations in individual characteristics, mentalities, habits, mannerisms, traditions, accomplishments, desires, fears, and shortcomings.

Colonel von Lindeiner thought the prisoners an interesting lot. Thinking about the Americans, British, Canadians, South Africans, Australians, New Zealanders, Dutch, Belgians, Poles, Czechoslovakians, and Russians under his care, he once remarked, "A budding diplomat could have received excellent schooling here, studying the mentality of almost all the peoples of the globe." He was no less intrigued by their varied skills and backgrounds. In addition to career soldiers, he found among them "tramway conductors, sons of millionaires, waiters, lords, Hindu princes, horse trainers, race car drivers, professional dancers, pro hockey and football players, bus and buggy drivers, cowboys, photographers, actors, policemen, traveling salesmen, moviehouse operators, ski instructors, artists, miners, veterinarians, reporters, missionaries, private detectives, singers, diamond miners, lawyers, organists, jockeys, bacteriologists, plantation owners, hotel managers, porters, cardsharps, chauffeurs, bandleaders, firemen, pianists and school teachers."

Like all good commandants, von Lindeiner was observant. And over a period of time he formed definite opinions about the prisoners. The British refused to accept materials for self-help projects, arguing that the Germans were obligated to do the work, and any help the British might give would only free German workers for the war effort. Their attitude, von Lindeiner felt, was rather shortsighted: "Not a single German worker was pulled from the war work force to undertake a beautification project in a prisoner of war camp." The Americans, on the other hand, "were quite different and helped make their quarters more livable whenever they could." The British were "much less careful with German property," perhaps thinking they were harming the German economy by destroying whatever they could. He concluded that the New Zealanders' "high intellect and life style directed toward peaceful and beautiful things were probably the result of life on an island without green borders and without neighbors to envy their wealth." The South Africans and Canadians "were also rather pleasant fellows," but the Australians, along with the British, "were the most defensive against the Germans." Concerning the other nationalities, he thought that the Dutch "tried to be more British than the British" and noticed that the Poles "were preoccupied with a deep worry about the future of their homeland, regardless of the outcome of the war."[1]

Von Lindeiner's sensitivity toward the Poles' plight was more than a patronizing gesture. He considered all the prisoners to be his wards, in the truest sense of the word. Perhaps nowhere is this more clearly seen than in his thoughts and comments about the Russian prisoners who worked for the Germans in the Vorlagers and around the camp.

Von Lindeiner's treatment of the Russians stood in refreshing contrast to the cruelty to which most prisoners from the East were subjected. There were about three hundred Russian prisoners, and they maintained the transportation unit (the cars and the horses and carts), ran the electrical plant, took care of the pigs and chickens, and worked in the big vegetable garden. When they arrived, they were in miserable condition—they were undernourished and wore rags. After consulting with doctors, von Lindeiner procured blood from nearby slaughterhouses and ordered that blood soups be cooked with stinging nettles and the tips of Scotch pine needles. Before long the Russians had regained their strength and their will to live. He was

1. Von Lindeiner, "Memoirs," 103–104.

pleased that there had been only two deaths, the result of advanced tuberculosis. And he was impressed with the Russians' ability to restore clothing, furniture, cooking utensils, and other items their fellow prisoners had thrown away. Struck by their striving for cleanliness, he observed that for the Russians "a piece of soap was a most treasured possession" and that their living quarters were always immaculate.

An avid student of government, von Lindeiner was fascinated by the Russian approach to self-rule. Virtually all the prisoners from the West turned to their senior officers or elected a Man of Confidence. There was, however, for the Russians a steady rotation of leaders. Inquiring about their motive, von Lindeiner was surprised to learn that they wanted to avoid taking sides, even unknowingly, and transgressing the laws of camaraderie, something they felt could easily happen with the prolonged rule of one individual. Perhaps he should have expected such an answer, for of all the hundreds of Russians he met during the war, he "did not find one who was not a devout communist." They were also ardent nationalists—to them "Mother Russia, the holy soil of Russia, represented more than their own being." From everything he could see, the Russians had high moral standards, considered the family holy, and viewed the unmarried woman as untouchable.

Von Lindeiner was particularly interested in the Russians' attitudes toward their allies. From his vantage point, they apparently considered the Americans their greatest enemy, not the Germans. The Russians firmly believed that the Americans were the despised representatives of capitalism, though their power was something to be respected and feared. The British "were on their way down in the order of the world and therefore were to be less respected." And as for the other peoples of Europe, they "did not count at all, though the traditional sympathy of the Russians for the Germans was apparent." Von Lindeiner perhaps engaged in a little wishful thinking in this regard, but undoubtedly realized that the Russians regarded national socialism and communism as somewhat akin. But the Russians were quick to point out that Hitler and his cohorts were not drawing the correct conclusions from Communist teachings.

At first not fully appreciating the cleavage in Allied ranks, the Germans attempted one day to put some Russian and American prisoners together in the same hospital room. The doctor in charge conferred with the Americans, and they did not mind the situation.

But the Germans were greatly surprised the next morning that the Russians had chosen to sleep in the corridor. Asked why they had moved, the Russians replied that if at all possible, they "did not wish to live with capitalists in the same room." In a similarly revealing episode, von Lindeiner received an invitation to a Russian concert. There he found not only an excellent choir but also a rather large and well-equipped orchestra. Since the Russians were given only ten pfennigs a day, he asked where they had gotten the money to pay for all the instruments. After some hesitation came the reply, "Capitalists dumb, Russians smart." They then boasted that, serving as hospital attendants, they had played cards with the Americans and the British and had won the money for their purchases. Von Lindeiner concluded that the Russians might have thought that occasional cheating in a card game with capitalists was a virtue rather than a vice.[2]

Undoubtedly some in the Nazi hierarchy felt that von Lindeiner showed a little too much understanding and concern for the Russian prisoners. But that was a risk most members of the German camp staff came to accept and live with. Clearly they were in an awkward, and often dangerous, position. The main problem was that they had to serve three masters—the prisoners, their own superiors, and other German citizens. The difficulties at Barth alerted the staff that any signs of leniency would be interpreted outside the camp as coddling. At Sagan the staff was increasingly pressed and threatened by numerous decrees, rigorous war-laws, and orders. According to Simoleit, Goebbels' propaganda campaign against the Luftgangsters stirred the populace to such a pitch that many of the staff members "began to be regarded almost as traitors when they undertook to provide humane and correct treatment for the prisoners."

How the pressures increased over the months and years can be observed in the funeral services conducted by the Germans. Outside Sagan, there was a small cemetery for prisoners, and in the early years of the war, prisoners who died were buried with full military honors. A delegation of German officers and prisoners, each carrying a wreath of flowers, accompanied the body to the cemetery. A squad of German soldiers rendered the customary rifle salute, and the German national colors were placed on the grave. After 1943 all such chivalric customs were forbidden. Hitler gave strict orders that Luftwaffe prisoners be buried without military honors.

2. *Ibid.*, 109–15.

Orders such as this placed the German staff in an embarrassing position, and sometimes they risked a great deal to save face as well as placate the prisoners. In some cases it was also a matter of personal honor. Simoleit found himself in just such a predicament shortly after Hitler's order on military funerals had been issued. A prisoner en route to the camp had tried to escape from the train, was badly injured, and died in the hospital soon after his arrival at Sagan. Simoleit discovered evidence among the man's personal papers that he was not a pilot but a member of a ground crew. No sooner had Simoleit decided that military honors could be rendered at the funeral than it was learned that the man was a Jew. Nevertheless, Simoleit proceeded as planned, making sure that the man's Jewish identity remained a carefully guarded secret. The funeral service was dignified and chivalric. A Catholic priest administered the last rites, not even he knowing the real facts of the case. Very likely this was only one of many such incidents.

Simoleit used his own case to describe the plight of the German staff: "These two-sided duties to our own country and to the prisoners, the permanent pressure from both sides, and . . . the apprehension and anxiety that some catastrophe could occur every day, made our lives very unpleasant. From 1940 to 1945 I always suffered from sleeplessness and had to use sleeping pills almost every night." He concluded, rather dramatically but nevertheless truthfully: "In discussions about what our future life would be after the war I used to say 'My future is very clear and simple. Either the Germans will shoot me dead for treason or the Allies will hang me after the war because I was a jailer of prisoners.'"[3]

Von Lindeiner had a clear impression of what he wanted from his staff members in regard to their treatment of the prisoners. Shortly after assuming command, he spelled out his expectations:

The Geneva Convention is the basis for our behavior. It is against the tradition of the German soldier to violate the precept of law, humaneness, and chivalry even against an enemy. In the last war, there persisted even until the last days, especially between the German AF and its enemies, a spirit of chivalry and fellowship. Our commander in chief has expressed his wish that in this war also this spirit should guide the actions of the organizations under him. As representatives of the detaining power, we have to look upon the POWs as persons who had and still have the duty to fight for their country, as we are doing. The imprisoned enemy is defenseless, to violate his human

3.   Simoleit, "Organization and Administration."

dignity is contrary to the spirit of chivalry as mentioned before. Vexing insults are a part of this. Provoking or violent behavior towards defenseless people is proof of cowardice. It is absolutely essential that all German personnel employed here are aware of their rights and duties as representatives of the detaining power, and also of the rights and duties of the POWs. I ask the individual section commanders to make sure their subordinates are informed accordingly. The basis of our behavior is the correct conduct of the POWs. Violations of individual POWs are to be reported: they will be punished. However, the actions of a few should not prejudice you towards the others. I have personally warned the POWs about the consequences of repeat incidents. It is the right of a POW to rejoin his unit by trying to escape. It is our duty to prevent a successful escape. We shall try our utmost to do our duty with the resources at hand. I shall ask you not to forget one important fact: any war has to end sooner or later, and after a war the nations have to live together again. We cannot ask for the sympathy of the POW[s] we will release when this is over, but what we want to instill is a feeling of respect. They can say "I hate the Germans," but they must think "I respect them."[4]

In many important respects, von Lindeiner was an anachronism. His beliefs and practices represented the moral code of an earlier age, making him especially vulnerable in a period of Nazi decadence and modern warfare. Perhaps nowhere was this fact more evident than in the matter of escape.

In telling the prisoners that he planned to treat them as he would wish to be treated were he a prisoner of war, he stated that he only wanted them to "resign themselves honorably and quietly to their unfortunate position and behave accordingly." The prisoners quickly reminded him that it was not only their right but their duty to attempt to rejoin their troops. The ensuing discussion led to a gentleman's agreement: "The armed war is over for the POWs in this camp. They recognize the international laws and camp rules; however, they maintain the right to rejoin their units through escape. In the place of a war of weapons, they are now in a 'war of brains'. Absolute fairness is to be observed in all actions."

Von Lindeiner felt that both sides generally lived up to the agreement and pointed to two specific instances where fairness seemed to prevail. Two British officers approached Sergeant Pilz and asked for a map of the area surrounding Sagan in return for a handsome bribe. Pilz reported the incident and received orders to go ahead with the deal. After three weeks of haggling, the prisoners agreed to pay fifty Reichsmarks. The exchange would take place one morning during

4. Von Lindeiner, "Memoirs," 122–23.

roll call when the two officers would play sick so Pilz could bring the map to their room. Pilz appeared on time and pulled out the map; the British paid. Pilz quickly pocketed the money and the map and delivered everything to von Lindeiner. The English were rather indignant and called Pilz's behavior "unfair." They reported the incident to von Lindeiner, insisting that the gentleman's agreement had been broken. After lengthy debates, von Lindeiner felt he had convinced the prisoners that the Germans had merely shown more brains than had their adversaries. Before long, however, the shoe was on the other foot. One day a high-ranking friend of von Lindeiner's drove into North Compound with a fancy new car, a Tatra with a rear-mounted eight-cylinder engine. The visitor wanted his chauffeur to explain the car's construction to the ever-growing number of prisoners, who were arguing noisily among themselves. Well aware of the prisoners' uncanny ability to appropriate objects they could use, von Lindeiner argued against the idea but relented after satisfying himself that the doors and windows were securely locked. Shortly after he and his guest left for their discussion, the distraught chauffeur appeared and reported that a book had been stolen from the locked vehicle. Von Lindeiner asked the senior officer of North Compound to report to him and explained that since the car demonstration was a good-will gesture, he would have to regard the disappearance of the book as a violation of the gentleman's agreement. He demanded that the book be returned within two hours. It was, but there were two neatly stamped entries: "Passed by the British Censor" and "Seen by Winston Churchill."[5]

But in von Lindeiner's opinion, the agreement eventually was broken, and in a particularly tragic way. Barely three months after he assumed duties as commandant, von Lindeiner was warned by good friends in the German High Command that his behavior toward the prisoners had aroused indignation, especially at the Reich's Security Headquarters and in political circles around the party district director in Sagan. He nonetheless continued to contest the Gestapo's holding captured fliers rather than turning them over immediately to the armed forces. It took lengthy negotiations to secure the release of Roger Bushell after he was found incarcerated in a Gestapo prison in Prague. Returned to Stalag Luft III, he was once again whisked off to Security Headquarters in Berlin for further interrogation. When he

5. *Ibid.*, 118–19.

was not returned after what seemed an excessive amount of time, von Lindeiner personally intervened and eventually succeeded in getting him back to camp. A similar confrontation with the Gestapo involved Flight Lieutenant Bram Vanderstok. Having served in the Dutch Air Force at the beginning of the war and become a prisoner in the capitulation of March 14, 1940, Vanderstok escaped to England, where he joined the RAF. He was shot down, was taken prisoner, and ended up in Stalag Luft III. The Gestapo in Holland demanded his extradition for court-martial. Aware that two similar cases had resulted in the death penalty, von Lindeiner refused to release him. Intense and exceptionally harsh correspondence followed, but Vanderstok stayed.[6]

It would be some time before von Lindeiner would learn of the special role these two individuals would play in the Great Escape. Had he known that Bushell was the mastermind and that Vanderstok was one of the three who would make it all the way home, he might not have been so willing to compromise himself on their behalf. On the other hand, even he saw signs that it was no longer an easy matter to determine what was and what was not fair. In the fall of 1943, von Lindeiner met briefly with the Silesian Gestapo chief, Councillor Dr. Scharpwinkel, in the latter's office in Breslau. Von Lindeiner's first impression was that Scharpwinkel was "a well-bred and rather intelligent man living a spotless life." During the course of the conversation, however, the telephone rang, and though von Lindeiner could hear only one end of the discussion, he was disturbed by Scharpwinkel's closing words, "Will be liquidated." When he asked Scharpwinkel what that meant, he was told that "this man will not see the sun go down today!" Stunned, von Lindeiner wanted to know whether it bothered Scharpwinkel's conscience "to snuff out the life of a human being over the phone, whose reasons for committing the act he did not know and who might have a mother, wife, or children." The reply was not what von Lindeiner wanted to hear. "Three years ago," Scharpwinkel explained, "I was thinking just like you now. When I was confronted with that type of situation for the first time I argued like you and did not sleep for several nights. In the time that has passed since then I have come to the conclusion, however, that the life of a single human being cannot play a role if the destiny of the whole German race is at stake." Even more unsettling to von Lin-

6. *Ibid.*, 131–32.

deiner was the realization that Scharpwinkel was not alone in this belief. Encountering increasing numbers of Gestapo members whose senses had been dulled, men who "resembled beasts in their behavior," von Lindeiner nonetheless had to work with them and found that even "one look into their fanatically glowing eyes" was frightening.[7]

In time von Lindeiner's pleas that the prisoners accept their fate and peacefully sit out the war took on new meaning. His initial advice, to forgo escape activity, perhaps reflected little more than the wishful thinking of an old soldier who simply did not want any trouble on his watch. But his words began to take on a certain urgency. He spoke of the dangers the prisoners faced among the civilians whose patience with Allied air attacks had grown thin. Von Lindeiner begged the senior officers to "think of the mothers, women and children of your friends, whose happiness will be in jeopardy if some young hotheads try something foolish which has no bearing on the outcome of the war." Trying desperately to warn them without revealing all he knew about their probable fate should they escape, he went on: "Here, within the confines of this POW camp, I am responsible with my life for the lives of the POWs entrusted to me; here I will protect you within my means, outside of the barbed wire I am powerless. I beg of you to take my words very seriously and act accordingly."[8] But the prisoners either did not believe him or chose to accept the increased risks. Von Lindeiner watched ruefully as the prisoners tunneled their way toward death.

German records show that during the twenty-one months and twenty-four days von Lindeiner served as commandant, the prisoners made 262 escape attempts, 100 of them involving tunnels.[9] In addition to the gentleman's agreement, von Lindeiner felt he had an ally in Group Captain Massey, the Senior British Officer. Massey and von Lindeiner seemed to understand each other, and they did what they could to keep German-prisoner relations civil. Further, when a well-known English surgeon arrived in central Germany in the spring of 1943 to operate on Englishmen with complicated wounds, von Lindeiner had one of his doctors and a medic escort Massey to the hospital so the surgeon could treat his injured foot. About two months later,

7. *Ibid.*, 285–86.
8. *Ibid.*, 237.
9. *Ibid.*, 93.

von Lindeiner received a call from the commandant of the hospital: Massey was under suspicion of inciting his fellow prisoners to mutiny. The commandant asked von Lindeiner whether he thought Massey was capable of doing that. If so, proceedings against him would be started. Von Lindeiner vouched for Massey and later sent another escort to have him brought back to Stalag Luft III.

Having extended a helping hand, he felt confident that Massey would respond in kind if the need ever arose. So he turned to Massey when he discovered that the prisoners were still digging tunnels despite his warnings. Still hoping to avert disaster, he talked seriously and at length with Massey, reminding him that after two years of working together, Massey should know him well enough to pay attention to his warnings. Von Lindeiner was deeply hurt to discover later that Massey had let him down, that he not only knew every detail of the escape plan but also had approved the prisoners' actions. His concluding thoughts about Massey's apparent betrayal hark back to the moral code of an earlier, simpler age: "I believed that he, being responsible for the well-being and future of so many young men, would stop them from going through with this senseless if not childish adventure. How bitterly I was deceived."[10]

The Germans had to work throughout the night and into the next day after the Great Escape to discover how many prisoners had escaped. For von Lindeiner, "the result was earth-shaking, 76 were missing." Hordes of investigators descended upon the camp, asking the same questions over and over again, talking to almost everyone but von Lindeiner, piling up the evidence for his court-martial. At 1400 hours on March 26, two staff officers of Luftgau Command III in Dahlem arrived with Deputy Judge Advocate General Dr. Garbe and handed von Lindeiner the writ he had been expecting. In stoic silence he read: "Colonel von Lindeiner gen. von Wildau is hereby relieved of his duty as commander of the POW camp and a court-martial investigation is hereby ordered. Col. von Lindeiner is to remain in the camp at Sagan until the start of the court-martial proceedings. Command of the camp is to be taken over by the next senior officer."[11]

The two staff officers returned to Dahlem while Garbe remained in Stalag Luft III to continue the investigation, again excluding von Lindeiner from the discussions. Then, on March 29, having been

10.   *Ibid.*, 236–40.
11.   *Ibid.*, 246, 248.

unable to eat or rest properly for several days and suffering tremendous mental and emotional strain, von Lindeiner collapsed with acute heart palpitations. A doctor living several rooms away swiftly came to his aid and pulled him out of danger. But it now was obvious that he could not go on. He reluctantly resigned himself to a period of recuperation at his estate, Jeschkendorf Manor, outside Sagan. There he spent much time preparing his defense, should he be allowed to testify on his own behalf.[12]

Eleven weeks passed before he was finally questioned officially. In the meantime, it was said that staff members at Stalag Luft III were undergoing the inevitable interrogations. Tension and fear increased daily; charges and countercharges served to worsen the situation. Reports reached von Lindeiner that there were repeated scenes of "the unfortunate ones . . . rolling around the floor screaming and covered with blood." Out of the investigation came a 200-page report destined for the Reich's Security Office.

Five more weeks passed without incident, but suddenly, late in the evening of September 16, von Lindeiner heard loud knocking. When he opened the door he saw one of his loyal subordinates with a clearly agitated expression on his face. "Thank God you are still here," he said. "We were afraid you had been picked up already. You have to get away immediately!" When von Lindeiner asked why, the man replied: "An order was signed this afternoon at 1:30 at the Reich's Military Tribunal in Berlin-Grunewald demanding your immediate arrest and incarceration at the military prison Berlin Kruppstrasse." Von Lindeiner thanked his visitor and advised him to leave at once.

Von Lindeiner probably could have slipped away then with the help of long-standing friends in counterintelligence. But he feared "kin incarcerations," a common Gestapo practice. In addition, despite all the documents against him that were being assembled, he was aware that the immediate investigation had cleared him of any wrongdoing and that Garbe personally had concluded there was no evidence to convict him. Thus it was important for him to "publicly confront the scandalous methods" of those who insisted on making a false case against him. Knowing that the Gestapo's preferred time for dirty work was before daybreak, he said nothing to his wife but packed a small suitcase with necessary items and awaited the morning.

12. *Ibid.*, 251.

Nothing happened. The ensuing weeks were calm and peaceful as well. Finally, on October 2 while von Lindeiner was in Sagan, an acquaintance approached him and asked, "When are you going to Guben?" Surprised, von Lindeiner asked, "What would I do in Guben?" The friend replied that that was where his court-martial would be held on October 5. Twenty-one witnesses had been called from Sagan alone. Crushed once again that everybody but him seemed to know about the court-martial, von Lindeiner paused to ponder his next move. Suddenly it occurred to him that he likely had misinterpreted what had happened. There was no intentional slight: his ignorance was the result of a friend's intervening to ensure that the original arrest order was not carried out, in hopes that the case would not come to trial. But now the date had been set, and he learned that experts from numerous Reich offices as well as a number of high-ranking officers had been ordered to attend. Not to show up would endanger the lives of those who had failed to arrest him. In addition, he still felt a strong desire to clear his name.

At 9:00 a.m. on October 5, von Lindeiner took his seat on the bench for the accused, together with Captains Pieber and Broili, seven soldiers of various ranks, and one civil servant, all from Stalag Luft III. During the opening session he saw the list of accusations for the first time.

The first witness for the prosecution was the paymaster, Schmidt. At the end of his testimony the presiding judge asked, "Are you telling me that you cannot uphold the accusations against Colonel Lindeiner?" "No," Schmidt answered, whereupon the judge said, "Then take your seat." The judge asked the second witness whether he held a grudge against von Lindeiner. The man answered, "No, not against Colonel von Lindeiner, but against all officers." Later, when the O.K.W. representative was asked for his opinion on a particular accusation, he replied: "Mr. President, if this is a point for the prosecution, then all I can say is that this is going to make the chicken laugh." The witness was given four weeks' room arrest for disorderly conduct in court. And later yet, Colonel Braune, von Lindeiner's successor as commandant, said, "Mr. President, if this can be used as a point for the prosecution, then I request to take a seat next to Colonel von Lindeiner on the bench."

Overall von Lindeiner felt that the trial was conducted in a factual and honorable way. But he was surprised when the prosecution asked for demotion and eighteen months in prison. But given the investigation and the Reich's interest in sending a clear message to other commandants about leniency toward prisoners, von Lindeiner was not surprised about the final sentence—twelve months' confinement in a fortress. And since the last appeal in such cases was Himmler himself, von Lindeiner knew better than to try.

But there was another way, one cleverly adapted from the prisoners' escape log. What went on behind closed doors can no longer be determined, but numerous individuals were working on von Lindeiner's behalf. After the sentence was handed down on October 9, von Lindeiner returned to Sagan, where he was warmly greeted by some of his former co-workers. During the latter part of October a medical commission arrived on orders from certain military authorities. A renowned psychiatrist said that von Lindeiner suffered from "an advanced stage of mental disturbance" and ordered his admittance to Reserve Lazarett I at Görlitz. Prisoners faked mental illness to get out of Stalag Luft III and return to their homeland. Von Lindeiner wanted to avoid the Gestapo and feigned mental illness so he could enjoy the relative safety of an army hospital. It worked. Although his troubles were far from over, the Gestapo never imprisoned him. The ruse bought him time, but not enough. The likely Allied victory made him wonder if he might not have to live as a prisoner of war and be on the inside of a camp looking out. His concerns were to prove well founded.

In addition to von Lindeiner and his staff, there were other people living and working in Germany who were able to view Stalag Luft III from the outside. Among them were members of the protecting-power staff, the Red Cross visitors, and the YMCA field delegates. Henry Soderberg, a young Swedish lawyer fresh out of law school, was with the YMCA and was a frequent visitor. Because he was neither captor nor captive, and because his duties took him to numerous camps, his observations are particularly revealing.

Soderberg had been involved with the YMCA in Sweden for a long time and had become a firm believer in its goal of nurturing young men in their pursuit of a sound and balanced body, soul, and mind and a life of service to others. When a broken arm forced him out of the military officers training program, he accepted an offer to serve in Germany as a YMCA field delegate in the War Prisoners Aid branch. In the spring of 1943 he boarded the train for Germany and suddenly found himself in another world. "After all," he recalls, "in Sweden everything was light, cheerful, peaceful and good, with no air attacks. We read about the bombings and so on in the newspapers, and many people thought I was crazy to go there." Originally signed up for only one year, he continued his work until well after the end of the war.[13]

During his stay in Germany, Henry Soderberg lived through approximately 250 bombings. In a very real sense, they personified the surrealism of his life and work on behalf of prisoners in war-torn Germany. Huddled in a bomb shelter in Berlin late on August 24, 1943, Henry witnessed an often repeated scene. Awakened at midnight by the air-raid sirens, he waited for the bombers to come. When the anti-aircraft fire played out, the noise from the falling bombs became crushing, and he realized that the entire city was under attack and there was no hope that his neighborhood would be spared. Even in the shelter he found that the noise hurt his ears. As his eyes adjusted to the dim light, he saw the family from the house next door: they were stunned, and all the children were crying. The ground shook, and fires began to light the entire area. The deafening noise became even more intense as several searchlights illuminated some British bombers. The anti-aircraft guns situated nearby rejoined the fray, and the combination of explosions sounded like "one uninterrupted scream." Amid the turmoil more neighbors arrived, crying, their house having just been destroyed. Seeing their plight, someone shouted above the din, "Damn British!" Whispering directly into Soderberg's ear, Dr. Vogt, one of whose parents was Jewish, responded, "Damn Hitler!"

The raid lasted a long time. In the aftermath, Soderberg felt the tension leave his body, but he could not stop trembling. Joining neighbors, he spent most of the night filling and passing buckets of water to help extinguish the fires. The next morning he set out for work, only to find that his office no longer existed. He and the other YMCA workers then transferred their base of operations to Sagan, hoping there they would be spared the dangers that encumbered their life and work in Berlin.

Suitable quarters for the Sagan YMCA office were found in an old restaurant, Augustiner. As usual, the workers rented rooms from the townsfolk. Where Soderberg took up residence, the father was somewhere on the front and the seventeen-year-old son had left to serve in the army, leaving only the housewife and her elderly mother at home. He was able to give them coffee and soap sometimes, and since he

---

13. Interview with Henry Soderberg, September 15, 1979. Unless otherwise specified, the account of Soderberg's experiences is based on this interview.

was young they tended to treat him as a son. The day he moved in, the landlady said: "You know, Mr. Soderberg what kind of family we are. My brother is in a concentration camp. But I would like you from now on, and forever, never to mention that you know about that, and never to ask me questions about it. The situation is such that the person you mention it to might talk about it and the discussion could lead to my being picked up by the Gestapo the next morning." His sin against the state, she said, occurred during a military parade. On one wall of his house he had hung the flag of the Weimar Republic.

The Germans often expressed reservations about Henry's work. "Why do you want to help American and British Luftgangsters?" The word *Luftgangsters* was used often, he recalls, and in at least one instance he heard irate German citizens shrieking it as they rushed toward some descending parachutes. But overall, he felt he was well received as a YMCA representative, in part perhaps because the populace and officials he worked with knew that similar efforts were being made among German prisoners held by the Western Allies.

Henry had a clear and proper understanding of his duties and responsibilities: he came to the prisoners as a representative from the outside world, they were hungry for such contact, and he was one of the few channels through which they could receive aid. He sensed that, above all, he had to keep the lines of communication open, a task that required tact and diplomacy, not to mention a conscious sub-jugation of personal freedoms and feelings. Recalling when some of his co-workers allowed themselves to take sides and accordingly were expelled from Germany, he emphasized: "I never, never, at any moment did anything which would put me and my work in danger. It was a balancing sometimes between feelings and loyalties. But we were indoctrinated from the outset of our work to never do anything which could endanger the well-being of the prisoners of war." Only by observing the rules of strict neutrality, he felt, could he hope to accomplish his goal of "reducing depression and bad feelings and encouraging, inspiring, and creating a joyful atmosphere" among the prisoners. So he took every opportunity to mingle with them. A com-posed, handsome figure, he was an outgoing individual who pos-sessed the requisite linguistic talents to succeed in a highly fluid environment that sometimes brought him into contact with individ-uals from forty different nationalities in a single day.

Like von Lindeiner, Soderberg was fascinated by the distinctive traits exhibited by members of various nationalities. The British and the Germans were a bit formal in comparison with "the gum-chewing Americans who preferred to ask their questions sitting on the table with their hands deep in their pant pockets." He was especially pleased that the Americans immediately called him by his first name, and he reciprocated by calling Colonel Spivey "Del" and General Vanaman "Arthur."

Soderberg developed "a very sympathetic feeling towards Lindeiner," a true German aristocrat. "A little bit remote from the people he dealt with, perhaps because of his aristocratic upbringing," von Lindeiner was nevertheless "very kind." He also noticed that von Lindeiner "had a distaste for the political gang on top in Germany, even if he never said it directly." Beyond a doubt, Soderberg concluded, von Lindeiner "was very much concerned about the well-being of the prisoners in his camp and recognized the necessity for them to have an occupation. Therefore he welcomed our efforts to assist when their own resources were not sufficient and he understood that these young men were very active and very dynamic." As for Simoleit, Soderberg found him to be "very correct. A little bit tense. A little bit nervous, always emphasizing that he was not a professional soldier. He always wanted to stick to the rules and not do anything wrong in one direction or the other." Wings Day, Soderberg perceived, was prominent in camp. Noticing that Wings was not the senior officer when they met, Soderberg did not immediately see why Wings had such an air of authority. Unable to discover the answer at the time, he could only conclude that he "never knew what Wings was doing," but knew "he was doing something important." Soderberg had difficulty understanding Goodrich's southern accent, but observed that the colonel knew his men well and understood the problems in camp.

Soderberg was struck by the distinct personalities the camps themselves seemed to have. "In walking in and out of the camps," he said, "you could feel and experience a variety of atmospheres in various respects. In some camps, the spirit was low; in others it was generally high. In some they were very active. In others they were very idle." The differences even extended to the way each camp smelled:

I think the answer lies in the fact that the various nationalities were used to differences in their eating habits and, therefore, the components of the meals were different. I mean if you got into a compound where you only had Indians from the British Imperial army, for instance, you could smell the Indian smells, which are unexplainable but similar to the ones I experienced in India when I went down the narrow streets of Calcutta or Bombay. But it was the same way when you entered a Russian compound. They had a very distinct smell also, and the Belgians had one too. The Russians were fed only potatoes, and there was the smell of sour potatoes in their camp. The French use lots of onions and garlic in their meals; you could smell that. The British and Americans and South Africans and some others used the Red Cross parcels from home which were more normal ingredients, and they too had a special smell in their barracks.

And Soderberg knew from experience how important the availability or absence of hygienic facilities and bathrooms was. The smells had other sources as well: "Since water was scarce in the camps, many people did not get their regular showers. When it was raining, and in the winter, of course, they had to hang up their coats and pants to dry during the night, and they were hung in the barracks where they were sleeping. Also, in order to keep the cold away in many camps, they had to keep the windows shut during the night. And you can imagine if you have 150 men jammed up in a small little hut what a smell it was in the morning." The interesting aspect of all this, Soderberg recalls, is that of all the camps, Stalag Luft III stood out as having the least distinctive smell. Like all camps, it too gave off an odor, but it was "nothing sharp." No matter which camp he visited, however, he took the smell home with him on his clothes: "I didn't notice that myself, of course, as I got used to it," he later stated. "But my friends in the office would say, 'Aha, you have been in the French camp' or 'Aha, you have been in the Dutch camp.'" When they would say, "Why do you smell so horrible today?" Soderberg usually replied, "Unfortunately, today I had to visit the camp of the poor Russians." He explained that "these undernourished creatures live in the highest degree of misery. They hang their clothes all over and do their cooking in the barracks with no way to let the smoke out."

The job of being a YMCA field representative proved to be a very satisfying task for Henry Söderberg. In addition to providing the normal sports and music equipment, he dealt with an array of requests that challenged his resourcefulness. Employed by a Christian organization, he supplied copies of the Koran to Moslem prisoners. When a medical doctor asked for a human cranium for his biology class, Soderberg procured one. And when von Lindeiner commented that the prisoners' practice of reserving one barracks as a chapel was against the law, the YMCA attempted to provide the lumber for a building that could be consecrated. The effort failed, but the idea itself illustrates how far the YMCA was willing to go to help the prisoners.

Soderberg disliked most not being able to satisfy everyone's needs, much less their desires. In his words, "Stalag Luft III was the most dynamic camp in Germany," and he recognized that the prisoners from affluent societies were suffering both relative and real deprivation. So he felt that it was not his duty to pass judgment on the requests. Rather, he sought to fulfill them as best he could. But when the American prisoners asked for ten typewriters so they could offer a typing class, he knew they were asking for the impossible. And while none of the prisoners had much, there were some who had nothing. "If you got into an American camp," he later recalled, "you might get a request for a hundred footballs," a number that was not unreasonable to satisfy the crowds there. But then in a Russian camp, the commandant might well say: "This whole camp, consisting of 10,000 Russians, would be more than happy if you gave them one football."

Another unpleasant aspect of his work was that he and his co-workers did not ever feel safe. They understood the risks and adjusted somewhat to the bombings and strafing attacks and the general inconveniences and scarcities in a war-time economy. But the one thing they never got accustomed to was the tactics of the Gestapo and SS agents.

Soderberg carried an elaborate set of papers at all times. The Germans generally were impressed with the physical size of some of the documents and especially with the numerous stamps. But sometimes he did not have time to show his credentials.

In November, 1943, Soderberg was surprised to find himself in a hotel with a large group of SA (Sturmabteilung) soldiers and officials celebrating a party reunion in Poznań, Poland. Deciding to take a walk, he donned his hat and his trench coat. Before long, crowds started to gather along the sidewalk. He asked a man why. The passerby replied, "Don't you know? Himmler is here and will be giving a lecture in the square in about an hour." Suddenly he heard music and saw a band approaching, accompanied by ranks of Hitler Youth and other groups. He also saw a man in a brown uniform who, without warning, slapped a spectator in the face and threw his hat to the ground. In rapid succession he did the same thing to several other people. Soderberg could hardly believe his eyes. As the music played and the sound of heavy boots echoed in his ears, he walked down the street, keeping well ahead of the parade. But within moments the SA man came up beside him, struck his right ear, grabbed his hat, and threw it over a fence. A fanatical glow in his eyes, the SA agent shouted in Soderberg's face repeatedly, "You didn't salute the flags, you devil, you!" Not yet having seen any flags, Soderberg shouted back, "Just what do you think you are doing. I am Swedish." The SA man countercharged, "Either you are Swedish, or American, or English." Soderberg was infuriated by the accusation. Then another agent arrived and began to shout and swear at him. Realizing how serious the situation had become, Soderberg pulled himself together. He knew they would shoot him if he hit one of them. But then the agents suddenly moved down the street to stay abreast of the parade, leaving Soderberg and others who were punched and mauled in the confusion.

Angry and frustrated, Soderberg filed a complaint at the local police station. The officials there admitted they could do nothing since it was a political matter, but they agreed to send it on to Gestapo headquarters. The next day, Soderberg was summoned to the office of the Gestapo chief in Poznań. Outwardly friendly, the chief expressed his regrets: "Please do not think that this action was personally directed against you. We cannot always control our men, and you must understand, Herr Soderberg, that when you have been staying very long among these unreliable Poles you have to work with some harder methods. The Poles will not learn anything. They will not accept the new situation. They lack tactfulness and education. It is a well-known fact that they should take off their hats for the German flags and symbols, and the man who hit you, of course, thought you were a Pole." The chief's words only served to make Soderberg angrier. He snapped back, saying he could not see how anybody could have mistaken him for a Pole. Rising to his full height and drawing attention to his fair skin, blond hair, and clean facial features, Soderberg pointed out that he was not only a Swede but was in fact of Ostrogothian birth, a heritage recognized by all Nazi theories as Aryan at its finest and purest. Astonished, the chief immediately stood up and asked in awe, "Are you really an Ostrogothian?" Suddenly assuming a special air of politeness, he promised that the man who attacked Soderberg would be caught and sent to apologize in person. Knowing that nothing more could be done, Soderberg agreed to the terms. In the ensuing conversation, the chief inquired about Soderberg's work and commented, "Well, the Gestapo knows what you are doing, and we follow your travels and know you are doing a very fine job. But it would be much better if the Ostrogothians could join with us Germans in the fight against Bolshevism."

Soderberg instinctively knew that such an encounter with the Gestapo could not do him any harm. But he also knew they would continue to watch him closely, and he found that disconcerting. Since he could do nothing about it, he simply carried on with his visits to the camps. He was careful not to give the Gestapo an opportunity to arrest or expel him. Unfortunately, however, there were circumstances beyond his control.

When Soderberg visited Stalag Luft III in February, 1944, the Germans were tense. They were convinced that the prisoners were tunneling again, and von Lindeiner was afraid they had ignored his warning about dangers on the outside. On March 26, Soderberg was having a glass of beer with some German officers in a distant town in Upper Silesia. Two Gestapo men approached and asked to see their papers. Finding everything in order, they apologized, saying, "We have to be careful. Quite a lot of English officers, Luftgangsters, have escaped from Stalag Luft III in Sagan." Excusing himself, Soderberg left immediately to prepare for the trip home. He probably knew at least some of the escapers personally and wanted to get back as quickly as possible to learn of their fate.

Returning to Sagan, he found that the atmosphere in the YMCA office was filled with tension. The Gestapo had already stopped by several times to try to discover whether the YMCA had helped the British escape. Shortly thereafter, Soderberg paid an unannounced visit to the camp. As he approached Major Simoleit, he realized he had never seen a man as tense and nervous. "Mr. Soderberg, for heaven's sake keep away from Stalag Luft III until further notice," Simoleit warned. "Things are terrible here." Soderberg said he simply wanted to speak to Colonel von Lindeiner. Simoleit curtly informed him, "Colonel Lindeiner was taken away two days ago. We do not know what has happened to him."

Denied permission to visit the camp, Soderberg turned his attention elsewhere for a time. Badly needing a rest, he traveled to a nearby town to spend Easter weekend with friends. Upon his return, he was startled to discover that the Gestapo had taken three of his office mates—a Dutch girl, a Swedish girl, and a Danish Lutheran priest who led the YMCA work in Germany. At first he could not determine what happened to them, but eventually he pieced the story together.

After the YMCA office moved to Sagan, one of the local girls began to visit the workers. The Swedish girl, Gertrude, befriended her, and

Henry did not give it much thought. But the visitor was Jewish and had no ration card and could not buy any clothes. Gertrude and the Dutch girl, with the priest's assistance, extended a helping hand. They gave her a ration card and clothes, but one dress still had the owner's initials on it. The Gestapo eventually discovered the girl's true identity. When they came for her, she committed suicide. Her three accomplices were then taken. Soderberg immediately notified the Swedish embassy, and after much diplomatic maneuvering and bargaining, the three were released and deported about a month later. Soderberg understood the human side of their involvement, but he felt they had improperly jeopardized the work of the YMCA. Now operating out of an understaffed office and himself the object of suspicion, he struggled on through the summer. His mood matched that of the prisoners. They were despondent about the fifty escapers shot by the Gestapo. In addition, the guards' tactics were increasingly heavy-handed, and relations with the German camp staff were difficult.

At the end of the summer, Soderberg returned to Sweden for new instructions. Back in Suhudyomrt, he saw in the kitchen an attractive brunette, a young Swiss girl sent to work in the office. She was an excellent linguist and an able worker. They soon were an effective team. And with the Allied landing in France now secure, things began to look much brighter, at least in some respects, for both Soderberg and the prisoners.

Soderberg continued to visit Stalag Luft III whenever he could. Always happy to see him, the prisoners were amused by his car with the large charcoal burner on the back and numerous bags of coal stacked up on the roof. It trundled along at about thirty-five miles per hour. Every so often Soderberg had to stop to shake the grate on the burner a bit to ensure a steady flow of coal gas to the engine.

His most memorable visits to Stalag Luft III occurred during the Christmas holidays of 1944. Red Cross parcels had become scarce that fall, and the prisoners were not looking forward to another bleak Christmas in captivity. Nonetheless, they decorated their barracks and seemed determined to make the best of it. Soderberg was sure it would be appropriate for him to go into the camp under such circumstances to wish the prisoners Merry Christmas. But he petitioned the commandant anyway, asking if he could stay three days.

Much to everybody's surprise and relief, a special shipment of Red Cross Christmas parcels arrived just a few days before the big holiday: they contained "canned turkey and plum pudding, all kinds of goodies, candles and everything that the prisoners only in their wildest dreams thought belonged in a prisoner of war camp." Overnight, "as through a wizard, the prisoners' spirit turned around and the preparations for the Christmas celebrations became hectic, nearly as in a fever."

Soderberg spent Christmas Eve day with the British prisoners. He had trouble getting his car across the railroad tracks in the fresh snow, but he was warmly greeted by hosts of prisoners shouting Merry Christmas. The camp was brightly decorated with garlands, home-made Christmas trees, and empty tins cut into shiny stars. Going from barracks to barracks, he wished everyone Merry Christmas, stopping often to taste the cookies they baked that he aptly described as "formidable things both in regard to taste and shape."

Entering sick quarters, Henry spotted a live Christmas tree. Because of the holiday those who were really ill had been given clean white sheets from the Red Cross supplies. He sensed that the men were happy to see someone from the outside world on that particular day, realizing that "I was the visitor who personified all the warm thoughts and wishes from back home."

Soderberg also encountered a group of Norwegian prisoners who had joined the RAF. Strict orders dictated that only English or German be spoken in the camp. But on this day the Germans made an exception, and Soderberg was allowed to speak to them in a Nordic language. Speaking their native language for the first time in ages, the prisoners laughed and joked at length. The German guard in the corner smiled and laughed as though he understood what was being said. Soderberg was certain that the guard had not the slightest idea what they were talking about.

The visit on Christmas Day started with a religious service in the Center Compound theater. The room was packed. In fact, Soderberg recalled, "it nearly exploded." At the end of the service he was asked to say a few words. Emotionally touched, he related: "It was a fantastic sight that met my eye when I mounted the stage. It was not a very long speech that I gave, but I hope it was friendly because in that moment I felt with the prisoners as I had never felt before. And there were thousands of men. They were well dressed and they had lots of blankets over themselves because it was very cold. They were very packed together and they all had their eyes on the man from the outside."

Making the most of the contents of their Red Cross parcels, the prisoners shared their noontime feast with Soderberg. He sat with General Vanaman and about fifteen colonels.

Everybody forgot completely about their surroundings, the barbed wire and captivity. Some of the German officers sitting in the corner watching us tried to look very grim and untouched by what they saw. But the tiniest joy of the Americans they could not resist. The Christmas table with Red Cross parcels also became too tempting to them. It was very meager and sparse on the German table that Christmas, and very soon these German officers were sitting in our circle and were happy like bees even if they did not dare go so far as to put the paper caps on their heads.

Realizing the breach of discipline obviously involved, Soderberg went on to say, "Of course, it could have been a very great scandal. The Gestapo generals could have come in very suddenly to visit the camp that Christmas day and found these officers sitting with the Americans. You never felt really sure and safe from the secret police, neither the prisoners of war nor we foreigners in international positions, nor even the German army officers themselves."

Scenes such as these caused Soderberg to say of Stalag Luft III: "Joys and sorrows, they really went together here." Then, recognizing that the prisoners' merriment covered a mountain of hurt and loneliness, he pensively added: "I didn't see the worst side."

The Christmas celebrations could not blot out the nagging question on everyone's mind: what would the new year bring? Having experienced excitement at the Normandy invasion, the prisoners realized that the slow march across the Continent meant that the war might go on for some time. Just a few days before Christmas, in fact, Chaplain Daniel had visited Simoleit in his office and noticed an ominous-looking arrow on a huge map hanging on the wall. The broad yellow arrow pointed toward Antwerp. Although the prisoners knew that the German counteroffensive had begun on December 16, Daniel asked Simoleit what the arrow meant. His answer would not bolster the prisoners' flagging spirits. "We have started a great drive which will split the Allied forces in the West," Simoleit said gleefully, "and then Hitler's armies will defeat each of the divided forces, thus ending the war in our favor."

The sense of gloom and uncertainty carried over into the new year. One day in early January, Chaplain Daniel paid another visit to Simoleit's office. The yellow arrow was gone. Simoleit did not mention the western front. Shortly thereafter, in the quiet of the night, the prisoners began to hear the rumble of Russian guns. Spirits began to rise. [14]

14. Daniel, *In the Presence*, 74.

16

Evacuation

At 1500 hours on January 17, 1945, the German news broadcast announced unprecedented Russian advances toward the camp. That same day, the prisoners heard that shipments of Red Cross food parcels had arrived from Lübeck. In light of these developments, the senior officers decided that it was time to put the prisoners back on full rations (for the first time in four and one-half months) so that they could "fatten up" and be "ready for any eventuality."[1]

The news electrified the men and gave everyone much to think about. They had heard that prisoner of war camps farther east already had been evacuated and on very short notice. Clearly their own preparations had to be speeded up. For some time the men had been making extra trips around the circuit in an effort to get in better condition for a possible forced march. Now they began to prepare bedrolls and build various containers for their few personal belongings and supplies.

For a few days the camp seemed to be in limbo. Prisoners tried to carry on normally in the theater and outdoors, but their attention was glued to events outside the camp. More and more refugees were seen not only passing the camp but also in Sagan. Stalag Luft III was on the combat air route to the eastern front, and the men gazed up frequently at German planes, including the startling new ME-262 jet fighter.

The prisoners also watched the German camp personnel closely for their reactions to the impending crisis. Some of the Germans seemed more willing to curry favor with the prisoners. Most of them, however, calmly said that the prisoners' preparations for a march were "foolish and over cautious." They also told the men in Center that the pris-

1. Mulligan, Burbank, and Brunn, "History of Center Compound," Pt. III (Diary), January 17, 1945.

oners in the other compounds were not making preparations, when in fact they were. Understandably, the Germans wanted to confiscate all the bedrolls, but finally consented, in Center Compound at least, to let the prisoners sign a parole that the materials would not be used for escape. The kit bags then were stored in the block commander's room in each barracks. In at least one instance, a German called the prisoners' work inadequate and then showed them a better method of packing their goods. The men reviewed their contingency plans to ensure that medics, engineers, and camp leaders would be among the marching ranks and that everyone concerned knew what he was to do if the German staff should desert or attempt to liquidate them.[2]

Tensions among the prisoners mounted as the Russians drew nearer. On January 25, news arrived that a Russian spearhead had reached the Oder at Steinau, only forty-eight miles due east of Stalag Luft III.[3] All the Germans and the prisoners could do, however, was wait and try to carry on as usual. The Germans conducted a routine search of the barracks in Center Compound; the prisoners in Center and West compounds enjoyed a hockey match on the afternoon of January 26. That night the men attended performances in the compound theaters. Most prisoners thought that the time had passed when they could expect to be evacuated. This belief was apparently confirmed when the commandant received an order from Berlin on Saturday morning, January 27: the prisoners were not to be moved.

That evening the order was countermanded. About seven o'clock the Germans announced that the camp would be evacuated. The prisoners in North Compound were rehearsing *The Wind and the Rain* when suddenly the curtains were drawn and the adjutant called out, "All pack up and be ready to move out in an hour's time." A similar scene occurred in East Compound, where the adjutant looked in the

2.   *Ibid.*, January 17–25, 1945; Goodrich, "History of South Compound," Pt. II; Neary, *Stalag Luft III: Sagan*, 26; Crawley, *Escape from Germany*, 215–17.

3.   At this point the records left by the prisoners begin to reflect the confusion that undoubtedly prevailed in the camp, and dates, times, and distances vary with the source. The discrepancies are generally insignificant, and thus little attempt is made here to reconcile the differences. The emphasis instead is upon the trend that can be deciphered from the documents. Examples can be seen in the Center Compound diary, which states in one place (January 25, 1945, entry) that the bedrolls were kept in the block commanders' rooms and in another place (Pt. IV) that they were held in the Red Cross parcel store. Further, one source puts the Russians forty-eight miles from Sagan on January 25 (January 25 entry), while a second account ("History of Center Compound," Pt. IV) places them only thirty-eight miles away on January 23. Neither of these discrepancies is important.

door of the theater and said, "I'd be moving if I were you. We leave at 11:00 P.M." The prisoners in South Compound were enjoying the play *You Can't Take It With You* when Colonel Goodrich walked onto the stage and reportedly proclaimed, "The goons have just come and given us thirty minutes to be at the front gate."[4]

There was a mad rush, then much delay and confusion. Some prisoners felt that stalling might allow the Russians to overtake the columns fairly close to camp; others simply had a lot to do just before their departure. Bedrolls had to be repacked to accommodate available food. The men cleaned out cupboards and quickly "bashed" what could not be carried. They tried to consume as much nutritional food as possible. Also, they were careful to destroy anything that might be of value to the Germans. Into the bonfires went piles of old clothes, furniture, and other items. Somehow barracks 104, from which the Great Escape tunnel had been dug, went up in smoke. Not until eleven o'clock that night did the last man from South Compound leave.

The remaining compounds departed at various times throughout the night and the next day. West Compound left at 12:30 A.M., North Compound cleared the camp by 3:45 A.M., Center Compound followed immediately, and East Compound brought up the rear at about 6:00 Sunday morning. The prisoners in Belaria did not leave until late that evening.[5]

In spite of their best efforts the prisoners had to leave a great deal behind. All the instruments and sports equipment remained, most of which was collected by YMCA personnel who were still working out of their headquarters in Sagan. Estimates suggest that between

4. Crawley, *Escape from Germany*, 219; John Toland, *The Last 100 Days* (New York, 1970), 19.
5. Goodrich, "History of South Compound," Pt. II; Neary, *Stalag Luft III: Sagan*, 26; Mulligan, Burbank, and Brunn, "History of Center Compound," Pt. IV; Crawley, *Escape from Germany*, 220–21. See Spivey, *POW Odyssey*, 118ff., for a different order of march that places Center Compound at the end of the line. This account agrees that the prisoners in Center began passing through the gate at 3:30 A.M., however, and it can then be deduced that Center was not the last to leave. Other evidence indicates that East Compound left at 6:00 A.M. and Belaria later that same day. In confirmation are arrival times of the various compounds at points along the route. The best explanation for this discrepancy is that part of East Compound passed Center during one of the latter's layovers and that the rest of the men from East later joined the prisoners from Belaria, who traveled a somewhat different route, thus placing Center Compound at the end of the columns by the time they entrained at Spremberg.

25,000 and 55,000 Red Cross food parcels were left. The senior officers had gained permission at the last minute to allow some of the prisoners to pass by the Red Cross store and take choice items from the packages, and most of the men gathered up additional cigarettes, chocolate, and other goods that were valued for barter or extra nutrition. After the prisoners departed, thousands upon thousands of food cans littered the area around the Red Cross stores and down the road where the prisoners discarded items in order to lighten their load. One report indicates that approximately 1 million books were left behind and that more than 2.5 million cigarettes were abandoned in East and North compounds alone.[6]

Approximately five hundred prisoners were too sick to be moved, and a few medical personnel, clergymen, and healthy prisoners also remained to help care for them. These men received little assistance from the Germans, but managed to find plenty to eat and drink by scrounging through the various compounds. Finally, on February 6, 1945, they too were removed from the camp, placed inside boxcars, and taken westward to a camp outside Nuremberg where, on February 10, they rejoined the prisoners from West Compound, who had arrived shortly before.[7] With the departure of the sick and wounded, Stalag Luft III ceased to exist as a Luftwaffe prisoner of war camp. What happened to the facilities is not known. At least one prisoner returned to the scene immediately after the war in an effort to locate certain documents and the carefully hidden copies of the *Kriegie Klarion*. The camp was still standing, but he could not find what he sought. At some later date the camp was torn down. Today all one sees at the site is an open field with a monument built by the Polish government in memory of the men who died in the complex of prisoner of war camps in the vicinity of Sagan.[8]

The demise of the camp, unfortunately, did not mark the end of the prisoners' travail. Snow had begun to fall several days before the

---

6.   Crawley, *Escape from Germany*, 220; Mulligan, Burbank, and Brunn, "History of Center Compound," Pt. IV.
7.   Full details are in Mulligan, Burbank, and Brunn, "History of Center Compound," in a section "The Evacuation of the Hospital Party from Sagan and the Period Before the Evacuation."
8.   Interview with Dreyer, February 25, 1976. Dreyer named one Major Eggen as the man who revisited the site immediately after the war. Eggen is now deceased. For comments on the monument, see Toland, *The Last 100 Days*, 663. A picture is in a pamphlet in the Clark Collection that depicts war monuments throughout Poland.

march started, and about six inches had accumulated by the time the men left the camp. In some ways the snow was a blessing. Taking advantage of the time between the departure of the first and last compounds, many prisoners were able to build sleds upon which to carry their possessions. In some cases the sleds were nothing more than overturned benches with runners attached, but however makeshift they might have been, they proved to be a boon.

The low temperatures were another matter. Estimates range from ten degrees below zero to twenty degrees above zero (the latter is perhaps the more accurate figure, though the chill factor could have been significant) the night the march began, and from ten to twenty degrees above zero the next day. Snow fell during the night, and the wind created blizzard conditions at times.[9] For a brief period the prisoners were festive, for they had the exhilarating realization that they were at last outside of the wire. The harsh weather soon took its toll upon the weakened men, however, and the columns began to stretch out as fatigued men fell farther and farther behind. The prisoners generally believed that stragglers would be shot, and rumors spread quickly whenever shooting was heard nearby. While some prisoners witnessed isolated shootings, there were apparently few such instances. The guards themselves, in fact, were mostly older men who were in worse condition than the prisoners were. In addition, some exhausted marchers were returned to Stalag Luft III, and others who were picked up later by search parties were sent back along the route after the columns stopped to rest. Many men were found where they had fallen, worn out and half frozen but otherwise unharmed.[10]

The prisoners realized that the march provided ample opportunities for escape but only a few of them took advantage of the situation. The BBC had broadcast an order that the men stay together for safety and ease of identification. South and Belaria compounds did not receive the message banning escape, however, and prisoners

9. Crawley, *Escape from Germany*, 221; Mulligan, Burbank, and Brunn, "History of Center Compound," Pt. IV, "The Evacuation of the Hospital Party"; interview with Albert P. Clark, March 22, 1976. The trying conditions on the march are vividly portrayed in a novel written by Joe Klaas. *Maybe I'm Dead* exemplifies the prisoners' tendency to exaggerate (he says the temperature on the first night was forty below), but the work is well worth reading because the author skillfully describes the prisoners' moods and the intangible fears and hardships they endured on the march.

10. Mulligan, Burbank, and Brunn, "History of Center Compound," Pt. IV, "The Evacuation of the Hospital Party"; Crawley, *Escape from Germany*, 222–23.

from there did escape. Colonel Goodrich, seeing no advantage to escaping in central Germany during winter, ordered the men of South Compound not to escape, even though at times they carried rifles for some of the exhausted guards. When their group arrived in the vicinity of Munich, interest in escape increased, and before their train arrived at Moosburg, the station near their final destination, the prisoners were given permission to escape. Thirty-two men jumped out of the boxcars. Not only were the escapers physically worn out, they did not know the terrain and the local populace. They were all captured within five days and sent to Moosburg, where they rejoined their fellow prisoners. Fifteen prisoners from Belaria Compound also escaped, but their fate is not known.[11]

Knowing that escape was not a practical alternative, the prisoners had little choice but to suffer through the hardships of the march. It soon became clear that the Germans had made little or no provision for their care on the journey. A few wagonloads of bread were sent along with several of the columns, but the prisoners ate mostly the food they carried on their backs. They bartered for some additional food and water along the way. The people they met were generally kind and considerate. But the isolated groups of SS men who crossed the prisoners' path berated the people for associating with the Luftgangsters. The men in South Compound seem to have suffered the most on the march. The prisoners blamed the German officer in command of their group, and he may have intentionally abused the men. It is also possible that higher authorities were pressing him to keep South Compound moving. The lead column had to travel long distances with only brief rest stops so succeeding groups would have room. Had they not moved rapidly, the advancing Russian forces might have overtaken them. Russian guns could still be heard in the distance after the men got on the road, and with the columns stretching out some twenty miles, there undoubtedly was concern over the progress of the first compound. Article 7 of the Geneva Convention specifies that prisoners of war are not to march more than 20 kilometers (12.5 miles) a day. The men of South walked 34.5 miles in the first twenty-seven hours and had one four-hour stop. At 2:20 A.M.,

---

11. Goodrich, "History of South Compound," Pt. III; Albert A. Kadler, "Special Report on Conditions During the Forced March of American and British Prisoners of War from Their Former Camps to Stalag III A, Luckenwalde," n.d., File 383.6–15, SHAEF 1–6, Record Group 331, Modern Military Branch, National Archives.

January 29, they reached Muskau, where they found quarters in a brick factory and a heating plant. The factory's furnaces were white hot, and the prisoners reveled in the warmth. The facility also had running water, and those who were still physically able washed themselves and cooked some food. About 15 percent of the men could not walk without assistance, and many more were to suffer from exposure and exhaustion.[12]

All the compounds but Belaria followed the same route from Sagan to Spremberg, where the men boarded trains and traveled in different directions. South Compound remained in the lead but had a somewhat easier trek during the final 15.5 miles from Muskau to Spremberg. West Compound came next and covered 17.3 miles in eleven hours. They stopped to rest, and the prisoners took two-hour turns getting warm in some concentration camp buildings. The column then moved on at about 6:00 P.M. Early on January 29, exhausted groups began seeking shelter in barns and roadside inns. The men later resumed the march under their own direction and continued toward Muskau, where they found the brick factory the South Compound prisoners had used. They demanded extra time to rest and recuperate next to the furnaces. The factory soon became a jumble of humanity. South Compound, with a thirty-hour rest, was still present when the men arrived from West Compound, and they stayed there two days.[13] The prisoners from West then covered the remaining 15.5 miles to Spremberg in two more days, stopping overnight in some barns near Graustein.

The five hundred Americans of North Compound covered the distance in three stages. They marched 20.5 miles, then less than 20, and, after a three-day rest at Muskau, walked the 15.5 miles to Spremberg with half the prisoners from East who had caught up with them at Muskau.

The complete lack of organization is revealed in the problems faced by the North Compound prisoners. Anticipating a rest at Halbau, the first logical stopping point along the way, the prisoners learned upon arrival there that they were to billet at Friedwaldau, some four miles farther on. When they reached that village about noon, they found

12. Crawley, *Escape from Germany*, 222; Goodrich, "History of South Compound," Pt. III.

13. Neary, *Stalag Luft III: Sagan*, 27; Goodrich, "History of South Compound," Pt. III.

only two halls capable of holding 350 men each. The German officer in charge of the compound left the men waiting in the street while he went to look for more accommodations. After about an hour, during which time the prisoners' wet clothing began to freeze, some prisoners began to look for shelter themselves. The local populace offered to let them come into their houses. Within minutes, however, shouts echoed down the streets, and members of the SS and the local police went to each house and ordered the prisoners out. The whole column then had to march four more miles to the village of Leippe, where it was rumored that a large barn was available. Once there, they discovered that the barn would hold at the most 600 men. As many as possible were crowded in, and the rest of the column was halted on the road. There they waited for four hours while the Germans tried to find more places. The temperature on this second night of the march reportedly dipped below zero. Most of the Germans gave up the search before long and retired for the night, leaving the prisoners in the cold. Hermann Glemnitz, however, continued to look for quarters. Eventually he got almost all the men under a roof, but fifty prisoners had to sleep on straw placed on the leeward side of a farmyard wall. The march was resumed at 8:00 the next morning and ended that evening in Muskau. The brick factory was still occupied by other prisoners, so the men from North stayed in a riding school, the stables of a palace, a laundry, a pottery, and a section of a French prisoner of war camp three miles outside town.[14]

The prisoners in Center and East compounds encountered difficulties also. General Vanaman walked the entire distance at the head of Center Compound's column. The prisoners from Center found refuge in Halbau, but the church and attached buildings they occupied were so small that virtually no one got any rest that night. The next day they marched some ten miles to the village of Barrau, where they rested on January 30. Then they went on to Muskau and stayed there until February 3. That day they marched to Graustein and spent the night in barns. On February 4, the eighth day of their journey, the prisoners from Center Compound completed the trip to Spremberg, where, like all the others, they boarded trains for unknown destinations.[15]

14. Crawley, *Escape from Germany*, 228–30.
15. For detailed accounts of their journey, see Spivey, *POW Odyssey*, 118–32; and Mulligan, Burbank, and Brunn, "History of Center Compound," Pt. IV.

Lieutenant Walter G. Johnson recalls the march vividly. The night they left Stalag Luft III, "the chill factor was about −20 degrees. There was a very bright moon. We marched all that night and all the next day until 8:00 P.M. We'd had several stops of 10–15 minutes each. At one point I went to sleep. My shoes were in bad disrepair because I'd worn them for over a year, and they were cracked and water got inside. While I was sleeping they froze. It didn't seem too important to me at the time, so when the march resumed I kept walking." As they approached Muskau, Johnson decided to attempt an escape he had been planning. He pretended to be ill and fell out, hoping the guards would take him to a hospital. There, he thought, he could more easily carry out the rest of his plan. But he was taken to the home of the Bürgermeister, or mayor. "This was an interesting experience," he later recalled:

Both the mayor and his wife were very devout Catholics. He was a rather short fella, about 5′6″ or so, wore jackboots, and looked very proper. Outwardly he gave the appearance of being a Nazi, but his wife made no bones about the fact that she was a very ardent Catholic and tremendously interested in the welfare of the POWs that were being moved. They took about 20 of us into their home, pulled down comforters off the beds, put mattresses on the floor and gave us pillows. She and some other ladies took what rations we had with us, along with some of their own foodstuffs and made soups and meals for us.

Turned back over to the guards the next day, Johnson again feigned illness and fell as though he was too weak to walk. This time he was taken to a German hospital. Staying there one day until the prisoners marched on, he then joined with several Romanian soldiers who also were interested in fleeing toward the Russian lines. Unfortunately, after they climbed out a window, they walked down the street and ran directly into members of the Gestapo. At headquarters, Johnson and the others were "worked over in good Gestapo style." They wanted to know who had helped him, but since no one had, he had nothing to tell them. Now with superficial head wounds and body bruises inflicted by the Gestapo, he was taken back to the hospital. About that time, his feet began to hurt, and the doctor determined that they had indeed frozen during the rest stop while Johnson slept. Then "the Germans concluded I had gangrenous feet and in their usual thorough manner wished to amputate both feet, but I refused adamantly. So they left them alone and treated them with some sulfur powder and whatever else they had on hand for an antibiotic." Johnson's feet were saved, though he lost his toenails and they did not grow back properly. Before long he was on a train, going to rejoin the other prisoners.[16]

At Muskau and later at Spremberg, the prisoners were divided into groups and sent in different directions.[17] The Americans from West Compound went to Stalag XIII D outside Nuremberg, and those from South and Center went to Stalag VII A near Moosburg. The British from North Compound (and some from East) went to Marlag-Milag, a camp near Tarmstedt originally for naval prisoners and merchant marine internees. The prisoners from Belaria Compound and the men from East who joined them went to Luckenwalde, a large camp about twenty miles southwest of Berlin.[18]

The train rides, like the marches, entailed hardships and dangers. Forty to fifty men and several guards were crowded into each boxcar, so only a few men could lie down. Many were sick by this time, and vomit and human excrement accumulated on the floors. For long periods the prisoners received no water and were allowed no opportunities to prepare food or relieve themselves. And, as was true throughout the march, everyone was exposed to attacks by Allied aircraft. There is no proof that any of the columns from Stalag Luft III were attacked while on foot or aboard the trains in January and February, but Allied planes did fire on them in the spring. Reports of strafing circulated frequently among the men, and on numerous occasions they passed through or near areas that were being heavily bombed. The boxcars seldom carried proper markings that would identify the passengers as prisoners. And they never knew where they were being sent. Some suspected that the Germans might place them in large cities to try to discourage Allied bombings.[19]

16. Interview with Walter G. Johnson, November 25, 1978.
17. At Muskau the five hundred American prisoners from North Compound joined one of the all-American compounds and traveled with them to Spremberg. And half of the men from East went with North Compound toward Spremberg; the other half remained behind and joined with Belaria Compound, which followed twenty-four hours later (Crawley, *Escape from Germany*, 234–36).
18. Details of the British movements are in Crawley, *Escape from Germany*, 237–81. Only the Americans' experiences are recounted here.
19. Such a plan actually did exist: the Luftwaffe Operations Staff proposed that camps for British and American air force prisoners be established in the centers of towns, and Alfred Jodl approved the measure on behalf of the General Staff of the High Command. Keitel wrote only two words on the first page of the document—"No objections"—and added his initials (*IMT*, VII, 114–15). However, Article 9 of the Geneva Convention reads in part: "No prisoner may, at any time, be sent into a region where he

After the war, members of the Judge Advocate General's Office, seeking evidence for use in the war crimes trials, took numerous affidavits from prisoners that had to do with the hardships on the march.[20] The prisoners had also registered many complaints with the protecting power. They charged individual Germans, as well as the German prisoner of war system as a whole, with gross violations of the Geneva Convention. Especially noted were marches in inclement weather over distances exceeding the twenty-kilometer limitation and with inadequate food, water, rest, and shelter. They had often been exposed to hostile fire, and there were not even minimal efforts to identify the columns of marching men or the boxcars in which they later rode.

The widespread agreement in the prisoners' reports clearly shows they suffered severe hardships and abuse during the final months of the war. The difficulty of singling out and passing judgment on the Germans, however, is aptly pointed out in a perceptive report by a staff officer of the Supreme Headquarters, Allied Expeditionary Force (SHAEF):

While the Annex to the Hague Convention, and the Geneva Convention prescribe certain rules as to the treatment of prisoners such as treating them humanely, avoiding exposing them to fire in a combat zone, evacuating them at stages of not more than 20 kilometers a day and supplying them a food ration equal in quantity and quality to that of troops at base camps, there is no indication as to the duty of the detaining power when these conditions cannot be met. There is nothing that requires the detaining power to offer the prisoners a choice of (1) being overrun by the forces of their own or Allied nations or (2) of undergoing severe forced marches with inadequate food and shelter.

The problems facing SHAEF personnel in their efforts to alleviate the prisoners' plight also were clearly seen. The report continues: "Cha-

---

might be exposed to the fire of the combat zone, nor used to give protection from bombardment to certain points or certain regions by his presence." Berger claims that he never saw the order, stating that Goebbels had repeatedly asked that British and American air force prisoners be placed in cities where they would serve as "living air defense." Further, Berger joined forces with Albert Speer, and they convinced Reich leaders that sufficient barbed wire could not be found to prepare such camps and that adequate forces were no longer available to guard the prisoners in the cities (Discussion among Delmar T. Spivey, Dr. Helmut Haubold, and Gottlob Berger, April 16–17, 1968. [Transcript in Berger Folder, Spivey Collection], 10–11, hereinafter cited as "Berger Interview Transcript").

20.   See Entry 321b, Record Group 153, Records of the Judge Advocate General's Office, Washington National Record Center, for individual affidavits on to apparent violations of the Geneva Convention in the treatment of prisoners of war.

otic conditions in Germany due to the Russian advance and Allied air assaults were undoubtedly the main cause of the violations although there is some indication of willful refusal to better their condition. At this stage of the proceedings, while a protest would be proper, it is extremely doubtful if it would be effective particularly in view of the great mass of crimes awaiting investigation and action. Nor would it be advisable to speculate as to the effect of retaliation against German prisoners of war since this would only produce greater hardships against our own personnel in German hands."[21]

Realizing that the Allies could most help the prisoners by approaching the Germans in a spirit of cooperation and compromise was a step in the right direction. The real problems, however, were what kinds of aid the prisoners needed most and how it might be sent to them.

SHAEF personnel had begun in early 1944 to lay contingency plans for the care of Allied prisoners during the final months of the war and after Germany's collapse. Little concrete work could be done, however, until Germany's intentions became clear. Throughout January and February, 1945, the Allies watched the prisoners' migration and set to work with representatives of the International Red Cross to see what could be done to get obviously needed food and medical supplies to the prisoners while they were en route and after they had arrived at their destinations. Soon the planners realized that nothing short of drastic emergency measures could save the prisoners from large-scale suffering, disease, and death.[22] One report indicated that as of February 26, 1945, three broad migration routes had emerged. About 100,000 prisoners were in the northern line of march, all moving westward along the German coast. Approximately 60,000 pris-

21. Lieutenant Colonel C. S. Bushman to Colonel Brooks, April 2, 1945, memorandum in File 383.6–15, RG 331.
22. For detailed accounts of the contingency plans and the factors that affected their formation, see the following items located in the Simpson Center, Maxwell AFB: USSTAF, "Information on current problems confronting the AAF in the ETO, 1944–45 [concerning] the protection, evacuation, relief, and maintenance of U.S. and British prisoners of war after cessation of hostilities" (tab 9), File 519.979; USSTAF, "ECLIPSE Memorandum No. 8: The care and evacuation of prisoners of war in Greater Germany under ECLIPSE conditions," May 19, 1945, Flle No. 519.9731–3, 13; USSTAF, "Folder of miscellaneous post hostilities planning data for treatment and evacuation of POWs, January-March 1945," File 519.9731–13; USSTAF, "Minutes and notes of planning meetings and conferences on supply, protection and evacuation of Allied Prisoners of War, PW sec. on file, November 1944-May 1945," File 519.9731–3.

oners on the central line of march were moving westward in an area delimited by Berlin, Dresden, and Leipzig. The third group, about 80,000 men, was mostly moving westward along a line from the Sudetenland through the towns of Böhmisch-Leippe, Königgrätz, Gitschin, and Teplitz-Schönau. The prisoners were then assembled and split into two groups, one of which went to Karlsbad and the other to Marienbad and thence to Nuremberg, Stuttgart, and Munich.[23]

On February 24, SHAEF announced that an agreement had been concluded (apparently with representatives of the International Red Cross in Geneva) for transporting supplies from Switzerland into Germany by truck. The first convoy was scheduled to cross the border the next day. The trucks did not, in fact, begin to cross the border until March 6, but thereafter a steady stream of supplies was sent into Germany on a fleet of two hundred specially marked trucks and several trains that operated out of Geneva in the south and Lübeck in the north.[24]

The delay may have occurred for several reasons. The shipping of emergency relief supplies was a gigantic undertaking and the operation may simply have taken longer to arrange than the planners originally expected. Second, some doubt still existed whether the Germans would grant safe passage. The British secretary of state for war pointed out in the House of Commons on February 27, 1945: "It is impossible to make anything effective without the agreement of the German authorities. . . . I would . . . just like to say that the assumption in some quarters that the only thing necessary to solve the problem is for the united nations to place at the disposal of the International Red Cross Committee large numbers of lorries or railway wagons, together with large quantities of petrol, oil and so on . . . has no foundation. It is no use piling up lorries and railway wagons at Geneva if there is no outlet into Germany for them."[25] At some point prior to March 6, the Germans did agree to let the convoys enter

23. Mr. Harrison to Ambassador Fullerton, February 28, 1945, in File 383.6–15, RG 331.
24. Mr. Caffery to Secretary of State, February 24, 1945, in File 740.00114 EW/2–2445, RG 59; résumé of report by Dr. Rossel, March 17, 1945, concerning the First Emergency Relief Motor Convoy, in File 383.6/6, "Supplies for POWs," SHAEF G–1, RG 331.
25. Transcript of message in John G. Winnant to Secretary of State, February 27, 1945, in File 740.00114 EW/2–2745, RG 59.

Germany. After that date the vehicles did travel safely through the country.

Henry Soderberg was among the first to benefit from advance Allied planning. In 1945 he was given a gasoline-powered car to replace his coal burner. At first his travels were more pleasant, but obtaining gas grew steadily more difficult as Germany neared total collapse. Just when it seemed as though he would have to curtail his trips, the YMCA, the United States, and Germany struck a deal—the Allies would deliver specified quantities of gasoline to Lübeck. The Germans would then issue equal amounts of gasoline to the YMCA field delegates wherever they needed it. To get gas, a delegate drove to a military installation, handed the fuel-supply custodian a coupon, and filled his tank. Soderberg was astonished how well the system worked. If gas was available anywhere in the area he was traveling, it was easy for him to get what he needed.[26]

The prisoners had no way of knowing about the extensive relief efforts and became increasingly concerned about their survival. Some of the men from Stalag Luft III felt they had one factor in their favor, however—the presence of a brigadier general. They assumed that General Vanaman could gain concessions that would be denied to lower-ranking prisoners. Many questions arose, therefore, when suddenly Vanaman, Spivey, and three other officers were removed from the columns at Spremberg and sent to Berlin. Conflicting stories about their departure circulated among the prisoners both then and later. The official word from the Germans was that these men were being prepared for early repatriation because of their fine work conducting the march in an "orderly and efficient" manner. This explanation put the members of the "repatriation party" in an awkward position. Because of the instructions from home to remain together and not escape, the prisoners had in fact conducted themselves well. In this case, however, their actions made the story about early repatriation seem plausible. Spivey wanted to stay with his men, as did Vanaman, but the Germans left them no choice. They not only had to leave, they had to go along with the official word on their departing as well.

Vanaman, however, had some concrete reasons, unknown to the other prisoners, for agreeing to the German cover story. Ever since his

26.   Interview with Soderberg, September 15, 1979.

capture, he had felt that the Germans would try to use him in some manner. He was convinced that they wanted him in Berlin for their own purposes. But the trip also offered Vanaman many opportunities, for he felt that decisions affecting the prisoners were still being made there and that perhaps he could have an influence on some of them. What would happen to him and the other men in the repatriation party when they got to Berlin was anybody's guess.[27]

Their route took them north to the bombed-out city of Berlin and then back south to Luckenwalde. As Vanaman's group had feared, nobody there knew anything about plans for repatriation. They waited two weeks before receiving any indication of what might happen to them.

One day a young German captain, Helmut Bauer, introduced himself as a member of General Berger's staff and asked if he could help them. Vanaman, thinking that this might be the opportunity he had been hoping for, said he would like to go to Switzerland and arrange with United States government representatives to send the food being stored there to the various camps in Germany. Vanaman promised that he would come back and remain a prisoner of war.

In a few days, Bauer returned with news that Berger had approved Vanaman's trip. Unfortunately, the journey had to be canceled because of Berger's "difficulties" with Goebbels and Bormann. The general had special plans for Vanaman that he had revealed to few men in the German hierarchy. Goebbels, Bormann, and Himmler were not among them. At the suggestion of a staff member, Dr. Helmut Haubold, and in keeping with his interest in providing humane treatment for the prisoners, Berger had agreed to hold a medical conference in Berlin to help alleviate some of the worst problems facing the prisoners under his control. Berger insisted, however, that Vanaman, as a high-ranking prisoner, be present so that the medical personnel from the various camps would take the conference seriously and not dismiss it as a mere Nazi propaganda scheme. Berger kept Vanaman's presence in the area a closely guarded secret because he feared that Bormann, Goebbels, and Himmler would try

27. Interview with Vanaman, April 2–3, 1973. More detailed accounts of the experiences of the repatriation party are found in Spivey, *POW Odyssey*, 133–67; and Spivey and Durand, "Secret Mission to Berlin," 115–20. The information presented here is derived from the interview with Vanaman and these two sources.

to use Vanaman for their own purposes. So Berger canceled the trip to Switzerland. But with the help of his staff, he worked directly with International Red Cross and protecting power representatives in an effort to have the supplies brought into Germany in specially marked trucks.

The medical conference began on March 28, 1945. A great deal was accomplished. The members arranged, for example, to pool medical supplies and disperse them, at least in part, through two teams of doctors. An American physician and a German physician were to visit prisoner of war camps throughout southern Germany for the purpose of stopping epidemics. And a British doctor and a German doctor were assigned the same mission in camps in northern Germany.

After the conference Vanaman and Spivey remained in Berlin upon orders of Berger, who had further plans for them. He summoned them to his headquarters on the outskirts of the city and asked them to carry special radio codes to the Allied armies. Berger wanted to establish clandestine communication with General Eisenhower. He sought to negotiate a separate peace with the West so that the remaining German forces could concentrate all their strength upon the advancing Russian armies. He was prepared to circumvent Hitler, Himmler, and all the rest of the Nazi hierarchy in order to save the fatherland.

Berger certainly was not alone in thinking that such a plan would work—it is widely known that other Reich leaders were putting out secret peace feelers. Berger's attempt is interesting because he chose one of the prisoners under his control to serve as his emissary, and because the prisoner stipulated that he would carry the codes to Switzerland only if Berger continued his efforts to get supplies to the men and did his utmost to stop the prisoners being moved.

Vanaman, Spivey, and Berger did not meet until the night of April 3, so one cannot be sure that Vanaman's stipulations to Berger were responsible for the continued arrival of the specially marked Red Cross trucks that had begun entering Germany on March 6, 1945. It is possible, however, that Berger granted the all-important safe conducts without which Allied authorities would not have allowed the convoys to move. It is also possible that he was motivated, at least in part, by the knowledge that if he wanted the Americans and the British to accept the messages carried by Vanaman, he would have to do something rather spectacular to establish his credibility. What better way to exhibit his sincere desire to cooperate than to assure the safety and well-being of the prisoners about whom they had expressed so much concern.[28]

Berger arranged for Vanaman and Spivey to be smuggled into Switzerland. Because of circumstances beyond Berger's control, however, the two men did not cross the border until April 23, 1945. The war was almost over and the codes received little attention, though Vanaman was flown to Washington, where he made a full report to American authorities. In the meantime, much had happened to the other prisoners from Stalag Luft III, all of whom were anxiously awaiting the day of liberation.

When the prisoners arrived at their destinations after the march, the conditions all around them were deplorable. As might be expected, the camps were exceedingly crowded, and more prisoners were arriving every day. In spite of the Germans' best efforts, latrines overflowed and garbage accumulated faster than it could be carried away. The danger of epidemics arose again, only this time the prisoners could do little to help themselves. Inadequate rations throughout the march and during the weeks before the emergency supplies arrived sapped the men's health and strength. Many had become ill and were prostrate by the time the first parcels were delivered.

The prisoners at Nuremberg found it necessary to send a long list of complaints to the protecting power on March 13, 1945. The most serious charge was that the Germans had violated the Geneva Convention by placing the prisoners within 3 kilometers (1.86 miles) of a major military target, the marshaling yard. During the three weeks before the submission of the report, the target had been bombed repeatedly, and many bombs had fallen near the camp.

George Sweanor found the bombing raids horrible and fascinating. The first attack of the "heavies" came only a few nights after his arrival at Nuremberg. At first aware only of distant air-raid sirens wailing in the night, he was summoned to instant wakefulness when nearby sirens sounded a more urgent cry. He opened the windows so less

28. This line of reasoning involves much speculation. However, Berger himself openly claimed after the war that he was responsible for arranging for the shipments inside Germany. In lengthy interviews with General Spivey, Berger listed many things he did to safeguard the prisoners' interests as the end of the war approached and asserted that supporting documents existed somewhere in German archives. Since the war, pieces of evidence, some of which are outlined here, have emerged, and they substantiate his statements. See "Berger Interview Transcript," *passim.*

glass would be shattered when the bombs landed. Re-creating the scene, he stated: "Soon, the drone of high-flying Merlin engines became perceptible and, as the throb grew inexorably in volume, it seemed to chant: 'You've had it, chum, here we come, *rumm rumm*; you've had it, chum, here we come, *rumm rumm*'; over and over again. Our nervousness increased with the aerial armada's approach. We milled about in the dark, and the pail in the corner never lacked patrons." Some raids, especially those conducted by the fast and usually single Mosquito aircraft, were short and sharp. With the Lancasters and Halifaxes, however, it was like watching a play. "Following the 'Imminent Attack' siren wail," Sweanor continued, "the sharp cracks of hundreds of flak guns ushered in the next act with ear-splitting din; then red and green marker flares cascaded from the depths of the night sky as someone shouted, 'Markers are down!' There was no doubt now as to the target for tonight. I watched, fascinated, as the brilliant markers seemed to be drifting straight for my open mouth." His eyes remained glued to the scene. Suddenly, "two walls of flame erupted in front of us as the sound of exploding bombs deafened us; I could feel the heat on my face." The bombs were close, and the barracks seemed increasingly frail. There were slit trenches, but the guards had been instructed to shoot anyone who ventured outside during an air raid. Before long, however, hundreds of prisoners dove out the windows and raced for the trenches. No shots were fired—the guards were busy looking out for themselves. "The scene before us was one that had to be seen to be believed," he later recalled. "It was a most beautiful maze of light and color that hid the stench of death. Powerful blue and white searchlights made an ever-changing lattice of colors, and died. Every few seconds a particularly large blossom would go streaking downwards followed by an orange trail of light as another bomber and crew were written off. At the base of this huge lattice work were countless tongues of flames, growing in size and number; their dance pausing frequently to merge with dull red glows as two-ton bombs exploded."

As the inferno raged the smell of burning was everywhere. Then "a high-pitched scream, the like of which I never want to hear again, tore at us, increasing in agony until it spoke for all the tortures of the ages. We did not comprehend its meaning, but it was coming at us from all directions, blotting out the rest of the universe. There was absolutely nothing left but our small slit trench; there was nowhere to run. I crouched low, not knowing what to expect. Immeasurably long seconds later, the tortured metal of a blazing Lancaster screamed overhead, barely missing our hut, and, escaping its tormentors, plunged to its death in the trees just outside the wire." The scene brought back vivid memories to Sweanor and numerous others: "We were all several shades whiter. Most of us had escaped from aircraft in similar death plunges; but this one was different—we had heard the soul of a dying aircraft, crying out in terrified protest." Turning again toward Nuremberg, Sweanor watched as the final scenes unfolded. "The raid lasted no more than half an hour; it seemed an eternity. As the last bombers turned for home to bacon and eggs and soft beds, ugly black smoke, welling up from the fires of Nuremberg, blotted out the stars as though man, now ashamed of his deeds, was trying to hide his handiwork from the eyes of God."[29]

The prisoners' report to the protecting power also noted that their diet consisted of approximately thirteen hundred calories per day, and the dehydrated vegetables were consistently wormy. Crowded conditions, and the lack of fuel for the stoves, had increased the prisoners' susceptibility to disease, especially influenza and pneumonia. At the time, 1,159 men had no beds and were sleeping on cold, damp floors. The available palliasses were vermin-ridden. Rats, mice, bedbugs, lice, and fleas were everywhere, and no adequate disinfectants or antivermin powders had been distributed. There was no space available for education or entertainment or even calisthenics. The report ended with a proposal that the prisoners sign paroles and be allowed to march (no more than twenty kilometers a day) until they reached Switzerland, where they would remain interned until the end of the war. The second plan they offered called for them to march to another camp where adequate facilities existed and where Red Cross parcels could be more easily obtained.[30]

When the Allied armies began to approach Nuremberg, the Germans accepted the second offer. On April 4, 1945, the prisoners from Stalag Luft III who had been transferred to Nuremberg set out on the road once again, this time in the direction of Moosburg, where the other Americans had been sent. Fortunately, the weather was much warmer this time. And other notable differences existed between this

---

29. Sweanor, *Pensionable Time*, 173–74.
30. Darr H. Alkire, "Complaints Respecting Conditions of Captivity," March 13, 1945, as found in Goodrich, "History of South Compound," Annex III, "Protecting Power File."

march and the one that marked the departure from Sagan. Second
Lieutenant George W. Wenthe recorded in his daily log:

4 April: 10:00 A.M. Left Nurnberg—nearly 10,000 men. Marched 25 KM to a
small village. Arrived at 9:30 P.M. Slept in barn. Saw American fighters
during day, bombing and strafing—two kriegies killed.

5 April: Up early and cooked breakfast. Civilians very hospitable. A small
boy showed us American and British flags he had for use soon. All think the
war soon over. Marched 3 KM to Neumarkt. At 10:00 A.M. watched 100's of
bombers and fighters hit Nurnburg. Later heard 147 American kriegies
killed, 2000 Russ-Serbs, and 40 goons. Our camp was leveled—lucky so far.
Had first goon issue [of] brot soup at 1:00 P.M. Marched on. Saw some
bombed areas in Neumarkt. Kriegies starting to straggle, also goons. Start of
complete disorder of march. Moved on 18 KM to Berching—after spending
afternoon in woods south of Neumarkt. Rained all the way. Arrived at 3:00
A.M. and was bedded in a Catholic church. Slept near altar. Very tired feet
and wounded leg. . . .

6 April: Up early and started bargaining with civilians. Soap and cigarettes
for brot and eggs—whatever else we could get. Had first fresh eggs in over a
year. At 10:00 A.M. we assembled. Got 1/2 Red Cross parcel and 1/2 loaf of
bread. Left the town (very old and picturesque) and started to straggle—too
difficult to keep up. Walked about 5 KM and dropped off to side to cook. Four
of us made a big pot of oatmeal and eggs in a driving rain. Good eating. Left
the spot at 5 P.M. and walked 7 KM to Paulustrin, still raining. Funniest
sight, an old goon walking as if on last leg. Unteroffizier asked Bill Dunlap
and I to walk slow with him and watch over him. We went up a long hill and
some of us carried his gun. What a war! Stopped in town and told a housewife we were ill, asked for a bed. She gave us a room all to ourselves. Plenty
of straw, hot water, fire, potatoes and brot. Ate, dried our clothes and went
to bed.

7 April: Slept until 9 A.M. Made breakfast and roamed about town. . . . Col.
Jenkins—friend from the hospital in Paris in charge said ok to stay on. At
noon, Pappy Yochim and Fran Flynn came by and we moved them in. Ate
again and built a deluxe kriegie pie, 15" x 10" x 3" for 4 men. The Frauen
were astounded upon tasting same. This plus salmon potato loaf stalled us
out. We now had the run of the house, guards living next to us—we helped
them cook. Chatted a bit and then to bed again. Rumors aplenty. Kriegie
stories astounding—a movie of this would be priceless.[31]

Not all the prisoners were having such a relaxed time of it. When
the men from Nuremberg arrived at Moosburg, they found conditions similar to those they had just left. On April 9 the prisoners from
South Compound had transferred into the area occupied by Center.
The five large tents proved insufficient, and prisoners slept outside.

---

31.   George W. Wenthe, "Daily Log, April 4–June 4, 1945" (Copy in the possession
of the author; original held by Mr. Wenthe).

Crude lean-tos also were hastily constructed. The camp resembled a hobo village. The four hundred prisoners in each barracks (which were only a little larger than those at Sagan) obtained their water from one faucet and one hand pump. Again, sanitation measures were totally inadequate.

Interest in escape was keen at Moosburg, even though the war was rapidly drawing to a close. The most obvious temptation was the relative proximity of the Swiss border and the Allied forces. In addition, escape was relatively easy. Moosburg supervised numerous small work camps, which were poorly guarded and which had French, Serbians, Russians, British, Americans, and Italians in them. These men, together with the thousands of foreign workers throughout the area, were willing to help the fliers. Contact with them was established through the prisoners in the labor camps and was maintained through the Man of Confidence of that particular nationality in Moosburg. The officers soon found that the best way to get out of the camp was to sneak into the enlisted men's compounds and then go with them on a work detail and later break away and find the friendly workers. Another method was to switch identities with enlisted men who entered the officers' compound for one reason or another. The enlisted men were only too happy to enjoy the better living conditions available to the officers. At least sixteen officers made identity switches. On two different occasions two officers, using a key the prisoners made for the front gate, walked out of the compound. A tunnel also was started between the officers' and enlisted men's compounds, but it was never completed. Finally, near the end of the war, members of the German garrison expressed a willingness to help Americans to escape if they could go along. Several officers availed themselves of such opportunities, and most of them hid out in the town of Moosburg until the American forces arrived. Their primary motive was to avoid the fighting that might occur if die-hard Germans refused to surrender the camp.

There was yet another reason why the prisoners thought about escape during the last hectic days of the war. They had frequently heard rumors that Hitler intended to use captives as hostages for better truce terms and would hold them in the redoubt area of southern Germany. One day in mid-April, the prisoners from Stalag Luft III and an unknown number of other men at Moosburg were ordered to prepare for a march into the redoubt. The prisoners, upset at being removed once again from the path of the liberating armies, discussed what they should do. The senior officers concluded that everyone should abide by the order and hope that the Allies would intervene before the men reached the redoubt. That night the prisoners heard a news broadcast from Luxemburg stating that the Allies had reached an agreement with Germany: no more German captives would be removed from the Continent and no more Allied prisoners would be moved from their present locations. The next morning the prisoners confronted the Germans with this information. They in turn asked higher authorities and discovered that the report was true.[32]

It is not known whether Vanaman's request to Berger influenced that agreement. But Berger was involved in the redoubt operation. Recent findings clearly demonstrate he was a true friend of the prisoners and definitely knew how to deal with important persons in the Reich to achieve his ends. Glenn Infield, who argues that Eva Braun had much more influence upon Hitler than is generally believed, has noted:

When, late in the war, Hitler decided to use thirty-five thousand prisoners of war as hostages, it was Eva who saved them. Hitler had instructed General Gottlob Berger of the Waffen-SS to take the hostages to the mountains south of Munich and hold them there until he could obtain a satisfactory truce from the Allies. If he was unsuccessful the prisoners were to be executed. Eva learned that Berger opposed the plan, that even if ordered he would not kill the prisoners. She decided that it would be best if Hitler gave the signed orders to Berger rather than to some other officer who would carry out the Fuhrer's command. She and Berger, both convinced that such executions were morally wrong, entered into an agreement. She arranged for him to have an appointment with Hitler, and while Hitler was discussing the matter with the general, Eva brought the typed orders pertaining to the executions into the room and handed them to the Führer. He immediately and automatically signed them and Berger left the room with the documents in his possession. Both he and Eva knew that he could stall off Hitler until the war ended without carrying out a single execution, and that is exactly what happened.[33]

Infield's point about Eva is well taken, but the information he presents casts a favorable light upon Berger as well.

As the prisoners struggled through their last days in captivity, Colonel von Lindeiner continued his own battle for survival. Just two days before the Germans evacuated Stalag Luft III, the chief medical

---

32. Interview with Clark, March 22, 1976; Goodrich, "History of South Compound," Pt. III.
33. Glenn B. Infield, *Eva and Adolf* (New York, 1974), 194.

officer of the facility in which von Lindeiner had found refuge announced that the hospital also was being moved westward. The officer explained that he could not take von Lindeiner with him.

It took more than fifteen hours for him to travel the 28.5 miles from the hospital to his home in Sagan. The next day he reported to the Bóbr River sector commander for duty and was promptly made his deputy. On February 9, the commander was killed in combat and von Lindeiner subordinated his forces to the battle commander, Sagan, who had at his disposal seven companies of retreating soldiers who had been stopped at check points and regrouped into hundred-man units. Each had been issued a weapon and sixty-five rounds of ammunition.

Early on February 12, von Lindeiner and another officer made a reconnaissance trip by motorcycle into the northern battle sector. When the fog lifted, they could see Russian guards on the eastern shore of the Bóbr. They approached the village of Greisitz, believing it occupied by German troops whom they had telephoned before their departure. Instead, they encountered Russian troops, who quickly opened fire on them. Von Lindeiner was hit in the shoulder and foot, and he fell off the bike. The Russians, thinking him dead, pursued his escort officer.

Von Lindeiner managed to crawl to the edge of the woods, and he reached Sagan after a grueling three hours. The bullet was removed from his foot, and that night he turned his command over to his highest-ranking staff officer. Boarding a heavily damaged armored scout vehicle, he set out on February 13 and finally stopped for treatment at Reserve Lazarett IV G in Leipzig. On April 5, he was transferred to the Reserve Lazarett at Blankenburg in the Harz, where he soon became a prisoner of the Americans and then of the British. The British, he quickly discovered, wanted to implicate him in the death of the fifty prisoners murdered after the Great Escape. About this time he must have been wondering if there was anything resembling justice left in the world.[34]

Henry Soderberg also spent a great deal of time on the roads during the waning months of the war. In January he returned to Sweden and was directed to do whatever he could for the prisoners being marched westward, even if communications were totally severed and he had to work without instructions. Upon returning to Germany, he discov-

---

34. Von Lindeiner, "Memoirs," 261–64.

ered that his co-workers at Sagan had already begun to move the office to Meissen. There, on the night of February 13, he watched the destruction of Dresden. In his diary he wrote:

It was a horrible spectacle that was repeated three times. First around 10:00 P.M., then at 1:00 A.M., and then again early this morning. We were standing in the window of the tower of the castle and we saw the whole thing. It was as a very mean and unreal dream. It was a horrible noise from the bomb explosions and our castle was shaking from the bottom. The air was full of English and American bombers. The heavens were [lit] up with searchlights and the whole sky was red from the fires going on in Dresden, the bombing so intensive we had to ask ourselves if not the whole city has been completely rubbed out. We know that there are 100,000 or so refugees in the city right now.

Then, perhaps sensing the controversy such bombings would engender, he wrote: "The people in Dresden during the last days have taken the view that their city never should be bombed. Some-body has said that Churchill has a relative there. Further, they say that Dresden should not be bombed because the Germans never bombed Oxford. Now, the horrible thing has taken place. Well, bombed out and full of fears, people seeking help have been coming to us today from Dresden. What they are telling about the bombings and the effects of the bombings in the city surpasses everything I have heard earlier in any context."

Before heading farther south, Soderberg found Paul Garçon, one of his former French helpers, at Sagan and asked if he could take Gar-çon along as his driver. The Germans agreed. Just before they departed, however, Soderberg encountered another heart-rending situation in which he had to suppress his desire to help someone because he could not risk the prisoners' safety and welfare. "Just as we were about to start," he wrote, "Katie came running. Katie was one of the pretty blonde girls who worked with the SS troops in the castle. She had been very friendly with us during our stay in Meissen. 'Take me along with you away from these horrible people,' she cried. 'Please take me along with you for heaven's sake. Just away from here. No one will notice for several hours if I run away. There are no com-munications in Germany. You will save my life. Everything is chaos,' she cried and pleaded." Katie was a decent 18-year-old girl from a good family in northern Germany. But Soderberg could not allow tears to move him at that moment. He finally concluded that he could not drive through Germany with an SS girl in the car. Furthermore,

Garçon flatly stated that he would rather commit suicide than sit in the same car with a member of the SS, however innocent the girl might be. While feeling pity for her, Soderberg could not even think of sacrificing Paul for Katie. Realizing she could not go with them, she cried loudly and said that she must now take her life. She made one last plea: "If you cannot take me along, please give me a piece of soap." Soderberg did and then drove away.

On the way Soderberg drove through the ruins of Dresden, where Russian prisoners were working slowly at removing debris. "The devastation was beyond description," he wrote, "and every day they are finding hundreds of dead bodies. The stench is horrible." Heading toward Czechoslovakia, they traveled along roads jammed with caravans of refugees, soldiers, and prisoners of war. At times they could hear American artillery in the west, and the Russians were pressing in hard from the east. He concluded that the myth about the last resistance at the Führer's Eagle's Nest in the south had deeply impressed many headquarters and government departments. Everybody seemed determined to fight through to the last line of defense.

Arriving in Eger just minutes after an air raid, he found the town burning and people slowly emerging from their shelters. They just stood there along the streets, seemingly unable to do anything or even move along. Whenever he stopped the car, the people asked, "When are the Americans coming?" Stories about Russian atrocities abounded, and everywhere he turned, people had the same question.

Suddenly they began to run, and Soderberg realized that another bombing attack was imminent. Driving wildly, he and Garçon hurried toward Regensburg. By now they could hear and smell that the fighting was near. Flocks of German soldiers were "running around like wing-clipped ducks without weapons, without helmets, many of them barefoot." It was strange to see the army that had been victorious during the past five years now run around panic-stricken. By the thousands, people moved along the roads, also panic-sticken and full of fear. "They are waiting, but waiting for what?" he asked. Then, knowing the answer, he added: "Just one thing . . . that the Americans will come before the Russians."

Along the way he encountered large columns of prisoners of war. Some men recognized him and waved frantically. He also watched as groups of Russian prisoners moved forward with heavy steps, and many of them had sacks or newspapers wound around bleeding feet. There also were SS officers here and there. Worried that they would try to take his car, he became suspicious when one of them tried to force him off the road. Soderberg and Garçon drove away at high speed, only to discover that the SS man had been warning them of an impending strafing. Blue planes came down, turned in over the road, and started shooting. People began to scream, and Soderberg and Garçon scrambled out of the car and into the ditch. As quickly as it started, the attack was over. Just as quickly the crowds jammed the roads again.

Proceeding through bombed-out Regensburg, now little more than a ghost town, Soderberg noticed they were getting low on gas. He drove to half a dozen gas stations—there was no fuel to be had anywhere. At a police station, he was assured that they would give him fuel if they had it since his coupons were good. On the way to Munich, he stopped at a military installation, but there was no gas there either. Finally he found a place that still had some left. They filled his tank, and he went on his way, feeling very fortunate indeed.

On April 16, Soderberg approached Moosburg and Stalag VII A. During normal times the camp held 30,000 prisoners. Now 100,000 men milled around on the grounds. Everywhere he turned he saw prisoners. "Thousands and thousands of them," he wrote, "live in barns and stables and bombed-out houses and in the small forest around Moosburg. There are new streams of prisoners marching in every day." He joined forces with another field delegate, Eric Berg, who was already on the scene, and together they set about sending the prisoners food, medicine, and other necessities. After systematically combing the area for ten days, Soderberg spent a week working north of Salzburg. While there he received welcome news—the prisoners in Stalag VII A had been liberated. Knowing that there were still prisoners held farther to the southeast, he set out on April 30 for the Italian border.[35]

35. Interview with Soderberg, September 15, 1979.

17

Liberation

Within days of the threatened move to the redoubt, the sound of gunfire could again be heard by the prisoners in Stalag VII A. By the last week in April, everyone knew that the end had to come soon. On the evening of April 28, the prisoners spotted armored vehicles pulling into town, and for a short time some thought it might be the Allies. Instead it was an SS contingent. They had been negotiating with the attacking army, attempting to arrange the peaceful surrender of the camp in exchange for securing several Esir River bridges that led back to more secure lines. Several high-ranking prisoners, including Colonel Paul Goode, captured at Normandy early on, were escorted to the site of the negotiations and remained throughout the night. When the discussions broke down, they were told to get back to camp and keep down because the attack would begin the next day at 9:00 A.M. The German troops, in turn, pulled back into town to prepare a last-ditch defense.

Alexander MacArthur was standing with his good friend Emmett Dedmon inside the camp that memorable Sunday morning, April 29, 1945, when the invading forces approached. A P-51 fighter flew low over the camp. It had wet mud on its wings. They correctly concluded that it had taken off from a nearby airstrip, and that the Allies held the surrounding terrain. One of the guard towers began to shoot at the plane. After a single chandelle turn, the P-51 came down with its powerful guns spitting bullets, ripping the tower into kindling.[1] To observers, the episode seemed like the starting klaxon. Within a minute or two, mortar shells landed in the town and stray bullets whistled into the camp. All but a few prisoners wisely took cover and waited for the brief battle to end.

1. Interview with Alexander MacArthur, April 29, 1944; interview with Wells, January 26–27, 1975.

Captain John Bennett and Lieutenant Elwin F. ("Dick") Schrupp were among those who did not wait. Both men still had the cameras and film they had used for intelligence work at Sagan, and they were instructed by senior members of the intelligence staff to shoot scenes of the German surrender. Schrupp spoke German fluently and easily got them through the front gate. As they walked toward the town an American vehicle painted white with big red crosses on it drove in. The British and the American senior officers got out. Colonel Goode, just coming from the overnight negotiating session, told Bennett and Schrupp that they had better find a hole because the war was going to start at 9:00 A.M.

The two photographers were standing with some German soldiers when the fighting began. They could see the SS troops lying behind a railroad embankment about three hundred yards away. American forces were coming directly toward the camp and moving fast. Puffs of smoke rose above the tanks and smaller vehicles. Schrupp and Bennett jumped into a nearby trench; so did the Germans. Bennett later recalled: "There we were, squeezed into a trench with small-arms fire and some heavier stuff howling all around us. The Germans were scared. Dick and I were scared. We just hunched down for a while and then, in a lull, we decided to get the hell out of the trenches with the Germans. So we ran like blazes and dashed behind a building which served as the mail censoring room. When we got there we lay down along the concrete foundation, feeling for the moment that we wanted a lot of concrete between us and the fighting." Since the retreating SS forces might well come that way and see them, they decided to move again and broke a window in the mail building. Once inside, they found that there still was no easy place to hide. Then a tank shell blew a huge hole in the brick wall they were leaning against. Sprayed with brick dust and fragments but unhurt, they began to retreat. Using a shutter, they smashed their way through the windows of several buildings until they arrived at the barbed wire. Small arms fire kept hitting the roofs. They used a heavy ladder as a battering ram and broke through the rusty wire. Finding a hole in the ground, they stayed put until the fighting stopped. Then they dashed back to the front gate to take pictures. The scenes they snapped were everlastingly imprinted on the prisoners' minds that morning.[2]

2. John M. Bennett, "Memoirs," *ca.* 1950 (Copy in possession of the author), 157–60.

The prisoners cheered with unrestrained joy as an American tank drove right through the barbed wire into the camp. Immediately the tank was surrounded as Kriegies rushed to welcome the liberators, and within seconds it was invisible. Men stood on top and everywhere there was an inch of space. Wild cheers, and the sounds of thousands of men laughing and crying, were the only anthem needed when the Nazi flag came down and the Stars and Stripes was raised.

Shortly thereafter, some war correspondents arrived. One of them jumped out of the jeep and asked if anyone was from Illinois. Alexander MacArthur, standing nearby, immediately said he was. Looking more closely, MacArthur realized that the correspondent was Hal Faust from the Chicago *Tribune*. He ran up and said, "MacArthur, Chicago *Times*. Emmett Dedmon is here too." Dedmon had worked at the *Times* and also knew Faust. MacArthur quickly found Dedmon and led him back to Faust, who was frantically scribbling down names. At 2:00 A.M., MacArthur's father answered the telephone in Chicago and received a welcome message from the *Tribune* City Desk: "We have just gotten a message from our foreign correspondent in Moosburg, Germany. He has talked to your son and Emmett Dedmon. They both have been liberated by a tank spearhead."[3]

Other unexpected reunions occurred amid the turmoil. Melton McCracken had been a prisoner of war since May 10, 1944. His brother Harry, serving at Camp Maxey in Texas, learned that the 99th Infantry Division would soon be departing for Europe. Harry told his mother not to worry, that he would set Melton free. He ordered a complete set of new clothes, including shoes for Melton, and took them with him overseas.

Harry's sister kept him informed of Red Cross reports on the prison camps, and eventually he narrowed the likely choices down to Nuremberg and Moosburg. Unfortunately, the camp at Nuremberg had been evacuated when he arrived. The remainder of the 99th continued on to the north, and Harry's specific unit, the 395th Regiment, was assigned to accompany some tanks heading south. As a medic, he rode in one of the lead jeeps and entered Stalag VII A only minutes after the tank plowed through the wire.

Finding the Senior American Officer, he inquired whether there were any McCrackens in the camp. The answer was, "Yes, several.

3. Interview with MacArthur, April 29, 1944.

But I doubt if we could find any of them in this commotion. Come back tomorrow morning and if we find him he'll be here waiting for you." Disappointed but still hopeful, Harry turned to leave, and his eyes came to rest on a man standing near the door. It was Melton. Melton said he thought the man in the jeep looked like Harry, but he did not even know that Harry was in Germany. They had a great reunion, and that evening Harry handed Melton the new clothes.[4] (Two other McCracken brothers also found each other that day, as the former prisoners discovered some thirty-eight years later at a reunion.)

The prisoners rejoiced in their new freedom, tore holes in the wires around the camp, and walked out into the fields to look around. Somewhat later, General Patton arrived in his command car. It was not the dull green usually seen at the front, but brightly shined and suitably decorated with sirens, spotlights, and a four-star flag. Walter Johnson was in awe of this man, who first toured a building or two and then mounted the hood of the car to speak. As usual, Patton was immaculately dressed in whipcord trousers, boots, battle jacket, two ivory-handled pistols, and a helmet polished to a high sheen. The prisoners crowded around, but this time kept a respectful three or four feet away, and no one touched the command car. From Johnson's perspective, Patton was an imposing figure: with his harsh face, he stood rigidly at attention, a man more than six feet tall, weighing 190 to 200 pounds. Then, according to Johnson, the most surprising thing happened. This Greek god–like general grabbed the microphone attached to the loudspeakers on his car and addressed the crowd in a high-pitched, almost falsetto voice. That distracted Johnson only momentarily. Thereafter he hung on every word the general uttered and is confident he remembers them verbatim to this day. After holding up his hand and getting complete silence, Johnson recalls, General Patton looked up and saw a Nazi flag still flying. Pointing toward it, he said: "I want that son-of-a-bitch cut down, and the man that cuts it down, I want him to wipe his ass with it." Then he said, "Well, I guess all you sons-a-bitches are glad to see me." Immediately a great roar went up. After the noise died down, he went on: "I'd like to stay with you awhile, but I've got a date with a woman in Munich, it's 40 kilometers away, and I've got to fight every damned

4. Harry E. McCracken to the author, May 1, 1983, Melton McCracken to the author, May 24, 1983.

inch of the way. God bless you and thank you for what you've done."
Within seconds he stepped back into his car and drove away.[5]

To the prisoners, the days until they could be sent home seemed
like an eternity. Bub Clark remembers the wait as extremely trying.
The army was totally unprepared for the huge number of prisoners
turned loose in such a short time. In addition, many Russian prisoners and concentration camp internees were on a rampage, seeking
revenge, committing rape, and stealing food. Germans with their
families and all their belongings were hastily fleeing the Russians
and added to the chaos. General Eisenhower repeatedly ordered that
the former prisoners "stay put" and not create confusion within the
Allied lines. Many could not restrain themselves and hitchhiked to
Paris or elsewhere. Most of the men obeyed their superiors, however,
and proceeded eventually to Le Havre, where they were placed on
ships and sent home.

In the years since their liberation, most of the prisoners have
reflected upon their experiences during the war. They have drawn a
variety of conclusions about the days they spent behind barbed wire.
Some have come to view their time in captivity as a loss of their best
years; others have concluded that it marked one of their most productive and spiritually enriching periods. The prevailing sentiment both
then and now, however, reflects a renewed appreciation for the country to which they returned. As Bob Neary aptly expressed it: "I had
never fully realized before going overseas just how wonderful this
country of ours is. I had always taken for granted my complete liberty,
freedom of speech and countless luxuries that I considered my heritage as an American. . . . My year and a day of oppression and want in
prison camp have changed my perspective completely. I think I have
learned my lesson well and feel that I shall never forget it. . . . I am an
American! And I am grateful."[6]

5. Interview with Johnson, November 25, 1978. Unfortunately, there is little
agreement among the prisoners about this event. Lyman Burbank, for example, says
Patton looked like anything but a Greek god, and Bub Clark remembered Patton
driving up in a jeep.
6. Neary, *Stalag Luft III: Sagan*, 52.

Epilogue

For years after the end of World War II, several hundred former prisoners from Stalag Luft III met each spring to celebrate the anniversary of their liberation. As time went by, the participants found it expedient to hold the reunions every five years, but the decision by no means reflected a lessening of interest. Since 1960, attendance has steadily increased, as has the public stature of many of those who took time away from their busy schedules to gather with their former comrades to swap war stories and share memories of the days they spent together as Kriegies. The 1960 guest list included Brigadier General Melvin McNickle (later promoted to major general), Major General John D. Stevenson, General Jacob Smart, Major General Robert M. Stillman, Major General Albert P. Clark (later promoted to lieutenant general), Major General Delmar T. Spivey, and Major General Richard Klocko.

Perhaps the most notable reunion, however, took place in Dayton, Ohio, in 1965, when the prisoners created a nationwide stir by inviting four of their former German captors: Gustav Simoleit, camp adjutant; Hermann Glemnitz, chief ferret; Wilhelm Stranghoner, chief NCO in Center Compound; and Dr. Helmut Haubold, who arranged the medical conference in Berlin in March, 1945. General Spivey saw nothing strange about hosting the Germans on an all-expense-paid trip to America. "We cannot help but give the German Luftwaffe credit for the fairly good treatment we received," he said.[1] Most of the prisoners from Stalag Luft III agreed.

The Germans' presence in the United States evoked a different

---

1. Spivey quoted in the Mexico City *Times*, April 24, 1965, clipping enclosed in "Lists and Miscellaneous Correspondence-POW" Folder, Spivey Collection.

response among prisoners from other camps. A former army NCO wrote to General Spivey:

In reaction to the newspaper account today which quotes you as saying that you were fairly well treated at StaLag Luft 3, I must say that my experience was quite different: we were packed 96 in a 40 and 8 for 72 hours at one stretch, 86 for 48 hours, with no food or water, and without the doors even being opened. We were marched for days without food and finally arrived at Stalag IVB in pitiable condition.

Men who worked on Kommando [work parties outside the main camps] returned (when too sick to work) to see their bodies for the first time in months when taking a shower, and would break down and cry at what they saw of themselves. I went from 135 pounds to 95 pounds in four months of imprisonment. All we were given to eat was a cup of soup and a piece of ersatz bread each day. This was a systematic brutality to keep us dependent on the next meal and too weak to try to escape, for the number of guards was small. There was enough food, as we discovered, in towns, warehouses, etc., when we broke out. We found the remains of Red Cross parcels in some houses.

I had frozen feet, jaundice, fleas, lice, dysentery, two foot infections, and general malnutrition. Our stomachs were . . . swollen . . . and some died. . . . We had no sexual potency. . . . It is not that I want us to continue hating Germans, but that so often officers and Air Force men had better treatment by the Luftwaffe guards than did the enlisted men in the ground forces. We could always spot an air force man in the showers at the rest camp; they had buttocks!

I can appreciate that you did receive good treatment at your Stalag, but you are quoted as saying that you think the POW camps were run humanely, in contrast to the concentration camps. The only difference between the concentration camps and the Stalag I was in was that we were not killed off with gas or bullets. . . .

In short, General, I do not think you can speak for the rest of the Stalags occupied by the plain dogfaces who were POWs. The Luftwaffe had some chivalry: three of our airmen parachuted into our Stalag and were immediately sent to a Luft Stalag. I do not remember one act of mercy or compassion all the while I was a prisoner of war, on the part of the Germans.[2]

General Spivey was not ignorant of the suffering of prisoners held by the German Army. In fact, precisely because he and the other prisoners in Stalag Luft III were aware of the inhumane treatment given almost everyone but air force personnel, the men attending the reunion concluded that members of the Luftwaffe should receive commendation.[3] In their own way, the air force prisoners were

2.   NCO to Spivey, May 8, 1965, *ibid.*
3.   It should be mentioned that Spivey may have been quoted out of context or may inadvertently have given the impression that he was equating treatment by the Luftwaffe and that by other parts of the German prisoner of war system. In the Foreword to

addressing the paradox that holds the key to much of Stalag Luft III's history.

Directing the German prisoner of war system as a whole was a complex and nebulous command structure that permitted diversity in administering the camps. Under these circumstances, an influential man like Göring could not only secure control of virtually all the Allied airmen but also determine which provisions of the Geneva Convention would be observed in the camps. His decision to abide rather closely by the convention benefited the captured fliers, if only by making it possible for lower-echelon Luftwaffe personnel to run the camps in accordance with their own sense of duty and their professional standards and without undue outside interference.

Since not enough is known about the other Luftwaffe camps and especially about those that held airmen of other ranks, generalizations about camp administrators are not warranted. The evidence suggests, however, that those personnel in charge of Stalag Luft III, at least, acquitted themselves well and were among the heroic figures of the war. Men such as von Lindeiner, Simoleit, and Glemnitz, to mention only a few, performed their duties in a professional manner and conducted themselves honorably despite severe handicaps and at great personal risk. More than once they bent the rules when it appeared that the prisoners' burdens could be lightened without seriously endangering the Reich. These men seem to have done as much for the prisoners as one could reasonably expect, given the state of affairs in Germany at the time and the government's insistence that the Luftgangsters were already receiving better treatment than they deserved.

Von Lindeiner did not reach London until August 12, 1945. At one point, he spent forty-eight hours with only a bare board to sit and sleep on and without eating utensils, and then was handcuffed and placed under heavy guard when he was moved. He often asked what he had done to deserve such shabby treatment. After numerous and

---

his 1946 manuscript, he said: "There were great numbers who were killed during combat and some were killed by the Germans during or after capture . . . but those who fell into prisoner of war channels were, almost without exception, treated quite decently by German military personnel" ("History of Center Compound"). If this statement were published as it stands, it would undoubtedly give the impression that he was making an unwarranted generalization. Earlier in the Foreword, however, he clearly states that he is speaking primarily about air force officers, not about the other ranks or the members of other services. This subtle yet extremely important distinction might not have been noted in a newspaper article.

lengthy interrogations, he finally was exonerated of any wrongdoing in connection with the deaths after the Great Escape. Nonetheless, he remained a prisoner for more than two years, returning to the British Zone of Germany in July, 1947. Not until November, 1947, did he receive permission to rejoin his wife. She escaped from Silesia with only a small suitcase and had been vegetating in the American Zone for two and a half years, keeping herself barely alive by giving English and French lessons and teaching music. Their property in Silesia now was in Russian hands, the apartment in Berlin had been bombed to the ground, and their extensive landholdings in the Netherlands had been confiscated as enemy property.[4] Now an old and broken man, von Lindeiner might well have found himself identifying closely with the main character in a Shakespearean tragedy.

It was Major Simoleit who supervised the surrender of the German personnel at Stalag VII A. He accomplished the task in an orderly manner and then joined his colleagues who had been crowded into trucks and taken away to serve their term as prisoners of war. Simoleit fared very poorly after the war. His nominal membership in the Nazi party kept him from gainful employment for several years, and he and his family lived in abject poverty for quite some time.[5]

Lieutenant Colonel Clark saw Glemnitz in the back of one of the trucks. There was some straw on his uniform, and he looked desolate. "Germany has lost another war!" he said. " Vat am I going to do? Vat am I going to do?" Glemnitz was released after only a few weeks, but his house in Breslau had been badly damaged. Not until two days before Christmas were all the family members brought back together. A survivor by instinct, Glemnitz managed to find work in early 1946 and through a succession of jobs, ranging from road repair to translation, eventually gained a goodly measure of financial stability and the physical comforts of life. Today, at age eighty-six, he lives comfortably in West Berlin and attends the Stalag Luft III reunions in England, Canada, and the United States whenever he can.[6]

General Gottlob Berger was convicted at the war crimes trials and sentenced to twenty years. Colonel Spivey testified for the defense,

4. Von Lindeiner, "Memoirs," 265–74.
5. See postwar letters from Simoleit to Spivey, in Simoleit Folder, Spivey Collection.
6. Albert P. Clark, "Some Reminiscences of Stalag Luft III," January 20, 1978 (MS in Clark Collection), 4; Clark and Schrupp, interview with Glemnitz, April 9–10, 1984.

and that likely led to Berger's release after he had served only two years.[7]

The relatively independent position of the Luftwaffe camps in the German prisoner of war system, the decision to abide by the letter if not the spirit of the Geneva Convention (at least in regard to captured fliers of officer rank from the West), and the professionalism and personal honor exhibited by most members of the German camp staff, all contributed to the prisoners' well-being in Stalag Luft III. These factors in themselves, however, were not the camp's lifeblood.

The vitality so evident throughout the camp resulted from the efforts of outside agencies and from the prisoners themselves. The prisoners' home governments made it abundantly clear that they were interested in the treatment accorded their soldiers and that they were willing to work reciprocally in determining how German soldiers held by the Allies would be treated. Furthermore, the home governments gave material aid and moral support to the prisoners in Stalag Luft III. This was important because resources in camp were scarce and because the prisoners were thereby convinced of their inherent worth to the Allies and that their governments had not forsaken them. Russian prisoners seldom, if ever, had this assurance, and one can only guess how adversely this must have affected their will to survive. Because the home governments exhibited a genuine interest in the prisoners' welfare, the protecting power was able to act more effectively on the prisoners' behalf. The Germans knew that the information gathered and sent out by the protecting power received close attention in the United States and the Commonwealth countries.

That interest also greatly facilitated the work of the YMCA and the Red Cross. Without the invaluable services of these two organizations, the prisoners in Stalag Luft III might indeed have fared little better than those in concentration camps. There is no evidence that the German government would have provided the necessary food, educational, recreational, and religious items the prisoners needed to sustain themselves as healthy and productive human beings.

The prisoners possessed the means to help themselves and deserve credit for exhibiting the willingness and expending the effort to do so.

---

7.   See postwar letters from Berger to Spivey, in Berger Folder, Spivey Collection.

As a group, they had a high degree of native intelligence and benefited from generally good mental and physical health. They could boast a variety of special abilities, many of which had been developed in college and through their professions. Capable leaders emerged and used the chain of command to exercise effective control. The senior officers established workable policies that suited the prisoners' particular situations from the early days until the end of the war. The decision to pool their resources and share them undoubtedly eliminated much divisiveness, as did transforming escape from an individual enterprise into an operational mission. Good leadership and wise policies contributed, in turn, to the growing sense of community among the prisoners. That spirit, the basis of their society, accounts in large part for their success in transferring community functions from one compound to another without serious loss of continuity.

All these factors help to explain the unique history of Stalag Luft III. But what do they tell us about the camp's place overall? In theoretical terms, the evidence reveals that conditions in Stalag Luft III did not measure up to the standards set by the Geneva Convention of 1929. The men went hungry, lived in overcrowded quarters, lacked adequate sanitation facilities, had insufficient clothing and bedding, suffered from barbed-wire psychosis, and had inadequate medical care. They lived in constant fear of what the Gestapo and the SS might do to them, were shot at repeatedly inside their compounds, and in some cases were murdered in cold blood.

At the same time, it must be remembered that World War II was a total war, and the suffering inflicted upon all its victims was correspondingly severe. Not even the Geneva Convention outlined all the obligations of the detaining power when the fighting was destined to continue until the bitter end. Furthermore, the occupants of Stalag Luft III were not always model prisoners. Their making escape an operational mission distinguished them from prisoners who saw it as an individual duty, and their espionage clearly took them beyond the law.

In the final analysis, what occurred in Stalag Luft III says more about the state of confusion in prisoner of war affairs in modern times than it does about either the Germans or the prisoners. Both parties acted as they did because of forces so complex and changeable that they defy man's best efforts to define and control them. The prisoners were exposed to virtually every hardship and danger that prisoners of war have ever encountered. And the Germans faced the same problems that detaining powers have always faced. The experiences of those who have become prisoners since World War II indicates that mankind has made little progress toward agreeing on the prisoners' status and the detaining power's obligations.

There is still something to be gained by scrutinizing the experiences of these men. Just because man has not yet come to terms with all the implications of wartime captivity is no reason to despair. Studying what happened to them is of value even if it does no more than remind us that prisoners of war cannot yet count on receiving humane treatment or an early parole to prevent wasting valuable years. If that day should ever come, prisoners would not have to write as Joe Boyle did in "The Fate We Share as Prisoners":

> The fate we share as prisoners
> Is drab and often grim,
> Existing on such scanty fare
> As Reich-bread, spuds and klim.
>
> Beds and books and little else
> To fill Time's flapping sail,
> She makes or loses headway all
> Depending on the mail.
>
> Oh! Drab the days and slow to pass
> Within this barbed-wire fence,
> When all the joys of living are
> Still in the future tense.
>
> So here's to happy days ahead
> When you and I are free,
> To look back on this interlude
> And call it history.

Appendix

A HISTORY OF PRISONERS OF WAR
From Ancient Times to the American Civil War

Down through the ages, prisoners of war have had many fates, each reflecting the standards of the society that held them captive, these standards in turn exhibiting as many variations as civilization itself. There are, however, certain notable events or trends, the sources of recent policies around the world. It therefore is appropriate to survey the history of prisoners of war in an effort to understand the basis for the beliefs and attitudes that exist in modern times. Numerous factors determined the fate of prisoners of war from ancient times to the eve of the American Civil War, the first of the modern wars that brought a host of new problems for the POW.

The oldest branch of international law consisted of efforts to establish rules for the conduct of warfare.[1] It should not surprise us that the treatment accorded prisoners of war was a major concern. It is surprising, however, that so much time elapsed before anything approaching modern ideas of that treatment appeared.

Some scholars believe that in the early years of recorded time the concept of the prisoner of war was unknown. Among ancient peoples, they claim, a tribal mentality prevailed and dictated harsh treatment and almost certain death for anyone captured by the enemy. The usual explanation is Georg Friedrich von Martens': "The ancient world had not grasped the fundamental notions of the law of nations;

---

1. Joseph L. Kunz, "The Chaotic Status of the Laws of War and the Urgent Necessity for Their Revision," *American Journal of International Law*, XLV (January, 1951), 38*n*2.

. . . it had no regard *for man as man*." At least as early as Greek and Roman times, however, a form of international law had developed. By then, as Coleman Phillipson pointed out, the ancients "were by no means entirely indifferent to the moral obligations of justice and humanity between peoples; . . . they were not regardless of the elementary rights of the individual." Robert F. Grady, in his excellent study, finds himself in agreement with this conclusion. He suggests that ancient peoples were able to sense, at times, "some common bond other than tribal, political, or religious kinship." With the appearance of the Greek city-states, their common culture and shared language, the stage was set for moving beyond a strict tribal mentality. Genuine cosmopolitanism emerged after Alexander the Great's conquests. He was the first to try unifying a large geographical area. And the unity attained by the Roman Empire greatly advanced this trend in human affairs.[2]

The growing sense of oneness led to efforts to restrain the evils of warfare. One element discussed by philosophers was the proper disposition of prisoners of war. Whatever philosophers' expectations, Grady tells us, the plight of prisoners of war during ancient times was, by any standard, desperate. It was universally conceded that the captor held full dominion over his captive, and if the captive was spared anything, including his life, it was only through pure generosity. Those fortunate enough to escape execution remained the property of the captor. They were frequently branded and used as slaves or were sold into slavery. The captor acted with no compunction whatever; indeed, his actions were very much in keeping with the law.[3]

Prisoners could be disposed of in other ways. Sometimes they were released without any penalty, and sometimes they had to pay ransom. Granting paroles and arranging for exchanges of prisoners were also known during ancient times. Sometimes, however, parole merely meant that a prisoner would be released upon his word that a ransom would be paid after his safe return to his homeland. It could also

2. Howard S. Levie, "Penal Sanctions for Maltreatment of Prisoners of War," *American Journal of International Law*, LVI (April, 1962), 433; Martens and Phillipson quoted in Robert F. Grady, "The Evolution of Ethical and Legal Concern for the Prisoner of War" (Ph.D. dissertation, Catholic University of America, 1971), 2–3. (emphasis added by Grady).

3. Grady, "Ethical and Legal Concerns," 4–7, 11–13.

involve, as it frequently does today, certain freedoms in return for the prisoner's word that he will not use them to escape.[4] The matter of exchanges is clearly enough described in the term itself.

Before concluding this discussion, we should note two features of Roman law that called for slightly different forms of treatment. The Romans thought of prisoners taken in war as the property of the conqueror. But Roman rule encouraged preferential treatment under certain circumstances. Rome's interest in conciliating the conquered and winning their allegiance led to better treatment for many prisoners, especially those who surrendered voluntarily. Furthermore, if the prisoners were considered to be "civilized," they would usually be better treated than were "barbarians," the latter being thought subhuman. This distinction in treatment has manifested itself throughout the history of prisoners of war.

By the dawning of the Christian Era, then, a few harbingers of the modern ways to treat prisoners of war had surfaced. But little more than that can be said for ancient practices and attitudes. The unfortunate captive, viewed solely as private property, could be killed, sold into slavery, ransomed, paroled or exchanged, or given outright freedom by a generous captor. The last three—parole, exchange, and unqualified freedom—were rare.

Little change occurred during the early Christian Era. Over the centuries, however, Christian theology encouraged more humane treatment of prisoners of war. Also having an influence were the concept of chivalric warfare associated with knighthood, and the philosophies and laws that emerged during the Enlightenment and the Age of Reason.

Two contrasting features characterized Christian beliefs and practices regarding prisoners of war: the charity and love for members of the Christian brotherhood, and attachment to the holy war as derived from Jewish beliefs and customs. It is well known that wars involving religion can be the most inhumane of all. In antiquity, holy wars were the rule. They began at the gods' command, progressed as omens directed, and ended successfully only with proper sacrifices to the gods. But until the covenant between God and the people of Israel, the religious overtones in war were secondary. After the covenant, however, Israel's wars became sacred. The inspiration came from Yahweh's command: "When the Lord your God brings you into the land

4. *Ibid.*, 14, 19; Fooks, *Prisoners of War,* 205–206.

which you are entering to take possession of it, and clears away many nations before you . . . seven nations greater and mightier than yourselves, and when the Lord your God gives them over to you, and you defeat them; then you must utterly destroy them; you shall make no covenant with them, and show no mercy to them" (Deut. 7:1–3). As Grady points out, the Israelites' wars seldom matched the ferocity demanded in this passage. In fact, he asserts, prisoners were frequently taken and were usually treated with relative kindness. Those who were enslaved enjoyed better treatment than did their counterparts in other lands, and at times the captives "were treated with great condescension."[5]

The significance of this heritage for Christianity lies not so much in Jewish practice as it does in the tendency of later generations to find theological justification for barbaric conduct toward non-Christians and, in some cases, toward fellow Christians whose beliefs were slightly different. This spirit was vividly exhibited in the Crusades and the notorious inquisitions in post-Reformation Europe. As late as the seventeenth century, Christian leaders echoed Calvin and urged that religious wars "be fought with fervor in the name of the Lord God of hosts, and the more holy the cause the less restrained would be the means." And since "no consideration could be paid to humanity when the honor of God was at stake," the fate of war prisoners was not an enviable one.[6]

Offsetting these attitudes in the Christian world was a more humanitarian instinct that mitigated the tendency toward harshness. Although few Christians have lived up to the dictum "Love thy enemy" to the extent many feel they should, there is abundant evidence that Christian doctrines and practices improved both the status and the treatment of prisoners of war. For example, early Christians were concerned about prisoners taken by the heathens. When they realized that large numbers could be brought back into the Christian fold if they paid ransom, they worked hard to raise the money. Saint Ambrose expressed the church's viewpoint: "It is especially noble to redeem captives, particularly from the barbarous enemy who shows no humanity for mercy's sake, but only what avarice promotes him to accord in view of the ransom money." Grady asserts that by the seventh century "the ransoming of captives by the

5. Grady, "Ethical and Legal Concern," 9, 41–42.
6. Calvin quoted *ibid.*, 43.

Church was a well-established, time-honored practice of the corporal works of mercy."[7]

A more significant development resulted from the adoption of Saint Augustine's just-war theory. In short, as "necessity leads us to slay an enemy who shows fight, . . . so the vanquished or the captive is entitled to mercy."[8] The mercy was not remarkable by present-day standards. It proscribed the killing of prisoners but still permitted their being sold into slavery or held for ransom. It did, however, support a principle that was becoming important in the budding field of international law: that punishment meted out to prisoners of war must never exceed that which is absolutely necessary for the safety of the state.

Francisco de Vitoria was among the first writers who dealt systematically with international law, and in the work he completed in the 1540s and 1550s, one can see his applying the principle that prisoners were not to be subjected to unnecessarily harsh treatment. To evaluate any warlike act, Vitoria proposed that it be illegal, first, to do greater harm than attaining of the war objective warrants and, second, to injure those innocent of taking active part in the hostilities, except when there is no other way of carrying on the war. It followed, then, that slaughtering captives was no longer appropriate since that act was not necessary to attain victory. The fruition of the just-war theory is clear here. The next major improvement was the release without ransom of the prisoners captured in the Thirty Years' War. With notable exceptions, this can be designated as the point after which the practice of enslaving captives declined rapidly.[9]

In 1748, Montesquieu, in his famous *L'Espirit des lois*, enunciated his belief that war gave no other right over prisoners than that they be prevented from doing further harm by securing their persons, since all nations had concurred that killing prisoners in cold blood was detestable. Furthermore, he declared, this position was in keeping with the general principle expressed in international law that the various nations must do each other the greatest good during peace and the least possible harm during war without injuring their true interests.

Rousseau declared in 1762 that he conceived of war as a struggle

7. *Ibid.*, 32 (quoting Saint Ambrose), 36.
8. Saint Augustine quoted in *ibid.*, 44.
9. Flory, *Prisoners of War*, 13–14, 15.

not between man and man but rather between states in which individuals are enemies by accident and merely as soldiers: "No state could have anything but other states for enemies, not men. The aim of war being the destruction of the enemy state, the right to kill its soldiers exists so long as they are armed, but as soon as they surrender, ceasing to be instruments of the enemy, they become once again ordinary men." This realization, in my estimation, marks the greatest single development in the history of prisoners of war. Its significance lies not in the restriction on taking a prisoner's life, but in the line of reasoning, which encouraged the adoption of entirely new attitudes and laws regarding the treatment of prisoners of war. The legislative assemblies in France, for example, said in 1792 that prisoners of war would no longer be considered the property of the individual captor, but would henceforth be given over to the care and protection of the nation.[10]

Certain prisoners of war have received humanitarian treatment since ancient times. It was not until the eighteenth century, however, that such care was sought for all prisoners. And even from that time until the present, humanitarianism has often been most conspicuous by its absence. Why did this development come so late, and why have the appeals for humanitarian treatment so often gone unheeded? There are at least seven contributing factors: the persistence of doubt; disagreement over who qualifies as a prisoner of war; the absence, until recently, of a clear definition of what constitutes humane treatment for such prisoners; the difficulty of striking a proper balance between humanitarianism and military necessity; the decision by some societies to place themselves above the law; the absence of effective sanctions to be used against those who violate the laws of war; and the assignment of untrained or unsympathetic personnel to prison camp duties. These philosophical and practical issues deserve a closer look.

Those who express skepticism about granting humanitarian care to the captured enemy during times of war do, at first glance, seem right. There is something inherently contradictory and hypocritical about the entire notion. The concept is as difficult to grasp as the one that attempts to reconcile rules or laws and warfare itself. One observer has noted: "At first sight law and war are terms which negate each other. Law generally implies an orderly polity where human relationship and behavior are governed by inescapable rules. . . . War,

10.   Flory, *Prisoners of War,* 16; Fooks, *Prisoners of War,* 12.

on the other hand, appears to connote the abandonment of the restraint of rules of behavior in international intercourse, by substituting in their place reliance on brute force. No judicial consideration of rights and wrongs resolves the issue between warring nations. That is decided by might alone. . . . What, therefore, has law to do with war, and war with law?" The answer is that warfare has always been vicious and destructive and has become even more so with the invention of more and more powerful weapons. Man has nevertheless come to realize that there are definite advantages to placing some restraints upon the conduct of war. For example, honoring a white flag as a means of communicating the intention to surrender or negotiate is recognized as beneficial to all parties. That the rules governing its use and sanctity are often violated does not diminish either its standing in law or the respect that combatants generally accord it. The credence given such matters of international law is enduring: prosecutions for war crimes, for example, antedated the Nuremberg trials by at least five centuries.[11]

In a sense the same may be said by way of justifying adherence to humanitarian principles during war. The possibility of reprisals against a nation's own soldiers held captive by the enemy is reason enough to provide adequate treatment for the prisoners under that nation's control. But the rationale extends beyond that. Most people agree that it is simply the proper thing to do since human beings are involved.

The question of who qualifies as a prisoner of war is complex. Jurists have struggled for years to ascertain the status of various combatants. Uniformed soldiers captured with their units generally pose no problem. But commandos, guerrillas, insurrectionists, parachutists, and soldiers temporarily out of uniform can all be treated as rebels, spies, or saboteurs rather than as war prisoners.

Once a soldier had been classified as a prisoner of war, he was, at least after the middle of the eighteenth century, entitled to humane treatment. But until recently, there was no clear definition of such treatment. Not until the twentieth century did a document appear that outlined specific criteria. This advance occurred in 1929 when the Geneva Convention Relative to the Treatment of Prisoners of War was successfully concluded.

Until 1929, and to a certain extent even afterward (some articles

11. Greenspan, *The Modern Law of Land Warfare*, 3, 4.

needed revision), officials in charge of prisoners of war had to make their own judgments about what constituted humane treatment. Opinions varied widely. And then, as now, a balance had to be struck between humanitarian interests and military necessity. It is not always possible to remove prisoners from combat zones or provide sufficient rations. In times of serious crises, civilian populations often suffer grievously. No captor can long allow his captives to live better than any major group of citizens do. Charges of coddling arise quickly when prisoners are seemingly being treated too well. When the general population is starving, "coddling" may mean sharing subsistence rations with the prisoners. In the search for standards applicable in such circumstances, each case must be judged on its merits. For instance, as war draws to a close, prisoners held by the losing side often face starvation along with the citizenry. Reason suggests that the detaining power has no right to continue its prosecution of the war once that condition exists. This position is the one taken in international law today. The court at Nuremberg rejected the claim that wanton suffering could be imposed upon people facing the crises that always occur in the final phases of a war. The decision read in part: "It is an essence of war that one or the other side must lose and the experienced generals and statesmen knew this when they drafted the rules and customs of land warfare. In short these rules and customs of land warfare are designed specifically for all phases of war. They comprise the law for such emergency. To claim that they can be wantonly—and at the sole discretion of any one belligerent—disregarded when he considers his own situation to be critical, means nothing more or less than to abrogate the laws and customs of war entirely."[12]

Questions of judgment and balance are involved here. When does humane treatment become synonymous with coddling? Or, conversely, at what point does a harsh situation forced upon everyone by military necessity render humane treatment impossible? The difficulty of answering helps explain why demands for humanitarian treatment

12. Lothar Kotzsch, *The Concept of War in Contemporary History and International Law* (Geneva, 1956), 119–20. He points out: "Besides military necessity which States are prevented from invoking on grounds of State emergency, there remains the genuine concept of tactical military necessity as a plight of a single military unit. Tactical military necessity which prevails in the fight of a military unit cannot be explained in a general way because of its being individually settled with regard to each of the rules of warfare" (*ibid.*, 120).

occurred late and why they are not always recognized even today. Civilization had to be well advanced before these questions could be adequately addressed. And the absence prior to the eighteenth century of clear pronouncements, such as those by Montesquieu and Rousseau, suggests that only in recent times has mankind achieved the required level of civilization. But to the extent that such considerations have received short shrift since the eighteenth century, one must question modern man's claims to being civilized.

In this connection, what is to be said for societies that overtly or covertly reject humanitarian principles? The cultural and historical milieu within which that decision was taken should be considered. Although most westerners find it difficult to accept ill-treatment of prisoners of war, Americans can comprehend the Asians' conduct in World War II (they in fact had historically different ideas about prisoners of war) more easily than they can the actions of the Germans, who had openly espoused Western standards as outlined in international law. Germany's conduct is a clear example of a nation placing itself above the law. That usually occurs in the name of a cause more highly valued than are the interests of humanity itself or of certain segments of humanity. In this sense, Germany's actions are reminiscent of those associated with holy wars. Holy wars, whether inspired by devotion to God, state, or ideology, are no longer recognized in international law. Nevertheless, few effective sanctions exist for use against those peoples who undertake holy wars or otherwise place themselves above the law.

It is, however, beyond the scope of this study to discuss the reasons why there are no sanctions for those who treat prisoners inhumanely.[13] It is sufficient to point out here that the search for effective sanctions against those who violate all the rules of war has been going on for centuries. We should, therefore, sympathize with those who failed to impose effective sanctions when prisoners of war received less than humane treatment.

Finally, let us consider the personnel assigned to prison camp duties. One observer has noted that "humane officers should be detailed for this duty,—men who by nature are kind and sympathetic to persons in unfortunate circumstances,—yet officers who have the necessary firmness of will, and strength of character to deal with

---

13. For excellent discussions of this matter, see Levie, "Penal Sanctions," 433–68; and Kunz, "The Chaotic Status of the Laws of War," 37–61.

prisoners of war who are unruly, disorderly, and who do not respond to kind treatment. There should be made a special effort before the outbreak of war, and during the continuance of hostilities to determine the characteristics of officers for assignment to duty with prisoners of war."[14] It appears that such care was seldom exercised. All too often, camp personnel were chosen because they were unfit for active combat due to wounds, old age, or other disabilities including pure and simple ineptitude. National policies calling for humane treatment have often been rendered ineffective by administrators who ignore or are ignorant of the most basic procedures and measures for the proper care of prisoners of war. In the final analysis, the individuals who control the immediate situation can do either great good or untold harm merely by the manner in which they execute their duties. The absence of adequate training for prison camp administrators usually dictates that prisoners suffer while the unskilled jailers learn their jobs. And when the camp personnel are hostile and unsympathetic, approach their duties grudgingly because they dislike the job or they could not continue as fighting men, or are otherwise unsuited to the task, the prisoners can expect to derive little comfort from the best of laws.

Interestingly, the call for humanitarianism in the treatment of prisoners of war was made prior to the first great war in American history. Theoretically, the prisoners taken during the American Revolution, and in every war thereafter, should have received humane treatment. And the number of times men did receive such treatment indicates that by the end of the eighteenth century, the appreciation of civilized standards had become quite sophisticated. When prisoners were badly treated, we have a right to ask why. The answer can probably be found among the seven factors discussed here.

As a word of caution, let me emphasize that the record seldom speaks solely for one side or the other. In real situations, even in hindsight, right and wrong are extremely difficult to determine. Prisoners of war often suffer when their interests must be weighed against military necessity. Allowing for the confusion and passion of war, we can readily understand the need for controlling our outrage.

The difficulty of distinguishing right and wrong is clearly demonstrated in the American Revolution. To the colonists, it was a war of inde-

14. Fooks, *Prisoners of War*, 174–75.

pendence; to the British, it was nothing less than rebellion. Americans would come to appreciate the implications of such distinctions when the Civil War raised similar questions.

The British position can be ascertained from a notation Captain Frederick Mackenzie made in his journal in the autumn of 1775: "An exchange of prisoners is talked of. The measure may be right and polite; but it appears rather extraordinary that under the present circumstances we should treat with them as if on an equality. . . . Rebels taken in arms forfeit their lives by the laws of all countries." The British government itself adopted a policy of dealing with American prisoners as common malefactors and outlaws. Not until 1782 did an act of Parliament officially recognize Americans as prisoners of war rather than traitors.[15]

The fruits of such policies are easy to imagine. American prisoners were treated very harshly by the British. According to one report, American soldiers died in greater numbers aboard the infamous British prison ships than from being hit by British rifle fire.[16] Captain William Cunningham confessed:

When the war commenced I was appointed Provost Marshal to the Royal Army; which placed me in a situation to wreak my vengeance on the Americans. I shudder to think of the murders I have been accessory to, both with and without orders from government, especially while in New York, during which time there were more than 2000 prisoners starved in the different churches, by stopping their rations, which I sold. There were also 275 American prisoners and obnoxious persons executed, out of all which number there were only one dozen public executions, which chiefly consisted of British and Hessian deserters.[17]

These policies and actions contrasted sharply with the Continental Congress' call for humane treatment of British prisoners. On January 2, 1776, the Congress declared that being a prisoner of war involved "a restraint of honor only" and sought to apply humanitarian concepts

15. Grady, "Ethical and Legal Concern," 55, 55n3, 56.
16. *Ibid.*, 57. For a brief but authoritative discussion of the deaths among captives from the revolutionary armies, see Howard H. Peckham (ed.), *The Toll of Independence: Engagements and Battle Casualties of the American Revolution*, Clements Library Bicentennial Studies (Chicago, 1974), 132. This source does not include figures that can be used to confirm or deny the claim, but it does strongly support the conclusion that fatalities among prisoners were outrageously high. Of the 18,182 men held by the British, an estimated 8,500 captives died (*ibid.*, 130).
17. Fooks, *Prisoners of War*, 176.

to the treatment of prisoners.[18] Since the British continued to mistreat American prisoners, Washington lowered the standards of treatment so British prisoners were similarly dealt with. At the same time, he appealed to the British to reconsider their position, and at one point he protested:

I am sorry that I am again under the necessity of remonstrating with you upon the treatment which our prisoners continue to receive. . . . Those who have lately been sent out, give the most shocking accounts of their barbarous usage, which their miserable emaciated countenance confirm. . . . How very different was their appearance from that of your soldiers, who lately have been returned to you, after a captivity of twelve months. . . . I would beg that some certain rule of conduct towards prisoners may be settled: if you are determined to make captivity as distressing as possible, to those whose lot it is to fall into it, let me know it, that we may be upon equal terms for your conduct must and shall match mine.

Washington had cause for his frustration and irritation. He had read reports about prison camp conditions: in Philadelphia, food shortages were so critical among prisoners that rats were considered a luxury and that mortar and rotten wood were scraped from the walls and greedily eaten for the temporary sensation of nourishment. In the end, American threats of reprisal materialized in brutal fashion. The Continental Congress ordered that all captured seamen be incarcerated aboard prison ships and be subjected to the same treatment American prisoners got. Subsequently, hundreds of British sailors reportedly died from privation and disease.[19] In the final analysis, it appears that a compromise was struck. During the American Revolution, the British treated American prisoners brutally, but not as brutally as was permissible under law in quelling domestic disturbances. The Americans, in turn, set out with good intentions but succumbed to the temptation to use reprisals as a means of securing better treatment for their own soldiers.

The lessons learned in the Revolution were not lost on Americans. In 1785 the United States and Prussia signed a treaty that was one of the earliest formal agreements on the treatment of prisoners of war concluded by nations not at war with each other. It also expressed all

18.   George G. Lewis and John Mewha, *History of Prisoner of War Utilization by the United States Army, 1776-1945* (Washington, D.C., 1955), 1, 2; Washington quoted in Grady, "Ethical and Legal Concern," 59.
19.   Grady, "Ethical and Legal Concern," 59, 61.

the new theories about their treatment. The parties pledged that prisoners of war would not be sent into distant, inclement countries and should not be confined in dungeons, prison ships, prisons, put in irons, or bound, or otherwise restrained. It is generally conceded that this treaty "furnished the precedent that formally specified the duty of the captor toward its prisoners, and, as such, was the forerunner for the multilateral conventions among nations relative to the treatment accorded prisoners of war." The treaty was reenacted in 1799 and extended in 1828. Surprisingly, it was the only effective agreement between the United States and Germany on the treatment of prisoners of war during World War I.[20]

Historically, prisoners of war in the War of 1812 have received little attention. A highly respected authority on the treatment of prisoners of war, William Flory, dismisses the entire matter: "Probably prisoners of war, during the War of 1812, were satisfactorily treated, since the evidence to the contrary is extremely meager." Grady skips the war entirely. Lewis and Mewha devote little more than three pages to the subject, and their account is good as far as it goes. The first really adequate coverage of this topic seems to have awaited Anthony George Dietz. Although he deals primarily with the treatment of British soldiers held by Americans, he does discuss a heretofore neglected subject and brings to light important facts about the conditions that then prevailed.[21]

One major difference between the American Revolution and the War of 1812 affected prisoners of war. In the latter war, the British no longer considered most American soldiers traitors and rebels. The same could not be said for those unfortunates whom Britain impressed or otherwise attempted to control under the guise of perpetual citizenship. However, their numbers were relatively small. More important, the War of 1812 represented one of the better eras in the history of prisoners of war. The United States and Great Britain generally accepted the prevailing philosophies and the laws govern-

20. Flory, *Prisoners of War*, 17; Fooks, *Prisoners of War*, 11–12; "Treaty of Amity and Commerce Between the United States and Prussia, 1785," in William M. Malloy (ed.), *Treaties, Conventions, International Acts, Protocols and Agreements Between the United States of America and Other Powers* (4 vols.; Washington, D.C., 1910–38), II, l484–85, 1494–95; Lewis and Mewha, *History of Prisoner of War Utilization*, 21.

21. Flory, *Prisoners of War*, 17; Anthony George Dietz, "The Prisoner of War in the United States During the War of 1812" (Ph.D. dissertation, American University, 1964).

ing prisoners. Stipulations in the Cartel of 1813 called for "prisoners to be subjects of humane treatment 'conformable to the usage and practice of the most civilized nations during war,'" but such statements did not guarantee that prisoners' rights would be respected. Dietz says that though the United States and Great Britain were not in complete accord on how to treat prisoners, both nations were "influenced by the value of a common heritage" and "had a high regard for law." There were instances of brutality and mistreatment, and there were reprisals to force the British to forgo holding their past subjects to perpetual citizenship. But, in general, the prisoners in the War of 1812 fared remarkably well because the views and practices of the United States and Great Britain were similar. Dietz concludes: "Their recognition of and general acceptance of the growing body of customs or rules which were applied to prisoners of war and their furtherance of the principles involved attest to this high regard and support the view that the two nations were, in a genuine sense, the servants of the rule of law."[22]

As the years went by, the United States could boast of a consistently humane policy toward prisoners of war. Although its good intentions had been largely frustrated during the American Revolution, its record in the War of 1812 was good. The same can be said for its conduct in the Mexican War.

Both sides were generally satisfied with the treatment afforded prisoners in the Mexican War. The Americans took many prisoners, but most were released on parole and permitted to return to their homes. The Mexicans treated the American prisoners well: in 1847 the commander of the American Home Squadron referred to their "kind and liberal treatment."[23]

The philosophy underlying the policies followed throughout these early years of nationhood was succinctly outlined by Daniel Webster in 1842:

Prisoners of war are to be considered as unfortunate and not as criminal, and are to be treated accordingly, although the question of detention or liberation is one affecting the interest of the captor alone, and therefore one with which no other government ought to interfere in any way; yet the right to detain by

22. Dietz, "The Prisoner of War . . . 1812," pp. 376, 379.
23. Lewis and Mewha, *History of Prisoner of War Utilization*, 25–26; Commodore M. C. Perry to Don Manuel Baranda, April 27, 1847, in *House Executive Documents*, 30th Cong., 1st Sess., No. 60, Ser. No. 520, p. 983.

no means implies the right to dispose of the prisoners at the pleasure of the captor. That right involves certain duties, among them that of providing the prisoners with the necessaries of Life and abstaining from the infliction of any punishment upon them which they may not have merited by an offense against the laws of the country since they were taken.[24]

This philosophy governed American prisoner of war affairs in the rest of the nineteenth and the twentieth centuries. The advent of total war, however, posed new problems. And the future faced by prisoners seemed increasingly dim. At the same time, the realities of modern war gave impetus to a reform movement that succeeded in either eliminating or significantly reducing the impact of a few of the limiting factors and paved the way for civilians to work against the destructive forces of total war.

From the Civil War to the Present

On the eve of the American Civil War, the United States could look back with pride upon the humane theories and practices that had governed its conduct toward prisoners of war during the previous fifty years. Its record was later tarnished, during the Civil War and the Indian wars, but otherwise has been maintained down to the present.[25] That achievement is remarkable in view of the significant changes in warfare since 1860, especially man's increasing capacity to engage in total war.

Unfortunately, enemy captors did not always adhere to policies as humane as those of the United States. There were primarily two reasons. First and foremost, the consequences of total war were less strongly and less immediately felt in America. Second, the previously mentioned seven factors could thus reign more freely in the war zone.

Still, with the exception of the treatment accorded Americans in Asian wars, prisoners from United States forces fared better than most. The United States apparently benefited from the success of a civilian reform movement under way in the West in the mid-nineteenth century. It effectively mitigated many of the evils confronting

24. Webster quoted in Flory, *Prisoners of War*, 17–18.
25. This is the only reference that will be made to United States prisoner of war policies in regard to the American Indian. The nature of those policies was unique and so falls outside the scope of this study.

prisoners of war in modern conflicts. These reforms bore little fruit in the East—thus the tragic suffering encountered in Asian conflicts.

The evil influences of total war on prisoners' lives were not entirely removed, as became evident during the two world wars and even in the post-world-war era, when limited warfare again seemed to be in vogue. In Korea and in Vietnam, restraint was considered wise in the use of arms but not in the treatment of prisoners. Americans held captive in these two wars suffered all the abuses one would expect them to have encountered in a total war.

The American Civil War, one of the first modern or total wars, provides a convenient introduction to the fate of prisoners in modern times. During that conflict, prisoners fared badly. There were two reasons for this tainted record: the uncertain status of Southern captives, and the totality of the war.[26]

In 1861 the United States government found itself in a position similar to that of the British in 1775. Since it refused to admit the "right of secession," those who took up arms on behalf of the South were traitors or rebels. The terminology often applied to captives from the Confederacy reveals the attitudes of Northerners: Southern soldiers were "insurgents," privateers were "pirates." Grady points out that "to the extent that this mentality prevailed, to that extent the opportunities for ameliorating the condition of prisoners of war remained remote."[27]

The South sought proper recognition for its captured soldiers and threatened reprisals against Northern captives if Southerners were imprisoned or executed as rebels and pirates. At first, these threats were ignored, but then the Confederacy came to hold increasingly large numbers of Northern prisoners. In time the North and the South concluded a series of arrangements for paroles and exchanges.

These gains were largely offset, however, when the Civil War soon evolved into a form of total war, and once again the clash between military expediency and full involvement on one hand and concern for prisoners' rights and humane treatment on the other came into focus. The results are generally well known. There were instances of mutual respect and consideration for the needs of enemy captives, but the overall record is most unworthy of that previously established

---

26. Grady, "Ethical and Legal Concern," 66; Dietz, "The Prisoner of War . . . 1812," p. 379.
27. Grady, "Ethical and Legal Concern," 66.

in the United States. Sensational stories about Andersonville, Libby, and Belle Isle have frozen in the public mind vivid images of the horrors perpetrated by the South. Many complaints arose about the camps in the North also, and the evidence indicates that the Union permitted, and in some cases even fostered, poor treatment of Southern prisoners.

William B. Hesseltine fully recognizes the unsanitary conditions and inadequate diet in the Northern camps in 1861–1862, but concludes that in general the food was "of good quality" and that "proper police of the prisons kept disease and death at a minimum." Hesseltine says that the same was true for the treatment of the prisoners held by the South during the early years of the war. But the rapid influx of prisoners, as well as inadequate resources, quickly led to overcrowding and widespread privation. He confirms the intolerable situation at Andersonville, but carefully outlines the contributing factors. One of the least of these was the camp personnel's improper behavior. Prisoners were moved from camp to camp in an effort to find locations safe from Northern armies. Hesseltine regards this movement as but another manifestation of the South's desperation near the end of the war, implying that the poor treatment during the moves was but one more consequence of the South's general collapse.

In time the rumored mistreatment of prisoners was believed on both sides. Northerners especially came to feel that the "vindictive spirit" among Confederates was in stark contrast to the "excellent treatment" accorded prisoners in the North. Inevitably Northerners demanded that the Southerners held in Northern prison camps be given similar treatment. Accordingly, rations were cut and further improvements in the Northern camps were curtailed.[28]

That acute shortage of supplies was a major factor in Southern mistreatment of prisoners was only vaguely recognized by the North. It is not surprising to find that after the war "the psychosis which had been engendered in the minds of the people during the conflict" led the nation to demand proper restitution from the responsible parties in the South. Numerous accusations were made, but only three of the men charged with atrocities against the prisoners were ever brought

28.   William B. Hesseltine, *Civil War Prisons: A Study in War Psychology* (New York, 1930), 45, 54, 175, 177ff.

to trial and only two of them were convicted.[29] Nevertheless, the polemical nature of the entire controversy and the literature that nurtured it contributed to the poisonous atmosphere that lingered long after the war ended. The psychosis Hesseltine describes is not uncommon in war. People often attribute their enemies' actions to pure vindictiveness and reply in kind. Perhaps the environment of total war encountered during the Civil War caused the psychosis to become more widespread and vitriolic than would normally be the case. If so, the danger posed both then and now by this phenomenon can be added to the many new factors that adversely affect prisoners whenever total war occurs. A list of these factors would include, but not be limited to, the following: First, total war reaches deep into a nation's hinterland, so prisoners are often in combat zones long after their capture. Second, the massive destruction deprives the population of not only the comforts but the necessities of life. Prisoners interned in their midst can anticipate sharing those privations, which may become serious enough to cause death. Third, the hatred that often arises as a result of total war can readily be turned against the prisoners, easy targets of abuse. Fourth, as conditions deteriorate, or as the opposing forces commit more and more of their resources to the war, prisoners sometimes become a resource and are active combatants long after they have been disarmed. This situation may occur when the captor somehow endangers their lives or when the prisoners harass and embarrass their captors for propaganda purposes, even though such actions might lead to riots or otherwise endanger life and limb. More will be said about prisoners who, for one reason or another, continue as combatants. The difficulties they confront, though almost unfathomable, are worthy of careful thought.

Most of these evils affect the lives of prisoners in every form of warfare. But the intensity so increases during total war that prisoners caught up in such conflicts face an entirely new environment with problems unique to it.

29. *Ibid.*, 233. Captain Henry Wirz was tried, convicted, and sentenced to death by hanging for the cruel treatment and unlawful killing of prisoners of war at Andersonville. (See Hesseltine, *Civil War Prisons*, for evidence that the trial was a sham.) One of Wirz's civilian employees, James W. Duncan, was tried in Savannah in March, 1866, for the same offense, was convicted, and was sentenced to fifteen years at hard labor. Major John H. Gee was tried in Raleigh in 1866 for his failure to take proper care of the prisoners at Salisbury, N.C., and for causing the deaths of several. He was acquitted (Levie, "Penal Sanctions," 436–37).

The poor treatment and abuses suffered by prisoners during the Civil War, then, were apparently harbingers. But many of the threatened dangers were ameliorated or staved off entirely by a movement to alleviate the plight of all victims of war. Headed by civilians, this movement rekindled public interest in the fate of prisoners of war and secured new safeguards in their behalf. The civilians worked to codify laws, publish army field manuals, organize aid societies, and promote international agreements.

The explanation for that growing interest can be found in the history of civilian involvement in warfare. Prior to the French Revolution and the Napoleonic Wars, the general populace had little to do with the actual fighting. The unpleasant realities of war were known primarily to mercenary and professional soldiers. Under these circumstances, the public was little interested in the conditions encountered by the fighting men. With few exceptions, only religious organizations, such as the Knights of Saint John of Jerusalem, the Knights of Saint George, and the Sisters of Charity of Saint Vincent de Paul, showed any serious concern for the victims of war.[30]

In the nineteenth century, however, civilian aloofness was no longer possible. From the French Revolution onward, the general populace was enlisted in large national armies. Furthermore, fighting was no longer restricted to the battlefield—those who did not journey to the front encountered war on their doorstep. The American Civil War provided the first clear example when total war came to the South and no segment of the population remained unscathed. Civilians were increasingly reluctant to allow professional soldiers sole power for the conduct of warfare. As the distinctions between the home front and the battlefield disappeared, concern for the victims of war was also transformed. Civilians mistrusted the military's seeming readiness to sacrifice everything in the name of military necessity. The survival instincts of man asserted themselves. At the very time when the realities of total war seemed to demand complete submission to the dictates of war, spokesmen for humanitarian interests called for increased, rather than decreased, safeguards for every individual in society.[31]

---

30. William Howard Taft (ed.), *Service with Fighting Men: An Account of the Work of the Young Men's Christian Association in the World War* (2 vols.; New York, 1922), II, 39–40.

31. *Ibid.*, 39–41. The idea that civilian concern for war victims arose in response to national armies and modern warfare is more fully outlined in Taft's text.

One of the most significant achievements of the entire reform effort came during the Civil War itself. In 1863, Francis Lieber, a refugee from Germany and at the time professor of history and political economy at Columbia College in New York, drew up a set of instructions concerning prisoners of war for use by the Union armies. His work probably was the first comprehensive codification of international law on this subject issued by a government. Published as General Orders No. 100 and entitled *Instructions for the Government of Armies in the Field*, it was the forerunner of the present-day Army Field Manual 27–10, *The Law of Land Warfare*, and served as the foundation statement for later international conferences that considered the plight of prisoners of war.[32] Two of its articles are of particular relevance here. Article 56 states: "A prisoner of war is subject to no punishment for being a public enemy nor is any revenge wreaked upon him by the intentional infliction of any suffering, or disgrace, by cruel imprisonment, want of food, by mutilation, death, or any other barbarity." And Article 79 says: "Whoever intentionally inflicts additional wounds on an enemy already disabled, or kills such an enemy, or who orders or encourages soldiers to do so; shall suffer death, if duly convicted, whether he belongs to the Army of the United States, or is an enemy captured after having committed his misdeed."[33] These articles indicate that American policies still emphasized high standards of treatment. Although neither the North nor the South upheld them, the standards themselves were not lowered. Furthermore, introducing a clear statement of sanctions against violators was important. Applying the sanctions was and still is a problem since the victor often enforces the rules only against the vanquished.

Other efforts to improve conditions and establish safeguards for prisoners of war were under way at this time. The terrible suffering experienced by the victims of the Crimean War, and Florence Nightingale's pioneering work in ministering to the soldiers' needs, sparked a wave

32. Flory, *Prisoners of War*, 18; John Brown Mason, "German Prisoners of War in the United States," *American Journal of International Law*, XXIV (April, 1945), 199; Frank Freidel, *Francis Lieber: Nineteenth-Century Liberal* (Baton Rouge, 1948), 337, 353–56; Lamar F. Peyton, "Treatment and Utilization of Prisoners of War by the United States During World War II" (M.A. thesis, Louisiana State University, 1973), 9; George B. Davis, "The Prisoners of War," *American Journal of International Law*, VII (July, 1913), 530.

33. Articles quoted in Levie, "Penal Sanctions," 436. Levie points out that Wirz, Duncan, and Gee were prosecuted because they violated these rules.

of civilian action that, though earlier in time, nobly complemented the spirit of Lieber's work.

Building upon the momentum stirred by Nightingale's work, the Swiss government called a convention in 1864 to be held in Geneva for the express purpose of obtaining better protection through the provisions of an international agreement for those who cared for the sick and wounded in the war zone. The Geneva Convention of 1864 for the Amelioration of the Condition of the Wounded and Sick of Armies in the Field, or the Red Cross Convention of 1864, was adopted and won wide support.[34] It also brought into existence the famous Red Cross (the Swiss flag with colors reversed) as an emblem signifying relief work in the field. National Red Cross societies were organized to provide equipment and workers who would take full advantage of the opportunities offered by the convention. And the International Committee of the Red Cross, with headquarters in Geneva, was established as a clearinghouse for Red Cross activities worldwide.[35]

The United States sent delegates in 1864 but was preoccupied with the Civil War and did not immediately join the international effort. Civilians, however, did participate in relief work in an organized manner through the United States Sanitary Commission, which coordinated the efforts of many "Soldiers Aid Societies" that sprang up throughout the North.[36]

Closely related to relief work, but still somewhat different in nature, is welfare. In the military context, relief is identified primarily with easing of physical pain and suffering. Welfare, on the other hand, encompasses the spiritual, social, recreational, educational, and religious needs of the able-bodied soldier. It is to fulfilling these needs that the Young Men's Christian Association has devoted itself since the mid-nineteenth century. YMCA delegates were active in the United States during the Civil War, but they were concerned almost entirely with religious matters. In succeeding years, however, the YMCA came to be associated with all forms of welfare work among soldiers.

34. This convention is still in force, having been revised in 1906, 1929, and 1949 (Levie, "Penal Sanctions," 379n15).

35. Taft (ed.), *Service with Fighting Men*, II, 46–47.

36. *Ibid.*, 47; William Quentin Maxwell, *Lincoln's Fifth Wheel: The Political History of the United States Sanitary Commission* (New York, 1956), 279, 307–308.

Partly as a result of and certainly in conjunction with these endeavors, there were many efforts to enlarge upon, clarify, and codify the body of national and international law that pertained to prisoners of war. During the Spanish-American War, for example, the United States government asked the protecting powers to inspect prisoner of war camps. Although no substitute for effective sanctions, the moral and popular pressure brought to bear on those guilty of abusing or neglecting the prisoners were the result.[37]

The designation "protecting power" refers to "a state which has accepted the responsibility of protecting the interests of another state in the territory of a third, with which, for some reason such as war, the second state does not maintain diplomatic relations."[38] The concept of using a third nation as a protecting power or intermediary dates back at least to the thirteenth century, but appeared in its present form less than a century ago. During the Franco-Prussian War, all the belligerents were represented by protecting powers in the territory of the enemy. Since enemy consuls were expelled and stringent restrictions were imposed on enemy aliens, the protecting power seemed an appropriate instrument for executing such duties.[39] It was a logical progression for the protecting power to inspect the camps where prisoners of war were confined and check on their food and how they were treated. The protecting power played an increasingly important role as its involvement with prisoners of war became more clearly recognized and defined in international law.

Meanwhile, a series of international meetings sought agreement on the rules of war. Also considered were questions about the care of prisoners of war. The first conference occurred in 1874 at Brussels, and the declaration, based largely on Lieber's work, called for improvements in the treatment of prisoners. The first Hague Conference (1899) adopted many of its provisions. The rest of its work dealt with

---

37. Flory, *Prisoners of War*, 108.
38. Howard S. Levie, "Prisoners of War and the Protecting Power," *American Journal of International Law*, LV (April, 1961), 374. Levie goes on to point out: "Because the protection is most frequently rendered to nationals of the protected state found in the third state, the former is often referred to as the *Power of Origin* and the latter as the *Power of Residence*. For obvious reasons, in the case of prisoners of war the state by which they are held is known as the *Detaining Power* rather than as the *Power of Residence*" (ibid., 374–75).
39. *Ibid.*, 375n3, 376.

establishing information bureaus, granting facilities to relief societies, and officers' pay.[40]

The need for revising the articles adopted in 1899 was evident by 1907 when the second Hague Conference met. At that time, there were several changes. First, internment was distinguished from confinement, which was the more rigorous and was to be used sparingly and only as long as circumstances necessitated. Second, officers were exempted from work while prisoners of war. Third, since the 1899 provisions for information bureaus proved inadequate in the Russo-Japanese War, efforts were made in 1907 to improve their operation. And fourth, officer prisoners would receive full pay, the amount to be paid to the detaining power by their own government.[41]

The provisions of the second Hague Conference influenced the treatment accorded prisoners of war in the years ahead, but only indirectly. The terms of the conference were considered binding only upon those who ratified them and only if ratified by all belligerents. Since Montenegro and Serbia did not do so, during World War I all signatories were released from their obligations. The document did stand, however, as a declaration of existing international law, and many nations, including the United States, adhered closely to its stipulations.[42]

There were also bilateral agreements. The United States still considered its 1785 treaty with Prussia to be in force. The United States also secured a special agreement with Germany concerning the treatment of prisoners of war, but the Armistice occurred before it could be ratified.

None of these measures successfully offset the erosion of human rights that occurred during World War I. An estimated six million enemy soldiers were captured.[43] It was all but impossible to provide adequate shelter and transportation for them. Equally important, the economic blockade against the Central Powers and the unrestricted submarine warfare against Great Britain and its allies lowered all

40. Flory, *Prisoners of War*, 20; A. Pearce Higgins, *The Hague Peace Conferences and Other International Conferences Concerning the Laws and Usages of War* (Cambridge, 1909), 221–32, 262, 276–78.

41. *Ibid.*, 261–63. In both conferences the documentary material relating to prisoners of war appears in the Fourth Convention, Chapter II, Articles 4–20.

42. Flory, *Prisoners of War*, 22.

43. *Summary of World War Work of the American Y.M.C.A.* (N.p., 1920), 100; Taft (ed.), *Service with Fighting Men*, II, 302.

participants' standard of living. And many prisoners suffered griev-
iously, especially in Germany.

The approximately twenty-six hundred American soldiers captured by Germany during World War I were treated rather well.[44] At
first they were scattered throughout Germany. Upon the suggestion
of Conrad Hoffman, a YMCA representative who inspected the
various camps, however, the Americans were gathered into one location. Unfortunately, the Germans assigned them to Tuchel, a camp in
East Prussia that consisted of dugouts and root cellars. As a result of
persistent efforts by the American secretary of the YMCA, the prisoners were transferred in August, 1918, to Rastatt. This camp had
been a showplace, and the facilities were much more satisfactory. A
great deal was done to make life more comfortable at Rastatt:
"Through cooperation with Berne and Copenhagen, a complete [line
of] athletic equipment was provided; a piano and musical instruments were furnished and a band organized; books were sent
through the Swiss office, a camp newspaper was started. Regularly
on Sunday mornings church services were held, with an attendance
at times of 500 men. The appearance and spirit of the camp on subsequent visits differed radically from the early melancholy days—base-
ball games, football matches, band practice, chess, checkers, and
dominoes, reading and studying all going forward simultaneously to
make a kaleidoscopic pattern of activity." Such conditions were the
exception rather than the rule. Carl Dennett states that the American
prisoners in Germany received preferential treatment for at least
three reasons. First, the Germans held them only briefly (the United
States entered the war late), thereby lessening the discomforts that
occurred during lengthy periods of imprisonment. Second, the number of German prisoners held by the United States always exceeded
the total number of Americans in German hands; furthermore, the
United States saw to it that they were well fed and cared for. The
Germans were thus obliged to reciprocate and provide good care to
their American prisoners. Third, the Germans respected the Americans. As Dennett observed, when the prisoners' state of origin
neglected them, the Germans seemed to feel safe in indulging in
brutality and harshness. But if the prisoners were cared for by their

44. Taft (ed.), *Service with Fighting Men*, II, 302; Grady, "Ethical and Legal
Concern," 103.

own government, the German government and prison authorities respected them and treated them well.[45]

By the 1920s, most observers agreed that the existing protections in international law and custom were still insufficient to ensure the well-being of prisoners of war. The Red Cross and the YMCA had done a creditable job of ministering to their needs, and the prisoners fared better than if the reform efforts had never been undertaken. But the toll exacted by total war was still too high. Further safeguards were needed.

At the tenth annual conference of the International Red Cross (1921), work began on a new code. The result was the Geneva Convention of 1929 Relative to the Treatment of Prisoners of War. This work was the basic document governing conduct toward and by prisoners of war in World War II. With its appearance, a seemingly comprehensive definition of humane care came into existence. Ninety-seven articles outlined the duties and responsibilities of everyone concerned from capture through repatriation.[46] Despite its apparent thoroughness and the care with which it was written, the Geneva Convention of 1929 proved inadequate in World War II.

All the factors that eroded the prisoner's rights and contributed to his misery in World War I were present in World War II, though on a much larger and more serious scale than ever before. First, the 1929 agreement did not accommodate the full spectrum of views. Neither Russia nor Japan agreed with or ratified the convention. And despite Japan's stated intention to abide by its spirit, gross violations were predictable since Japan did not recognize surrender as a viable option for soldiers.[47] Second, the Geneva Convention could not provide adequate protection against the machinations of totalitarian states engaged in ideological strife. A definition of humane treatment meant little when the Germans felt justified in adopting one standard for prisoners from the East and another for those from the West. And third, the extensive use of airpower in World War II took the war into the hinterland of almost every nation in unprecedented fashion.

The dangers and difficulties that prisoners of war encountered in

45. Taft (ed.), *Service with Fighting Men*, II, 303; Carl P. Dennett, "American Prisoners of War, 1918" (Typescript in Archives Division, American Red Cross Headquarters, Washington, D.C.), 95–96ff.

46. *Treaty Series No. 846*, pp. 35–66.

47. Grady, "Ethical and Legal Concern," 123.

World War II suggested the need for revising the rules. Another convention met in Geneva in 1949, and sought once again, as had the 1929 convention, to go beyond a mere statement of principles. The second Hague Convention (1907) produced 17 articles on the treatment of prisoners of war, and the 1929 convention listed 97. But the 1949 convention included 143 articles. Its purpose was to impose on the signatories specific, detailed objectives in terms of care and safeguards. Jean S. Pictet asserted: "It is no exaggeration to say that prisoners of war in present or future conflicts are covered by a veritable humanitarian and administrative statute which not only protects them from the dangers of war, but also ensures that the conditions in which they are interned are as satisfactory as possible." Little comfort, however, could be gained from his words, for some felt that prisoners of war had been so favored long before 1949. As early as 1911, J. M. Spaight charged: "Today the prisoner of war is a spoilt darling: he is treated with a solicitude for his wants and feelings which borders on sentimentalism. [POW captivity] is usually a halcyon time, a pleasant experience to be nursed fondly in the memory, a kind of inexpensive rest-cure after the wearisome turmoil of fighting." History proved Spaight's sarcastic optimism to be ill-founded and made Pictet's words seem somewhat hollow. There is much truth to the observation that "the way to international hell seems paved with 'good' conventions."[48]

Despite the notable work of those who strove to secure prisoners' rights and interests through international agreements, there has been no real progress in enforcing these laws and customs. In the absence of adequate sanctions, disagreement continues over who qualifies as a prisoner of war, and some nations choose to place themselves above the law.[49] This situation is to be especially regretted since organizations such as the international branches of the YMCA

---

48. *Geneva Convention Relative to the Treatment of Prisoners of War*; Commentary by Jean S. Pictet, vol. III of *The Geneva Conventions of 12 August 1949* (Geneva, 1960), 10; Spaight quoted in George S. Prugh, "Prisoners at War: The POW Battleground," *Dickinson Law Review*, LX (October, 1955–June, 1956), 125n10; Levie, "Penal Sanctions," 468n139, attributes the remark to one Mr. Roling who lectured at the Hague Academy of International Law in the early 1960s.

49. This disagreement has become an increasingly important problem in combat that is a "police action" rather than a declared war. Under these circumstances, a nation bent upon ignoring the spirit and letter of the law can easily label as "war criminals" soldiers who actually meet all the criteria of prisoners, for example, being members of recognized armed forces, wearing uniforms, openly displaying arms, etc.

and the Red Cross have less and less influence (many countries do not allow either group to operate within their boundaries) and since the tendency is not to use protecting powers. The latter development also stems in part from national jealousies, but no less important is the lack of suitable candidates. The large number of belligerents in World War II left no strong neutrals from which to select protecting powers. Both then and now, even if the few uncommitted powers are offended by violations of the rules of war, the public outcry would be relatively slight.[50]

All these factors suggest that the prisoner of war could anticipate as many or more difficulties in the post–World War II era than ever before. The American experience in Korea and Vietnam confirmed these suspicions. Though the inhumane treatment accorded American prisoners is vividly remembered and needs no further elaboration here, several observations seem appropriate.

First, the world still is capable of expressing outrage whenever prisoners of war are abused and mistreated, but certain closed societies can engage in brutal practices over extended periods of time without much risk of detection. Maintaining such secrecy inevitably means that the prisoners are deprived of the benefits available to them through the Red Cross, the YMCA, and the protecting power. Second, even after evidence proves that prisoners are being badly treated, there is still no adequate way to secure relief for them. Third, the evils of total war persist even when conflicts are limited. In the past quarter-century, two notable examples are the revival of the holy war in pursuit of ideological ends and the change from prisoner *of* war to prisoner *at* war.[51]

Between the sixteenth and eighteenth centuries, it became generally accepted in international law and custom that a soldier posed a danger only so long as he was an integral part of his nation's armed forces. As an active combatant, he was subject to all the perils associated with warfare. Once he was taken captive and disarmed, however, his status changed, and he immediately regained those protections and rights that he forfeited when he took up arms. The conquering nation felt safe in taking minimal safeguards against the relatively

50. Levie, "Prisoners of War," 380.
51. Excellent discussions of the prisoner at war and the prisoner of war can be found in Grady, "Ethical and Legal Concern," 169–77; and Prugh, "Prisoners at War," 123–38. Both the ideas and the facts presented on this topic were in large part gleaned from these two works.

passive prisoner. Thus the captor could treat the prisoner humanely and with consideration. Although this status did not guarantee good care, it did justify the demands for humane care levied against the captor.

The same cannot be said for a captive who is assigned the status of prisoner at war. He does not relinquish his role as a fighting man because he has been disarmed. But his own government requires that he do more than merely try to escape or force his captor to withdraw many men from the front lines for guard duty. Unarmed, he must be as violent as he would be if he still had weapons. The Chinese prepared their soldiers for such a role. The results in the Korean War can only be viewed, according to Western standards, as a regression in the dismal history of prisoners of war. Chinese prisoners formed well-disciplined military organizations within their camps and frequently used them to inflict corporal punishment and death upon fellow prisoners and to stage riots for propaganda purposes. The response forced upon the detaining power is seen as a tragedy by those who have sought to alleviate the prisoners' plight. The prisoner is no longer a relatively passive human being in need of care and protection until the end of the war; he is, in effect, still an active combatant of the most vicious sort, and must be treated as such. The small ratio of guards to prisoners dictates that whenever prisoners act in a threatening manner, either individually or en masse, unarmed though they may be, arms will be used against them. That often is only the most visible response; the detaining power frequently has other countermeasures. Once initiated, this regressive process can only lead to partial or complete abandonment of the Geneva conventions.

Some see the United States Military Code of Conduct as an example of the trend initiated by the Chinese in the Korean War. Disturbed that American soldiers betrayed their country and fellow servicemen in that war, the United States adopted a code that requires a captive to conduct himself at all times not just as a soldier but, in stronger terms, as a fighting man. This requirement does not, however, make American captives prisoners at war, for their training stresses that the duty to remain a fighting man does not justify resorting to violence, except, of course, in self-defense.[52]

52. Grady, "Ethical and Legal Concern," 172–77. *U.S. Fighting Man's Code* (Washington, D.C., 1955), Art. 3, pp. 59ff., states in part: "The POW should never give

It is clear, then, that the ideological nature of the conflicts that have dominated recent warfare have led to a significant change in the status of certain prisoners of war. The tendency to fight fire with fire is strong in this instance: innocent prisoners are caught in a form of struggle in which they are sometimes expected to use their lives and limbs as weapons. To encourage such barbaric sacrifices in the name of warfare is to ignore the hard-won heritage of civilization itself.

---

his captor any valid reason to label him a war criminal and treat him as one. Except in extremely desperate circumstances, the POW should avoid violence." In all fairness, it must be admitted that Grady's argument covers issues other than violence. Among them are questions of the right to accept parole and the right to refuse to attempt to escape. I have chosen not to address these two issues at this point primarily because I feel they are not inherently contained in the prisoner of war concept in the same sense that violence is (see Prugh, "Prisoners at War," 137).

Bibliography

PRIMARY SOURCES

MANUSCRIPT MATERIALS

AIR FORCE MUSEUM, WRIGHT-PATTERSON AFB, OHIO
"Stalag Luft III" File, "Prisoners of War" Drawer, Research Division
"Education and Entertainment" Folder
"Equipment and Supplies" Folder
"History" Folder
"Medical Care" Folder
"Miscellaneous" Folder
"Personnel" Folder
"Religious Activities" Folder

ALBERT F. SIMPSON HISTORICAL RESEARCH CENTER, MAXWELL AFB, ALA.
Combined Services Detailed Interrogation Center. S.R.G.G. Report 1303.
Goodrich, Charles G. "History of the USAAF, Prisoners of War of the South Compound, Stalag Luft III." 1945.
Mulligan, Thomas E., Lyman B. Burbank, and Robert R. Brunn. "History of Center Compound, Stalag Luft III, Sagan, Germany." 1945.
United States Strategic Air Force (USSTAF). "ECLIPSE Memorandum No. 8: The care and evacuation of prisoners of war in Greater Germany under ECLIPSE conditions," May 19, 1945, File No. 519.9731-3, 13.
———. "Folder of miscellaneous post hostilities planning data for treatment and evacuation of POWs, January-March 1945," File 519.9731-13.
———. "Information on current problems confronting the AAF in the ETO, 1944–45 [concerning] the protection, evacuation, relief, and maintenance of U.S. and British prisoners of war after cessation of hostilities" (tab 9), File 519.979.
———. "Minutes and notes of planning meetings and conferences on supply, protection and evacuation of Allied Prisoners of War, PW Section on file, November 1944–May 1945," File 519.9731-3.

AMERICAN RED CROSS HEADQUARTERS, WASHINGTON, D.C.
Archives Division
Dennett, Carl P. "American Prisoners of War." 1918.

File 619.2, "American and Allied POWs-Europe-Germany."

File 619.2/43, "Food and Subsistence, American and Allied Internees and POW."

File 619.2/08, "Reports and Statistics, American and Allied Internees and POW."

Military Intelligence, War Department. "American Prisoners of War in Germany." November 1, 1945.

"Red Cross, U.S., ANRC, Prisoners of War Activities (Miscellaneous-European)."

Robinson, Arthur W. "Relief to Prisoners of War in World War II." 1950. Vol. XXII of "The History of the American Red Cross."

IN AUTHOR'S POSSESSION

Bennett, John M. "Memoirs." *ca.* 1950.

Broach, Bob. "The Last Mission." 1943. Copy. Original held by Broach.

————. Notes on Armistice Day Pool. Copy. Original held by Broach.

Emanos, Josepe, to Colonel Saltsman, February 9, 1976. Copy.

Gorse, Norville J. "There I Was." N.d. Copy.

Saltsman, Ralph H. "My Story." September 14, 1944.

Spivey, Delmar T. "History of Center Compound." 1946. Copy.

Von Lindeiner, Friedrich-Wilhelm. "Memoirs of Colonel Friedrich-Wilhelm von Lindeiner-Wildau, Kommandant, Stalag Luft III." Translated by Berthold Geiss. Edited by Arthur A. Durand. N.d.

Wenthe, George W. "Daily Log, April 4–June 4, 1945." Copy. Original held by Wenthe.

————. "Diary." Copy. Original held by Wenthe.

MANUSCRIPTS DIVISION, LIBRARY OF CONGRESS

McCright, E. R. "Urkunden Stalag 3 fur die altesten offiziere (Record for the Senior Officer), giving names and addresses of dead flying comrades."

NATIONAL ARCHIVES

Diplomatic Branch

File 711.62114 Mail/—. Record Group 59.

File 711.62114 A/—, "United States Prisoners of War Detained by Germany." Record Group 59.

File 711.62114 A.I.R./—, "Reports of Inspection of Camps for American Prisoners in Germany." Record Group 59.

File 740.00114 European War 1939/—, "Prisoners of War—European War, 1939." Record Group 59.

Modern Military Branch

"Dulag Luft" Folder, "Camp Reports-Germany-Air Force Transit Camps" File, Record Group 389.

File 383.6-15, "Transfer of Allied Prisoners of War from Central Germany," SHAEF 1-6. Record Group 331.

File 383.6/6, "Supplies for POWs," SHAEF G-1. Record Group 331.

"Stalag Luft III" Folder, "Camp Reports-Germany-Stalag Luft III" File, American POW Information Bureau, Office of the Provost Marshal General. Record Group 389.

TROY H. MIDDLETON LIBRARY, LOUISIANA STATE UNIVERSITY, BATON ROUGE

Newspaper and Microfilm Room

"Auswertestelle West," A.D.I. (K) Report 328/1945, microfilm roll A5405. "Great Escapes," Doc. F164.

"German Methods and Experiences of Prisoner Interrogation," A.D.I. (K) Report 388, microfilm roll A5405. "Great Escapes," Doc. F164.

U.S. AIR FORCE ACADEMY LIBRARY, COLO.

Albert P. Clark Collection, 1942–1975, Special Collections Room

Clark, Albert P. "Photographic Work." 1945.

————. "Radio and News Service." 1945.

————. Scrapbook.

————. "Signals." 1945.

————. "Some Reminiscences of Stalag Luft III." January 20, 1978.

"A History of Stalag Luft III." N.d.

Interview between Albert P. Clark and Ben Pollard, March 22, 1974.

Interview with Herman Glemnitz by Albert P. Clark and Elwin F. Schrupp, April 9–10, 1984.

Delmar T. Spivey Collection, 1943–1975, Special Collections Room

Berger Folder

"Dulag Luft." N.d.

Eggen Folder

Galathovics Folder

Glemnitz Folder

Haubold Folder

Lange Folder

"Lists and Miscellaneous Correspondence-POW" Folder

"POW Letters-General" Folder

"Red Cross Clothing Store" Folder

Simoleit Folder

Stark, Bob. "Intelligence Operations in Air Force Officer Prisoner-of-War Camps in Germany, 1939–1945." N.d.

Stranghoner Folder

Von Lindeiner Folder

WASHINGTON NATIONAL RECORD CENTER, SUITLAND, MD.

Entry 321b, Records of the Judge Advocate General's Office. Record Group 153.

"The Kriegsgefangenenwesen," Combined Services Detailed Interrogation Center, S.R.G.G. Report 315, File 100-411-23, Records of the Office of the Judge Advocate General. Record Group 153.

CORRESPONDENCE WITH AUTHOR

Bland, Edwin A., Jr., May 14, 1975.

Brennan, Thomas G., February 16, 1975.

Carrigan, William E., February 25, 1975.

Chamberlain, Mervin A., February 25, 1975.
Charland, Donald G., May 8, June 23, 1975.
Cooper, James R., April 24, 1975.
Dreyer, Arthur, November 24, 1975.
Ferrell, Robert L., February 3, 1975.
Fier, Reuben, April 22, 1975.
Fortman, Robert W., February 28, 1975.
Goodrich, Charles G., November 21, 1975.
Hartney, Charles W., February 8, 1975.
Heckman, Willard L., January 21, 1975.
Hopewell, Clifford, July 29, 1982.
Jackson, Loren E., February 2, 1975.
James, B. A., August 6, 1982.
LaChasse, Al, January 23, 1975.
McCracken, Harry E., May 1, 1983.
McCracken, Melton, May 24, 1983.
McNickle, Melvin F., January 14, 1975.
Mitchell, Merlin P., August 18, 1975.
Schrupp, Elwin F., February 12, 1975.
Spivey, Delmar T., March 24, September 18, November 11, 1973, Febru-
    ary 4, 21, April 7, 28, September 25, 1974, April 27, May 12, July 21,
    1975.
Stevens, Donald M., January 11, 1975.
Stillman, Donald L., January 26, 1975.
Turkington, William J., April 21, 1975.
Vanaman, Arthur W., April 27, September 24, 1973, August 8, 1974,
    December 19, 1975.
Wendell, Karl W., January 24, 1975.
Wiley, Eugene M., July 1, 1980.
Zapinski, L. E., March 6, 1975.

GOVERNMENT DOCUMENTS AND PUBLICATIONS

House Executive Documents, 30th Cong., 1st Sess., No. 60, Ser. No. 520.
*Treaty Series No. 846: Prisoners of War. Convention between the United
    States of America and Other Powers.* Washington, D.C., 1932.
U.S. Fighting Man's Code. Washington, D.C., 1955.

NEWSPAPERS

Gefangenen Gazette, December 19, 30, 1943, April 26, August 30, 1944.
New York *Times*, May 27, 1944.
Stars and Stripes, March 27, 1983.

BOOKS

Daniel, Eugene L., Jr. *In the Presence of Mine Enemies: Memoirs of
    German Prisoner of War Life, February 16, 1943 to April 29, 1945.*
    Attleboro, Mass., 1985.

James, B. A. *Moonless Night: One Man's Struggle for Freedom, 1940–1945.* London, 1983.

Kimball, R. W., and O. M. Chiesl. *Clipped Wings.* N.p., n.d.

Neary, Bob. *Stalag Luft III: Sagan . . . Nurenberg . . . Moosburg. A Collection of German Prison Camp Sketches with Descriptive Text Based on Personal Experiences.* North Wales, Pa., 1946.

Sage, Jerry. *Sage.* Wayne, Pa., 1985.

Spivey, Delmar T. *POW Odyssey: Recollections of Center Compound, Stalag Luft III and the Secret German Peace Mission in World War II.* Edited by George Gibb and Hilma Gibb. Attleboro, Mass., 1984.

Sweanor, George W. *It's All Pensionable Time: 25 Years in the Royal Canadian Air Force.* Woodland Park, Colo., 1979.

Trial of the Major Criminals before the International Military Tribunal: Nuremberg, 14 November 1945–1 October 1946. Vols. I, II, IV, VII, X, XI, XX. Nuremberg, Germany, 1948.

Trials of War Criminals before the Nuremberg Military Tribunals. Vols. XI, XIII. Washington, D.C., 1952.

U.S. Office of United States Chief of Counsel for Prosecution of Nazi Criminality. *Nazi Conspiracy and Aggression.* Washington, D.C., 1946–48. Supplement B, section III.

INTERVIEWS

Broach, Bob, April 19, 1975.

Clark, Albert P., April 7, 1973, November 7–8, 1975, March 8, 1976, March 22, 1976, April 15, 1976, July 4, 1984.

Daniel, Eugene L., Jr., April 14–15, 1983.

Dreyer, Arthur, February 25, 1976.

Frey, Royal D., February 25, 1975.

Goodrich, Charles G., February 25, November 18, 1975.

Hackwith, Robert, July 14, 1984.

Houston, John W., November 7, 1984.

Johnson, Walter G., November 25, 1978.

Keeffe, James, March 12, 1979.

LaChasse, Al, October 13, 1975.

MacArthur, Alexander, September 7, 1979, April 29, 1984.

Orozco, Raymond, April 15, 1983.

Powell, Bill, November 7, 1984.

Saltsman, Ralph, July 17, November 28, 1979.

Sargent, Roland L., June 24, 1980.

Soderberg, Henry, September 15, 1979.

Spivey, Delmar T., approximately fifteen sessions, January, 1973–November, 1981.

Storer, John M., April 19, 1975.

Sweanor, George, February, 1979.

Vanaman, Arthur W., April 2–3, 1973.

Wells, John, January 26–27, 1975.
Widen, Norman L., April 11–13, 1979.

SECONDARY WORKS

Books

Andrews, Allen. *Exemplary Justice.* London, 1976.
Barker, A. J. *Prisoners of War.* New York, 1975.
Brickhill, Paul. *The Great Escape.* With an Introduction by George Harsh. Greenwich, Conn., 1950.
Burt, Kendal, and James Leasor. *The One that Got Away.* London, 1956.
Cadoret, Roland A. *The Battle of Grounded Eagles.* N.p., 1970.
Crawley, Aidan. *Escape from Germany: A History of R.A.F. Escapes During the War.* New York, 1956.
Datner, Szymon. *Crimes Against POWs: Responsibility of the Wehrmacht.* Warsaw, 1964.
Dominy, John. *The Sergeant Escapers.* London, 1974.
Dulles, Foster Rhea. *The American Red Cross: A History.* New York, 1950.
Feilchenfeld, Ernst H. *Prisoners of War.* Washington, D.C., 1948.
Flory, William E. S. *Prisoners of War: A Study in the Development of International Law.* With an Introduction by Norman H. Davis. Washington, D.C., 1942.
Fooks, Herbert C. *Prisoners of War.* Federalsburg, Md., 1924.
Freidel, Frank. *Francis Lieber: Nineteenth-Century Liberal.* Baton Rouge, 1947.
Geneva Convention Relative to the Treatment of Prisoners of War. Commentary by Jean S. Pictet. Vol. III of *The Geneva Conventions of 12 August 1949.* Geneva, 1960.
Giovannitti, Len. *The Prisoners of Combine D.* New York, 1957.
Greenspan, Morris. *The Modern Law of Land Warfare.* Berkeley and Los Angeles, 1959.
Haugland, Vern. *The Eagle Squadrons: Yanks in the RAF, 1940–1942.* New York, 1979.
Hesseltine, William B. *Civil War Prisons: A Study in War Psychology.* New York, 1930.
Higgins, A. Pearce. *The Hague Peace Conferences and Other International Conferences Concerning the Laws and Usages of War.* Cambridge, 1909.
Infield, Glenn B. *Eva and Adolf.* New York, 1974.
Klaas, Joe. *Maybe I'm Dead.* New York, 1955.
Kotzsch, Lothar. *The Concept of War in Contemporary History and International Law.* Geneva, 1956.
Lewis, George G., and John Mewha. *History of Prisoner of War Utilization by the United States Army, 1776–1945.* Washington, D.C., 1955.

Malloy, William M., ed. *Treaties, Conventions, International Acts, Protocols and Agreements Between the United States of America and Other Powers.* Vol. II of 4 vols. Washington, D.C., 1910–38.

Maxwell, William Quentin. *Lincoln's Fifth Wheel: The Political History of the United States Sanitary Commission.* New York, 1956.

Morgan, Guy. *P.O.W.* New York, 1946.

Neumann, Franz. *Behemoth: The Structure and Practice of National Socialism, 1933–1944.* New York, 1966.

Peckham, Howard H., ed. *The Toll of Independence: Engagements and Battle Casualties of the American Revolution.* Clements Library Bicentennial Studies. Chicago, 1974.

Philpot, Oliver. *Stolen Journey.* New York, 1952.

Risner, Robinson. *The Passing of the Night: My Seven Years as a Prisoner of the North Vietnamese.* New York, 1975.

Simmons, Kenneth W. *Kriegie.* New York, 1960.

Smith, Sydney. *Mission Escape.* New York, 1969.

Summary of World War Work of the American Y.M.C.A. N.p., 1920.

Taft, William Howard, ed. *Service with Fighting Men: An Account of the Work of the Young Men's Christian Association in the World War.* Vol. II. New York, 1922.

Toland, John. *The Last 100 Days.* New York, 1970.

Toliver, Raymond. *The Interrogator: The Story of Hans Scharff, Luftwaffe's Master Interrogator.* Fallbrook, Calif., 1978.

Vietor, John A. *Time Out: American Airmen at Stalag Luft I.* New York, 1951.

Williams, Eric. *The Wooden Horse.* New York, 1949.

Wright, Gordon. *The Ordeal of Total War, 1939–1945.* New York, 1968.

Young, Peter, ed. *The World Almanac Book of World War II.* New York, 1981.

ARTICLES

Cole, James L. "Dulag Luft Recalled and Revisited." *Aerospace Historian,* XIX (June, 1972), 62–65.

Davis, George B. "The Prisoners of War." *American Journal of International Law,* VII (July, 1913), 521–45.

Dreyer, Arthur. "The 'Kriegie' Press." *Air Force,* XXIX (March-April, 1946), 16–18, 47.

Friedheim, Eric. "Welcome to Dulag Luft." *Air Force,* XXVIII (September, 1945), 16–17, 43.

Kahn, David. "World War II History: The Biggest Hole." *Military Affairs,* XXXIX (April, 1975), 74–76.

Kunz, Joseph L. "The Chaotic Status of the Laws of War and the Urgent Necessity for Their Revision." *American Journal of International Law,* XLV (January, 1951), 37–61.

Levie, Howard S. "Penal Sanctions for Maltreatment of Prisoners of War." *American Journal of International Law,* LVI (April, 1962), 433–68.

————. "Prisoners of War and the Protecting Power." *American Journal of International Law*, LV (April, 1961), 374–97.

Lunden, Walter A. "Captivity Psychosis Among Prisoners of War." *Journal of Criminal Law and Criminology*, XXXIX (March-April, 1949), 721–33.

Mason, John Brown. "German Prisoners of War in the United States." *American Journal of International Law*, XXIV (April, 1945), 198–215.

Plammer, Philip, ed. "Dulag Luft." *Aerospace Historian*, XIX (June, 1972), 58–62.

Prugh, George S. "Prisoners at War: The POW Battleground." *Dickinson Law Review*, LX (October, 1955–June, 1956), 123–38.

Rundell, Walter, Jr. "Paying the POW in World War II." *Military Affairs*, XXII (Fall, 1958), 121–34.

Scharff, Hans Joachim."Without Torture." *Argosy* (May, 1950), 38–39, 87–91.

Spivey, Delmar T., and Arthur A. Durand. "Secret Mission to Berlin." *Air Force Magazine*, LVIII (September, 1975), 115–20.

DISSERTATIONS AND THESES

Bland, Edwin A., Jr. "German Methods for Interrogation of Captured Allied Aircrews." Thesis, Air Command and Staff School of Air University, Maxwell Air Force Base, Ala., 1948.

Burbank, Lyman B. "A History of the American Air Force Prisoners of War in Center Compound, Stalag Luft III, Germany." M.A. thesis, University of Chicago, 1946.

Dietz, Anthony George."The Prisoner of War in the United States during the War of 1812." Ph.D. dissertation, American University, 1964.

Grady, Robert F. "The Evolution of Ethical and Legal Concern for the Prisoner of War." Ph.D. dissertation, Catholic University of America, 1971.

Ingenhutt, William W. "Something was Missing." Thesis, Air Command and Staff School of Air University, Maxwell Air Force Base, Ala., 1948.

Peyton, Lamar F. "Treatment and Utilization of Prisoners of War by the United States During World War II." M.A. thesis, Louisiana State University, 1973.

Index